Mobilizing New York

MOBILIZING
New York

AIDS, Antipoverty, and Feminist Activism

Tamar W. Carroll

The University of North Carolina Press / Chapel Hill

Publication of this book was supported in part by the Paul and Francena Miller
Research Fellowship at Rochester Institute of Technology.

Set in 10.2/13.5 Utopia by Westchester Publishing Services
Manufactured in the United States of America

The paper in this book meets the guidelines for permanence and durability
of the Committee on Production Guidelines for Book Longevity of the Council on
Library Resources. The University of North Carolina Press has been a member
of the Green Press Initiative since 2003.

Cover illustration Top: NCNW members at the 1977 National Women's Conference,
courtesy of Janie Eisenberg. Middle: ACT UP demonstrates at the Food and Drug
Administration in Washington, D.C. in 1988, © Donna Binder. Bottom: Film still from
Roberta Hodes's *The Game* featuring MFY Cultural Arts students on a street on the
Lower East Side, from Grove Press Records, Special Collections Research Center,
Syracuse University Libraries.

Library of Congress Cataloging-in-Publication Data
Carroll, Tamar W.
   Mobilizing New York : AIDS, antipoverty, and feminist activism / Tamar W.
Carroll. — 1 Edition.
       pages cm. — (Gender and American culture)
   Includes bibliographical references and index.
   ISBN 978-1-4696-1988-0 (pbk : alk. paper) — ISBN 978-1-4696-1989-7 (ebook)
   1. Economic assistance, Domestic—New York (State)—New York—History—20th
century.   2. Feminism—New York (State)—New York—History—20th century.
3. AIDS activists—New York (State)—New York—History—20th century.   4. ACT UP
New York (Organization)—History—20th century.   I. Title.
   HC108.N7C29 2015
   322.4'3097471—dc23
                                                                    2014034905

THIS BOOK WAS DIGITALLY PRINTED.

Contents

Maps and Figures

Preface
Making History

This book examines the ways in which otherwise ordinary New Yorkers participated in social movements that made history: the War on Poverty, second-wave feminism, and AIDS and reproductive rights activism. When I began this project, I had in mind a different subject: the intellectual and glamorous spokeswoman for American feminism, Gloria Steinem, whose archives are at Smith College in Northampton, Massachusetts. When I visited Smith, archivist Nanci Young suggested I might be interested in a new collection, the records of the National Congress of Neighborhood Women (NCNW), founded by Janet Peterson in 1974–75. I had never heard of the group, but their brochure's photograph of a multiracial group of confident, apparently working-class women on the steps of the U.S. capitol intrigued me, as did their list of "Original Goals." They aspired to not only "look seriously at sexism," but also to "help women identify, perceive and assume power without feeling that it was a threat to family" and to "validate women as part of a family." They remarked that "most poor people are women" and expressed the hope that they could "bridge [the] gap between black and white women whose issues were the same." And they wanted to build an organization that "their mother felt comfortable in."[1]

I found this list of goals exciting, in part because it contradicted much of what I thought I knew about American feminists in the 1970s: that they were mostly well-off, college-educated white women who yearned to break free from oppressive family obligations and were either rebelling against their own mothers, or being encouraged by aspiring or college-educated mothers who never felt that being a housewife with children was all that a woman could do.[2] Among these working-class women, I was especially curious to find out how they managed to reconcile women's empowerment with strong family relationships. The NCNW's vision appealed to me as a young woman raised in a conservative Irish Catholic household and drawn to the study of feminism; I valued gender equality yet loved my family members. Thus, I found understanding difference, and the obligation that women took upon themselves to work together across difference, intellectually compelling. The group of community activists in New York City that I studied formed coalitions across class, race, ethnicity, gender, and sexuality. From the beginning of my research I hoped to discover the productive role of difference in these coalitions.

Nanci Young was the first, but not the only archivist to help me hone my research questions. Michael Nash of New York University's Tamiment Library led me to the records of Women's Health Action and Mobilization (WHAM!), a group of reproductive rights feminists who partnered with gay men in the AIDS Coalition To Unleash Power (ACT UP) in the 1980s and 1990s. Like the NCNW, WHAM! intrigued me because it contradicted prevailing assumptions that lesbians and gay men had parted ways in the 1970s, and, like so many identity-based political movements of the post–World War II era, diverged to follow separate paths.[3] In fact many historians of the United States still view political movements based on difference—a core value of identity politics—as a hindrance to social movements seeking to expand social justice.[4] Once I discovered these archives, I began to doubt prevailing assumptions that a strong group identity is likely a barrier to social movement building, and I wanted to learn more about how these coalitions maneuvered within the difficult terrain of identity and power.

Meeting WHAM! organizer Elizabeth Meixell was another revelation. A woman in late middle age, she regularly dresses up as a nun and performs with a group of gay men in drag known as the Church Ladies for Choice, singing songs about reproductive rights. Before she would grant me access to the WHAM! records, Meixell wanted to make sure I was legitimate. Although she did not specifically say so, I imagine that she wanted to be confident that I would be fair and respectful, sympathetic but honest in my appraisal of the activism to which she has dedicated so much of her life. She invited me to join her at a series of counterprotests across New York City in response to the antigay demonstrations by opponents of Harvey Milk High School, and I conducted impromptu interviews on the spot.[5] Fortunately, by virtue of continuing to show up, I passed the test. Meixell introduced me to the rest of the Church Ladies for Choice, whose subversive humor I saw in action several times, most notably during the historic April 2004 March for Women's Lives in Washington, D.C., when almost a million people gathered to support reproductive rights. Watching Meixell and the Church Ladies perform taught me firsthand the importance of direct action and of supporting your partners in coalition, as well of being bold and laughing often.

When it came to my learning about Mobilization for Youth (MFY), a social welfare agency that became a model for the War on Poverty, I experienced a different kind of intellectual discovery. I had read about the welfare rights and legal services movements that grew out of Mobilization for Youth,[6] but I wanted to better understand their origins, and especially the variety of interactions among social workers, lawyers, and low-income Puerto Rican and African American mothers living on New York's Lower East Side. As I did more research, I discovered that NCNW founder Janice Peterson, as well as other feminist activists and scholars such as Rosalyn Baxandall, Barbara Hunter Randall Joseph, and Terry Mizrahi had all begun their careers in social work at MFY. This early cohort of organizers gained skills and experience at MFY that allowed them to transition seamlessly into the community activism that was taking place across New York City.

Like theirs, my story must begin with MFY. As community organizer Ezra Birnbaum once reminded me, MFY was an important pioneering organization, but its legacy can be assessed best by examining "what kind of effect it ha[d] on other organizations" and on the subsequent social movements such groups helped initiate.[7] Through its popularization of the idea of "maximum feasible participation" within the policymaking process, MFY captured the early 1960s commitment to broadening the democratic promise of a nation that was still learning from the African American civil rights movement and its larger message that change was worth fighting for. This rich history continues to animate my optimism today.

In the more than fifty oral history interviews I conducted while researching this book, my narrators analyzed their personal political development as well as the successes and failures of the social movements for which they worked. Many viewed their childhoods and upbringings as crucial to the emergence of their political consciousness. Birnbaum, for example, explained how his family's Orthodox Jewish background meant that the "thrust for social justice in general" was "always present in the house."[8] Similarly, the noted social theorist and welfare rights activist Frances Fox Piven recalled the influence of her Russian Jewish father in shaping her independence and her intellectual interests: "I was always interested in social movements and social action. . . . I mean, I had to go to school because I was bred to be an intellectual. . . . [My] father, in particular expected [us] to [consider the question:] What do you want to be when you grow up? Getting married and having children was not an answer. It's not. You're supposed to get married and have children, but it was not an answer to the question."[9] Public housing activist Ethel Velez shared Piven's early consciousness of women's equality: her first organizing project was establishing a girls' basketball team in junior high when "they were only letting the boys play." Growing up African American in a public housing project gave Velez a strong sense of community that translated into taking responsibility for one's civic participation. Velez explained that she had always been organizing, even before she knew what the word meant. She participated in the antiwar and school integration movements when she was in high school in the 1960s; for her it was about "just right and wrong."[10]

As I listened to the stories of their family backgrounds and experiences coming of age, my narrators also asked about my coming of age. Because several of my interviewees were Jewish and my first name, "Tamar," is often understood to be a Hebrew name, while my last name is the Irish-sounding "Carroll," my informants asked me about my ethnic identity. My mixed ancestry contains Welsh, Irish, and Albanian roots, but culturally my family is Massachusetts Irish Catholic, and I grew up in a prosperous suburb of Boston. Though one grandfather worked as a boiler inspector and attended night school with the assistance of the GI Bill to earn his engineering degree, my parents were the first in their families to attend college full-time. While I am not a native New Yorker, I nevertheless fell in love with the city when, as an undergraduate at the University of Massachusetts, I first visited the Big Apple.

Like Frances Fox Piven, my father encouraged me to pursue graduate education, and like Velez, my family nurtured in me a strong sense of civic engagement and of the obligation to fight for my belief in what was right. My mother, a woman so empathetic strangers often choose to tell her their life stories, taught me to be a good listener. That skill, along with my youth and status as a graduate student, helped me establish trust with my narrators. In my late twenties, as I gathered the experiences of women and men twice my age and even older, it became immediately clear that I was there to learn from them. My narrators were authorities of the past, and their stories attempted to explain both to me and themselves how they came to hold a feminist perspective. While some interviewees credited their upbringing in general for their social activism, others recalled a specific event that altered their understanding of how society worked. For a number of women, the difficulty of trying to obtain an abortion shaped not only their political consciousness, but also their understanding of a range of constraints, both legal and cultural, on women. Karen Stamm first became involved in women's issues when she obtained an illegal abortion in 1963. She never forgot "the hoops I had to jump through in order to get a psychiatric abortion." She made "a commitment to myself that if the opportunity ever arose to fix the situation I was going to fix it."[11]

Struggles to obtain reproductive freedom, economic independence, and day care for their children while they worked drew many women into community activism. For others, however, the death of relative or close friend from AIDS led to the development of a feminist consciousness. Virginia Kennedy's uncle, a closeted gay man, became ill and died prematurely. The tragedy made her aware of how homophobia had shaped his life and his interactions with her parents, who were staunchly Roman Catholic. As a child, she recalled, "the male authority figure was very prominent" but she "learn[ed] to start to resist this authoritarian paradigm." Her grief at her uncle's death catalyzed a political and personal transformation. No longer "an obedient woman," she became "steadily more politically active," ultimately breaking with the Catholic Church, because she felt it had "no place for me, for gay men, and for women who want to choose what to do with their bodies."[12]

My own feminism as well as my commitment to women's history as a discipline also helped me establish trust with my narrators. Like me, many of them had been raised in traditional Catholic families and later developed a feminist consciousness. This enabled them to trust me, and sometimes even perceive me as a younger version of themselves, or as a younger sister. In addition, my training as a journalist and historian comes with it the assumption that we are primarily chroniclers of the past, rather than activists ourselves. Generally, my subjects accepted my attempts to record and interpret the past as accurately as I could and seemed pleased that I considered their work important enough to insist that their place in history be recognized. Often I was thanked for my persistence and hard work. It is also true that not everyone I contacted was willing to be interviewed. One person even opposed my attempt to gather WHAM! members together for a reflective reunion, feeling strongly that time could be better spent in activism itself, rather than in sentimental reminiscence.

After tracing their political development, my narrators discussed the challenges they encountered trying to achieve their goals. For some, the dangers of crossing boundaries were palpable. At the close of a few interviews, after I had already shut off my recorder, several present expressed fear for my safety; one even insisted on walking me out of her neighborhood. This kind concern indicated that they perceived me as "other," vulnerable because of my outsider status and my appearance as a white woman from a background of relative privilege. These interactions reinforced the saliency of race and class difference, which shapes daily social relations in New York City.

My narrators helped me appreciate the courage involved in participating in cross-race and cross-class coalitional politics and the limitations of my own experience as a basis for understanding. They also changed the way I thought about priorities. Velez explained that after many years of organizing, when her Tenants' Association finally won federal funds to renovate the public housing complex where they lived, the first thing on their agenda was building a six-foot fence around the perimeter to keep out people with guns who were running through the grounds.[13] Before that conversation, I had never thought of "fences" as an asset to social justice activism, but Velez taught me that unless people feel safe it is hard to work on other issues. This book celebrates not only what I learned from women like Velez, but also the strengths and insights that diverse people and perspectives can bring to social movements. On the other hand, it also acknowledges the profound pain and discord that is the outcome of social and economic oppression, so often justified by theories of difference.

My narrators faced difficulties and setbacks unimaginable to me before I began this project, yet the great majority of them continued to participate in community-based activism well into their advanced years. Their example has convinced me, as Elizabeth Meixell put it, that "We're here and we might as well do something."[14] Ethel Velez is currently trying to "organize the whole city" to prevent the privatization of public housing, while Jan Peterson is a leader in the global feminist movement and founder of Grassroots Organizations Operating Together in Sisterhood (GROOTS International), a nonprofit dedicated to increasing the participation of women in development of their communities. Steven Wizner, a former staff attorney for MFY, supervises Yale law school students working with low-income and undocumented New Haven residents in clinics run by Immigration Legal Services and Legal Services for Immigrant Communities. When I interviewed Ezra Birnbaum at age seventy-four in 2005, he was retired, but still working full-time as an organizer; at the time he was recruiting pharmacists, EMTs, paramedics, and other health care workers to join Chapter 1199 of the Service Employees International Union. He explained, "It's always worthwhile to be part of and help create movements for social change . . . because one never knows what it's going to turn into."[15]

While I did not always know where my graduate training would lead, the more I studied and taught history, the more I found myself drawn to those accounts of ordinary people transforming their own lives in an attempt to change the course of events. I wanted to know: How do people make meaning in their own lives? How might I emulate them in addressing the issues facing my own generation? My idea to turn to grassroots activists for answers was confirmed when, during the NCNW reunion at Smith College in 2004, attendees were granted an unusual privilege: access to the archival storage vault. As we entered the vast climate-controlled room filled with floor-to-ceiling shelves, a staff member pointed to the NCNW records, which interestingly enough are shelved alongside Gloria Steinem's papers. Several NCNW members grew teary-eyed, moved by this visual recognition that they are as important to history as the best-known American spokeswoman for feminism.[16] Our visit to the vault that day confirmed for me the importance of documenting and disseminating the history of community activists who, while seldom recognized for their contributions, have important stories to tell about social change in the United States.

Abbreviations

ACLU	American Civil Liberties Union
ACORN	Association of Community Organizations for Reform Now
ACT UP	AIDS Coalition To Unleash Power
AFDC	Aid to Families with Dependent Children
BID	Business Improvement District
CAP	Community Action Program
CARASA	Committee for Abortion Rights and Against Sterilization Abuse
CDC	Centers for Disease Control
CETA	Comprehensive Employment and Training Act
CORE	Congress of Racial Equality
FHA	Federal Housing Authority
GRID	Gay-Related Immune Deficiency
GROOTS	Grassroots Organizations Operating Together in Sisterhood
HOLC	Home Owners' Loan Corporation
HUD	Department of Housing and Urban Development
JTPA	Job Training Partnership Act
LENA	Lower Eastside Neighborhood Association
MOM	Mobilization of Mothers
MFY	Mobilization for Youth
NAACP	National Association for the Advancement of Colored People
NAG	Negro Action Group
NAN	National Association of Neighborhoods
NCNW	National Congress of Neighborhood Women
NEA	National Endowment for the Arts

NGO	Nongovernmental Organization
NIH	National Institutes of Health
NOW	National Organization for Women
NNC	Northside Neighborhood Committee
NYCPHA	New York City Public Housing Authority
OEO	Office of Economic Opportunity
PATCO	Professional Air Traffic Controllers Organization
PCJD	President's Committee on Juvenile Deliquency and Youth Crime
RRC	Reproductive Rights Coalition
TANF	Temporary Aid to Needy Families
TOP	Tenant Opportunity Program
UFT	United Federation of Teachers
UN	United Nations
UNB	United Bronx Parents
WEP	Work Experience Program
WHAM!	Women's Health Action and Mobilization
YAAG	Young Adult Action Group
YELL	Youth Education Life Line

Mobilizing New York

Introduction

In July 1991, a group of gay men from the AIDS Coalition to Unleash Power (ACT UP) joined activists from Women's Health Action and Mobilization (WHAM!) on a memorable ferry ride to the Statue of Liberty. It was not the first time that gay men and reproductive rights feminists had traveled to the iconic monument together; rather, this excursion was a culmination of "many, many, many reconnaissance trips" and detailed planning. Dressed conservatively, they carried balloons and concrete blocks covered in colorful wrapping paper, which they deliberately displayed for the benefit of the security cameras. Once they reached Liberty Island, they headed to the top of the statue, used keys to open the windows, and placed a banner over Lady Liberty's face reading "No Choice, No Liberty." This "gag" was designed to represent the Supreme Court's recent "gag rule" in *Rust v. Sullivan,* which upheld a domestic ban on abortion counseling at federally funded family-planning clinics. Simultaneously, other activists draped a 900-foot-long banner over the statue's pedestal that read "Abortion is Healthcare—Healthcare is a Right." Park rangers hurriedly removed the banners, a move WHAM! had anticipated; photographer Meryl Levin captured a shot of the display before rangers could remove it.[1] (See figure 1.)

The Statue of Liberty protest and similar direct actions conducted between the 1960s and the early 1990s allowed social activists to appropriate New York's landmarks and give them new meaning. WHAM!'s powerful image of impingement on women's freedom reached a broad audience

1

Abortion is healthcare. Healthcare is a right.

ABORTION IS HEALTHCARE HEALTHCARE IS A RIGHT

WHAM!

WOMEN'S HEALTH ACTION AND MOBILIZATION

Figure 1. Poster with photograph of WHAM!'s Statue of Liberty action, July 29, 1991, photograph by Meryl Levin. WHAM! Records, Tamiment Library, NYU, Box 9, Folder "Resume." Courtesy of Meryl Levin.

when Levin's photograph and accompanying stories ran in newspapers across the United States and internationally.[2] As WHAM! member Karen Ramspacher explained, "Whenever we conceived an action . . . we tried to do it in such a way that the media could access it and get the message quickly, so that they would cover it, so that more people would read about it."[3] By selecting the Statue of Liberty as the site of their protest, WHAM! ensured that reporters and editors, as well as onlookers, would rapidly understand the connection they were drawing between individual freedom, misunderstandings of American exceptionalism, and women's reproductive autonomy.

New York's many landmarks provide a range of unique venues for activism. Demonstrations, marches, strikes, acts of civil disobedience, and even poster campaigns are ensured global reach as print, broadcast, and online media inform the greater public. In addition, New Yorkers often travel by foot, rub shoulders on the subways and sidewalks, and utilize the city's many parks during lunch breaks or after work. Along with the tens of millions of tourists the city hosts every year, these residents and workers provide a built-in audience for activists, whose attention-grabbing graphics, words, and performances transform the city's spaces into forums for critical and creative expression. Activists can usually rely on their fellow New Yorkers to be open-minded enough to listen and savvy enough to "get" their jokes.

New Yorkers' long history of direct action provides resources to activists as well. Labor militancy, rent strikes, and mass gatherings have drawn in generations of New Yorkers, many of them immigrants learning strategies from one another. In the twentieth century, New York was the site of significant demonstrations for labor unions and workers' rights, women's suffrage, peace, civil rights, economic justice, opposition to urban renewal, gay rights, feminism, and a nuclear freeze, among other causes. Free expression is part of the city's enduring appeal, along with diversity of all kinds and vibrant intellectual and artistic communities engaged with the metropolis around them, often contributing ideas and members to movements. Frequently, mass demonstrations in New York have influenced activists in other places, and led to changes in social policy.[4]

One such example was the devastating Triangle Shirtwaist Factory Fire of 1911, in which 146 people—mostly young Italian and Eastern European Jewish immigrant women—died in a locked building in Washington Square. The tragedy strengthened the resolve of garment workers to unionize and to demand government regulation of working conditions. They took to the streets by the hundreds of thousands, held mass meetings in the Great Hall of Cooper Union, went on strike, and worked with allies, including middle-class progressive reformers and liberal politicians, to enact protective labor legislation at the state level. Later, during the New Deal, Congress adopted New York's model labor legislation at the national level: the 1935 National Labor Relations (Wagner) Act guaranteed workers the right to unionize and to bargain collectively, and the 1935 Social Security Act established federal unemployment income, old-age insurance, and workers' compensation.[5]

In the mid-twentieth century, urban studies theorist and activist Jane Jacobs led a movement to oppose city plans to extend Fifth Avenue through Washington Square Park, a design that included the construction of the Lower Manhattan Expressway (Lomex) through SoHo and the Lower East Side. Jacobs mobilized city dwellers and changed the way urban planners in cities across North America and Europe thought about redevelopment and community participation in planning processes.[6] Jacobs collaborated with other leaders, including Catholic priest Gerald La Mountain and Puerto Rican activist Ernesto Martinez, to organize residents and to challenge city plans for construction of the highway through some of the oldest neighborhoods in the city.[7] Through her writing, public speaking, and willingness to be arrested during acts of civil disobedience—and her committed defiance of powerful development czar Robert Moses—Jacobs succeeded not only in stopping the Lomex but in inspiring other resident-led "freeway revolts" that eliminated highways planned in thickly settled urban neighborhoods in Boston, San Francisco, Baltimore, Milwaukee, New Orleans, Philadelphia, and Toronto.[8]

In June 1969 in Jacobs's beloved Greenwich Village, gay men and lesbians at the Stonewall Inn on Christopher Street fought back against police trying to arrest them. The "Stonewall Riots" led to a sea change in the consciousness of gay men and lesbians and sparked the birth of the modern gay and lesbian rights movement; pioneering gay rights leader Lilli Vincenz recalled "people who had felt oppressed now felt empowered."[9] Inspired by the uprising, activists formed the Gay Liberation Front and the Gay Activist Alliance, both of which attacked institutionalized homophobia and encouraged gay men and lesbians to come out of the closet and live openly as homosexuals. In 1970, gay men and lesbians gathered to commemorate the Stonewall Uprising and marched from Christopher Street to Central Park in the first New York Gay Pride March, while simultaneous demonstrations took place in Los Angeles and Chicago. The gay and lesbian rights movement quickly achieved victories including the 1973 removal of homosexuality from the American Psychiatric Association's *Diagnostic and Statistical Manual of Mental Disorders* (DSM) and the passage of civil rights ordinances banning discrimination based on sexual orientation.[10]

Recent events such as the centennial commemorations of the Triangle Shirtwaist Factory Fire in 2011, the celebrations of Jane Jacobs's life in 2007–8, and the annual New York Gay Pride March have ensured that the legacies of the early actions persist in the collective memory of New Yorkers, providing models and, in some cases, continuities between social movements in terms of participants, goals, strategies, and tactics. These public remembrances give even the most recent of New Yorkers a sense of the historical significance of their city, and implicitly, their own potential to make history. Most importantly, commemorations of these events convey the message that ordinary people, through collective action, can advance change in the world.[11]

While the rich activist histories of some sites, like the Stonewall Inn or the Triangle Building, are periodically excavated and harnessed for new movement goals during commemorations, New York's many landmarks provide activists with immediately recognizable symbols. Wall Street, Madison Avenue, Times Square, Broadway, the United Nations, and even Trump Tower: all these places resonate as centers of American economic, cultural, and political power. The stock exchange and Federal Reserve Bank on Wall Street epitomize the free-market system, while the advertising firms and luxury retailers on Madison Avenue reflect the consumer culture and the wealth and inequality it generates. Countless young women have hoped for an engagement ring from Tiffany & Co., the jewelry store featured in Truman Capote's *Breakfast at Tiffany's* and its 1961 film version starring Audrey Hepburn; they plan pilgrimages to the company's 5th Avenue flagship and neighboring stores, and Tiffany's iconic shopping bags symbolize success and upward mobility. To the poor people and antipoverty workers who staged a 1966 demonstration at the nearby New York headquarters of the Office of Economic Opportunity, in contrast, Madison Avenue represented money being unfairly withheld from people who need it by "savages."[12] Home to broadcast stations and theaters, Times Square and Broadway conjure up American media and cultural dominance, while the United Nations and One World Trade Center represent America's post–World War II global leadership as well as the challenges to it. They are icons not just of New York, but of the United States and its role in the world.

Just as its landmarks can be read in multiple ways, symbolizing both freedom and repression, New York has long been perceived as simultaneously distinctive and representative of America. On the one hand, Americans recognize New York's central role in generating economic growth, developing cultural and media dominance, and shaping national politics. On the other hand, New York's large foreign-born population leads critics to label it un-American, and its combination of great wealth and deep poverty has led to its association with social problems. The city is identified both with the elite, the movers and shakers who make this country rich and powerful, and with the poor, foreign, bohemian, and dangerous. New York is at once both the core of the nation and on the periphery of the heartland. As one WHAM! poster, responding to anti-abortion activists in the National Right to Life Committee who planned a "human cross" demonstration in Midtown Manhattan in 1991, put it, "New York isn't Wichita" (See figure 2).[13]

To residents of Middle America, New York can indeed seem like its own country, and yet Americans' sense of identity in the decades following World War II has been tied to the fortunes of the United States' largest city. During the early years of the Cold War, New York showcased the growing

prosperity of the nation as massive urban renewal projects, including public housing in East Harlem, the Lincoln Center for the Performing Arts on Manhattan's West Side, the middle-class housing developments of Stuyvesant Town and Peter Cooper Village on the Lower East Side, and the United Nations complex transformed the landscape of the city, while the Cross-Bronx Expressway and new parkways, bridges, and tunnels channeled commuters into the rapidly spreading suburbs.[14] Although federal transportation, housing, and defense policy was shifting the nation's center of gravity to the Sunbelt and the suburbs, New York City remained important. "By general consent," *Time* magazine declared in 1962, "Manhattan is the U.S.'s cultural capital, the greatest concentration of taste and wealth in the nation."[15] Artists, in particular abstract expressionists, and the concentration of world-class universities helped realize city boosters' dreams of New York becoming an international cultural capital as well.[16]

New York's model social welfare system that allowed average Americans to partake in the nation's economic success and enjoy a high quality of life was also a source of pride. Buoyed by strong labor unions and liberal political leadership from Democratic mayor Robert F. Wagner Jr. (1954–65) and moderate Republican governor Nelson A. Rockefeller (1959–73), New York built what Joshua Freeman has termed a "municipal social democracy" that offered white working- and middle-class New Yorkers affordable housing, health care, pensions, cost-of-living wage increases, access to public higher education, and public transit.[17] Civil rights leaders fought to win the inclusion of African Americans in New York's social democracy, and they valued public provision of social welfare programs and sought to hold government responsible for ensuring access to good jobs, housing, education and health care, as well as an end to police brutality.[18] With the support of their allies in New York's communist left, civil rights activists won landmark legislation, including the 1945 Ives-Quinn Law banning discrimination in private employment and the 1951 Brown-Isaacs Law barring discrimination in all publicly assisted private housing, an impetus and model for the federal Fair Housing Act of 1968.[19]

Although city officials and white residents did not grant the city's growing population of African Americans and Puerto Ricans equal access to good jobs and high-quality housing and schools, those families that were able to move into public housing shared in some of the city's benefits and laid claim to part of the fruits of citizenship. Moreover, in New York and throughout the urban North in the years following World War II, African American women participated in what Lisa Levenstein terms a "movement without marches," using public institutions to secure housing, education, health care, financial support for childrearing, and protection from domestic violence. Through their daily interactions with public institutions, in spite of frequent and ongoing efforts to deny them the resources they sought, low-income African American women sought to realize their vision of an expansive citizenship in which the state met its obligations to ensure their well-being and dignity.[20]

Public housing served as a particularly important site for women's enactment of citizenship. By implying a right to decent living conditions for citizens and bridging the private, domestic sphere with the political sphere of government, public housing linked "familial duties with community participation and political activism."[21] This was certainly the case for African American community activist Ethel Velez, who traced her lifelong involvement in social justice causes to her experiences growing up in public housing in the 1950s and 1960s. She recalled her childhood home fondly, explaining that it gave her a strong sense of what scholars call social citizenship, or the ability of all citizens, particularly those with low incomes, to enjoy meaningful inclusion in society: "It was just really fun growing up in the projects. Particularly, I didn't know I was poor. I didn't even know I was poor, because we had food, we had clothing, we had a house. . . . It took me a long time to realize I was poor."[22]

For African Americans and Puerto Ricans, New York represented both the promises of postwar liberalism and its persistent exclusions. While on the one hand the successes of the civil rights movement in New York City inspired activists across the country and raised hopes among New Yorkers themselves, as in other northern cities, segregation in housing and schools worsened in the 1950s and 1960s, due to a combination of poor law enforcement and federally financed urban redevelopment and suburbanization.[23] Increasingly in the 1960s, New Yorkers were inspired by the mass demonstrations and dramatic nonviolent civil disobedience of the southern civil right movement, even as New York's leaders used media depictions of southern racism to deflect rising calls for change at home.[24] Soon New York's social democracy faced not only challenges from movements seeking greater inclusion and fairness, but also counterattacks from capital insistent on reducing social welfare spending and weakening labor's influence.

My first chapter begins in the Cold War years with Mobilization for Youth (MFY), a social program funded by the Kennedy administration and the Ford Foundation. It aimed to assist Puerto Rican and African American male youths in achieving upward mobility and full inclusion in American society. MFY was located in the Lower East Side, a neighborhood inhabited by successive waves of poor immigrants, including Irish in the 1840s and 1850s, Germans in the 1860s through the 1880s, Eastern European Jews and Italians from the 1880s until World War I, African Americans and Puerto Ricans from the 1940s through the 1970s, and Chinese, particularly after immigration reform in 1965. (See map 1.) Some of its crowded tenements had been replaced by low-income public housing projects and middle-income cooperatives, but in the 1950s and 1960s many families continued to live in substandard apartments without hot water and central heating, "run-down in every way."[25] The Lower East Side had an early tradition of radical politics, based on the largely Eastern European and Italian garment workers' labor unions, as well as of progressive reform, based in the early twentieth-century settlement house movement, which sought to regulate industrial capitalism, improve public health, ameliorate poverty, and promote the assimilation of immigrants to American culture.[26]

By the 1950s, however, the increasingly impoverished and nonwhite neighborhood was becoming known for gang violence and heroin, a "junkies' paradise." In 1963 the *Daily News* characterized it as the worst neighborhood in New York.[27] The Lower East Side provided a perfect social laboratory for Lloyd Ohlin and Richard Cloward, Columbia University sociologists who were eager to test out their opportunity theory thesis, which posited that the cause of juvenile delinquency was blocked ambitions among poor youth, who had little opportunity to achieve the middle-class status that American culture promoted and they desired, and who therefore turned to antisocial behavior.[28] Ohlin and Cloward caught the eye of the Kennedy administration, which responded to growing concerns about gang violence and drug use among teenagers by funding Mobilization for Youth as a comprehensive social service agency. As Attorney General Robert F. Kennedy explained in 1962, "Our great challenge is to offer new and expanded opportunities to young people, opportunities in education and employment, and recreation, opportunities to overcome barriers based on race and religion. We must help these young people so that they will want to lead decent, useful lives, rather than lives of crime and self-destruction."[29]

Ohlin and Cloward initially conceptualized MFY as a top-down, expert intervention program aimed at low-income Puerto Rican and African American male youths and focused on remedial education and job training. Indeed, no one involved in its founding anticipated MFY's generative role in the welfare rights movement. In chapter 1, I show how low-income Puerto Rican and African American mothers reoriented the agency's focus from juvenile delinquency to the broader problems of low-income mothers and families.[30] As these mothers came to MFY's storefront offices for help with securing decent housing, the welfare benefits they were entitled to but often denied, and quality education for their children, they pushed social workers to develop a new model of client advocacy. MFY's clients, along with the larger civil rights movement, helped to transform technocratic liberalism from below. As MFY program director George Brager later reflected, "I think our grassroots involvement and notions of self-determination came as we were on the streets, and engaged with people."[31] Inspired by the mass demonstrations of the southern civil rights movement and by their participation in consciousness-raising groups sponsored by MFY's social workers, Puerto Rican and African American mothers used direct-action politics, including school boycotts, rent strikes, and sit-ins at the city welfare department, to demand that their needs be met and their rights as citizens be realized. Through their collaboration with social workers and lawyers and their coalitions with civil rights groups, these activists achieved important victories, including an end to midnight raids into the homes of women receiving welfare to determine if there was a man present.[32]

Very quickly, MFY's frontal attacks on landlords, the public schools, and the welfare and police departments resulted in a city council–led backlash against the agency. *The Daily News* accused MFY of harboring communists and sponsoring un-American activities, particularly the July 1964 New York race riots, which were actually sparked by police brutality and by frustration with the glacial pace of school and residential integration. Chapter 2 demonstrates that in the mid- and late 1960s, even as MFY was forced to curtail its more radical programs, it helped generate and influence the development of the legal services, welfare rights, and Black Arts movements. Moreover, as Lyndon Johnson pledged to wage a national War on Poverty, his administration took many of MFY's innovations and included them in the 1964 Economic Opportunity Act, in particular the employment of paraprofessionals, neighborhood residents who did not have formal education but who were valued for their experiential knowledge, and the concept of maximum feasible participation, the idea that poor people themselves should be involved in decision making in antipoverty programs.[33]

When Frances Fox Piven joined the staff of MFY as a researcher, Richard Cloward met his intellectual equal. It was not long before the two became partners in work and life. Together, they developed a theory of political participation that helped explain how disruptive poor people's mobilizations could be to existing power relationships. They encouraged a range of grassroots activity, including suggesting that welfare rights groups proactively canvass individuals and families eligible for benefits and help sign them up. This dramatic increase in the welfare rolls led to budget shortfalls at city and state levels. Piven and Cloward anticipated that the resulting crises would encourage the federal government to step in and provide a guaranteed minimum income to all, a sort of negative income tax that they believed would end poverty.[34] The time was ripe for such innovation, and they came close to achieving their goal. In New York City from 1965 to 1969 "the number of families receiving AFDC [Aid to Families with Dependent Children] more than doubled from 130,000 to 272,000." By 1969, liberal Republican mayor John Lindsay was writing to President Richard Nixon for help in addressing New York's budget crunch.[35] In response to concerns about rising welfare rolls nationally and the mounting political pressure to relieve cities and states from increased costs, Nixon proposed a Family Assistance Plan (FAP) that would have replaced AFDC with a guaranteed minimum income, albeit at a much lower rate than that sought by welfare rights' activists. Opposition from powerful Southern Democrats, always wary of challenges to white supremacy, ensured that the FAP legislation never made it out of the Senate Finance Committee. In the end, controversy over the program encouraged Nixon to withdraw his support for the legislation prior to the 1972 presidential campaign.[36]

Cloward and Piven's book, *The Politics of Turmoil* (1974) argues that the most significant accomplishment of the federal government's antipoverty programs of the 1960s, including MFY and the War on Poverty, was to direct federal funds to African American residents in the urban North, which secured their allegiance to the Democratic Party. MFY, Piven argued, was "influential . . . not as a programmatic model" but rather because it showed how federal agencies could bypass city hall and administrators' reluctance to alienate white voters by visibly spending money on services for African Americans.[37] Certainly both the Kennedy and Johnson administrations hoped to stave off unrest in poor ghettos through channeling funding to those communities. David Hackett, who toured Harlem, Watts, and Appalachia with Attorney General Robert Kennedy in 1961 and 1962, recalled "I can remember very distinctly his [RFK] beginning to talk about the riots and what we were going to have in this country, were riots. It didn't take much genius; it's just the fact that we went into ghettos."[38] Those encounters helped solidify the Kennedy brothers' commitment to funding antipoverty programs. For antipoverty workers and low-income community activists themselves, however, the commitment of the federal government to the concept of maximum feasible participation was significant not only because it allowed for federal funds to flow more directly to poor and non-white communities, but also because it enabled them to imagine and enact new relationships and novel solutions to community problems.

Social worker Janet Peterson worked at MFY's storefront offices and helped Lower East residents figure out "how to get the services they were supposed to be entitled to from the city." (See figure 3.) She defined maximum feasible participation as the belief "that the poor deserved to be part of their own problem solving" and explained that "there really was a very different tone" at MFY:

> You felt like you were in service to [poor residents]. It wasn't like the Department of Welfare where people are lined up and you're going to

Figure 3. MFY social worker and NCNW founder Jan Peterson, ca. 1977, photograph by Janie Eisenberg. Courtesy of Janie Eisenberg.

decide who is deserving and who is not deserving. You were there as part of the whole community. You were working with the poor themselves to try to figure out what to do, and if nothing else, on any given day, even if all you were able to do was to get the government to deal with the person that you were seeing—you know, I saw probably ninety people a day, I remember, it's unbelievable. And they got their coat, they got their heat turned on . . . And you did it together. I mean, we were working together . . . you felt that you were actually really part of something, and that you were building, and that the government of the country you lived in actually cared about this kind of work.[39]

As soon as MFY created opportunity for the Lower East Side's poor to participate, people flooded its programs. Interactions with each other and with staff workers were significant, particularly when they acted together in groups. Puerto Rican activist Manny Diaz described his coworkers at MFY as "innovators" whose willingness to experiment left him feeling "liberated." He recalled "I had never felt more influential or more powerful than I did when I was running these programs at MFY. Why? Because they seemed to be meaningful."[40] Maximum feasible participation, in historian

Christina Green's words, "fostered a climate for creative community projects and interracial alliances."[41]

As the Community Action Programs (CAPs) of the War on Poverty spread MFY's innovations and optimism nationally, some of MFY's social workers and community organizers secured funding through these programs to start their own community agencies in New York. There, as in other places, the dynamism of the CAPs was a result of the convergence of multiple social movements of the late 1960s and early 1970s, including the civil rights, Black Power, New Left, women's liberation, gay and lesbian rights, and white ethnic movements, and the availability of federal funding for these local efforts.[42] Locally, the city was losing manufacturing jobs and white middle-class residents to suburbia and sliding towards racial polarization; yet Johnson's Great Society and the election of liberal Republican mayor John Lindsay (1966–73) rekindled hope that New York could fulfill its promise of full inclusion. Donald Elliot, chair of the City Planning Commission under Lindsay, later explained that when Lindsay took office even Republicans believed "government was expected to make society better and everybody believed it could do so."[43]

Janet Peterson's story illustrates the determination and optimism as well as some of the tensions that emerged during the 1960s. A Wisconsin-born social worker of Swedish descent, Peterson was drawn to New York City specifically because of its culture of social movement activism. Twenty-two years old in 1963, she "got on a bus" to New York "to look for the civil rights movement." She found it in the Harlem chapter of the interracial Congress of Racial Equality (CORE), a group that advocated a community control model that encouraged black self-determination and leadership in black neighborhoods.[44] Peterson's experience at CORE was exhilarating, but she was eventually challenged by organization leader Marshall England, who was also her romantic partner, to organize in a white community.

In the late 1960s, Peterson also participated in the New York Chapter of the National Organization for Women (NOW), as well as more radical feminist and socialist feminist groups, from which she gained "a new awareness: women, myself." As Peterson put it, she was "combining all of these movements in my body." While MFY's leadership anticipated their organization would be relatively short-lived because of the controversial nature of mobilizing poor people to hold landlords, school officials, and city government accountable, Peterson became increasingly interested in long-term development and hoped to build a community organization that would nurture its members and become a part of the social fabric of the neighborhood. In 1969, heeding England's challenge, Peterson moved to

Williamsburg, Brooklyn, where she was determined to apply what she had learned at MFY, CORE, and in the women's movement to organizing the white ethnic working-class community with the War on Poverty CAP funding she had obtained.[45]

Part II of this book follows Peterson to Williamsburg-Greenpoint, another neighborhood settled in the early 1900s by Italian and Jewish immigrants. (See map 2.) On Manhattan's periphery, the area exhibited the convergence of deindustrialization and the white ethnic and feminist movements in the 1970s. As skyscrapers sprung up across Midtown Manhattan in the 1950s and 1960s, they signified a shift in New York's economy toward banking, finance, advertising, and entertainment, all sectors employing primarily white-collar workers.[46] Across the East River, Williamsburg and Greenpoint offered residents a landscape of abandoned factories and derelict warehouses, including the shuttered Brooklyn Navy Yard.[47] The loss of manufacturing jobs eroded the city's tax base and middle-class residents abandoned the area, while the costs of social welfare programs and public services surged. Budget shortfalls became common. When rising energy costs triggered a national recession in the early 1970s, New York City's finances veered into crisis.

For Williamsburg-Greenpoint's white ethnic working-class residents, the city's fiscal crisis meant the loss of services, as Abraham Beame's mayoral administration (1974–77) implemented "planned shrinkage." The program included the withdrawal of police and fire stations and the closure of schools, hospitals, and subway stations in poor and nonwhite areas at Manhattan's periphery. As was often the case in the 1970s, federal funding for antipoverty programs continued even as cities cut services to the poor and working class, and local residents formed a CAP. In chapter 3, I argue that federally funded community organizing programs channeled Williamsburg-Greenpoint residents' anger against the city government rather than at racial others, allowing the neighborhood to avoid the violent white racial backlash against school busing that broke out in nearby Canarsie in 1972.[48] Building on this mobilization and using War on Poverty funds, Peterson worked closely with a group of Italian American women to open the neighborhood's first day care and senior citizens' center. The creation of Small World Day Care and the Swinging Sixties Senior Center turned out to be a contentious project opposed by many male leaders in the neighborhood, and one that drew the women into feminist organizing in the National Congress of Neighborhood Women (NCNW), which Peterson founded in Brooklyn in 1974.

In 1975, the NCNW developed an innovative neighborhood-based college program for Williamsburg-Greenpoint's women, many of whom had not graduated from high school and who increasingly needed to enter the paid workforce to support their families, as working-class men's real wages fell and divorce became more common. Peterson recruited African American and Puerto Rican women, who were leaders in their public housing tenants' association, to join the NCNW, and through group education and consciousness-raising members formed alliances across racial and ethnic differences. In 1976, in partnership with the Brooklyn YWCA, the NCNW founded the Women's Survival Space, the first battered women's shelter in New York City. Using federal funds generated through the Comprehensive Employment and Training Act (CETA), from 1975 to 1982 the NCNW administered a job-training program, Project Open Doors, which employed 200 women in feminist nonprofits across the city. NCNW placements ranged from Women Make Movies, a film and video training program, to Building for Women, a carpentry program for female ex-offenders, to the Brooklyn Women's Martial Arts Union and the New York City branch of the National Organization for Women (NOW). The NCNW developed an inclusive, class-conscious feminism that "funded the entire women's movement of the City of New York."[49]

Like New York itself, liberalism was embattled in the 1970s; yet federal funding enabled the working-class feminism of the NCNW to flourish. While historians have chronicled white racial backlash and New York's descent into urban crisis, especially the widespread arson in the Bronx and Bushwick, looking at the grassroots efforts in Brooklyn in these years reveals previously untold stories of interracial and cross-class collaboration, of the strengthening rather than destruction of communities, and of the continuing importance of federal funds to sustaining community programs. The NCNW's achievements in the 1970s also capture the vibrancy, diversity, and wide reach of feminism.[50]

Sally Martino Fisher, who grew up in a working-class Italian American family in Williamsburg, graduated from the NCNW college program and worked as an administrator in Project Open Doors. She recalled those years as the best of her life, saying that she felt a deep sense of accomplishment and belonging as a result of her participation in the NCNW:

I mean, we're telling poor, working-class women that National Congress is a vehicle for a voice for them in the women's movement. Not the traditional women's movement, and we're going to bring your issues, your

Figure 4. NCNW members Sally Martino Fisher and Diane Jackson at the 1977 National Women's Conference in Houston, Tex., photograph by Janie Eisenberg. Courtesy of Janie Eisenberg.

bread-and-butter issues to that movement for support. So that you could move. And you know, that's what we did, exactly what we promised. We came up with job training, we came up with women getting jobs. All of what we said, getting their high school diplomas, learning how to speak English; I mean, all of the things that we said that we would do. And that's why I feel so good about organizing around that, because I saw the outcome and that made me feel that I really had a place. I really helped them and I guess that's another reason I feel so great about those years.[51] (See figure 4.)

Chapter 4 chronicles the Reagan administration's elimination of CETA and its massive cutbacks on funding for community programs in the 1980s, which marked a turning point for both the NCNW and for wider progressive activism. As federal funding became scarce and highly restrictive, activists increasingly relied on foundations and the nonprofit sector. However, foundations were also influenced by the ascendancy of conservative critiques of social programs and implemented their own requirements for evaluation; in the practice of random assignment research, one person seeking services would have to be turned away for each person receiving them in order to have a "control group" against which to measure program effectiveness. The restrictions on both public and private funding mandated a more hierarchical model that undermined the empowerment of community residents and the principle of inclusion to which the NCNW was dedicated.[52] While the organization found some success working on tenant management programs with public housing leaders, for the most part its local programs diminished in the 1980s, and Peterson instead turned toward the United Nations and the international women's movement.

Locally, Mayor Ed Koch (Democrat, 1978–89), like Reagan, championed conservative social causes and radically cut funding to poverty and community organizing programs. When the city's economy rebounded in the 1980s, it was the banking, finance, and real estate sectors at Manhattan's core that experienced the most gains, even as poverty substantially worsened.[53] Koch signaled his allegiance to real estate investors with plans for more luxury housing developments, declaring "We're not catering to the poor any more. . . . They don't have to live in Manhattan."[54] In 1986, real estate tycoon Donald Trump epitomized the ascendance of the private sector and the degradation of the public when he rebuilt Central Park's ice-skating rink in five months, after the city's attempt to do so had dragged on for more than six years.[55] Increasingly, New York in the 1980s was characterized by gentrification, conspicuous consumption, and speculative finance on the one hand, and the crack epidemic, homelessness, and mass incarceration on the other.[56]

Part III enters this changed political landscape by charting the development of a different kind of community-based organization and a new vision of social justice that emerged from a younger generation of activists. Like Jan Peterson, artist Patrick Moore traveled from the Midwest in search of a community. After arriving in New York from Iowa in 1984, he recalled, "I sought connections to the gay world but could find none." The advent of the AIDS epidemic and the Koch administration's subsequent closure of gay bathhouses, along with gentrification's elimination of traditional cruising grounds, had greatly reduced the visibility of gay culture. Soon a movement to reclaim space in the city, to reclaim gay sexuality, and to call for treatment and prevention of AIDS emerged in dramatic form. Moore remembered the first time he saw the strikingly powerful "Silence = Death" poster, created by the Gran Fury art collective in 1987 and adopted by ACT UP as its logo, pasted on construction walls and over subway advertisements. (See figure 5.) "Suddenly, though I knew nothing about it, I felt intuitively that there was in fact a gay world that I could not only identify with but aspire to join."[57] Through their use of stunning visual art and spectacular street theater, AIDS activists reshaped the social geography of Lower Manhattan, subverting both the

Figure 5. Protestor wearing "Silence = Death" T-shirt at the Ashes Demonstration, Washington, D.C., October 11, 1992, photograph by Meg Handler. Courtesy of Meg Handler.

commercialization of public space and homophobic responses to the epidemic and allowing Moore and hundreds of others to connect.

In chapter 5 I show how ACT UP created a supportive queer community that proved essential to those ravaged by the virus, as well as how it changed the nation's response to the AIDS crisis. Through its art and actions, ACT UP developed an oppositional understanding of AIDS that rejected homophobia and sexual shame and instead called for universal health care and sexual privacy as human rights. Though many members lived in the East or West Villages, ACT UP, unlike MFY or NCNW, was not a neighborhood-based movement; the community it generated was instead based on affiliation, shared consciousness, and desire. Jettisoning binary understandings of sex and gender, ACT UP members embraced a fluid rather than fixed sexual identity, embracing the term "queer" to signify their rejection of normative sexuality. They also repudiated the "sex-negative" attitudes of those gay activists who responded to the AIDS epidemic by calling for gay men in particular to emulate heterosexual marriage and form long-term, monogamous partnerships. Instead, ACT UP members embraced a "sex-positive" approach, which favored harm-reduction policies such as comprehensive sex education and the provision of condoms and clean needles, while valuing the expression of homosexual and other forms of non-normative sexuality. As sociologist and ACT UP member Deborah Gould explains, "a sense of difference from straight *and* gay worlds created a strong shared identity among participants."[58]

While many ACT UP members were white, gay men, women and people of color made important contributions and formed their own caucuses within the larger organization, calling attention to issues they prioritized, including pushing the Centers for Disease Control (CDC) to expand its definition of HIV/AIDS to recognize opportunistic infections that targeted women. Indeed, though ACT UP's membership included poor and working-class New Yorkers, its significant number of highly educated middle- and upper-class people represented the city's new core of white-collar workers in finance, law, and the arts. Despite their financial successes, their queer identities placed them on the periphery as social outsiders.

While MFY and NCNW had viewed liberal political administrations as allies, ACT UP addressed a changing political environment. It mobilized in opposition to the Religious Right and its political affiliates, which had staunchly opposed gay rights and feminism in public since the early 1970s, when they gained a powerful political voice. The political realignment that began in the 1960s culminated in the 1980 presidential election, when Ronald Reagan successfully brought together the fiscal and social conservatives who came to dominate the Republican Party. Reagan spoke out against abortion and issued an executive order banning international family-planning services financed by the United States from discussing it, an action that became known as the global gag rule. Reagan also offered symbolic leadership posts to conservative religious leaders: he appointed James Dobson, head of the influential group Focus on the Family, to the Meese Commission on Pornography. Where Johnson had dreamed of a Great Society where government assistance would help all Americans fulfill their potential, Reagan argued that welfare programs encouraged out-of-wedlock births and unemployment and should be drastically curtailed. Increasingly, more Americans came to accept conservatives' rejection of postwar liberalism and the elevation of the market over the state as the best arena for solving social problems. The political atmosphere of the 1980s not only promoted a conservative social agenda, but redirected public funds to the private sector.

This turn toward privatization often meant contracting out state services to third parties. In New York as elsewhere, the Roman Catholic Church received substantial public funding to provide health and eldercare. Cardinal John O'Connor, who served on Reagan's Presidential

Commission on AIDS, denounced the provision of condoms or clean needles to people with AIDS and forbade health-care workers employed by the church from discussing condoms or other forms of contraception with patients—in effect, mandating abstinence. In one of its most controversial and influential demonstrations, ACT UP protested the cardinal's policies and the provision of public funding to the church during mass at St. Patrick's Cathedral in December 1989. (See map 3.)

This "Stop the Church" protest was cosponsored by WHAM!, which also called attention to the role of Cardinal O'Connor and the Catholic Church in opposing abortion and contraception. In chapter 6, I argue that the Religious Right's attack on gay rights and feminism helped to unify a coalition between gay men and women who were reproductive rights activists. Together they called for improved prevention and treatment for HIV/AIDS and supported women's rights to bodily autonomy. In the early 1990s, Operation Rescue and other antiabortion groups barricaded women's health clinics in often successful attempts to close them. Men and women from ACT UP joined WHAM! members in performing clinic defense and escorting patients past antiabortion demonstrators, as well as in staging and marching in demonstrations in favor of reproductive rights. Just as ACT UP had rejected sexual shame in relation to the AIDS epidemic, WHAM! argued that women should not be made to feel ashamed for expressing their sexuality and controlling their reproduction, including via abortion. Through their demonstrations, marches, and clinic defense, WHAM! offered New Yorkers—and, via the media, the world—a different model for thinking about reproductive rights as a necessary part of health care for women and of access to high-quality health care as a human right.

Mobilizing New York chronicles the efforts of women and men who participated in direct action and coalition building as community activists in New York City, crossing boundaries of race, class, gender, and sexuality in the process. Many but not all of the activists in this study self-identified as feminists, but they also shared the goal of expanding social justice through participatory democracy. They brought previously excluded groups from the margins to the center of political decision making and made voices heard and needs recognized. By claiming their rights and those of others, they helped envision and practice a more inclusive, egalitarian citizenship. They helped us see that the embrace of difference and the conflict that emerges from demands for social justice can be a dynamic motor of social change. They made history, and even when things did not turn out the way they had hoped, they represented the best aspirations of our country's recent democratic promise.

Organizers were absolutely essential to the success of these movements, but so were ordinary people who decided to act. The oral history interviews I conducted with a broad range of participants and observers of social movements aided me in accurately representing the multiple perspectives in this book. I have been committed to exploring commonalities as well as points of contention and divergence. My sympathy with those who demand equality has not hampered my efforts to provide a balanced account of activists' successes and failures; indeed, students of social movements need to understand both if they ever hope to participate in social change themselves. In addition to the more than fifty oral histories I conducted, I have drawn upon the more than 150 interviews in the ACT UP Oral History Project, and the dozens more interviews conducted by researchers studying Mobilization for Youth and the National Congress of Neighborhood Women. I have included activists' own analyses of social movement dynamics in crafting my narrative.

To provide context to the vast oral interview archives I have studied, the rich historical record of local and national politics in this period has helped me assess both the challenges activists faced and their many achievements and setbacks. I have combed archival collections at Smith College, New York University, Columbia University, the New York Public Library, the Centro Center for Puerto Rican Studies at Hunter College, the National Archives, and the John F. Kennedy and Lyndon Johnson Presidential Libraries for information that helped me synthesize the political contexts of social movement activism and governmental action at the federal, state, and local levels. Newspaper records have also been crucial. Because much of the activism was expressed by means of artistic endeavor, including aesthetic messages, performance art, films, photographs, and posters were also important sources.

ACT UP member Steve Quester gleefully recalled that when participants finished draping the Statue of Liberty, ACT UP and WHAM! members got back on the boat just as the park police arrived; the police "searched some hapless Italian tourists who were wearing all black, because they figured these must be the activists . . . and they didn't touch us, because we were all in Republican drag." He himself was wearing "gray slacks and a nice button-down shirt" with his hair "parted on the side." "It was great," he recalled.[59] I have very much enjoyed discovering activists in unexpected places, disguised as ordinary New Yorkers, and I hope that you, the reader, will as well.

CHAPTER ONE

A Cauldron within Which
New Ideas Can Be Tested Out

MFY and the Early War on Poverty

The *New York Times* heralded the launching of Mobilization for Youth in June 1962 with a front-page photograph featuring President John F. Kennedy announcing the federal grant that would fund the organization. Kennedy held his press conference at the White House Rose Garden while flanked by Attorney General Robert Kennedy and New York City mayor Robert Wagner, along with cabinet officials. "Using the Lower East Side area as a giant laboratory," the *Times* explained, "project officials will seek to reform the social patterns of an entire community as a way of guiding youth into conforming with the accepted patterns of American life." In their 600-page proposal, MFY's directors promised to "bring together the actionist and the researcher in a joint program of social engineering."[1] With $12.6 million in funds to be distributed over five years from the federal government, the city of New York, and the Ford Foundation, MFY represented the early Cold War era's faith in government intervention, expert knowledge, and social science research and planning.

Mobilization for Youth emerged during an era of technocratic liberalism, at the forefront of the federal government's adoption of social science research and planning as a means of creating a better and more harmonious nation.[2] The program's founding reflected long-term concerns over juvenile delinquency and the country's Cold War emphasis on domesticity and breadwinner-based masculinity at a time when married women with children were entering the labor force in increasing numbers.[3] The growth of the civil rights movement had drawn attention to the widespread poverty among African Americans and Latinos, prompting the Kennedy brothers and the Ford Foundation to seek to improve conditions in the ghettoes of the urban North. Together, these forces generated support for MFY.

Initially, MFY designers Richard Cloward and Lloyd Ohlin created a program emphasizing job training and enhanced social services. They explained that "the Cloward-Ohlin view of the sources and causes of delinquency is that poverty imposes handicaps upon the potential of young people for achievement, as does discrimination based on race and religion. . . . Efforts to prevent delinquency will succeed only if they provide young people with genuine opportunities to behave differently—especially through creative educational and exciting work programs—and if they involve residents directly."[4] Because Cloward and Ohlin conceived of juvenile delinquency as primarily a male phenomenon, the programs initially targeted only young men. According to Rosalyn Baxandall, who was employed as a community worker in one of MFY's neighborhood service centers on Stanton Street in New York's Lower East Side, "Everything was boys. Everything was boys. Everything was boys, and it really bothered me."[5]

Quickly, however, MFY's social workers found that it was low-income mothers who came into their offices seeking help as they contended with recalcitrant landlords, the mazelike city bureaucracy and its often demeaning welfare eligibility checks, and a school system unresponsive to their children's needs. Influenced by the civil rights movement and by their participation in consciousness-raising groups sponsored by MFY's social workers, these Puerto Rican and African American mothers took part in direct-action politics—including school boycotts, rent strikes, and sit-ins at the city welfare department—to demand that their needs be met and their rights as citizens be recognized. As Stanford Kravitz, an architect of the Economic Opportunity Act observed, their efforts "escalated long-festering problems into wide public view, so that discussion of them as critical national issues could no longer be avoided." In doing so, MFY participants and staff "prepared the ground" for the establishment of the Community Action Programs (CAPs) of the War on Poverty, which was launched by President Lyndon Johnson in 1964.

Like MFY, CAPs were agencies funded by public and private sources, dedicated to providing "services, assistance and other activities" in the effort to eliminate poverty. Importantly, CAPs had a mandate to involve poor people themselves in the planning and operation of programs directed at them. In accordance with Title II A of the Economic Opportunity Act, these programs were to be "developed, conducted, and administered with the maximum feasible participation of residents of the areas and members of the groups served."[6] Precisely what this mandate entailed in practice remains a subject of great controversy: Was it practical or desirable to involve poor people in decision making about social programs? Did CAPs actually do this?

While much has been written about Mobilization for Youth and its influence on the War on Poverty, we know far less about the grassroots members who pushed and enabled the organization to mount its most significant campaigns against racism in city schools, slum landlords, and discriminatory and inadequate welfare provision.[7] Scholars have focused on Ohlin, Cloward, and Cloward's partner, Frances Fox Piven, as the intellectual architects of MFY and the subsequent welfare rights movement that MFY helped spur. For example, in his 2007 comparative study of MFY and HARYOU-ACT, a sister CAP demonstration project in Harlem, sociologist Noel Cazenave used a framework of elite competition to demonstrate how Ohlin, Cloward, and other "elite, activist" social scientists "helped reshape democratic processes" through their support of the civil rights movement and, especially, by encouraging the "citizen participation revolution." Cazenave argues that CAPs in the War on Poverty succeeded in dramatically expanding democratic practices beyond the election of political representatives, but he credits social scientists rather than community participants themselves for making these changes. Cazenave concludes that "although community residents were enlisted as troops in the battles initiated by MFY professionals, the chief combatants were elite professionals."[8]

In contrast, my own research on MFY focuses on the relationships between neighborhood residents or clients and the frontline social workers and lawyers employed by MFY. What role did "the troops" actually play in setting the organization's agenda? Although the documentation on MFY is vast, most of the organization's records were written by administrators or supervisors. Therefore, my research strategies have included reading the official archives "against the grain," looking for neighborhood residents' presence in the extensive newspaper coverage of MFY, and conducting oral history interviews with both frontline MFY workers and neighborhood residents.

What I found was that between 1962 and 1964, paraprofessionals and mothers reshaped MFY's program to reflect the needs of low-income Puerto Rican and African American women in the Lower East Side. MFY programs originally operated under an outdated gender model, targeting women primarily as mothers of potentially or actually delinquent youth. In reality, the mothers' involvement in battles to integrate and improve the quality of education in their children's schools connected these low-income women to the broader citywide civil rights movement and radicalized them and the frontline MFY staff. Together, they in turn pushed MFY's board to support their school boycotts, rent strikes, and welfare rights organizing. By articulating their grievances and joining in interracial and cross-class protest movements, residents of the Lower East Side practiced "maximum feasible participation of the poor."

These women followed in the tradition of participatory democracy initiated by a civil rights leader well known for her work with the Student Nonviolent Coordinating Committee: Ella Baker, the standing president of New York City's branch of the NAACP. Living in Harlem in the 1950s, Baker encouraged African American and Puerto Rican parents to take control of their movement. Rather than depending on professionals and civil rights leaders, she urged them to call for school integration and more parental involvement in educational policymaking. Baker believed in the primacy of self-determination, that lasting social change occurred only when oppressed people analyzed their own situation, recognized their own power, and used it. This meant direct action such as pickets and demonstrations, considered the best form of political participation for marginalized groups who otherwise cannot influence policy decisions. Inspired by the civil rights movement Baker helped build, Lower East Side residents and MFY staff interpreted maximum feasible participation as a mandate for increasing participatory democracy through consciousness-raising, group education, and social protest.[9]

"The unfinished business of social change and social progress": MFY's Beginnings

In the late 1940s through the 1950s, headlines focused on New York's youth gangs, the colorfully named "Egyptian Kings, Dragons, Beacons, Imperial Knights, Fordham Baldies, and Comanches" among others, totaling 125 citywide according to *Time* magazine. The gangs' "thoroughly senseless" street violence threatened public safety and the city's reputation for racial liberalism and integration, as young men organized to protect their traditional turf in neighborhoods facing an influx of African American and Puerto Rican residents.[10] In July 1957, New Yorkers' concerns over juvenile delinquency reached a fever pitch after the widely publicized stabbing death of disabled fifteen-year-old Michael Farmer, son of a New York City firefighter. While going for a swim at the Highbridge Park pool in Washington Heights, Farmer found himself caught in the middle of a territorial dispute between Irish (Jesters) and Puerto Rican and African American (Egyptian Kings) youth gangs. Farmer's murder captured the public imagination because of his disability (caused by childhood polio), his presumed innocence as a non-gang member, and his whiteness.[11]

The Farmer case may have focused citywide attention on the gang problem, but local activists were already aware of the issue. Helen Hall, head of the Henry Street Settlement House in the Lower East Side, had long kept a watchful eye on youth violence. Often described as brilliant and dedicated, Hall was chosen to head the settlement in 1933 by Henry Street's founder, Lillian Wald, who established the first visiting nurses program in the country and who developed Henry Street into a renowned center for innovative social work and leadership in progressive reform. Well-educated, tall, attractive, and with an "imposing" personality, Hall was a skillful political agent.[12] In 1954, she had spearheaded the formation of the Lower Eastside Neighborhood Association (LENA), a coalition of "outstanding social and welfare leaders, educators, judges, law enforcement agencies, clergymen and public spirited citizens" who shared concerns over "the mounting tension among the young people of different racial groups" and "worsening living conditions" in the neighborhood, measured in part by the juvenile delinquency rate of 64 offenses per thousand compared to 44.2 per thousand citywide.[13]

The built environment and the population of the Lower East Side had changed rapidly during the 1950s, contributing to this social and racial stratification. Public and private investment in the suburbs and corresponding disinvestment in the urban core drew many Jewish and Italian residents out of the city and into new neighborhoods in Queens, Long Island, and New Jersey. Both official policies and unofficial practices of racial segregation in the massive new private and public housing projects built under urban renewal left Puerto Ricans and African Americans increasingly isolated.[14] Digna Sanchez moved with her family from Puerto Rico to New York City in 1950 and settled in the Lower East Side when Sanchez was about four years old. She remembered the apartment on Norfolk Street where they first lived, "a walk-up tenement, with the bathroom in the hallway and bathtub in the kitchen."[15]

The Sanchez family's building had been previously inhabited by Jews from Eastern Europe, but those tenants had since relocated to the newly constructed housing cooperatives built by the garment workers' unions. From the 1930s into the 1950s, the Amalgamated Clothing Workers Union and the International Ladies Garment Workers Union (ILGWU) built housing projects for members' families, financed in part by public subsidies. The 1953–56 construction of the largest, the East River Houses, required the clearance of thirteen acres of slums and resulted in 1,672 units in four buildings, the tallest reinforced concrete apartment structures in the United States at that time.[16] Soon, these co-ops became white ethnic "islands" set apart from the surrounding neighborhoods, and this residential segregation increased ethnic and racial tensions.[17]

In addition to the moderate-income housing cooperatives that were initially inhabited by Jewish and Italian garment workers and their families, the Lower East Side was transformed by the construction of high-rise low-income public housing ("tower in the park" projects), which had replaced many of the five- and six-story brick tenements by the end of the 1950s.[18] In 1961, the Sanchez family was able to move from their Norfolk Street tenement into the Lillian Wald housing development on Houston Street, which "was a definite move up," according to Sanchez: "We now had a bathroom and bathtub in one separate room and it was just for our family."[19]

Although Puerto Ricans and African Americans could sometimes access public housing and enjoy its improved material conditions, the developments were ethnically and racially homogenous. Urban renewal policy required that people living in an area targeted for slum clearance be given priority in the new housing developments; because Puerto Rican and African Americans were more likely to live in targeted areas, they made up the majority of new tenants. White flight and protests against the construction of public housing in white neighborhoods also contributed to racial segregation in public housing, with the result that "predominantly white, higher-income projects" existed in the outer boroughs while "primarily black or Puerto Rican projects" filled "the rebuilt slums."[20] Julio Colon, who like Sanchez was born in Puerto Rico and settled with his family in the Lower East Side, recalled, "There was a lot of racial separation between the various racial and ethnic lines. . . . La Guardia [Houses] belonged to the Puerto Ricans, the blacks were in the Vladecks. Grand Street

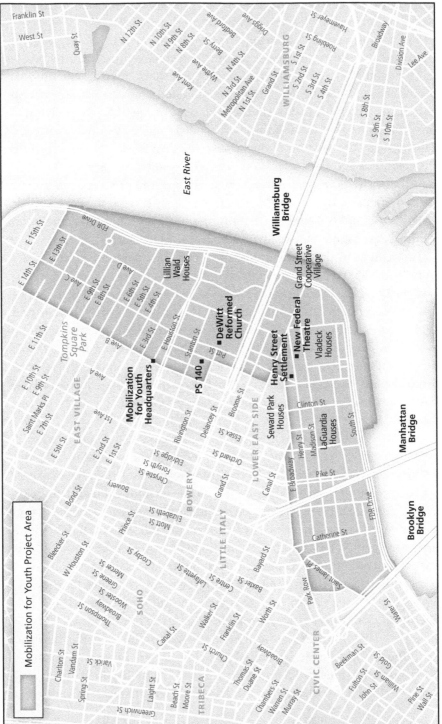

Map 1. Lower East Side

[Cooperative Village belonged] to the Jews. The park on Henry Street was our turf."[21] (See map 1, Lower East Side.)

Anxieties over racial change in the neighborhood found expression in part through the confrontations between youth gangs, estimated by the police to number forty-five in the Lower East Side. These groups of young men enforced racial segregation of public spaces, including parks, through intimidation and violence. In the early 1950s, as Puerto Ricans moved in, they faced attacks from the Mayrose, an Italian, Jewish, and Irish gang based on Henry Street and whose members targeted teenagers on their way home from school. Puerto Rican youth in turn formed a Lower East Side branch of the East Harlem Dragons, and African Americans joined the Sportsmen. In August 1956, a Puerto Rican youth from the Dragons shot an African American and badly wounded a Jewish young man, both from another rival gang, the Enchanters. The shooting further inflamed ethnic and racial tensions, stoking fears of greater violence. LENA responded by sponsoring recreational bus trips to upstate New York for the neighborhood's male youth and arranged for Peter Brown, a former U.S. attorney, to meet with representatives of the gangs. Brown successfully mediated a truce and headed off a feared citywide gang battle, but frequent skirmishes continued to plague the Lower East Side. The Henry Street Settlement House initiated a predelinquent program to reach young boys before they joined gangs; social workers found that progress depended on involving parents as well as religious and community leaders and providing recreation and job opportunities.[22]

Helen Hall saw in the Michael Farmer case and the rising national concern with delinquency an opportunity to build on the initial success of the LENA and Henry Street programs and secure new funding to replace the diminishing donations from the shrinking Jewish community in the Lower East Side.[23] In 1957–58, the Henry Street Settlement House board and LENA sought federal funding for a "saturation" project that included recreation, group work, and casework services to youths and families in the Lower East Side. The proposal emphasized the need for "professional social services," including more adult supervision and psychotherapy. According to Hall, "The basic thing was to do *enough*—we were tired of the inadequacy of our efforts here with juvenile delinquency."[24]

Hall was not the only one voicing concerns, as anxiety about youth gangs and urban violence was widespread. The U.S. Senate established a Subcommittee on Juvenile Delinquency in 1953, and that body would hold high-profile hearings through the rest of the decade. The national media's sensational coverage of the Farmer case and others raised public fears about an epidemic of juvenile delinquency.[25] Politicians, policymakers, and philanthropic organizations including the Ford Foundation were eager to find solutions to the problem. Social scientists hoped to validate their disciplines through successful application of their theoretical work to real-life "social laboratories." Thus, the National Institute of Mental Health (NIMH) looked favorably on the Henry Street proposal and eventually awarded $500,000 for planning a comprehensive demonstration project, Mobilization for Youth, but required that it add a research and evaluation component. Ultimately, the NIMH placed the project under the control of the Columbia University social scientists brought on board to implement the research, rather than Hall and LENA.[26]

In the late 1950s, Columbia University criminologists Lloyd Ohlin and Richard Cloward developed an analysis of juvenile delinquency that they articulated in *Delinquency and Opportunity: A Theory of Delinquent Gangs* (1960). Ohlin and Cloward proposed that delinquent behavior was an adaptation of low-income youths to stymied paths to success. "When pressures from unfulfilled aspirations and blocked opportunity become sufficiently intense, many lower-class youth turn away from legitimate channels, adopting other means, beyond conventional mores, which might offer a possible route to success-goals." It followed, then, that if government programs could increase legitimate opportunities for low-income youths, juvenile delinquency would be reduced.[27] Both men served as consultants to the Ford Foundation's Urban Social Problems Program, where they found receptive ears for their view that the institutional environment of the cities caused juvenile delinquency and that existing agencies, rather than individuals, should be the focus of social change efforts.[28]

Ohlin and Cloward set to work revising the proposal for MFY to place greater emphasis on changing bureaucracies, such as the public school and welfare systems, and less on individual treatment, in particular psychotherapy. The younger social scientists—in 1959, Ohlin was forty and Cloward thirty-four years old, while Hall was sixty-seven—saw themselves creating an innovative approach to combating delinquency. Ohlin and Cloward argued that people from the outside should be brought in to shake things up in the local bureaucracies. In contrast, the settlement house staff, as Hall explained, was "anxious not to pit one class against another, and cause cleavage in the neighborhood."[29] The Columbia proposal removed Hall from the project's center, relegating her to a position on the MFY board.[30] Voicing her displeasure at this move, Hall reminded an MFY researcher, "I have had twenty-nine years of experience here. There is nothing theoretical about that!"[31] Cloward countered that the settlement house services were "a fraud. These people needed jobs and they got recreation."[32]

The finished MFY proposal combined Cloward and Ohlin's emphasis on expanding opportunities through altering existing institutions and creating new ones with the settlement houses' "saturation" approach. The funding for MFY was also divided, with some going to the settlement houses for traditional programs and neighborhood organization under LENA's auspices and the rest used to form an independent organization to launch programs in youth employment and education and autonomous resident groups.[33] Ohlin and Cloward wrote that because delinquency resulted from "a deep sense of resentment against existing institutional arrangements," youths "must be shown . . . that there are nondeviant, if controversial, ways of expressing such sentiments." Accordingly, the MFY proposal listed in its "guidelines for action" the provision that programs should provide "opportunities for the collective expression of discontent and alienation, especially by opening channels for collective social action and protest against class and ethnic discrimination."[34] Despite concerns over the use of federal funds to initiate community protest against city and state governmental agencies and institutions, Ohlin's close link to the Kennedy brothers, who were committed to doing something to address the country's rising rates of juvenile delinquency and hoped to court minority urban voters, helped to ensure that the revised MFY proposal was funded.[35]

On May 11, 1961, President John F. Kennedy established the President's Committee on Juvenile Delinquency and Youth Crime (PCJD) by executive order and selected Attorney General Robert Kennedy as chair.[36] In a speech to Congress, the president proposed that the "malady" of the "lack of opportunity" be eliminated by the creation of a "more perfect educational and vocational training system, a more prosperous full employment economy, the removal of racial barriers, and the elimination of slum housing and dilapidated neighborhoods." Congress responded by passing the Juvenile Delinquency and Youth Offenses Control Act of 1961, which for the first time provided direct grants to community agencies for combating delinquency. The legislation authorized the expenditure of $10 million a year for three years, and Congress later increased the appropriation to $19 million. Mobilization for Youth was the first demonstration project to be funded.[37]

The PCJD was part of the Kennedy administration's "New Frontier" program, which aimed to spread democracy abroad. It featured a striking buildup of arms as well as military and humanitarian aid for underdeveloped countries; at the same time, it sought to further democracy at home through an expanded welfare state that would better meet the needs of disadvantaged and low-income Americans.[38] Program coordinator Stanford Kravitz conceived of the juvenile delinquency programs as an expansion of citizenship for the nation's poor and working classes. Casting the PCJD as part of a sweeping effort to complete "the unfinished business of social change and social progress," he described the demonstration projects as "an effort to bring into the mainstream of our society segments of the population who have never had the full privileges of economic security, personal dignity and self-respect."[39]

"I could not distance myself professionally": Developing Advocacy

On September 5, 1962, after five years of planning, ninety MFY staff members arrived in the Lower East Side to launch the "action phase" of the program, "a massive attempt at social engineering."[40] Their project area ranged from East 14th Street south to the Brooklyn Bridge and from Avenue B east to the East River, covering sixty-seven blocks.[41] (See map 1.) The MFY area had a population of 107,000, of whom 27 percent were Jewish, 26 percent Puerto Rican, 11 percent Italian, 25 percent "other" white, 8 percent "Negro," and 3 percent "other" nonwhite, mostly Chinese; however, 90 percent of the children were "Negro" or Puerto Rican.[42] Only 26 percent of adults in the study area had completed high school, and the unemployment rate was double that of New York City as a whole. According to the 1960 census, 62.4 percent of the tenements in the area were substandard. Small businesses, described by a reporter as a "jumble of tiny Puerto Rican groceries and restaurants, Chinese hand laundries, Italian bars, Jewish delicatessens and clothing stores," crowded among the old tenements.[43] The racial and ethnic makeup of the area was undergoing rapid change as the MFY program was being implemented: Between 1960 and 1967, the proportion of the population that was Puerto Rican or African American doubled, while many Jewish residents moved to the suburbs.[44]

MFY headquarters, located at Avenue B and East Second Street, was described by a visitor as a "dilapidated, seemingly centuries old building that appeared at one time to have been an entertainment house of some sort. The inside matches the outside: dirty, decrepit."[45] (See figure 6.) At the 1962 staff orientation, Cloward signaled that the no-frills office was a sign of the agency's solidarity with the neighborhood's residents, stating, "We're not only aiming for the reduction of delinquencies; we are also

Figure 6. Members of YAAG (Young Adult Action Group) in front of the MFY Youth Job Center and headquarters, located at Avenue B and East Second Street, January 1965. University of Minnesota Social Welfare Archives, Mobilization for Youth Collection, SW 58 84:13. Courtesy of Susan LaRosa, Henry Street Settlement.

concerned more generally with problems of low-income urban people. We have been remiss; the social workers have migrated to the suburbs also. They have left the 'problems of poverty.' "[46] MFY's seventy-five-member governing board took a hands-off approach, giving the triumvirate of administrators—Cloward, Columbia University Professor of Social Work George Brager, and head of the New York City Youth Board and former youth gang worker James McCarthy—a great deal of flexibility in designing and implementing programs.

From the start, Cloward communicated the expectation that since MFY was a demonstration project, staff members should see it not "as a permanent organization but rather as a cauldron within which new ideas can be tested out."[47] The staff, which would grow to more than 300, was encouraged to take innovative approaches in addressing the problems of the urban slum. Most MFY staffers had degrees in social work and were therefore outsiders in the neighborhood by virtue of their education and class position. As a counter, MFY hired approximately fifty "indigenous" paraprofessionals, or neighborhood residents, without formal education but possessing specific knowledge of the neighborhood and its residents, including Spanish-language skills. The collaboration between social work professionals and "indigenous" residents would prove central to MFY's ability to increase participatory democracy.[48]

MFY attracted social workers with experience in labor unions, the civil rights movement, and antiwar activism. They had a passion for social justice. Marilyn Bibb Gore, who headed the Community Development Division, explained, "I went into social work because I thought it had to do with radicalizing people."[49] The staff shared a strong dedication and the optimism of the Kennedy era. MFY social worker Barbara Hunter Randall Joseph recalled, "To think that we were now going to mobilize people, to change the conditions of their lives, was very exciting."[50] Over the first few months, interactions with residents would transform the MFY social services program, emphasizing the needs of poor people and turning staff members into client advocates.

Social worker Mary Anne Dowery came to Mobilization for Youth in 1961 to head the Parent Education Program, designed to promote Lower East Side parents' involvement in the public schools in order to improve the quality of education and lower the dropout rate. The daughter of middle-class African American teachers in Kentucky, she had previously worked with welfare mothers on the Upper West Side and Mexican American teenage girls in Los Angeles. Dowery later supervised the New York City Board of Education's after-school program. "Always, beneath it all, was some organizing. Always," she affirmed. Used to operating on a shoestring budget, at MFY Dowery had $300,000 and a staff that was "well educated, diverse, and committed to social change. That was an exciting time." She recruited paraprofessionals from the Lower East Side, ranging in age from twenty to thirty, including males and females, "black, Spanish, Filipino, and Chinese."[51] These paraprofessionals acted as a bridge between MFY and the neighborhood, translating information regarding programs to residents and conveying residents' needs and priorities to the MFY staff. Many would go on to become community leaders themselves.[52] Dowery began the program with sensitivity training, bringing in Frank Musminer, a noted psychologist and trainer, to instruct the staff on how to use role-playing and other techniques in working with the parents to enable them to confront the school bureaucracy: "when you're called to the school, how to deal with principals and the hierarchy and that kind of stuff."[53]

During the drafting of the MFY proposal, its authors identified "immense educational problems" in the Lower East Side that contributed to poverty.[54] Among all third-grade students in the MFY area, only 22 percent read at grade level, including just 9.8 percent of Puerto Rican students. Among eighth-graders, only 13.19 percent of all Puerto Ricans were reading at grade level, while 64.38 percent were more than three years behind.[55] Parents and MFY staff were particularly concerned about public schools' treatment of Puerto Rican students from Spanish-speaking homes, who were often placed in classes with learning-disabled children by teachers who spoke only English. Spanish-speaking students, parents, and MFY paraprofessionals faced "an attitude of muted hostility" from school administrators. By organizing parents, MFY hoped to create "pressure groups pushing for serious improvements in the schools" and better treatment of Puerto Rican students and their families in particular.[56]

Relations between the New York City Board of Education and the Puerto Rican and African American communities were uniformly bad. In the 1940s, as the African American and Puerto Rican populations of New York expanded, civil rights leaders argued that the Board of Education was purposefully drawing district lines to maintain racial segregation. Despite rebuffs from school officials and white politicians opposed to integration, who argued that the segregated schools were a "natural" result of housing patterns, throughout the 1940s and 1950s civil rights leaders continued to fight for integrated schools and quality education for all students. Under pressure from activists including Kenneth Clark, Hubert Delany, and Ella Baker following the Supreme Court's 1954 *Brown v. Board of Education* ruling, the city's Board of Education formed a commission on integration that called for improved quality of teachers in schools with African American and Puerto Rican students and for racial balancing in the student population. Yet the board rejected proposals to create integrated schools, and segregation actually increased over the course of the 1950s as the Board of Education continued to build new schools in segregated neighborhoods.[57]

Many parents in the Lower East Side shared the view that "the school system was not educating their children, especially the Hispanic children, properly." Before Dowery's staff could work with the parents in addressing their grievances against the school system, however, they found they "had to assist with a lot of the daily needs of the parents." Dowery explained that "My work was to assist them, accompany them where they had to go . . . the welfare office, the doctor, the schools, my staff would assist them, and they would meet with them in the home and help them with issues they had."[58] MFY sought to help needy individuals and families solve problems on a very practical, day-to-day basis, and providing information and assistance in negotiating bureaucracy proved to be essential. At first, MFY social workers attempted to maintain a neutral role, known as "brokerage," in connecting their clients with social service agencies. But soon, frustrated by the intransigence of the welfare system in particular, MFY's staff assumed a new role.

As client advocates, social workers adopted the "client's point of view" and "used all available techniques" to secure their clients' interests. MFY staff member Charles Grosser explained that under the advocacy framework, the social worker "is, in fact, a partisan in a social conflict. His expertise is available exclusively to serve client interests, since other actors in this social conflict may be using their expertise and resources against the client."[59] MFY social workers found that by intervening for Lower East Side residents in conversations with bureaucracies, they could improve the responsiveness of city agencies to their clients' needs.

MFY strove to make its social workers available to residents by operating four neighborhood walk-in centers where, as Cloward explained, people were "invited to describe their problems" while being "free to come and go." MFY staff organized parties at the neighborhood centers on holidays, and "young people were not discouraged from idling about the place." Importantly, neighborhood residents got jobs at the centers, working as paraprofessionals and translators as well as clerks and janitors.[60]

Social workers grew frustrated with their inability to compel the city welfare department to grant benefits to eligible recipients, and MFY decided to hire lawyers to work with the residents and the social workers for more expedient and successful outcomes. Neighborhood residents, whom MFY lawyer Stephen Wizner described as "poor people, Hispanics, African American, Jewish, Ukrainian, Poles, kids, gang members, drug addicts, people with mental illness," made use of the service centers, which were often packed. To Wizner's delight, the residents embraced the idea that MFY staff were there to work for them. He recalled his work as "transformative . . . feeling that I could be part of a community and also an advocate, and that I could not distance myself professionally. More than once, I can remember a woman storming in and demanding, 'Where's my lawyer?' I loved it."[61]

Because social workers found that many of the people who walked into the neighborhood service center had similar problems, MFY assigned community organizers to the centers to help residents form groups and devise their own solutions.[62] Petra Santiago, who was born in Puerto Rico in 1911 and settled in the Lower East Side in 1945, began her career as a community activist at her son's school, where she served as an interpreter for Latino parents who did not speak English. In the early 1960s, she helped found the Council of Puerto Rican and Hispanic Organizations of the Lower East Side and organized youth baseball leagues. In 1963, MFY hired her to "organize unaffiliated residents" in order to "help themselves combat the spectrum of poverty." Santiago recalled: "I made innumerable

Figure 7. Mobilization of Mothers (MOM) president Maria Lorenzi and
MFY community organizer Petra Santiago march wearing "mom" banners during the
MFY voter registration campaign, ca. 1963–64. According to Petra Santiago,
"A community parade celebrating the success of the voter registration campaign was
held at Lenox Hall on Second Street, with the presence of actor Sidney Poitier we
celebrated the participation of the community in all our programs." Quotation is from
"Petra Santiago Biography," p. 7, Petra Santiago Papers, Box 1, Folder 2. Photograph,
Petra Santiago Papers, Box 6, Folder 1, Archives of the Puerto Rican Diaspora.
Centro de Estudios Puertorriqueños, Hunter College, CUNY.

home visits and interviewed mainly women who either were separated
from their husbands or their boyfriends. I explained to them the aims of
Mobilization and urged them to actively participate in meetings. . . . When
I called the first meeting the place was completely full. . . . Six groups
were formed, each one adopting different issues that were affecting their
lives." Under Santiago's leadership, women formed buying clubs, took
English and job-training courses, and ran youth recreational programs.[63]
Soon, she and fellow resident Maria Lorenzi would channel mothers' frus-
trations with the poor quality of their children's education, taking part in
demonstrations against area schools. (See figure 7.) Santiago recalled, "It was
fantastic to see the community people so active against the bureaucracy."[64]

"Books should be provided to the children": The Politicization of Mothers

By the spring of 1962, Dowery and her staff were holding community meetings, attended by well over a hundred Puerto Rican and African American mothers, to discuss the quality of the education their children were receiving. When MFY staff members found the existing parent associations to be "almost totally under the control of school principals," they began organizing parents in autonomous groups. Because many principals would not allow these groups to meet at the schools, they held their meetings at MFY buildings or in parents' homes.[65]

In March 1962, with the support of MFY staff from the Stanton and Ridge Neighborhood Center, a group of Puerto Rican mothers formed Mobilization for Mothers (MOM) to lobby for after-school activities at their local school, P.S. 140. The group of forty-five mothers succeeded in getting an after-school center opened that summer. In late August, the mothers began meeting to discuss "what they, as parents, could do to help their children stay in school and get a good education. They wanted to know what work children are supposed to do in different grades, what books they should have, what homework they should do and how parents can work more closely with teachers."[66] The mothers were frustrated by the school's policy of not allowing students to take their books home with them and worried about their children's lack of proficiency in reading.

MOM president Maria Lorenzi, who had four children attending P.S. 140, applied for a permit to hold a meeting at the school and invited the principal, Irving Rosenblum, to come and speak to them. After voicing displeasure that he had been informed of the meeting only after it had already been scheduled, Rosenblum agreed to speak to the group. On October 22, 1962, Rosenblum addressed the crowd of seventy-five Spanish-speaking mothers after announcing that he would "speak briefly because you won't understand me anyhow." When questioned on why students in the second grade were unable to read, Rosenblum suggested that the students came from "culturally deprived" homes, which posed "problems for the school." Not surprisingly, "the meeting ended with many of the parents yelling at Mr. Rosenblum and his yelling back."[67]

At their next meeting, MOM members decided to petition the Board of Education for the removal of Rosenblum as principal "because of his lack of respectful cooperation with the parent body, [and his] handling of minority groups[, which] indicates his inability and incompetence as an educator and Principal." The petition also argued that "books should be provided to the children to be brought to their homes and specific assignments which will enable them to learn how to read and write."[68] On the advice of an MFY staff worker, the mothers began documenting their grievances against the school in general and Rosenblum in particular, and they held more meetings to gather additional parent support.

MOM members came to believe the school staff was retaliating against them for their petition. Teachers called parents into the school and asked them to cancel the group's meetings, and the guidance teachers "suddenly" argued that the children of MOM members had "serious problems," making other parents afraid to sign the MOM petition. MOM's subsequent meeting with Florence Becker, assistant superintendent of the Board of Education, was as disastrous as the meeting with Rosenblum. According to a Volunteer In Service To America (VISTA) observer present at the meeting, Becker "reproached the women for coming with 'demands'," informing them that they knew "nothing about educational policy or techniques" and were therefore unqualified to complain about Rosenblum or the system of education. Following the meeting, however, Becker issued a memo directing the principals in her district to acquire more books and allow students to take them home, to require that teachers give and grade homework assignments, and to ensure that principals and teachers meet with parents who wished to speak with them.[69] Even in light of those changes, Becker continued to publicly support Rosenblum, condemn MOM, and reproach MFY for its support of the group. Despite direct pressure from Becker and the principals on MFY director George Brager to disband the parent groups, MFY staffers continued to work with the mothers, who remained resolute in their call for Rosenblum's dismissal.[70]

Brager signaled his agency's support for the active participation of low-income and nonwhite Americans in democratic forms of government through both his support of MOM and his initiation of a voter registration campaign. In the spring of 1963, in preparation for the 1964 primaries, he announced a "massive" voter registration campaign requiring the "efforts of all Mobilization departments." MFY surveys found that 40 percent of the 63,000 adults living in the MFY area were not registered to vote.[71] Brager outlined the objectives of MFY's campaign: "a) to reduce the alienation of our citizenry from the authorities and the decision-making processes that affect their lives; and b) to help develop greater political power on the part of low income minority groups in the Lower East Side." He argued that while the voter registration campaign was most obviously related to the Community Organization division's goal of "organizing the unaffiliated," it was relevant to the entire agency, as increased voter turnout in the Lower

East Side would lead to "the improvement of housing conditions and codes, better educational opportunities, increased recreational facilities, etc."[72] Importantly, the voter registration campaign linked MFY to the southern civil rights movement, which was defying Jim Crow segregation and violent reprisals in its effort to register African Americans to vote.

In a speech to MFY staff in the summer of 1963, Cloward pointed out the connections between the opportunity theory of delinquency and the agenda of the civil rights movement and suggested that MFY build on and contribute to the activism the movement was unleashing:

> Far-reaching changes in our political life appear to be taking place. A new political energy is being generated in some of our most deprived groups, chiefly, of course, in the Negro communities. This burgeoning political thrust is not fundamentally for protection against poverty, for a higher welfare check: it is plainly and simply for dignity and opportunity. It is the right to enter the social and psychological mainstream of American life that is at issue here. . . . This political thrust is already altering the opinion climate of American life. The question for an organization like MFY is, then, how we ride this groundswell, exploiting its potential for programs, helping to give it momentum?[73]

In his July 1963 annual review of the Community Organization program, Director Harry Specht concluded that MFY, like the civil rights movement in the South, should focus on "highly visible and dramatic demonstrations, strikes, picketing, marches and mass meetings."[74]

That idea was quickly put into practice. In August 1963, MFY rented nine railroad cars to take 500 residents and staff members, including sixty-six participants from the Parent Education Program, to the March on Washington for Jobs and Freedom organized by A. Phillip Randolph.[75] Manny Diaz recalled drawing in "two thousand Puerto Ricans, mostly from the Lower East Side, using the resources of Mobilization for Youth" as well as those of Gilberto Gerena-Valentín, organizer of the District 65 Retail, Wholesale, and Department Stores Union, which had many Puerto Rican members. The participation of so many Lower East Side residents was an important turning point in bringing the African American and Puerto Rican communities together.[76] In D.C., they assembled under the banner of the Lower East Side Civil Rights Committee, bearing signs reading "We March Together CATHOLIC JEWS PROTESTANT For Dignity and Brotherhood of All Men Under God NOW!" and joined the crowd of 200,000 on the National Mall.[77] Piven recalled her sense of excitement on returning from the March on Washington: "Something *was* happening. On a late summer night, on the Lower East Side of New York, and in other neighborhoods, too, you could just sense" the energy. Indeed, the spirit of the civil rights movement was sweeping New York City and animating MFY.[78]

Returning to the Lower East Side after the March on Washington, MFY staff members organized community groups such as the Negro Action Group (NAG) and the Young Adult Action Group (YAAG) to fight for civil rights and economic justice. The formation of these young adult and other community groups took MFY in a broader, more democratic direction, expanding its initial emphasis on job training as a means to combat juvenile delinquency to one of embracing self-determination and systemic change. MFY organizer Sidney Pinsky explained that the new community development approach meant "to provide services, to get people to participate from the community, to start to fund through these small contracts, local, indigenous organizations, to develop them. Not to run these organizations—and we didn't. We actually had people from the community elected to manage these different community organizations."[79]

In addition to calling for school desegregation, NAG and other MFY groups demanded an end to racial discrimination in the market for skilled labor. In November 1963, NAG joined CORE in picketing the convention of the Building Trades Construction Union, which was notorious for its discrimination against African Americans and Puerto Ricans. Like other civil rights groups in the North, MFY's community groups emphasized the need to strike down de facto as well as de jure discrimination, arguing that until African American and Puerto Rican New Yorkers had access to quality education, jobs, and housing, formal legal equality held little meaning.[80]

Throughout the fall of 1963, MFY staff members worked with MOM and held community meetings on school integration. MOM's dispute with Rosenblum proved the spark that ignited the expression of wider dissatisfaction with the schools. In November 1963, MFY's Parent Education Program and MOM cosponsored a community meeting at the DeWitt Church. The meeting included civil rights leaders such as the Rev. Richard Johnson, chairman of the Lower East Side Civil Rights Committee, and Thelma Johnson of the Harlem Parents Committee. Thelma Johnson called the Board of Education's integration plan "garbage." Ellen Lurie, a Jewish Harlem-based civil rights leader and local school board member, argued that in order to please white parents whose children were in integrated schools, principals were placing Puerto Rican and black students in special-needs classes and thereby maintaining segregated classrooms. As the citywide civil rights movement pushed for school integration, MFY staff members offered their support.[81]

A large grassroots movement of parents spearheaded the effort to desegregate public schools. Clarence Taylor has chronicled the role of Rev. Milton Galamison, pastor of Siloam Presbyterian Church in Brooklyn, in crafting a broad interracial coalition, the Parents' Workshop for Equality in New York City Schools. Galamison's group demanded the Board of Education issue a concrete plan and timetable for citywide integration.[82] The grassroots movement joined with established civil rights groups to form the New York Citywide Committee for Integrated Schools, also headed by Reverend Galamison. When city schools superintendent Calvin Gross refused to support the involuntary transfer of students to achieve racial balancing, the Citywide Committee called for a boycott.

Negotiations between Gross and the Citywide Committee failed to produce a plan for integration, so on February 3, 1964, Galamison, with the help of Bayard Rustin, Diaz, and Gerena-Valentín, organized one of the largest civil rights protests in U.S. history. That day, 464,361 students, 45 percent of those enrolled in city schools, stayed out of school. About 150,000 were Puerto Rican. MFY cooperated with CORE, NAG, and a number of Puerto Rican civil rights organizations (some of which MFY had organized) to picket the schools. MFY also offered "Freedom School" classes and, with the Lower East Side Civil Rights Committee, distributed balloons reading "Teacher, please teach me." According to Marilyn Bibb Gore, MFY's efforts were responsible for the Lower East Side ranking third among districts with the highest proportion of students participating in the boycott: 80.3 percent stayed home or attended Freedom Schools. Demonstrators picketed at 300 schools throughout the city, including all those in the Lower East Side, and marched to the Board of Education building. MFY organizer Allen Simpson observed that "The Puerto Rican, Negro and white communities all contributed to the success of the boycott on the Lower East Side. What is most significant was the obvious awareness on the part of the Puerto Rican community of a common interest with the Negro community."[83]

Bridge-building between the African American and Puerto Rican communities was an achievement, given the language barriers, difference in racial consciousness, and competition for political representation, government jobs, and public funds that often sparked contestation rather than cooperation between these groups.[84] Historian Wendell Pritchett found that in the 1950s in Brownsville, Brooklyn, a neighborhood similar in many ways to the Lower East Side, generally, "black, white, and Puerto Rican adults did not mix."[85] According to scholars Sonia Lee and Ande Diaz, many Puerto Rican leaders feared that "joining black protest would jeopardize Puerto Ricans' own precarious status in the city."[86] Solidarity could not be taken for granted. The success of the school boycott revealed both the depth of community anger at the public school system and the inclusive approach of the organizers, which helped participants recognize common interests.

Following the success of the February 3 protest, Reverend Galamison announced plans for another boycott. Grassroots support for desegregation remained high, and on March 1, the Council of Puerto Rican and Spanish Organizations of the Lower East Side led a silent prayer march on City Hall and school headquarters, in which MFY participated. On March 10, 1964, MFY accompanied CORE and other labor and civil rights activists on a "March to Albany," advocating for a state minimum wage, greater availability of affordable housing, and civil rights enforcement.[87] A week later, on March 16, 267,459 students stayed out of school in the second city-wide boycott.[88] MFY staff, paraprofessionals, and residents of the Lower East Side embraced the boycott movement, and the Civil Rights Committee of the MFY board issued a statement in favor of school integration. Charging the Board of Education with ultimate responsibility for achieving racial balance, the statement called for Spanish-language classes and for "curriculum material stressing the historical and cultural heritage of minority groups." Finally, it suggested that "minority group and low income persons" be involved in "influencing and shaping community decisions." In conjunction with the Lower East Side Civil Rights Committee, MFY formed an Education Committee "to further their demands for quality, integrated education"; its first act was to petition Mayor Wagner for the removal of James Donovan, the president of the Board of Education.[89]

In the midst of the boycotts, as the MFY Civil Rights Committee prepared its statement and the community organizing staff worked closely with civil rights activists, Assistant Superintendent Becker and the principals made good on their threat to discredit MFY.[90] The principals sent telegrams to the *New York Times*; to David Hackett, executive director of the President's Committee on Juvenile Delinquency; and to Henry T. Heald, the president of the Ford Foundation, requesting an investigation of MFY and the removal of George Brager. MFY's parent educators and community organizers, they charged, were no more than "full-time paid agitators and organizers for extremist groups." The principals contended that MFY misappropriated funds and allowed "splinter groups" to harass teachers and wage "war against individual schools and their leaders."[91]

In response, the local school board held a public meeting on February 11 with 500 people present, largely Puerto Rican and African American parents. MOM president Maria Lorenzi detailed the women's grievances against the schools, including the fact that Parent-Teacher Association meetings were not conducted in Spanish, the lack of textbooks, and the use of children as hall monitors. Lorenzi denied the principals' charges that MOM members were "extremists" and stated, "We are organized through our own efforts and we will fight whenever necessary, because we want our children, as American citizens, to receive better education and so to attain the realization of their ambitions."[92] Ernesto Martinez, a member of the board of the Council of Puerto Rican Organizations, demanded Becker's resignation and observed that "not very long ago these same principals said we didn't participate because we didn't care. Now that we do, they call us Communists."[93]

MFY's leadership reinforced the legitimacy of the mothers' complaints. Board chairman Winslow Carlton stated, "These are groups that know their own minds, who are aware that they and their children have serious problems in education, housing, employment and discrimination generally." Carlton iterated that MFY "believes that effective citizen action on the real problems of our communities is essential to the solution of juvenile delinquency and to the healthy development of young people in our city."[94] Director James McCarthy characterized the mothers' protest as "a healthy sign of an awakening community."[95] But the February 11 meeting did nothing to resolve the conflict, and later that month, the principals of School Districts 1–4 issued a report on their grievances against George Brager.

In the introduction to the report, Becker argued that her principals had worked hard for years "to raise the aspirations and create ever-broadening opportunities for our young people whose cultural differences made difficult the achievement and upward mobility so desired by their parents and by us." She declared that the schools and MFY had been working harmoniously until "some staff members" of MFY led groups in "massive attacks" against the schools, issuing "destructive, vicious, false charges" against them. The principals acknowledged that recently "other school people throughout the city have been subjected to such attacks" but argued that MFY's professional staff, which was supported by public funds, had exacerbated the situation. More fundamentally, they charged, MFY never accepted the school system as a full "partner" in its education programs and instead treated the schools as "pawns for its purposes."[96] Teachers' morale had dropped precipitously since the conflict between MOM and Rosenblum began, dealing a crippling blow to the schools.[97] Despite Becker's tendency to blame educational problems on students' "cultural differences" and disputes between parents and principals on outsiders, the charges that MFY was using federal funds to make war on the city schools proved troublesome indeed.

The ongoing conflict in the Lower East Side worried the Kennedy administration, and key officials questioned the wisdom of organizing residents against the public school bureaucracy. After visiting the project area, Special Assistant to the Commissioner on Education David Seeley reported to David Hackett that if MFY continued the current direct conflict with the school system, it would "be detrimental not only to Mobilization itself but to the Juvenile Delinquency program nationally and to the poverty program now being planned. . . . School people across the country will fight to the death before letting into their midst a Trojan horse such as Mobilization is now viewed to be," he warned.[98] Seeley was correct in suggesting that the school administration viewed MFY's organizing of low-income Puerto Rican and African American parents as a threat; the depth of their unease with the newly vocal parents' groups was made clear when they accused the organization of fomenting "social revolution." In an odd twist on Cold War apocalyptic visions, the principals opined that they had "become the victims of a new kind of 'Dr. Strangelove' plot."[99]

"They had rights to confront this Board": Implementing Maximum Feasible Participation

When the principals wrote that MFY was "supposed to . . . promote good relations between school and community," they envisioned a very different role for the organization than it sought for itself.[100] In June 1963, the MFY Board of Directors had adopted a Statement of Objectives indicating MFY's support for the civil rights movement. Among its major objectives was "to increase the responsiveness of conventional and powerful persons and institutions to the needs, wants and culture of impoverished persons, to reduce discrimination based upon race, ethnicity, and social class, to increase the ability of lower income persons to affect the social conditions within which they are enmeshed."[101]

As Carlton described it, the organization had undergone a "gradual sea change" during the tumultuous years of 1963–64 as the agency "learned from experience."[102] While MFY devoted itself more fully to its social-change goals and to making maximum feasible participation a reality, school officials vigorously defended the education system and its hierarchical chain of command.[103] In the end, the conflict between MFY and the principals remained unresolved. Rosenblum took a six-month leave of absence but later returned to the same school.[104] Under pressure from the

President's Committee on Juvenile Delinquency and city officials, Brager disbanded the Parent Education Program, and the aides were transferred to working with block organizations.[105] Although the Parent Education Program was short-lived, it had important reverberations for both individual participants and MFY as an organization.

In a 1965 article, Frank Reissman explained that the agency's community organizing was the result of a long process of social workers getting to know residents in the Lower East Side. "The main emphasis in the beginning was on opening the store-front centers that received people with all kinds of problems from welfare to housing, to employment, to family and personal problems. Thousands of people flocked to these neighborhood service centers and the social workers quickly built up huge caseloads. . . . During this stage, community organizers were dispatched to talk to people standing on street corners, in the bars, and in front of buildings. These organizers tried to interest people in some kind of self-help group activity. The work was slow and immediate results were not forthcoming."[106]

More successful, Reissman believed, were the leadership-training programs employed in the Parent Education Program, in which neighborhood women practiced assertiveness, "negotiating and arguing to win's one point," and "on-the-spot caucusing," and learned "parliamentary procedure and meeting tactics."[107] The training program was extremely effective in empowering residents to bring their perspective on their children's education to citywide discussions. "This was a time when poor parents were utterly intimidated by the Board of Education, and all it represented. When a teacher spoke, the parents quivered, or did nothing. They might have felt extreme injustices against their children, but they didn't understand that they had rights to confront this Board of Education," Marilyn Bibb Gore explained. "That program helped a lot of parents in that community to be able to stand up for their rights of their children, to go to the Board of Education, to demand changes."[108]

The program's emphasis on the development of leadership capacity in neighborhood residents helps explain why the Parent Education staff took the lead in bringing MFY into the civil rights movement. Face-to-face relationships between social workers and residents and the skills acquired by paraprofessional staff members established the trust and reservoir of knowledge necessary to lay the groundwork for direct-action protests. According to Gore, MOM helped build cross-racial and cross-class alliances between white, middle-class Jewish residents and African American and Puerto Rican mothers, all of whom distrusted the Board of Education bureaucracy and wanted better schools for their children. Some of these alliances persisted as MFY entered into housing and welfare activism.[109]

By November 1964, MFY had disbanded the Parent Education Program. Dowery left the organization because her staff "no longer had the kind of freedom to go into the schools and back into the community." Dowery felt satisfied, nonetheless, that they "had paved the way for other groups to pick up and go on."[110] Indeed, in 1965 Puerto Rican mother and former Head Start staffer Evelina López Antonetty used War on Poverty funding to found United Bronx Parents (UBP), which was dedicated to empowering poor parents to advocate for high-quality public education. Lurie joined UBP as its training director, enrolling thousands of Puerto Rican and African American New Yorkers. She and Antonetty held workshops that taught "parents their legal rights" and how to use "those rights to demand improvements."[111] Like MOM, UBP actions revealed that the assumption frequently voiced by white school administrators—that low-income parents of color were not invested in their children's education—to be no more than a convenient excuse for the poor quality of education their children received. As in the South, civil rights activists were met with massive resistance from white parents, many of whom did not support integration of New York's public schools. This eventually led the movement to emphasize community control and put it on a collision course with the change-averse United Federation of Teachers (UFT).[112]

In the midst of battles between community control advocates and the UFT, the long struggle for high-quality public schools accountable to parents continued. Frank Espada, who had worked with MFY as a welfare rights organizer, and Digna Sanchez, who as a high school student was employed by MFY's Homework Helper Program, became leaders in Aspira, an organization dedicated to empowering Puerto Rican youth through education. Founded by Antonia Pantoja in 1961, Aspira emphasized Puerto Rican history and culture, leadership training and development, college preparation, and community responsibility. Aspirantes, as the group's young members were known, succeeded in establishing Puerto Rican studies courses in the city's high schools and colleges.[113] Aspira also fought for bilingual education in the public schools, finally winning a consent decree from the New York City Board of Education in 1974; the decree established bilingual education as a legal right and became a model for school systems throughout the United States.[114] As a result of community organizing in the Lower East Side, in 1972 Luis Fuentes became New York's first Puerto Rican school district superintendent. He worked to implement the "wishes of the community school board," which included bilingual education, cultural education, and "improvement of reading scores of all the students." Fuentes recalled, "It was also my responsibility to bring in educators who reflected those concerns and to hire teachers who shared the aspirations of parents to see their children succeed."[115]

Fuentes's understanding of his role as a champion of the wishes of parents in the community and of Puerto Rican, African American, and Chinese youth marked a departure from the attitudes of previous administrators. Ella Baker recalled that in the 1950s in Harlem, "At one point I've seen parents go into the school office, and the people would ignore them completely. Because you didn't have very many black teachers even in the school systems."[116] African American and Puerto Rican parents' activism on behalf of their children changed this dynamic, resulting in greater attention to students' needs as well as recognition of the importance of incorporating parents as partners in the public schools. Together, these activists challenged the idea that poor parents do not care about the education of their children by offering their own vision of high achievement coupled with appreciation for different racial and ethnic backgrounds.

MOM and the school boycott campaign served to radicalize low-income Puerto Rican and African American women in the Lower East Side, who went on to participate in additional community movements for better housing, health, education, and welfare. After the school boycotts, frustrated with the slow pace of change in New York City and inspired by the civil rights movement in the South, MFY adopted bolder protest strategies.[117] In the following months, MFY organized rent strikes, formed welfare rights groups, and took the battles of low-income residents to the courts, initiating the legal services movement.

CHAPTER TWO

A Grand Cooker of a Scene

MFY's Outgrowths

By the mid-1960s, many of New York's African American and Puerto Rican residents were "fighting mad," as one MFY social worker described them.[1] The public schools remained segregated; decent, affordable housing was in desperately short supply; and police brutality inflamed the wounds inflicted by inequality and poverty. The school integration campaign's inability to win improvements had led Milton Galamison to orchestrate the massive boycotts of February and March 1964; similarly, the fair housing movement's frustrated efforts to lessen residential segregation and secure more public housing for African Americans and Puerto Ricans prompted civil rights activists to embrace more disruptive tactics. In the fall of 1963, housing activist Jesse Gray organized tenants in Harlem for a coordinated rent strike designed to draw attention to the dismal conditions of the tenement apartments and to pressure city officials to enforce the building code and to fund more public housing. As development czar Robert Moses constructed his $1 billion 1964–65 World's Fair complex at Flushing Meadows, beckoning tourists from around the world, Gray suggested that Moses include a "guided tour of the ghetto in Harlem" for visitors to witness the tremendous gulf between the vision of consumer opulence and Space Age progress on display at the fair and the reality of dismal living conditions for so many of the city's African American and Puerto Rican residents.[2]

Following their participation in the 1963 March on Washington for Jobs and Freedom, MFY staff and Lower East Side residents alike were swept up in the civil rights movement. According to Frances Fox Piven, "As people showed themselves to really be ready and angry, the community organizing component of the project became much more important. . . . MFY professionals were learning and changing as the political situation changed."[3] Working with CORE leaders from the Harlem, New York University, Downtown, and Brooklyn chapters, MFY staff members helped organize rent strikes against slum landlords. In order to meet the needs of their largest constituency—low-income women of color—MFY staffers formed welfare rights groups. Lawyers in MFY's new Legal Service Division pressed the city courts to uphold the due process rights of their clients and advanced test cases that led to reforms in housing and welfare policy.

Property owners and city officials perceived low-income Lower East Side residents' calls for fair treatment—to receive what they were entitled to, by law—as attacks on themselves personally and on the social order. In the late summer of 1964 *The Daily News*, in conjunction with city councilman Paul Screvane, led a campaign against MFY, charging the organization with harboring communists and fostering subversion and, later, with mismanagement of public funds. Amid the still-heated Cold War atmosphere, the city government, New York State, and the U.S. Senate all launched inquiries into MFY's alleged communist ties.

While the agency was eventually cleared of charges regarding communist influence and misuse of funds, "the crisis," as MFY staffers later referred to the period between 1964 and 1965, had a chilling effect on the organization. The President's Committee on Juvenile Delinquency requested the resignations of MFY's top-level staff and installed a new head, Bertram Beck, with the directive to quell the community organizing program. The organization dissolved by 1970, but not before it left significant legacies, including the Community Action Programs of the Economic Opportunity Act of 1964, the welfare rights movement, and the legal services movement. Participation in MFY's community organizing proved to be a radicalizing experience for both residents and staff members, many of whom went on to become lifelong activists. MFY organizer Marilyn Bibb Gore reflected that "one of the greatest things that MFY did was help people learn to fight."[4] It fostered several social movements that changed the city's political and social landscape and inspired other activists across the nation.

"We are tired of being told to wait":
Living the Civil Rights Revolution

Living conditions in Puerto Rican and African American neighborhoods in New York City were extremely poor. As Puerto Ricans and African Americans moved into the Lower East Side, the South Bronx, East New York, Brownsville, and Bedford-Stuyvesant, many white residents moved to the suburbs, pulled by public and private investment in the new residential areas and pushed by the concurrent disinvestment in the old. Often the city reduced social services and ceased maintenance in those now majority African American and Latino neighborhoods, while landlords subdivided their apartments even further and allowed their buildings to deteriorate.[5] In the early 1960s, 900,000 families throughout the city still lived in 43,000 "Old Law" tenements, constructed prior to 1902, when "New Law" building requirements went into effect mandating an exterior window, running water, and bathroom facilities for each apartment.[6] The clearance or renovation of tenements brought little relief, as new apartments were often designated for middle-income tenants and were generally closed to African Americans and Puerto Ricans. For example, the massive Metropolitan Life housing development Stuyvesant Town, which stood immediately north of the Lower East Side and was subsidized by public funds, admitted just 47 African American individual residents out of 22,405 total tenants in 1960, and those few residents were admitted only after a sustained struggle by civil rights activists that began in 1943.[7] Public housing, too, was in short supply. By 1957, the New York City Housing Authority had a waiting list of 100,000 families, many of whom were African American and Puerto Rican, yet it gave priority to white applicants under its "Open Occupancy" program in an effort to bolster white voters' support for public housing.[8]

Puerto Ricans and African Americans paid more than white New Yorkers for their apartments and yet endured decrepit conditions, including lack of heat and hot water, no bathroom facilities, leaky ceilings, and rats, which posed health problems; in 1962 alone, the City Bureau of Sanitary Inspections reported 530 children bitten by rats in their homes.[9] Landlords often left doors unlocked, allowing narcotics addicts to enter, stash their drugs in holes in the walls, and occupy the stairways and halls of tenements, which quickly became unsanitary; one reporter described them as feeling "like a dank passage to despair."[10] Poor tenants faced a double bind, as the city welfare department would withdraw rent allowance if the building a tenant lived in was declared hazardous. In fear of losing their benefits should they bring a landlord's deficiencies to city authorities, renters had little recourse but to make do.[11]

In a telegram sent to city, state, and federal officials, a group of mothers living without heat or electricity in a tenement house in the Lower East Side summarized their plight and called on their government representatives to recognize their basic human rights:

> We are voters and Puerto Rican and Negro mothers asking for equal rights, for decent housing and enough room. Building has broken windows, no gas or electricity for four weeks, no heat or hot water, holes in floors, loose wiring. Twelve of forty-eight children in building sick. Welfare doctors refuse to walk up dark stairs. Are we human or what? Should innocent children suffer for landlords' brutality and city and state neglect? We are tired of being told to wait with children ill and unable to attend school. Negro and Puerto Rican tenants are forced out while buildings next door are renovated at high rents. We are not being treated as human beings.[12]

MFY staff became aware of the problems renters experienced through their daily contact with clients in the storefront offices. In March 1963, MFY opened up two clinics devoted solely to housing issues; social workers acted as brokers, bringing renters' complaints to landlords and city agencies. According to staff organizer Ezra Birnbaum, the result was "constant frustrating and bitter experiences with courts and city agencies," along with a growing understanding among staff members of how the system actually worked.[13] In addition to battling the bureaucracy via telephone and paper trail, MFY staffers engineered dramatic confrontations with absentee landlords who refused to repair their apartments. An MFY staffer contacted a local rabbi and asked him to denounce publicly, at temple, the list of slum landlords MFY provided. Another staff member dumped dead rats on a recalcitrant landlord's steps.[14] The maddening process of trying to aid tenants radicalized MFY staff members, who came to believe that only mass action could move the city agencies to punish delinquent landlords and provide decent low-income housing.

African American activist Jesse Gray, director of the Community Council on Housing, rose to prominence in the fall of 1963 and winter of 1964 after successfully organizing 225 tenements in Harlem with more than 2,000 residents to withhold rent payment until landlords completed repairs. Gray, one of ten children, was born in a rural town outside of Baton Rouge, Louisiana; attended college at Xavier University, a black Catholic institution in New Orleans; and joined the Merchant Marine, where he became a leader in the left-wing National Maritime Union, which championed racial equality and rank-and-file leadership. According to an interview with his good friend, fellow National Maritime Union member and important civil rights leader Jack O'Dell, Gray's political consciousness was shaped by both his international travels, which exposed him to movements for social justice such as the Tenants' Movement in Scotland, and his study of Marxism in the 1950s.[15] Gray had begun organizing tenants in Harlem in the 1950s; in 1963, seeking to apply greater pressure on city officials, Gray asked tenants to bring rats, living or dead, to court and to City Hall with them as ammunition in their battles with landlords and city bureaucracies. He also organized the "Rats to Rockefeller" campaign in which tenants mailed four-inch rubber rats to the governor and demanded more state support for public housing.[16]

In the fall of 1963, inspired by Gray's success, MFY shifted from supporting individual staff members in their actions against specific landlords to joining a citywide movement for fair housing conditions, rent control, an end to residential segregation, and the construction of adequate public housing for low-income families.[17] That winter, MFY changed its housing clinics to Tenants' Councils, designed to be membership organizations composed of building and block tenant leadership. The goal, Birnbaum explained, was to "convert as much of the service role as quickly as possible into direct action techniques, rent strikes, et cetera." While MFY staff members would still play a role in cultivating leadership, their objective was to form a resident-controlled movement of renters in the Lower East Side. Moreover, Birnbaum announced, MFY workers would "no longer work with individual tenants unless the tenant is prepared to help organize his building. Only emergencies will be exceptions to this." This directive marked a change in the conception of the role of the agency's social workers; no longer merely advocates, they were instructed to incite and participate in direct-action protests.[18]

"Tenants are tired of paying high rents for cold apartments where only the rats are comfortable! Harlem led the rent strikes. Now a Lower East Side Rent Strike organization has alerted our area! The strike is growing. Every day is important for organizing tenants," MFY's newsletter exhorted readers in January 1964. That month, MFY organized Lower East Side residents to march on City Hall for hearings on rent control. The campaign was an extension of the demonstrations and rallies in which activists explicitly tied the existence of racial ghettoes to white landlords' ability to exploit poor African Americans and Puerto Ricans. During one rally, author James Baldwin addressed a crowd in Foley Square and asked how a universal rent strike in Harlem would affect "the white economic power structure." Harlem activists called on the city to take action on 108 "slum" buildings in Harlem and to take immediately into receivership all buildings on 177th Street from Fifth to Madison.[19] Under Gray's leadership, the Harlem rent strike coordinating committee printed 50,000 leaflets urging tenants to join.[20] Gray also called on the Red Cross to declare lower Harlem a "disaster area" because of the large number of families without heat or hot water, some of whom attempted to heat their apartments using their gas cooking ovens.[21]

Also in January 1964, MFY staff invited Gray to address a community meeting and to help residents form their own rent strike organization. Gray's plan to extend the Harlem rent strikes to the Lower East Side found support from many MFY-affiliated groups, including the East Side Tenants Council, the Negro Action Group (NAG), the University Settlement Housing Clinic, the Council of Puerto Rican Organizations, the Fourth Street Housing Clinic, Puertorriqueños Unidos, the Metropolitan Conference on Housing, the NYU CORE chapter, and the downtown CORE chapter. Together, they formed a steering committee, elected Grace Cade of NAG as chair, and planned an outdoor rally at a vacant lot on Houston Street. The rally would include a huge bonfire to "dramatize the plight of many tenants whose homes were without heat and hot water."[22] Following Gray's appearance at the community meeting, the tenants of sixty Lower East Side buildings joined the citywide strike, which also spread to forty-five buildings in the Bronx and forty-five in Bedford-Stuyvesant, Brooklyn.[23]

East Harlem–based Puerto Rican activist Jose Fuentes joined the community organizing staff of MFY in 1961 and worked there for five years. Working with the Metropolitan Council on Housing, he formed the Comité Español de Organización (Spanish Organizing Committee) to "push the language barrier aside" and encourage Puerto Rican participation in the rent strike and broader tenants' movement.[24] Fuentes explained that, unlike the voter registration campaign, the rent strike campaign was hugely popular and touched a deep chord in the neighborhood, which had a history of influential rent strikes. The 1907 Lower East Side rent strike led by Pauline Newman had introduced the idea of rent control; it became law in the 1930s, another period of rent strike activity.[25] Fuentes recalled his organizing efforts:

> I remember that I would go through a project, trying to get people to come and vote, to register. It would take me about two weeks of knock-

ing on doors, and I might get ten people. With the rent strike situation, one leaflet—ten buildings in one block. And the next morning, at 9:00, I would have, maybe 180 people. . . . [It would say,] there's a rent strike, and we're going to have a meeting tomorrow. Everybody was there. That was in the air, that was what was happening. That was the language, and people were very responsive to that.[26]

As with MOM and the school boycott movement, MFY tapped into a preexisting sense of grievance, organized neighborhood groups and provided institutional support and mentoring, and linked Lower East Side residents with the citywide civil rights movement. The rent strike movement fostered Puerto Rican and African American collaboration, channeling frustration over poor living conditions toward the city government and landlords, rather than into inter-ethnic rivalry. This was not at all automatic. As recent migrants, Puerto Ricans competed with the more established African American community in New York for electoral representation and public-sector jobs, as well as for public funds for schools and antipoverty programs.[27] Sometimes resentments between ethnic groups turned violent. On August 31, 1964, for example, Puerto Rican youths tossed gasoline bombs "aimed at Negros" into a tenement on E. 10th Street between Avenues C and D in response to a shooting of a Puerto Rican man by an African American man the day before.[28] In response to the conflict, Joseph Maniscalco, a representative of the City Commission on Human Relations who claimed to have spoken to many Lower East Side youth, said the young men called for "a leader to tell of the conditions. They want someone to pay witness to the rats, the roaches, the drugs, the dirt, the unemployed. They want to talk about it."[29] MFY attempted to provide precisely such a forum for Lower East Side residents to name the problems they faced and to strategize together on ways to solve them. Through professional advocacy, MFY also hoped to make city bureaucracies more responsive to the needs of low-income New Yorkers.

In February 1964, as the rent strikes spread, MFY issued an official report declaring city enforcement of the Building Code "a sad flop" and suggesting that only "major rent strikes or similarly dramatic mass actions" would be effective in changing city policy and improving low-income housing.[30] MFY's Housing Program reported to the ad hoc committee on community organizing that a shortage of public housing and landlords' neglect of the safety and health of their tenants had resulted in the lack of "decent, safe, low-rent housing available for low-income people on the

Lower East Side." Inadequate government regulatory powers and the corruption of judges, MFY argued, resulted in a court system that was "real estate–controlled and a tool for landlords."[31] A *New York Times* editorial concurred, pointing out that fines assessed by judges in Housing Courts were so low that landlords had no incentive to complete necessary repairs.[32] Furthermore, landlords could evict tenants for nonpayment of rent, and the police department was responsible for enforcing the law and forcibly removing rent strikers from their apartments.

"There is no law for the people up here": The 1964 Harlem Riots

To augment the rent strike movement, MFY's newly founded Legal Services Unit began challenging slum landlords in the courts. In 1963, inspired by the successes of the NAACP Legal Defense Fund and the ACLU, the director of MFY's Legal Services, Ed Sparer, defined the task as using "the law as an instrument of social change."[33] In addition to educating the agency's social workers and clients about the law and creating handbooks on tenants' rights, staff lawyers were eager to test out novel theories of poor people's rights in the courts.[34] MFY's staff attorneys argued that "forgotten statutes" in New York City law permitted tenants to take out criminal summons against landlords who failed to provide essential services (Section 2040) and to pay rent money to the court in an escrow account when a landlord refused to repair an apartment (a 755 order). According to MFY staff historians Michael Appleby and Harold Weissman, prior to the Legal Service Unit's efforts, both of these statutes "were unknown and unused." MFY lawyers set about convincing the New York City courts that tenants had a right to hold landlords legally accountable for providing heat, hot water, and other basic necessities.[35]

As the rent strike cases wound through the judicial system, New York Criminal Court found Gray guilty of interfering with police when he had tried to prevent the eviction of a Harlem tenant.[36] His arrest angered civil rights activists and rent strikers and highlighted the tensions between the African American and Puerto Rican communities and the largely white and suburban police force. In 1962, Mayor Wagner had helped repeal the Lyons Law, which mandated that municipal employees live within the city, so white suburbanites increasingly staffed the police and fire departments. As Joshua Freeman explains, "not without reason, many residents of black and Puerto Rican neighborhoods came to see the police as an occupying army."[37] Following his arrest, Gray, who spoke fluent Spanish, organized a picket of the police station in East Harlem, where he called on police to "jail the slumlords" and protect the tenants.[38]

While Gray led citywide protests and the MFY Legal Service Unit represented 175 rent strike cases in the courts, Lower East Side women, including MFY paraprofessional Grace Cade, played a key role in organizing residents into tenants' councils and protecting tenants who faced eviction. At a meeting held at MFY's headquarters, Cade explained that while participants hoped for immediate action to remedy poor living conditions, they also sought long-term goals including "more public low-income housing in the area, emergency housing measures and an organized group of tenants to work on improving our neighborhood."[39] According to Fuentes, the rent strikes drew the Lower East Side community together in a cross-racial and, sometimes, cross-class movement for decent living conditions. The atmosphere in the neighborhoods was remarkably encouraging: "People supported each other because people refused to allow anyone to be thrown out in the street. . . . Somehow, you would find people that went to the court to get the necessary paperwork going to stop the eviction. You'd find people that would go to the landlord's house and picket his house."[40] When courts ruled in favor of the landlords, residents and MFY staffers organized rent parties to raise money for tenants in danger of eviction, turning the strikes into festive occasions. In some cases, the threat of a rent strike was enough to induce landlords to complete repairs.[41]

Like the Montgomery bus boycott and the Birmingham school integration campaign, the rent strike movement served both to generate solidarity among grassroots activists and to dramatize the plight of poor, non-white New Yorkers to a national audience. Tenants' grievances were widely publicized. A story in the *New York Times* described a television set as a poor Harlem family's "only solace," portraying a life the viewers "would never know, a life without squalor, vermin and rats."[42] Sympathetic, although voyeuristic reports gave credibility to civil rights activists' claims that the poor and nonwhite were cut off from the affluent society of the postwar United States. Predictably, the rent strikes also triggered a backlash, especially among those who saw them as symptoms of disorder and unlawfulness. Michael Bloom, head of the Democratic Party's Fourth Assembly District, denounced the rent strikes as "nonsense" steamed up by "red infiltrators." He claimed that the Lower East Side had "lived in harmony for years. Then all of a sudden this rent strike."[43] The police department, closely tied to the Democratic Party, was an important base of resistance to the rent strike movement.

Gray's confrontation with the police intensified as officers continued to try to forcibly evict rent strikers. Speaking in Harlem, Gray threatened, "There is no law for the people up here. The police work only for the landlords. Blood is going to flow if something isn't done."[44] Unfortunately, Gray proved prophetic. On July 16, 1964, Thomas Gilligan, an off-duty white police lieutenant wearing civilian clothes, fatally shot fifteen-year-old James Powell, an African American Harlem resident he alleged was carrying a knife, outside Powell's junior high school. Powell and two friends had been chasing a white building superintendent who had sprayed them with a water hose, and Gilligan decided to intervene. Witnesses testified that the youth was unarmed and had been shot without warning.[45]

For decades, African American Harlem residents had combated police brutality, including indiscriminate searches, station house beatings, and coerced confessions, with calls for federal intervention and the creation of an independent civilian complaint-review board. The police shooting of an African American soldier who intervened when an officer struck an African American woman triggered the 1943 Harlem Riot, and residents' anger remained simmering as the city refused to act on African American complaints.[46] The Powell slaying touched off five days of riots in Harlem and Bedford-Stuyvesant, including confrontations between Harlem youths throwing bottles and policemen who fired guns through tenement windows and at rooftops.[47] The riots left one person dead and more than 100 injured, as well as widespread damage to store windows and intense animosity between residents and the police.[48] During the rioting, a bruised and bleeding Gray, who accused the police of targeting him for beating, called for "100 skilled black revolutionaries who are ready to die" to correct "the police brutality situation in Harlem."[49]

After the riots, city officials increased pressure on Gray, charging him with inciting violence and serving him with a court injunction prohibiting him or his group from demonstrating in Harlem.[50] The injunction hindered Gray's ability to organize, and the rent strike movement, which was already slowing in the spring, ground to a halt by the fall of 1964.[51] By that time, however, Mayor Wagner began to respond to the demands of the tenants' movement. The city hired eighty-five new building inspectors and implemented cyclical inspections, reduced rents in buildings deemed substandard, put pressure on landlords to complete repairs and, under the receivership law of 1962, increased its takeover of buildings that landlords were unable to repair. By 1965, the city had taken over 117 buildings. This was a smaller number than activists hoped for, but city officials had little desire to become responsible for the bulk of low-income housing.[52]

In 1965, at the urging of Mayor Wagner, the New York State Assembly passed a bill mandating stiffer fines for landlords who violated housing codes and expanding the offenses for which tenants could legally conduct a rent strike to include rodent infestation and lack of heat, electricity, water, or adequate sewage disposal. The bill represented the codification of MFY's Legal Service Unit's claim that tenants had a right to withhold rent from delinquent landlords. The mayor also made plans for the construction of new low-income public housing, at least partially fulfilling the movement's demand for additional decent, affordable housing.[53]

Assessments of the efficacy of the rent strike campaign and the legal precedents won by MFY have differed considerably. Piven and Cloward argued that setting up escrow accounts to hold rent payments until landlords completed necessary repairs was too complicated for many poor residents and would benefit the middle class but not the poor.[54] (Indeed, the first group to withhold rent from their landlords under the new law comprised residents of a luxury East Side apartment house who charged that there were rats in the building and that the air-conditioners, washers and dryers, incinerators, and elevators did not function properly.[55]) Other actions had clearer benefits to lower-income residents; some Lower East Side residents who had taken part in the rent strikes formed tenants' unions and pressed the city to intervene and complete emergency repairs in "heat-and-hot water" campaigns in the winters of 1964–65 and 1965–66. In response, the city set up neighborhood centers for tenants to request repairs, and "a considerable number of people" obtained these necessary utilities, experiencing a significant improvement in their living conditions. Good, low-rent housing certainly remained in short supply across New York, but observers recorded a change in the tenor of tenant-landlord relationships as renters were granted more power: "The idea has spread . . . that tenants do not have to put up with intolerable conditions."[56] Importantly, as historian Roberta Gold argues, the rent strikes served to mobilize tenants more broadly, who then pressured the Wagner administration and the city council to retain rent control despite the efforts of the real estate lobby to eliminate it.[57]

The rent strike movement was important to participants, Fuentes claimed, because in addition to enhancing feelings of collective identity among residents it created a new and lasting sense of confidence in their own capacities: "People were taught to take over their buildings, to manage their rents, to keep the money away from the landlords."[58] The contest for space in the city is an ongoing one. The civil rights movement empowered low-income African Americans and Puerto Ricans to claim the right to live in New York in decent conditions and to call upon the state to extend them the benefits it previously reserved for white, middle-class residents. The vehemence of the attacks on MFY indicates that, although the campaign fell short of achieving activists' vision, their efforts to shift the balance of power were perceived as significant threats by those with a stake in the existing order.

"A suspected Red honeycomb for leftists": The Anticommunist Attacks

In July 1964, despite MFY's controversial involvement with the rent strike movement, the U.S. Department of Labor granted the agency an additional $1.5 million to expand its job-training program for unemployed youth who had dropped out of school. Announcing the grant, which was provided for by Manpower Act funds, President Johnson stated, "The Mobilization for Youth program has my deep interest and support."[59] At the same time it was enjoying federal support, MFY was making enemies locally. The Powell shooting and the riots against police brutality in Harlem and Bedford-Stuyvesant came just five days after Johnson's announcement. City Council president Paul Screvane charged that "the Harlem disorders" were incited in part by "fringe groups associated with the Communist party." Although he did not mention MFY by name, Screvane called for a Federal Bureau of Investigation (FBI) probe into groups that convened "very anti-American" rallies, including their funding sources. This move laid the groundwork for his attempt to tie MFY to communists and violent civil disorders.[60]

Many New Yorkers had supported the Communist Party (CP) or the activities that it and a variety of socialist and left-wing labor groups conducted during the 1930s, when communists organized councils of the unemployed, assisted tenants in resisting eviction, and conducted mass demonstrations for public relief. By the late 1930s, approximately half of the CP's national membership lived in New York City, the only place it regularly succeeded in electing candidates to municipal offices. Support for communism was high among labor unions, including the Transport Workers Union, National Maritime Union, United Electrical Workers, United Retail and Wholesale Employees, and American Newspaper Guild. The CP's support for racial equality, integration, and self-determination made it popular among African American and Puerto Rican New Yorkers, and it attracted support from the children of European immigrants who had brought radical views with them from their homelands and

sharpened their politics in labor struggles here. Communists Peter Cac-
chione of Brooklyn and Benjamin Davis of Harlem served openly on the
city council during World War II. So did Michael Quill, who ran as a candidate of the American Labor Party (ALP), which was founded by garment trades union leaders in 1936 and came under the control of the
Communist Party in the early 1940s. Like the CP, the ALP enjoyed strong
support in Jewish, African American, and Puerto Rican neighborhoods;
it garnered an average of 13 percent of the citywide vote between 1938
and 1949.[61]

New York's strong communist presence drew attacks from conservatives and some liberals as early as 1940–41, when the New York State legislature's Rapp-Coudert investigations into communist influence in New
York's municipal colleges resulted in the dismissal or resignation of dozens of faculty members, with most coming from the City College of New
York and Brooklyn College.[62] The scrutiny increased following the end of
World War II as anticommunist fervor dominated both national and local
politics. In the late 1940s, the New York City Board of Education targeted
the left-led Teachers Union, using "interrogation, firing teachers, forcing
them to resign or retire, banning the union from operating in schools, and
using undercover police agents and informers" in order to destroy the
union and remove more than 300 alleged communists from the city's
schools.[63] Many of the city's labor unions purged suspected communists
from leadership positions; left-wing activists who were naturalized U.S.
citizens had their citizenship revoked and were forcibly deported by the
federal government.

By 1956, the Communist Party in the United States was largely mori-
bund, and the anticommunist attacks had greatly weakened the institutions that had nourished leftist activism more broadly. Anticommunism
proved to be a powerful weapon directed at the strongest voices of support for racial equality and workers' rights. Benjamin Davis was jailed for
five years. Renowned actor and singer Paul Robeson was blacklisted,
banned from appearing on American television, and had his passport revoked for seven years. East Harlem–based congressman Vito Marcantonio was forced out of office. The eminent intellectual W. E. B. Du Bois was
put on trial at age eighty-two for leading a peace organization that the FBI
deemed suspect and had his passport revoked; he died in exile in newly
independent Ghana. Although McCarthyism reached its height in 1953–54,
the House Un-American Activities Committee (HUAC) continued to hold
hearings well into the 1960s, and red-baiting remained a viable strategy
to tar those on the left.[64]

Early in August 1964, in response to the riots in Harlem and Bedford-Stuyvesant, MFY called for the "immediate establishment of a Civilian Complaint Review Board, appointed by the Mayor and responsible only to him for its findings, to investigate charges of police brutality."[65] Supporting black New Yorkers' grievances against the police brought MFY under direct attack. On Sunday, August 16, 1964, the *Daily News* ran a banner headline: "YOUTH AGENCY EYED FOR REDS: City Cuts Off Project's Funds." The tabloid charged that its "lengthy investigation" revealed that "left wingers by the score have infiltrated Mobilization and diverted its funds and even its mimeograph machines to disruptive agitation." The report announced an "intensive federal-city investigation" of MFY "as a suspected Red honeycomb for leftists who have used its facilities—and juveniles—to foment rent strikes and racial disorders." Specifically, the *Daily News* charged that Gray, who was affiliated with MFY, led the Harlem riots and had used the group's facilities to print inflammatory handbills reading "Wanted for Murder: Gilligan the Cop." It claimed that a "spot check" of MFY personnel "disclosed that scores of them have signed petitions for Communist candidates for offices, demonstrated against nuclear testing, and participated in numerous other Red or Red-front activities." Screvane, who was angling for the 1965 Democratic mayoral nomination in a crowded field, announced that, pending the results of the investigation, the city "has clamped a stop-order on any further municipal expenditures or federal anti-poverty funds administered for Mobilization by the city."[66]

The FBI immediately mounted a background check of all of MFY's 380 employees. The charges came just days before President Johnson was scheduled to sign the Economic Opportunity Act, and his administration, fearing that its entire antipoverty program would be tainted by the accusations against MFY, summoned MFY director James McCarthy to Washington for an emergency meeting at the Department of Justice. MFY had lost its greatest champions in the administration when John F. Kennedy was assassinated in November 1963 and Robert F. Kennedy resigned in September 1964 to run for one of New York's U.S. Senate seats. McCarthy tried to defend the agency, noting that the controversial "Wanted for Murder" poster had been printed on an "offset press," which MFY did not own.[67] Hoping to clear itself of the charges, MFY launched its own internal investigation, headed by the noted anticommunist lawyer Phillip W. Haberman Jr. Despite these efforts, the charges unleashed a flood of complaints against the organization just as it was applying for federal grants to renew its projects for two additional years.[68] Journalist Jack Newfield reported that "in the wave of recent publicity over whether the MFY staff was Communist infiltrated, City Hall was bombarded with protests from real estate men outraged over the rent strike, police angered by endorsement of a civilian review board, and businessmen dismayed by the agency stand on building code revisions."[69]

MFY proved to be an easy target for charges of communist influence, enabling those with interests opposed to the agency's campaigns to impugn its integrity. The Lower East Side had long been home to communist and leftist organizations and institutions, many of which came under attack by anticommunists from the 1940s through the early 1960s. As James Smethurst explains, radicals remained in the neighborhood and retained their political commitments, forming an "interracial bohemia" while often eschewing formal membership in communist-affiliated groups to avoid persecution (and prosecution).[70] Not surprisingly, given both MFY's location and its goal of radical social change, leftists and current and former Communists joined the group's staff. The FBI found that two staff members were currently members of the Communist Party and three others belonged to leftist organizations that had split off from the CP. Additionally, it said that nine MFY staff members had belonged to the CP or to "communist front organizations" (that is, groups that were nominally independent but under the influence of the CP) during the 1930 and 1940s.

Immediate attention focused on the five staffers with current memberships, especially Leroy McRae, an African American community organizer who had aided Gray in the rent strike campaign and who had run as the Socialist Workers Party's candidate for state attorney general in 1962.[71] The investigation broadened to include MFY staff members with a past history of left-wing activism when the *Daily News* obtained a list of forty-five staff members who had signed a nuclear test ban petition.[72] MFY social worker Barbara Hunter Randall Joseph, who had protested the development and use of nuclear weapons, recalled her anxiousness during "The Crisis," as MFY termed the period of investigation: "All of us who had political backgrounds were called up and subpoenaed. . . . And, coming out of the 1950s, people were so terrified. I mean, such damage had been done to people's lives, for nothing. . . . It was so destructive."[73] Under Executive Order 9835, signed by President Harry Truman in 1947, present or past "membership in, affiliation with or sympathetic association with" any organization the U.S. government deemed "totalitarian, fascist, communist or subversive" constituted disloyalty to the United States and was grounds for dismissal from federal employment. In practice, the loyalty programs targeted Americans with leftist backgrounds, particularly those active in labor unions and civil rights groups, as well as those who had belonged to the CP. Most state and local governments, as well as many private employers, used the same broad criteria to determine "loyalty" to the United States.[74]

The FBI probe had a palpable chilling effect on the organization, as staff members worked to defend themselves against charges of present or past communist affiliation while they attempted to continue their organizing and day-to-day service provision. At that point, investigators warned Frances Fox Piven to stay out of the Lower East Side: "I had been hired by the Columbia University School of Social Work to do research," Piven said. "That's where I was supposed to be, said the investigators. A lot of investigators came in and everybody had our books and our files and was pouring over them. And so, I more or less left Mobilization at that point."[75] In addition to nine staff accused of links to the Communist Party, five other staffers with alleged leftist links resigned, supposedly "voluntarily . . . for better jobs," shortly after the *Daily News* report.[76]

As the charge that MFY was a communist front organization was discredited, Screvane refocused his criticism on the fact that a government-funded agency was assisting groups in protesting against city agencies. He argued that "the city government does not sanction or agree that lawless and disruptive activities should be encouraged by any organization that is financed by public funds."[77] MFY's directors contradicted Screvane's reasoning and suggested that protests by low-income minority New Yorkers were a positive step toward alleviating poverty and incorporating residents into responsible citizenship. The use of public funds to support protests was legitimate, they argued, even if it resulted in the embarrassment of city agencies.

Identifying itself with the American political tradition, MFY described its community organizing programs as "democracy in action."[78] In response to Screvane, Cloward contended that "part of our program is a war on apathy. The March on Washington was the greatest therapy in the lives of these kids."[79] McCarthy contended that "this is a self-help endeavor, to help people help themselves."[80] Moreover, MFY's directors warned, only "opportunities for constructive social action are an antidote to violence and riot."[81]

MFY garnered significant neighborhood support. Lower East Side leaders Rev. George Younger, Haydee Ortiz, and Esther Gollobin issued a statement urging residents to write letters to local, state, and federal officials detailing their support for the program: "Basically, MFY has helped our neighbors to help themselves become better citizens."[82] The United Tenants' Association of the Lower East Side, a group of Puerto Rican and African American residents, held a rally at which they praised MFY for helping them get relief from negligent landlords and argued that the attacks against the agency had been orchestrated by those landlords.[83] In September, community leaders delivered petitions with 13,000 signatures backing the agency to Mayor Wagner.[84] Beyond the neighborhood, a panel of social work experts headed by Leonard Cottrell, secretary of the Russell Sage Foundation, called MFY a "meritorious pioneering" effort and urged in a report to the PCJD that it continue to receive the "full support" of all levels of government.[85] The *New York Times* editorialized on behalf of MFY and sponsorship of local protests, declaring that "the right to fight city hall is as much a prerogative of the poor as of any other group of citizens."[86]

Despite support from Lower East Side residents, social work experts, and the *New York Times*, the negative publicity made MFY's funders anxious and cast doubt on the organization's future. The communist allegations seemed to threaten the PCJD's whole program of supporting new local agencies and innovative approaches to fighting poverty and delinquency. In September 1964, Ford Foundation director Paul Ylivisaker expressed concern about MFY's ability to institutionalize its programs beyond its initial five-year grant. Wondering whether MFY had developed techniques that would promote institutional change without alienating the existing leadership of the Lower East Side, he asked, "Has the protest method employed in the community organization effort fulfilled its promise? At what cost?"[87]

As the City of New York, New York State, and the Department of Justice conducted inquiries into MFY, Screvane and the *Daily News* kept up the pressure for an entire year, accusing McCarthy of misusing funds for his entertainment budget. The agency continued to function, with the city releasing funding on a month-to-month basis, for the duration of the investigations.[88] Although he was later cleared of significant financial impropriety, McCarthy resigned in September 1964, offering "ill health" as the reason. The crisis continued to unfold against the backdrop of the heated mayoral campaign, with Screvane and New Right leader William F. Buckley Jr. trying to make their anti-MFY stands testaments to their patriotism. Screvane and Buckley especially hoped to discredit liberal opponent John Lindsay, who won the Republican nomination and was supportive of the civil rights movement generally and of MFY specifically. Screvane and Buckley painted Lindsay as "dangerously ignorant" and "recklessly negligent" of the dangers posed by communists within the United States.[89]

MFY staff members showed a great deal of courage during the investigations, in many cases refusing to testify about their political affiliations or to testify against one another.[90] LeRoy McRae challenged New York State senator John Marchi (R-Staten Island), the head of the State Senate Committee on the Affairs of New York City that probed MFY, to prove in court that the Socialist Workers Party was "subversive" or that McRae was an "extremist."[91] Despite the fortitude of the group's staff members, MFY organizer Calvin Hicks believed that the lengthy investigations and the pressure to curtail organizing until the agency was cleared led to intense frustration: "These attacks have really finished Mobilization. There is vast demoralization of staff, and no freedom of programs."[92]

Ultimately, after the Marchi report failed to substantiate Screvane's allegations, the federal, state, and city governments cleared the organization and MFY received $1.5 million in funds for 1965–66.[93] By then, however, staff turnover had reduced much of the agency's organizing potential. In late December 1964, George Brager resigned from his post as codirector of MFY to take a position in the U.S. Department of Labor.[94] Brager was well-loved by his staff, and though he was replaced by Bertram Beck, an "eminently respectable" social-work expert, many felt that the agency's period of innovation had come to a close.[95]

"The idea that poor people had rights": Legacies

Although the anticommunist attacks weakened MFY, under Beck the group continued to incubate influential social movements based in the Lower East Side, including the welfare rights movement and the Black Arts Movement. Sensing that Mobilization's life span was nearing its end, its leaders were eager to accomplish as much change as possible through mobilization of disruptive social protest, which Cloward and Piven argued was poor people's most effective method for achieving results. Harry Specht, the head of the Community Organizing Program, wrote in March 1964 that "indigenous leadership is sought specifically for the social protest and not for the inherent value of developing leadership ability." With an increased focus on the goal of inspiring "bigger and better social action programs," MFY's administrators no longer placed as great a premium on training grassroots leaders.[96] In practice, many of the frontline staff continued to, however, and leadership development through face-to-face interaction and consciousness-raising among paraprofessionals and community residents was the hallmark of the Parent Education Program, the Tenants' Councils, and the welfare rights groups organized by MFY.

Ezra Birnbaum organized one of the first welfare rights groups on the Lower East Side, the Committee of Welfare Families. Born in 1931 to an Orthodox Jewish family in New York, he joined the Communist Party in his twenties and worked blue-collar jobs on the waterfront and the railroads. After the Soviet Union invaded Hungary in 1956, Birnbaum quit the CP and went to school to become a social worker. He worked with Italian gangs on the Lower East Side prior to joining MFY, where he remained until 1966–67, when he left to work for the Coordinated Committee of Welfare Rights Groups on a full-time basis. Birnbaum explained the evolution of the Community Organizing program of MFY into the welfare rights movement: "The idea was to take those ideas . . . of creating a ladder of opportunity and using government money, and begin to fight for your rights, not in a criminal manner but in terms of community-based activism. So, local leaders were hired. . . . And moving from that into organizing people and mobilizing people around what their own needs were, hiring them whenever possible to provide the organizing muscle, using the culture of the people rather than the culture of the professional. . . . So it naturally led into fighting for economic security."

He argued that women on the Lower East Side had a tradition of keeping their families together and striving to improve their children's lives, so that when MFY sought to employ paraprofessionals on its staff, local "leadership came out of the woodwork. . . . We didn't have to scrounge around and search for people who could be leaders. We simply had to bring them together."[97] Because Birnbaum himself lived in public housing in Chelsea and came from a working-class, union background, he said, it was "not strange at all" for him to "be in people's homes and sit down and talk." He remarked that "90 percent" of the leaders were women, many of them Puerto Ricans who belonged to Pentecostal churches. In the churches, he explained, "It was normal to get up in the audience and express yourself. So, we had a lot of interaction in our meetings, with people standing up and saying, 'Here's what happened to me today at the welfare rights center. And here's what's happening . . . and I will not stand for it any longer, and this is not fair'. . . . And the meetings were dominated by people getting up and giving their personal thoughts and their expression to their personal feelings, almost venting. And we would encourage that."[98] MFY workers helped the women connect their personal grievances to critiques of economic and political structures, and to join in larger movements. As community organizer Sidney Pinsksy noted, the agency popularized "the idea that poor people had rights, and that poor people could unite, and make demands, and push for those demands, and get something."[99]

While Lower East Side residents learned from the MFY staff, social workers and lawyers also learned from their interactions with clients. Barbara

Hunter Randall Joseph started the Welfare Action Group at MFY's Neighborhood Service Center on Avenue D and 10th Street, where she worked with Puerto Rican and African American women in a group that grew from six members to "about 600" and employed similar consciousness-raising techniques to Birnbaum's. She recalled her first attempt to organize low-income mothers into welfare rights groups as a failure, however. She had planned a public demonstration for the Puerto Rican women she was trying to organize: "I decided that we should have an open-air meeting, and the women sort of went along with this . . . and we had fliers everywhere, and women were going to come out and testify. . . . Very few people came. It taught me a good lesson."

Joseph was born during the Great Depression to African American parents with leftist political beliefs and studied social work at City College. Prior to joining MFY, she had been active in Women Strike for Peace, a largely middle-class, college-educated women's movement against nuclear weapons and the escalation of the Cold War. Her experience in Women Strike for Peace taught her that public protest was an effective form of political expression. As Joseph saw it, however, she had erred in conceptualizing an open-air meeting on welfare in the public housing complex her group members lived in, discounting both the stigma of being on welfare and the cultural taboo on women speaking out publicly in front of their husbands and families. Joseph pointed out that the same group of women later participated in a sit-in in a city welfare office and "stood firm" when the police came, recognizing that "over a period of time, they became very strong about what they believed."[100] But in order to organize effectively, Joseph had to change her own orientation to the group; she could not simply presume they would follow her lead.

Joseph worked with them to develop a "leadership packet" of information on "how to run a meeting" and "how to reach out to other members." Through consciousness-raising and ground rules for discussion, Joseph sought to create "an atmosphere of total respect and mutual appreciation and allowing different styles, different approaches by people," in order to facilitate cooperation between African American and Puerto Rican women. The group practiced collective decision-making and they made sure that both racial groups were represented in the leadership structure, as she explained: "We had a Latina president and an African American vice president and we had this matching on a conscious basis." Joseph encouraged participants to link welfare rights to civil rights, school desegregation, and other community issues. She recalled it as a "transformative" experience for both organizers and members.[101] Joseph's co-organizer Rosalyn Baxandall agreed, remarking that "we had meetings that went around the room and people weren't ashamed any more of saying they were on welfare and they were fighting as welfare mothers for their rights."[102]

Across the country, from 1963 to 1969, other groups of women receiving Aid to Families with Dependent Children (AFDC) began meeting to discuss their experiences with welfare. Some of the groups were organized by the Economic Research and Action Project (ERAP) of Students for a Democratic Society (SDS), while others grew out of CORE chapters, or from the neighborhood action centers of the Community Action Programs.[103] The groups organized by MFY were similar in many ways to other welfare rights groups, but they had a uniquely close relationship to attorneys in the agency's Legal Services Unit and to Piven and Cloward, who were interested in charting strategy for the emerging movement.

In 1965, while working with staff attorneys in a process similar to that employed by the rent strike movement, Birnbaum found in the New York City welfare regulations a provision for special grants of up to $150.00 for winter clothing for welfare recipients. This provision had been largely unused until MFY organized residents to place requests for winter clothing. The Lower East Side Committee of Welfare Families succeeded in obtaining these grants for 80 of its 110 member families and then publicized its victory, drawing more women into the movement. Over the next year, the group offered classes to women on welfare in order to educate them on what special provisions they were entitled to beyond the basic monthly grants. Hattie Bryant, the committee's business manager, explained that "If you don't know nothing, welfare's not going to give you nothing."[104]

Birnbaum also helped to organize a group of welfare workers who resented being forced to participate in "midnight raids" on welfare recipients' homes to see if there were men present, as well as in other repressive actions. At this time, any man found in the home of a woman receiving AFDC was presumed to be having a sexual relationship with the woman, and was therefore deemed to be financially responsible for supporting her and her children, allowing the city to cut off welfare payments. Generally, social workers in New York City supported the welfare rights groups and helped them by allocating their requests for special provisions, such as the winter clothing allowance and grants for household goods including couches and chairs.[105] At times the welfare workers' unions also offered public support to the movement. Judith Magee, president of the Social Service Employees Union in 1965, explained that the welfare rights movement could improve the relationship between caseworkers and clients by pressuring the city to change its policies: "We feel that many of their grievances can be related to the irrational policies of the department. The caseworker bears the brunt of their complaints and they may not understand that he is carrying out policy. But the clients can strengthen the union demands for changes in the policy so the workers will no longer be fettered."[106] In his role as the liaison between the Citywide Coordinating Committee and a group of about a dozen welfare workers committed to changing the system, Birnbaum organized sit-downs and takeovers of welfare centers by united groups of recipients and staff members.[107]

Working together with the Legal Aid Society and the Center on Social Welfare Policy and Law at Columbia, MFY staff attorneys discovered that under federal law, recipients had a right to a fair hearing after a welfare claim was denied. In 1966–67 they began filing hundreds of applications for fair hearings, and found that often, just filing the request led the welfare agency to grant the application. As historian Martha Davis observes, prior to this time, "fair hearings were rare . . . because virtually no poor people had lawyers and virtually no lawyers were familiar with the intricacies of the welfare system."[108] Meanwhile, Cloward and Birnbaum worked to connect their grassroots welfare rights leaders with the emerging national movement. In 1966, they traveled to Syracuse with Lower East Side residents to the national meeting of the Poor People's War Council on Poverty. There they met George Wiley, who in 1967 formed the National Welfare Rights Organization (NWRO). Cloward persuaded Wiley to adopt the "crisis theory" that he and Frances Fox Piven had developed from their work with Mobilization. By getting all eligible people on the welfare rolls and getting them what they were legally entitled to, including all special provision grants, Cloward and Piven hoped to create a fiscal crisis, which, they believed, would lead to political pressure for a national guaranteed minimum income.[109]

Joined by Legal Aid lawyer David Gilman in 1966, the MFY Legal Services Unit implemented this theory, filing thousands of fair hearing and special grant requests. By 1967, the city had paid out $5 million in special grants, with some clients receiving as much as $1,000 at a time.[110] As with the rent strike movement, the welfare rights movement generated considerable opposition. As early as January 1964, Republican city councilman Joseph Mondugno called for an official inquiry into the rising cost of welfare, which he warned was creating an "intolerable and unbearable" burden on the city's budget.[111] In the end, despite heated protests by welfare rights groups, the city implemented a flat grant in September 1968, eliminating special grants entirely and removing a powerful organizing tool from the welfare rights movement in New York.[112] This forced the movement's leaders to shift their focus to the federal government, which they pressed for a guaranteed national minimum income.

MFY legal services continued to provide assistance to New Yorkers on welfare, many of whom complained of arbitrary termination of benefits. In 1968, MFY lawyers filed suit against the city's welfare department, alleging that termination of benefits without a hearing violated due process rights. As a result of that case, in 1970 the Supreme Court in *Goldberg v. Kelly* held that the 14th Amendment's guarantee of due process required that recipients be given a formal hearing prior to termination of benefits. This landmark decision broadened the interpretation of constitutional due process and emphasized citizens' protection from arbitrary bureaucratic cutoffs. Importantly, *Goldberg v. Kelly* defined welfare benefits as an entitlement rather than a privilege. The decision resulted in a transformation in welfare administration, with many more hearings and a greater success rate among recipients challenging their termination.[113] MFY's lawyers achieved additional victories in the 1968 Supreme Court ruling in *King v. Smith*, which struck down "man in the home" laws as unconstitutional, and in the court's 1969 decision in *Shapiro v. Thompson*, which invalidated residency requirements for welfare benefits. Collectively, these cases resulted in concrete gains to individual welfare recipients. They also advanced thinking about a constitutional "right to live" that would make the federal government responsible for guaranteeing a minimum standard of living to citizens.[114] In his 1969 Family Assistance Plan (FAP), President Nixon proposed a negative income tax that would have done just that. However, welfare rights advocates deemed the amount proposed—$1,600 for a family of four—much too low, and amid criticism from both the left and right, Nixon abandoned his support for the FAP by 1972.[115] In the end, MFY legal services and the welfare rights movement were not able to secure a federally recognized right to live in the form of a guaranteed minimum income; however, future activists may well draw upon their models.

MFY left other important legacies, both in terms of the political development of its grassroots and professional participants and in how the category of "poor people" was understood by social workers, policy makers, the general public and, most importantly, poor people themselves. The idea of maximum feasible participation—the concept that poor people themselves should take part in decision making in programs directed at them—was not present in the original MFY proposal, but rather developed during the implementation of neighborhood organizing efforts. As George Brager recalled, "Essentially, we were liberal social reformists who went into a community, and wanted to do good work in the community, and decided what programs we thought would do good. . . . Our grassroots involvement and notions of self-determination came as we were on the street and engaged with people."[116] Influenced by the unfolding civil rights movement and residents' own leadership, MFY adopted participatory democracy, and in doing so, led to its inclusion in federal policy.

The Johnson administration replicated many of MFY's programs in the Economic Opportunity Act of 1964. In particular, policymakers used MFY's Urban Youth Work Corps as the model for the national Neighborhood Youth Corps and the agency's preschool education program as a basis for Head Start. The act's architects also drew on MFY's hiring of paraprofessional, indigenous workers in crafting the New Careers program.[117] The Johnson administration looked to MFY's storefront offices as the model for Title II of the Act, which established grants for Community Action Programs, and MFY's experience led policymakers to incorporate the idea of maximum feasible participation of the poor into those CAPs. In the rent strike and welfare rights movements, MFY attorneys pioneered new rights for their clients in the field of administrative law. The success of the Legal Services Unit, which won or settled advantageously more than 90 percent of its cases, led to a larger movement to provide neighborhood-based legal services. With federal funding from the Economic Opportunity Act, legal representation became more available to poor and working-class Americans, particularly in urban and rural areas.[118] Between 1966 and 1968, the Office of Economic Opportunity funded 850 community law offices staffed by 1,800 full-time lawyers who provided assistance to 600,000 families.[119]

Locally, MFY continued to provide services to Lower East Side residents, including literacy programs, job training, summer jobs for teenagers, and a health program featuring a roving van staffed with doctors and nurses that provided medical examinations on the spot. Yet, new restrictions on both public and private funding led to a decrease in social workers' involvement in protest. The 1967 Green and Quie Amendments to the Economic Opportunity Act gave local officials the authority to determine which community organizations were eligible for federal funding and mandated that one-third of Community Action Agency boards be composed of elected officials and another one third appointed by them, leaving just one-third representation by the poor themselves. The amendments also sought to reign in Community Action Programs and prevent their staffs from engaging in protests such as the rent strike movement while on the job. According to Robert Rosenbloom, the 1968 tax reform that banned private foundations from funding organizations involved in overtly political activities also caused the Ford Foundation to redirect its community funding away from advocacy and toward service provision and development, leading to an overall movement from protest to programming.[120]

Despite these new restrictions, MFY continued to support the efforts of community activists to maintain and increase the supply of affordable housing in the Lower East Side through the rehabilitation and renovation of slum housing as well as through renewed direct-action campaigns. MFY associate director Stanley Aronowitz, who was from a Jewish, left-wing background, recalled partnering with Puerto Rican leader Ernesto Martinez in 1968–69 to form the Coalition for Human Housing, with the goal of stopping the planned expansion of the Lower Manhattan Expressway through the Lower East Side and "resum[ing] the fight on recalcitrant landlords through rent strikes." Martinez and Aronowitz joined with Jane Jacobs and her allies in the West Village, as well as Italian leaders in the South Village, to oppose the construction of the Lomex, and won. According to Aronowitz, the Lower East Side residents had the highest rates of mobilization against the highway construction. As with the earlier rent strike movement and the retention of rent control, MFY's community organizing empowered residents to defy the city's leadership and fight for their own interests, changing the landscape of the city and its politics. By providing concrete resources, including spaces to hold meetings, publicity, and training, as well as a sense of legitimacy, MFY fostered interracial cooperation and effective grassroots organizing.[121]

From 1965 to 1970, under the leadership of Cultural Arts Program Director Woodie King Jr., MFY fostered another expression of creative resistance: the Black Arts Movement, which flourished in the Lower East Side and spread across the country. Nationally, the movement drew writers, artists, dancers, and musicians interested in exploring colonialism, black nationalism, and Marxism specifically and the relationship between art and politics broadly. Locally, teachers and students in the MFY Cultural Arts Program both adapted existing works and created new ones, exploring themes of racial identity and belonging, the difficulties and confusion associated with coming of age, and alienation and self-expression. They set their works in the Lower East Side and often portrayed the participants' experiences with heroin addiction, gang violence, joblessness, poverty, and domestic discord—or, in the case of their adaptation of Clifford Odet's 1935 play *Waiting for Lefty*, the rent strike movement.[122] As King explained, in art, "No matter what, we need our own existence corroborated," and thus the Cultural Arts program sought to document, publicize, and comment on the realities of existence in the Lower East Side in the late 1960s.[123]

King, who was then in his mid-twenties, was an actor and director who had already founded a black theater in Detroit. He had his own political and artistic consciousness shaped by attending programs at Detroit's Franklin Settlement run by radical Jewish and African American social workers, and the Will-o-Way School of Theatre in nearby Bloomfield Hills, Michigan. King drew on his training and network and brought a diverse group of artists to teach classes to the Lower East Side's multiethnic youth. According to King, the goal was to assist youth in taking "suppressed intellectual energy" and expressing it "artistically," thus combating drug use and delinquency, in addition to providing professional training that could lead to employment in the arts.

Students received a stipend in return for participating in training programs in modern dance, headed by Rod Rodger; drama (including filmmaking), headed by Olive Thurman Wong, Ed Cambridge, and Cliff Frazier; fine arts, headed by Jay Milder and Peter Martinez; and choral music, headed by Garrett Morris and Eva Texter. Guest instructors included influential African American playwright Lonnie Elder III, white experimental poets Diane Wakowski, Lawrence Ferlinghetti, and Allen Ginsberg, Black Arts Repertory Theater School founder and poet/activist Amiri Baraka (formerly LeRoi Jones), and African American jazz greats Jackie McLean, Kenny Dorham, and Archie Shepp.[124] "If they were in New York, I had money to pay them," King recalled. "I brought them in . . . These artists, if they were in town, they would come and talk about poetry . . . in the Sixties, these people were poeting in St. Marks . . . and these kids—they were there." He thus both assisted the careers of individual artists and exposed students to work that would prove influential in their own.[125]

MFY students performed Maryat Lee's *Dope!*, which depicts narcotic addiction, and George Houston Bass's *Games*, in which adolescents perpetuate violence while "playing" children's games. King explained that "we wanted plays that could speak to ghetto audiences, that, in the language of the ghetto, would deal with issues meaningful and important to its people. We wanted plays that accurately said what the actors were really thinking as youngsters living in the ghetto."[126] Performances took place in the streets on a vehicle known as the Dancemobile, or in Tompkins Square Park. "We would rent a truck, put a stage on it. It was street theater." The audience participated, shouting, cheering and booing characters— "sometimes they would throw eggs from their windows. There was all kind of stuff," King remembered.[127] Filmmaker Roberta Hodes was impressed by the MFY performances and decided to adapt Bass's play into a film starring the students and set in the Lower East Side. The film featured shots of urban renewal projects, the crumbling brownstones, the graveyard at St. Mark's-in-the-Bowery Church, and the playground at Jacob Riis Projects. (See figure 8.) *The Game* won numerous awards, including first prize, documentary class, at the 1967 Venice Film Festival, and was distributed by Grove Street Press.[128]

The Cultural Arts Program produced four other films, *You Dig It?*, *Epitaph*, *Where We Live*, and *Ghetto*, that received critical acclaim. *You Dig It?* depicts youth gang violence and was written by and starred Leon Williams, who was seventeen at the time. The film premiered at Lincoln Center and was shown on public television, at Expo '67 in Montreal, and at HemisFair '68 in San Antonio, Texas. The theater group was also invited to perform *Charades on East Fourth Street*, in which a Lower East Side gang holds a policeman captive and debates his fate, at Expo '67.[129] King recalled: "I think the art really burst on the scene. It was a new thing—people had never seen it before. . . . They had never seen this kind of expression, articulation. . . . They loved it."[130]

In his history of the movement, James Smethurst credits MFY for nurturing interracial and cross-ethnic institutions that fostered the breadth of the Black Arts Movement's vision, which emphasized self-determination and social justice. In just five years, the Cultural Arts Program succeeded in accomplishing many of its goals. The performances and films did give voice to the young residents of the Lower East Side, whose artistic visions continue to reach new audiences thanks to the many students in the Cultural Arts Program who did go on to careers in the arts. Evelyn Thomas, for example, won admittance to the Julliard School after beginning her dance training at MFY, and she went on to perform in many groups and to found and direct the Nuba Dance Theatre, in Oakland, California, dedicated to training dancers in a multiethnic and multigenerational setting. During her childhood, Thomas was sexually abused by her father, causing feelings of depression and suicide. In a 2013 interview, she credited the Cultural Arts Program with transforming her life and the lives of other troubled youths struggling with poverty, violence, and racism:

Understand that the cultural art program came along at a time that, if it didn't come along, we would have perished. It was more lifesaving than I can even describe, not just my story but so many people who aren't here, that I have to just put a voice in for them. If it wasn't for the cultural art program and the trickling effect, the domino effect that it's had over the years, to this moment, sitting here with you—and the story

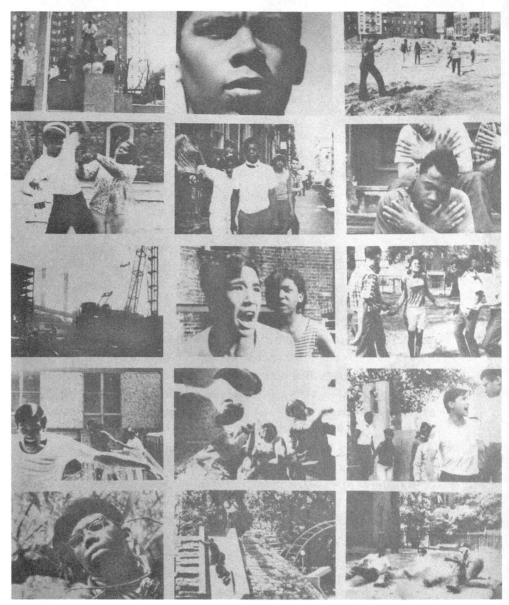

Figure 8. Poster of still images from Roberta Hodes' film
The Game (1967), starring MFY Cultural Arts students and filmed in the
Lower East Side. Courtesy of Woodie King Jr.

that I just told you—if it wasn't for Mobilization for Youth, there would be no existence for me.[131]

In addition to providing much-needed affirmation, nurturance, education, and inspiration to its young participants and launching individual artists' careers, the Cultural Arts Program nurtured important movement institutions: Woodie King's New Federal Theater, which grew out of MFY's theater program, opened in 1970 with the support of Henry Street Settlement. Its purpose was to serve as an "umbrella for a black theater, an Asian American theater, a Latina/o theater, and a Jewish theater." The New Federal Theater promoted works by playwrights of color and by women, including Ntozake Shange's *for colored girls who have considered suicide when the rainbow is enuf,* diversifying and revitalizing American drama.[132] Locally, the Black Arts Movement inspired Puerto Rican artists and writers, including Victor Hernandez Cruz, Miguel Algarín, and Miguel Piñero, who formed "Nuyorican" groups in the Lower East Side and East Harlem.[133] Like MFY, the Black Arts Movement was relatively short-lived but left a powerful legacy. The works it spawned are widely read and performed, and its members teach at universities across the country. As King put it: "We were passionate about the world, because what you learn early on is, a film is forever. It's a part of history."[134] Poet Hattie Gossett recalled that fertile time:

whoever would dreamed it woulda huh? Whoever
woulda thought a pizza/hotdog/souvlaki place
would usurp our house of dreams & visions on the
corner of 3rd avenue & 8th street major threshold to
an exalted state of mind known as the lower east side
a grand cooker of a scene which during those early
coldwar days shout out strong steady surges of music
writing civil disobedience painting anarchy dance free
sex political organizing that changed the world?[135]

Like Gossett, many former MFY members recalled their Lower East Side experiences with nostalgia and a sense of loss. Marilyn Bibb Gore commented that "I wouldn't have missed that experience for anything in life." Her coworker Sid Pinsky reminisced, "I didn't regret one day. It was such a profound experience."[136] MFY head George Brager recalled wistfully, "It felt to me like . . . what I was doing was really important. I've never had that feeling since. I'd never had it quite before."[137] Although MFY was unusually successful in having its policy goals adopted by the federal government, like most social movements, it may have had the greatest impact on its participants, many of whom became lifelong activists.

Following the crisis and the eventual dissolution of the organization, MFY staff and paraprofessionals continued to participate in the civil rights movement. Some went on to join the community health movement, the welfare rights movement, and the women's liberation movement. Others worked in the Community Action Programs, including Manny Diaz, who drew on his experiences and contacts in MFY to help found and secure federal funding for New York's Puerto Rican Community Development Project.[138] Terry Mizrahi, a social worker and LENA organizer who helped win four community health clinics for the Lower East Side in the late 1960s and early 1970s, argued that the federal government's acceptance of maximum feasible participation made her work involving residents in decision making over health-care provision possible: "The point is that, without the federal government mandating community participation, none of this could have happened in the way it did. There was an opening and a structure, there was an expectation that had to be filled."[139] Like Mizrahi and other professionals from the community organizing staff, many of MFY's paraprofessionals also went on to play leadership roles in the Lower East Side, including in local government, nonprofit organizations, and day care and health centers.[140]

Janet Peterson, founder of Brooklyn's National Congress of Neighborhood Women, which is the subject of the following two chapters, got her professional start as a social worker at MFY. Peterson worked first in an MFY storefront office and later in a housing office. During her time at Mobilization, "The real belief was that democracy could work and government could work, and that all people need to know was to organize." She took this philosophy, along with MFY's model of being "part of the fabric of the community" with her to Williamsburg, Brooklyn, where she directed a Community Action Program funded by the OEO. Many of these programs—including Peterson's—remained long after the official end of the War on Poverty, continuing to provide services and serve as conduits (albeit imperfect) for resident participation in governance.[141]

CHAPTER THREE

Everything Then Made Sense

Bridging the Neighborhood and Women's Movements

In 1969, Jan Peterson left the Lower East Side for Williamsburg, Brooklyn, heeding a challenge posed by her lover and former CORE leader Marshall England: to organize in a white neighborhood. Peterson's trajectory after Mobilization for Youth (MFY) captures much of the effervescent rise of social movements in the seventies, as well as the many tensions and contradictions building within the movements themselves and in American politics more broadly. Inspired by the example of the African American civil rights movement and the promise of the War on Poverty, many grassroots activists organized Community Action Programs (CAPs) with the goal of both improving the immediate material circumstances of their members and creating a mechanism for their voices to be heard and taken seriously in policymaking. While the 1970s are often remembered as a decade of racial and ethnic polarization, in many cases CAPs and their successors drew participants together in interracial efforts.[1] Brooklyn would become better known for the racially divisive battles over community-controlled schools at Ocean Hill-Brownsville and school busing in Canarsie in the late 1960s and 1970s, but during these same years interracial coalitions funded by CAPs emerged in opposition to local government's plans for urban renewal and disinvestment.[2]

Peterson took part in efforts to achieve community control of schools and to maintain the quality of life in Williamsburg. Based on these experiences, she found herself "getting really into what it means to do community-based work" and drawn into new social movements that sought to address the concerns of urban residents. As the African American civil rights movement inspired and influenced organizing by other racial and ethnic groups, including Chicanos, American Indians, and Asian Americans, some working-class white ethnics, predominantly Roman Catholic and of Eastern and Southern European descent, also began to organize and explore their own heritage and identity.[3] Based in the urban North, the white ethnic movement drew on the perception that the white working-class was being left behind by the white middle and upper classes who moved to the suburbs. During a time of widespread backlash against social welfare spending and growing anti-tax sentiment, these white ethnics were convinced of the need to organize themselves as African Americans had done in order to claim what they perceived to be their fair share of government spending.

Roman Catholic intellectual Michael Novak gave voice to the more conservative wing of the movement; he advocated ethnic pride, anti-elitism, a reassertion of traditional church and family practices as sources of authority and stability, the ending of busing and other desegregation programs, and government aid to the white urban working class.[4] At its most reactionary, the white ethnic movement channeled resentment of African Americans and their white liberal allies that was sometimes expressed violently, as in the 1970 "Hard Hat Riot" in Lower Manhattan during which white ethnic construction and office workers attacked and beat student antiwar protestors who had affronted their sense of patriotism and who symbolized the perceived betrayal of ordinary Americans by elites.[5] For Novak, who wrote that "the workingman's wife is psychologically 'passive,'" and that "she accepts things as they are given" and "tends to regard thinking as uncomfortable," the imagined champions of the white ethnic movement were masculine men, defined by their breadwinning status as husbands and fathers as well as by their physical prowess, most often displayed on the job.[6]

Less well known but equally important is the progressive wing of thought in the white ethnic movement, which raised awareness of the pain and sense of loss that assimilation engendered among many Southern and Eastern European immigrants to the United States, as well as the class shame, or feelings of inferiority and powerlessness, that constrained the lives of their working-class descendants.[7] In the nineteenth and early twentieth centuries, Catholic immigrants faced condescension, discrimination, and at times outright hostility from white Protestants who feared their loyalty to the pope and criticized their consumption of alcohol and their large families. Following the New Deal, World War II, and the implementation of the GI Bill, Catholics were better able to enter the mainstream middle class via suburban home ownership and higher education, but anti-Catholic sentiment remained potent enough to be a factor in John F. Kennedy's 1960 presidential campaign and a strong sense of difference between Catholics and Protestants persisted.[8] Thus, the white ethnic movement's affirmation of immigrant heritage and cultural traditions could be empowering, allowing participants to see middle-class, white Protestant norms as particular rather than universal and to validate their own belief systems.

As a community organizer in a racially mixed neighborhood, Peterson worked to mitigate feelings of racial distrust, drawing on the progressive strain of the white ethnic movement and its conviction that people who are "strong in their own ethnicity are better allies."[9] Consciousness-raising around ethnicity assisted in the formation of partnerships between white ethnic and African American and Latina activists by creating analytic tools for understanding multiple forms of oppression and deepening empathy for those with different identities.

Like the white ethnic movement, the neighborhood movement also embraced the New Left's tenets of participatory democracy, outlined in Students for a Democratic Society's 1962 Port Huron Statement, and the black left's emphasis on self-determination, a concept originating in Third World anticolonial movements.[10] The white ethnic and neighborhood movements shared overlapping membership, although leaders in the neighborhood movement, including Monsignor Geno Baroni, founder of the National Center for Urban Ethnic Affairs, and Wade Rathke, founder of the Association of Community Organizations for Reform Now (ACORN), emphasized the need for white ethnics to work together with African Americans and Latinas to preserve and restore the quality of life for residents.[11] Both nationally and locally in Brooklyn, the neighborhood movement drew residents together in opposition to urban renewal's large-scale redevelopment plans and the banking industry's practice of redlining, the refusal to grant loans for the purchase or renovation of housing in racially mixed urban neighborhoods, particularly those with African American residents.[12] The neighborhood movement's localism and opposition to bureaucratic central planning also fostered an ethic of do-it-yourself redevelopment, which included renovations of brownstones by gentrifying white middle-class professionals, poor people in sweat-equity programs, and the establishment of day care centers and other social service programs in addition to commercial ventures.[13]

The feminist movement shared the do-it-yourself impulse and program-building of the neighborhood movement as activists taught women to perform their own gynecological self-exams, shared knowledge, and built women's centers and domestic violence shelters.[14] Many feminists participated in the civil rights movement, and, like the neighborhood movement activists, they drew inspiration from the black freedom movement's use of direct action protests to achieve social change. The same year that she moved to Williamsburg, Peterson, who had earlier undergone an illegal abortion, went to an abortion rights march at St. Patrick's Cathedral in Manhattan organized by African American civil rights lawyer Flo Kennedy. As it turned out, Peterson was one of only five women protesting abortion laws on the steps of St. Pat's that day. She entered into a lengthy conversation with Kennedy and Ti-Grace Atkinson, the former president of New York NOW, and suddenly "everything then made sense . . . I was joining a movement that was about me," Peterson said. She participated in Atkinson's October Seventeenth Movement, a radical consciousness-raising group later known as The Feminists, whose members explored reversing women's internalized subordination to men in part through embracing female separatism and rejecting marriage.[15]

Peterson, who in her new home continued the advocacy and community organizing work she had begun in the Lower East Side, was "kicked out [of The Feminists] for missing a demonstration against family and marriage." (She had been busy helping a group of working-class Italian American women establish a day care and senior citizen center in Williamsburg, over the objections of local male leaders who accused them of undermining family relations.[16]) Aware of the irony in her ousting from The Feminists but still interested in the women's movement, Peterson joined New York Radical Feminists, a Manhattan group that included Kate Millet and Susan Brownmiller, authors of influential works on sexualized violence against women.[17] With New York Radical Feminists, she helped organize speak-outs on abortion and rape and participated in consciousness-raising around depression and gender oppression. It was a formative experience for Peterson, who recalled: "It was just totally electric. . . . You were going through every single day in a blaze of re-looking at who you were and what you thought and the empowerment of it." By the mid-1970s, Peterson was ready to bring the insights she had gained from her participation in feminist consciousness-raising groups to her work in Williamsburg.[18]

Conscious that "the way this whole ethnic, multi-cultural neighborhood-focused thing was going, was to have women still in the kitchen cooking the pasta," Peterson sought to carve out a new feminist space. She joined forces with Nancy Seifer of the American Jewish Committee and Baltimore councilwoman Barbara Mikulski, both of whom were prominent members of the white ethnic and neighborhood movements and interested in feminism.[19] Concerned that "the mainstream women's movement did not reach and touch a majority of women who were poor, working class or involved in neighborhoods," while male-led neighborhood groups were lacking and sometimes hostile to "a women's analysis," Peterson sought to establish "a new movement" in which "the fight for equal rights" would be "integrated with . . . efforts to improve the quality of life for . . . families and communities."[20]

"I was raised in a very white neighborhood": Housing and Racial Change

The North Brooklyn neighborhood Peterson moved to in 1969 was, like the Lower East Side, shaped by urban renewal, the loss of manufacturing jobs, and racial transition. Located on the northern tip of Brooklyn, Williamsburg and Greenpoint are connected to Manhattan by the Williamsburg Bridge across the East River. (See map 2.) Drawn by the neighborhoods' waterfront shipping industry and textile factories, Irish and German immigrants first settled in the area during the 1830s, 1840s, and 1850s, followed in the late 1880s by Russian Jews, Italians, and Poles. Throughout the first half of the twentieth century, immigrant men took jobs in construction, on the busy docks, at the Brooklyn Navy Yard, and in Williamsburg-Greenpoint's numerous textile, electronic, and meatpacking factories and warehouses. Immigrant women worked cleaning homes and offices or in textile factories.[21]

The numerous factories and modest homes gave North Williamsburg-Greenpoint, where Peterson settled, a distinctly working-class, industrial feel. By the mid-twentieth century, ethnic Italians, Poles, Russians, and Ukrainians predominated there, while in South Williamsburg a growing number of Puerto Ricans lived alongside Orthodox Jews.[22] Residents clustered together by kin and ethnicity and lived in multifamily two- and three-story wood-framed houses. Small, locally owned businesses were interspersed with the neatly kept but cheaply constructed and aging houses, while large warehouses and factories bordered the residential blocks. The Brooklyn-Queens Expressway lumbered overhead, dividing

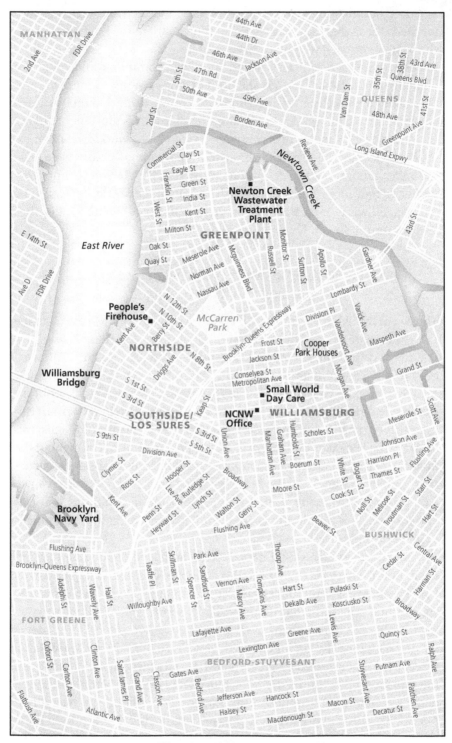

Map 2. Williamsburg and Greenpoint, Brooklyn

the neighborhood. Women kept their houses in "immaculate" condition and took care to clean the sidewalks and parks nearby.[23] Children lived at home until marriage, and then they often moved to another apartment in the same building. Neighbors knew each other and watched over each other's children.

Most residents were practicing Catholics, and many sent their children to parochial schools. They identified their parish as the center of their social and cultural lives.[24] The passage of time was marked by celebrations, including processions and feasts for saints' days such as St. Cono, Anthony of Padua, and Paulinas of Nola, when a huge tower, the Giglio, is lifted by hundreds of men.[25] These rituals featured elaborately carved statues of saints as well as Madonnas, including one from Our Lady of Mount Carmel, and included music, candles, prayer, and special foods. Feasts both linked immigrants and their descendants to their ancestral homelands and reinforced participants' sense of a religiously informed spatial understanding of Williamsburg-Greenpoint.[26]

Although in 1955 a *New York Times* reporter described the area as "drab," "dreary," and "deteriorating," residents were proud of their homes and felt strongly connected to their neighbors and their churches.[27] More than other groups, white Catholics in the urban North prioritized home ownership as a symbol of success. Given the importance and permanence of parishes, Catholics were more firmly rooted in their neighborhoods and slower to move to the suburbs than members of Jewish and Protestant congregations whose churches and synagogues could move to follow their congregations.[28] In addition, for many families, home ownership represented their most significant investment, and they were anxious about their houses losing value. They feared the block-busting and redlining that had recently taken place in Bedford-Stuyvesant, located just to the south. Bankers and real estate speculators, aided by federal housing authorities, encouraged white middle-class families to move out, often selling their homes at a loss, and African Americans to move in at artificially high prices, reaping huge profits for the real estate agents and bankers and accelerating racial change and declining property values in the neighborhoods. Among the victims were middle-class African American residents who saw their homes lose value and public services deteriorate.[29]

Unlike Bedford-Stuyvesant, North Williamsburg-Greenpoint did not become a target for block-busting. Nonetheless, African Americans and Puerto Ricans began moving there in the 1950s and 1960s when the New York City Housing Authority constructed public housing complexes in the neighborhood, often over the objections of white residents who opposed racial integration. Most private landlords in the vicinity refused to rent to nonwhites, making public housing the only option for people of color.[30] In 1952, the cornerstone was laid for Cooper Park Houses, composed of eleven seven-story buildings that provided low-income housing for 700 families, the majority of whom were African American and Puerto Rican.[31] In 1966, Greenpoint residents "vociferously" opposed the building of new public housing, claiming that their neighborhood was "already over-crowded." Despite residents' protests at the City Planning Commission, the New York City Housing Authority moved forward with construction. As the process accelerated, many young white ethnic families moved out.[32]

Unable to prevent the movement of people of color into their neighbor-hood, remaining white ethnics patrolled the boundaries between the proj-ects and surrounding residential blocks, subway stations, and public fa-cilities such as McCarren Park Pool. African American resident Mildred Tudy described Cooper Park Houses as being "located on an island . . . . And in order to reach the points of transportation, in order to go out to the schools and the shops, you have to go through a white, and often times it was a hostile, community."[33] Tudy recalled, "Black men and boys had trash cans thrown at them; I had to send my son across town to live with my step-sister so he could get to school without being hurt." When she took her chil-dren to a local Catholic church, "We found that when we sat down in a pew, people would move away from us."[34] Jewish ethnographer Ida Susser, who lived in Williamsburg from 1975 to 1976, observed whites intimidating African Americans who tried to live beyond the boundaries of public housing. Tactics ranged from posting racist signs to at least one incident of arson of an apartment where an African American family was living and "periodic" attacks on African American men, particularly those asso-ciating with white ethnic and Puerto Rican women.[35] Italian American Sally Martino Fisher recalled learning these racial boundaries as a child: her brother would hit her on the arm when they walked past the newly constructed Cooper Park Houses, warning her never to go in there. (See figure 4.) She explained, "I was ten when Cooper Projects were built. And it was forbidden [for me to go there] because it was . . . all minorities in there. . . . I was raised in a very white neighborhood."[36]

White men's regulation of women and children in their families and their attacks on African Americans and Latinos constituted a gendered as well as a race-based claim to the streets. Working-class men faced a sig-nificant erosion of status in New York's transition to a postindustrial econ-omy, as manufacturing jobs that paid a family wage became scarce and working-class women could more easily obtain employment in the expanding clerical and service sectors. The 1966 closure of the area's largest employer, the Brooklyn Navy Yard, was accompanied by the waning of the shipping and waterfront industry and followed by the shuttering of the Schaeffer and Rheingold breweries. Labor unions, which had reinforced working-class white masculinity, were also in decline. Even the beloved Brooklyn Dodgers abandoned their fans, having departed for Los Angeles in 1957. Taken together, these changes led to what sociologist Jonathan Reider terms a sense of "danger and dispossession" among working-class white ethnic men and their desire to protect the boundaries of home and family from racial others, using violence if they thought it necessary.[37]

Italian Americans, in particular, exhibited "fierce resistance to living with African Americans," often resorting to violent acts against them, according to Thomas Guglielmo.[38] In part because Italian Americans remained poor and working-class longer than other European immigrant groups in the United States, Jennifer Guglielmo writes, they evinced a "particular anxiety to assert a white identity in order to effectively distance themselves from their Brown and Black neighbors."[39] Some resented the civil rights and Black Power movements and believed that African Americans were gaining at the expense of Italian Americans.[40] While in the 1960s and 1970s Italian Americans were less likely to be poor than African American and Puerto Ricans in New York, they had higher high school dropout rates and fewer median years of schooling compared to the city's population as a whole, and those who remained were clustered in poor neighborhoods. The sentiment that "government was ignoring their needs" was widespread.[41]

Italian American Williamsburg resident Elizabeth Speranza founded the Conselyea St. Block Association in 1965 after attending a community meeting in an African American neighborhood in the Bronx, where members of the mayoral administration were dispensing "free tickets to the theaters, free everything." As Speranza explained, "I felt that this area never got anything because we were Italian—nobody really cared." With her female neighbors and friends, Speranza formed the block association so that their children could also reap the benefits of the mayor's donations to community groups.[42] Speranza's actions expressed both white ethnic resentment and a tradition of Italian American women's efforts to improve their families' living conditions and to knit their communities together.

Italian immigrant women had gravitated toward radical politics in the early twentieth century and played leading roles in the labor movement, where they drew upon protest traditions brought with them from Italy as well as their networks of kin and neighbors.[43] Many of the women of

Conselyea Street had mothers who were members of the International Ladies' Garment Workers' Union (ILGWU) and from whom they would have learned strategies of mutual aid and collective direct action. The ILGWU was a multiracial union, with ethnic locals that corresponded to ethnically segregated workplaces, and later, as workplaces integrated in the 1940s, multiethnic locals.[44] In the early twentieth century, the garment workers would have likely participated in multiethnic protests. By the 1960s, however, successive waves of anti-radical political repression and pressures to embrace whiteness meant that the second- and third-generation Italian American Conselyea Street women were more likely to organize in opposition to African Americans and Puerto Ricans than alongside them.[45] In time, however, Peterson's leadership as well the outreach efforts of African American women living in public housing in Williamsburg-Greenpoint helped to bring the Conselyea Street women into a multiracial alliance.

"There I was in the heart of *ethnicity!*": Identity-based Organizing

It was fitting that Peterson's first contacts in the neighborhood would be women from the Conselyea St. Block Association, as one of her primary goals was to lessen local working-class ethnic whites' distrust of government by putting antipoverty programs to work for them. Initially, however, Peterson was surprised by the differences she perceived between white Protestant culture, including both the working-class Swedish American community of her youth and the dominant middle-class norms she had been socialized into as a college student at the University of Wisconsin–Madison, and working-class Italian American culture. Years later, after rediscovering her own ethnic and cultural heritage, she recalled:

> I came here . . . because I was supposed to be in a white community, instead of being a white person in a black community. I thought I was in a white neighborhood, and lo and behold, I was in an Italian neighborhood. I was a nice, innocent Swedish person who didn't even know about my own working-class, Swedish ethnic background and there I was in the heart of *ethnicity*! Now all of a sudden I was one person in the middle of the Italian neighborhood.

The forthright combativeness and strong emphasis on family ties and tradition that characterized interactions among Italian Americans posed a challenge for Peterson, who remembered "I would get sick, I was nauseous, with all the organizing, because [of] the intensity."[46]

Just three months after arriving in Williamsburg with a $50,000 War on Poverty grant to work out of the School Settlement House, Peterson managed "to start a war in this neighborhood and get fired." She had ruffled feathers at the settlement when she tried to implement maximum feasible participation and hire Italian Americans, none of whom had previously been on the staff despite the settlement's location in an Italian American neighborhood. When the settlement board found out that at the request of a young woman's father Peterson had advised a pregnant teenager about her options, including abortion, they took it as an occasion to get rid of her. In the end the young woman decided not to have an abortion, but because Peterson had "talked to her about options and choices" the settlement house staged a community meeting in a local church to publicly chastise her. Peterson recalled feeling isolated and defeated: "Five hundred people went to this church, five hundred people were there to hear about this woman that was bringing discussions of abortion and other things to the neighborhood . . . which is a little scary, if you're the one person that's here." She planned to leave the community.[47]

Members of the Conselyea Block St. Association convinced her to stay. Speranza, whom Peterson had hired to work at the School Settlement, recognized that Peterson "knew where to open the doors"; while the Conselyea women had ideas about what they wanted to do, they "didn't know how to go about it."[48] Peterson used her grant to establish a new organization, the Education Action Center, where she worked with Speranza and a tightly knit group of Italian American women from the neighborhood, many of whom were related to each other. Italian American Tillie Tarantino, who became a lifelong community activist, recalled the organization's early days: "She [Peterson] would push us to do things. At the beginning we met on stoops, or we would meet in women's houses, for coffee klatches. Every night we would talk on different things." Together, they instituted educational programs such as English as a second language classes for Italian speakers, provided social services to the community, including a summer program for children and teenagers, and planted trees in the neighborhood.[49]

African American residents of Cooper Park Houses had begun to organize themselves a full decade before the women of Conselyea Street. Mildred Tudy's experience was representative of this early organizing. Born in 1927 in Macon, Georgia, Tudy grew up in East Harlem where she participated in civil rights activism with her grandmother and attended Julia

Richmond Public High School, where she was one of only a few African American students. Most African Americans were channeled into vocational rather than academic high schools at that time, but Tudy's grandmother pushed to get her academically talented granddaughter admitted. After graduation, Tudy spent one year at Fordham University before taking a job with the immigration bureau at Ellis Island. Tudy married in 1942 and quickly gave birth to twins, followed by another child. She settled in Cooper Park Houses in 1952, happy to have found space for her growing family. She recalled, however, that "the European immigrants . . . felt that this was their bailiwick. Where the housing went up it had been a wasteland, with a few secondhand shops and some goats that the Italians raised for cheese. But they still thought it was their community."[50] To the frustration of the new tenants, the New York City Housing Authority had left the sidewalks and roads inside the development unpaved.

Tudy explained that she helped found the Cooper Park Tenants' Association in 1955 because "we saw that in order to change the situation here, we had to have a strong organization here. I and others . . . some women who pulled together the men, and we started a strong tenants' association." Along with other African American women, including Margaret Carnegie and Mildred Johnson, Tudy worked to organize tenants and meet with officials in order to get the city to finish paving the roads and walkways and establish a community center and senior citizens' center in Cooper Park.[51] The tenants' association also conducted outreach to the white ethnic community to try to improve their relationship. Nonetheless, racial tensions in Williamsburg-Greenpoint boiled over in 1961 when an Italian American youth was stabbed by an African American youth in a fight in a laundromat. "All the vengeance from the years of people not wanting that project, and having it imposed on them—it all came out then. They threatened to blow up the projects, to get rid of us all," Tudy remembered.[52]

Following the incident, Tudy and other Cooper Park residents participated in meetings with white ethnics run by the Commission on Human Rights. She noted that the tenants' association's success in achieving its goals helped persuade white ethnics to work with them: "Slowly, some of the organizations started working together; we learned more about them, and they found out that we had expertise that they could use."[53] The tenants' association organized one of its first multiracial efforts, pressuring the city to install a traffic light at a dangerous intersection where several children had been hit by cars. Tudy remembered their collective act of civil disobedience as an important turning point: "We organized a picket line with the [baby] carriages, and this was a very wholesome thing, because not only were the black and Puerto Rican mothers from Cooper Park Houses out there, the Italians and Poles on the other side of the streets came out, too. And we blocked that traffic. The police came and yelled and screamed about arresting us, but there were too many to arrest. We got our traffic light."[54] Racial tensions in Williamsburg-Greenpoint remained high, but the Cooper Park leaders had forged personal relationships with white ethnic women that would endure and lead to further collective action.

In the early to mid-1970s, as New York's economy plunged into crisis, the city government made a series of decisions that mobilized community activism in Williamsburg-Greenpoint against the government, rather than against racialized others. In the late sixties and early seventies, a worldwide recession triggered a malign and unusual combination of rising unemployment and inflation. In addition, declining tax revenues as businesses and middle-class families moved out of New York City and severe cutbacks in aid from Washington and Albany shrank city coffers. The need for social services skyrocketed when the city could least afford to provide them, drawing it deeply into debt. Mayors John Lindsay and Abraham Beame, along with governors Nelson Rockefeller and Malcolm Wilson, coped with the recession and the intolerable rise in the cost of social services by turning to short-term debt to finance ongoing expenses. When in 1975 the banks refused to continue to issue short-term city notes, New York faced bankruptcy.[55]

In Williamsburg-Greenpoint, the first pangs of the fiscal crisis were felt in 1972, when the Lindsay administration rezoned the neighborhood for manufacturing, hoping to attract badly needed jobs. The rezoning led to the 1973 decision to condemn and demolish the homes of at least eighty-five families in the Northside in order to make way for the expansion of the S&S Corrugated Paper Machinery Company.[56] Seventy-five-year-old John Rzasa and his wife owned one of the homes the city condemned. They had emigrated from Poland in 1923 and saved money from their jobs at a rope factory and cleaning office buildings for twenty years in order to purchase the house. For the Rzasas and other Northside residents, the destruction of these houses symbolized a violation of property rights and a betrayal of the American dream.[57]

Led by Peterson, Northsiders including the Rzasas banded together to campaign against the demolition. They posted signs accusing the city of being "un-American" and held a dramatic sit-in in front of the wrecking ball. (See figure 9.) Residents did not succeed in getting the city to reverse

Figure 9. "Is This America?" House in Northside covered with banners from the S&S box factory fight, Greenpoint, Brooklyn, ca. 1973–74, photograph by Janie Eisenberg. Courtesy of Janie Eisenberg.

its decision, but they did persuade officials to build fourteen three-story homes nearby to house up to forty-one of the displaced families. Although they were subsidized, the new homes had to be purchased, making it impossible for many of the displaced families, who had been renters, to move in. Three years after the demolition, the factory had still not completed its planned expansion, making the destruction seem needless.

Building on the mobilization of Northside residents as well as on her work with the Conselyea Street women, Peterson applied for federal funds to establish a day care and senior citizen center for Williamsburg-Greenpoint. The use of federal antipoverty funds to contest local social service cuts is emblematic of the contradictory poverty policies enacted at the federal, state, and city levels during the 1970s.[58] In time, the center would become an important base of residents' opposition to the city's cuts in social spending.

As the deep recession continued to erode tax revenue, the unsympathetic New York State legislature, the Gerald Ford administration, and financial institutions all increased their calls for municipal budget cuts. In 1975, Gov. Hugh Carey wrested control of the city's budget from the Beame administration and clamped down on spending, resulting in the loss of many basic social services. In 1975–76, the city fired thousands of municipal employees, raised transit fares, cut welfare benefits, closed library branches and health facilities, and imposed tuition at city colleges for the first time in 129 years. The head of city housing and development, Roger Star, announced a policy of "planned shrinkage"—the withdrawal of police and fire stations and the closure of schools, hospitals, and subway stations—in poor and nonwhite areas of the city, which he suggested should "lie fallow until a change in economic and demographic assumptions makes the land useful again."[59]

Williamsburg-Greenpoint became one of the targets of the planned shrinkage strategy. By the mid-1970s Williamsburg, although by no means the worst neighborhood in the city, was described as a "war zone" littered with empty plots, potholed streets, and an active illegal drug trade. Between 1970 and 1980, it lost over 20 percent of its population and an estimated 50 percent of employment potential.[60] In the fall of 1975, Williamsburg-Greenpoint residents faced plans to eliminate schools, libraries, police stations, fire stations, bus lines, and hospitals. Angry about the planned cuts, as well as about noise and pollution from the expressway and leaking sewers at the derelict Brooklyn Navy Yard, residents conducted a series of dramatic protests.[61] Northside residents mobilized a long-term campaign to save their local firehouse, No. 212, which the city planned to close in November 1975 when it reduced its firefighting force by 900.[62] This threat made residents especially fearful for the safety of their homes and families because most housing in the area was old and wood-framed, with buildings connected by common garrets, making them burn quickly.[63] The recent spectacle of large swaths of the South Bronx, as well as neighboring Bedford-Stuyvesant, succumbing to arson made Northside residents anxious that absentee landlords might follow suit in their neighborhood and set fire to their unprofitable properties in order to claim insurance payments.[64]

With the aid of the local firefighters, residents organized an eighteen-month-long civil disobedience campaign designed to keep the firehouse open. On Thanksgiving Day 1975, when fire commissioner John T. O'Hagan sent a crew of twenty-four to remove Engine 212, more than 200 residents occupied the station, holding the engine and the firemen hostage. The next

Figure 10. Residents occupy firehouse and protest city plans to close it.
"Planned Shrinkage Stops at Northside," People's Firehouse, 1975, photograph by
Janie Eisenberg. Courtesy of Janie Eisenberg.

day, after negotiations with O'Hagan, the residents set the firemen free but continued to occupy the firehouse, which they renamed People's Firehouse No. 1. Polish American Northside grocer Adam Veneski moved into the firehouse with his wife and four children and organized volunteers to continue the occupation around the clock. For the next year and a half, residents decorated the firehouse, took turns sleeping in it, and held communal meals and dances there, turning it into a community center.[65] (See figures 10 and 11.) Every Wednesday night, a local Action Committee met at the firehouse to discuss the impact closing No. 212 would have on the response times of the fire department and strategized about how to get the city to respond. The committee documented the deaths of eight Northside residents in fires following the removal of Engine 212 and began a series of dramatic demonstrations across the city, dumping ashes from the burned-down houses at politicians' doorsteps, burning political figures in effigy, and blocking traffic on the Brooklyn-Queens Expressway during rush hour.[66]

The People's Firehouse gained media attention and citywide support when activists used it as a venue for hearings to bolster the passage of state legislation blocking further layoffs in the New York City police and

Figure 11. Mural inside
People's Firehouse,
1975, photograph by
Janie Eisenberg.
Courtesy of Janie
Eisenberg.

fire departments. Linking the struggle of the Northside residents to that of poor and minority groups, Harlem-based attorney and civil rights leader Basil Paterson negotiated with the city on behalf of the residents. The membership of the People's Firehouse, reflecting the demographics of the Northside, was largely Polish with a scattering of other white ethnics. Nonetheless, they solicited and received the support of African American and Puerto Rican leaders and residents in Williamsburg-Greenpoint, including the Cooper Park Tenants' Union.[67] Finally, in March 1977, O'Hagan agreed to keep the firehouse open and resume services, albeit with a reduced staff, and the residents moved out of the firehouse.[68] Members of the People's Firehouse decided to maintain their group as a local housing-development organization, and for the next three decades they mobilized whenever the city government announced plans to close Firehouse 212.[69]

Williamsburg-Greenpoint women played key roles in both the struggle over the S&S factory expansion and the People's Firehouse, even donning firemen's uniforms to march through the neighborhood. As Seifer put it, "The women on the Northside . . . got involved because their neighborhood was ready to be bulldozed. That was a survival issue for them."[70] The Conselyea Street women's simultaneous efforts to establish a senior citizen and day care center proved much more controversial, however, in part because their activism violated Italian American gender norms, which restricted women to taking care of family members within the home. Angie Giglios recalled that before joining Peterson's group, she "was a home person. I never went anywhere, like I never went to any places to speak in crowds or anything like that." While women exercised considerable power in this domestic role, they were also presumed to be subordinate to their husbands and brothers on issues outside of the home and were not supposed to engage in public speaking or other leadership activities.[71] Tarantino explained that "at that time, you are the woman; you're in the house; you stay in the background; you're not to talk. . . . You just bring up the children."[72]

Not only did the Conselyea Street women challenge traditional gender relations, they also violated norms of racial segregation. Opponents charged that the establishment of social services would bring "blacks here, and Hispanics," and race-baited Peterson and her supporters. Attempting to assert their control over their families and the space of their neighborhood, some white ethnic men responded to the proposed construction violently. Tarantino recalled the threats: "'You're going to bust the block and blacks will ruin the neighborhood.' I mean, they wanted to kill Jan Peterson in Our Lady of Mt. Carmel."[73] The controversy escalated to the point that the women were receiving phone calls warning them that if they didn't give up their project, their children would be killed.[74]

Despite their fear of reprisals and intense pressure from their families to stop their involvement, the women of Conselyea Street grew more determined. Anne Giordanno discussed her trajectory as an activist, recalling the anger and sense of injustice that motivated her to confront male officials:

What happened was, I started to go to meetings and I would listen to what was going on. But I would never speak. Then one day I got so mad, it was an issue that really affected me. I got up and started to speak, and they wouldn't recognize me. They refused to recognize my hand. I just insisted. I kept shouting over their voices. One guy yelled at me to go home and do my dirty dishes. I yelled back, "If you're so worried about my dirty dishes, why don't you do them?"[75]

The Conselyea Street women relied on their close network of female kin and friends for support and on Peterson for her intrepid and tireless leadership. Tarantino emphasized the importance of those personal relationships in sustaining her activism: "At that time I didn't have the confidence, so I did need Elizabeth [Speranza], I did need my mother [Molly Tarantino], my sister [Millie Tarantino]; I did need Marian Barielli and Angie [Giglios]. We had to work together, and if we had to go somewhere it had to be as a group."[76] The African American women leaders of Cooper Park, who tended to have more education than the Italian American women and had a strong tradition of women's leadership, also provided an inspirational model.[77]

In 1974, after years of fighting, the Swinging Sixties Senior Center and Small World Day Care opened in a multistory brick building in Williamsburg, where they continue to operate today.[78] Shortly afterward, Tarantino became the facilities' executive director.[79] The Conselyea Street women were thrilled with their success and eager to build on it. The sexism and racism of Williamsburg-Greenpoint's male leaders, as well as the national spread of feminism, made them receptive to the specifically gendered critique of power that Peterson helped them to develop. Soon Peterson drew them into a new and larger women's organization, using her ties to the white ethnic, neighborhood, and feminist movements.

"All of that is what feminism is to me": Joining the Women's Movement

With the help of Nancy Seifer and Barbara Mikulski, Peterson convinced Baroni's National Center for Urban Ethnic Affairs to fund a meeting of women activists in Washington, D.C. in 1974. According to Peterson, that first meeting of thirty people attracted mainly "women organizers, nuns . . . the usual people that leave out the working class. You know, the activists without the grassroots, the usual Left group." The following year, Peterson, Seifer, and Mikulski organized a larger conference of 150 women, also held in Washington, D.C. and funded by the National Center for Urban Ethnic Affairs. To this second meeting, Peterson brought fifty Italian American women from Brooklyn, veteran community activists she had met during the struggles over the S&S factory, the People's Firehouse, and the founding of the day care and senior centers. Although these women were already leaders in their communities, most had not yet identified with feminism as a movement. Peterson later remarked that, at the time, the women "thought they were probably going on a bus trip to Washington," similar to the summer outings they had organized for the enrichment and entertainment of the neighborhood's youth.[80] The other hundred women came from all over the country, including Tennessee, Texas, and Maryland.[81]

The group included women who had never traveled away from family before. In an emotional consciousness-raising session that was recorded on film, attendees testified to their struggles to provide for their families and to maintain their urban and rural communities in the face of economic recession, inflation, and mass migration to the suburbs and the booming Sunbelt. Participants linked their frustration with federal and local governments' contradictory poverty policies to their status as low-income women, often excluded from making policy decisions or even from obtaining a basic education.[82] Picking up on the wildfire spread of second-wave feminism, these working-class activists claimed the women's movement as their own, inflected by their specific class concerns.

Olga De Leon, a woman from Texas, described her background: a child of migrant workers, she was a single mother who joined the welfare rights movement and a feminist Chicana activist. Highlighting the theme of a unifying gender and class identity, De Leon noted, "I'm glad to be here, because I see a lot of people, women who have struggled like I have." Christine Noschese rejoiced in being able to shed class shame and talk openly about her family's working-class Italian background, noting that one of the best parts of the conference was "just dealing with who we are, and stopping hav[ing] to deny where we came from and what that means to us. I feel really good that we don't have to deny any of that anymore." Congresswoman Bella Abzug (D-New York) captured the spirit of the conference when she noted her own working-class background and eloquently proclaimed:

What I think most people don't understand . . . is that a women's movement is a movement of all women. And fundamental to the movement of women is the participation of all of us, as we come out of our neighborhoods, as we come out of our backgrounds, to come together, to exchange our ideas and to discuss our problems. . . . It's not some upper-middle class intellectual thing that people try to make it. It's our problems, it's ours, it's us. It's our today, and more than today, it's our tomorrow. . . . I believe that the women's movement is real, because this is real.[83]

Inspired by the strength they realized in sharing their creative responses to the challenges they faced, participants founded their own organization, naming it the National Congress of Neighborhood Women (NCNW), with headquarters in Williamsburg, Brooklyn. They defined "neighborhood women" as "welfare poor, working poor, and working-class women who live side by side." According to Peterson, "The fact that people choose the word 'neighborhood' as their most important word is very telling. . . . People didn't want to be called poor women; 'grassroots' was not in then, either. And 'neighborhood' fit. People felt comfortable with 'neighborhood.' "[84] The choice of neighborhood as a primary identity for the group reflected the influence of their sponsor, but it also recognized the way in which their organization built on preexisting relationships between relatives and neighbors even as it sought to broaden and transform women's networks across lines of race and class. In the future, their activism came to embrace issue-oriented social justice causes as well as those tied to specific locales.

Following the successful conference, Peterson worked hard to secure funding for the group by utilizing her War on Poverty ties. In 1975, she succeeded in obtaining federal grants to employ twenty-five Williamsburg women on the first NCNW staff, as well as in local community organizations.[85] The Brooklyn office Peterson established served not only as the headquarters of the national organization but also as the site of demonstration projects that other chapters could adopt. NCNW members continued to fight against redlining and for better social services in Brooklyn. Under Peterson's leadership, however, the group's activism broadened to encompass concerns more commonly marked as women's issues.[86] As Tarantino put it, Peterson was "the driving force," but together, with their mothers, daughters, sisters, friends, and neighbors, the group became "a coalition."[87]

Emphasizing women's education as the basis for their empowerment and the betterment of the community, the NCNW in its first year offered courses in driver's education (none of its local members had driver's licenses) and women's health. Then the NCNW created an innovative neighborhood-based college program to answer members' need for formal credentials to compete in the job market and their desire to become more effective agents of social change. Many NCNW members had not completed high school, and few had even dreamed of going to college. The program began by enhancing women's self-confidence through recognition of the skills they already had. As NCNW counselors noted: "Most of the women had little formal education, because of the traditional roles they were cast into by society. The feeling that education was basically for the man, because of his responsibility to maintain the family financially, was a general feeling among the women. The women felt they were not 'college material' because they had images of themselves as unskilled, unintelligent people. Meanwhile, most of these women were community activists, with skills ranging from local fund-raising to organizing block associations."[88]

Beginning in September 1975, the NCNW offered tuition-free courses in Williamsburg with a curriculum designed to meet the needs of the organization's largely middle-aged, homemaking membership in a two-year program. With funding from Pfizer (an important local employer), the New York Community Trust, and the Rockefeller Family Fund, and with the cooperation of Augusta Katner of LaGuardia Community College, the NCNW enrolled sixty women in an associate's degree program that students themselves planned in collaboration with NCNW staff. NCNW leaders recruited members of the Cooper Park Tenants' Association to the program, many of whom welcomed the opportunity to receive college credit.[89] As Noschese, the first director of the program, observed, group education became one of the NCNW's most effective tools for alliance building between women of different races and classes.

Drawing on the white ethnic movement's assertions that working-class whites had been neglected by government agencies and major cultural institutions, the NCNW worked to alleviate students' discomfort with bureaucratic settings and to engage them with course materials relevant to their daily lives. The college program gave priority to acknowledging and exploring differences of race, ethnicity, and class among students and teachers in order to improve communication and build trust. NCNW administrators stated that in designing the program, "special consideration is given to student inexperience in sustained multi-ethnic environments, to the importance to students of the geographic proximity of the classroom, and to the impact of students of being able to identify with other adult students and with the program staff." Much more participatory than a traditional college, the program encouraged students to take part in "decision making," including curriculum design and instructor hiring, and "to work in the college program office."[90] The NCNW employed peer counselors to ease communication between students and faculty and encouraged teachers to spend time in the neighborhood, familiarizing themselves with its traditions and outlook.[91]

Like Ella Baker, Peterson and Noschese believed that "students must learn how power is allocated on the community level in order to be effective citizens. We asked the faculty to prepare materials and procedures by which the students could analyze the social structures which most immediately affected their lives."[92] To improve "the status of the women in their families and community" and train them "to become more effective leaders and agents of political change," the program offered awareness-raising courses with titles such as "Getting Sick in New York," "Know Your Body," "Sociology of the Family," "The Urban Experience," and "Women in Society," which were unusual at most colleges at that time. The program also featured internships in local social work and activist organizations, as well as counseling support.[93] By fall 1977, the NCNW enlarged its program, the first of its kind in the country, to include 119 women and 29 men in its entering class.[94] By 1980, the college program had expanded to six locations: three in the Brooklyn neighborhoods of Bushwick, Carroll Gardens, and Williamsburg-Greenpoint, and, through NCNW affiliates, others in Pittsburgh, Philadelphia, and Rochester, New York.[95]

Students published their own newsletter, in which they included family histories, poems, essays, drawings, and other course assignments. The newsletter, along with end-of-the-semester college fairs and conferences, allowed students to celebrate the positive aspects of their working-class ethnic identities. As Irish American NCNW administrator Alice Quinn remarked, the NCNW college students needed to be allowed to affirm aspects of their ethnic backgrounds in order to stay linked to their support networks: "To function in their neighborhood, they have to maintain their ethnicity and close family ties. Having to choose between the values of the college and of the neighborhood produced enormous psychological pressure and impedes the women's effectiveness both in the college program and in their neighborhoods."[96] Participants formed student support groups, which combined consciousness-raising with formal and informal peer counseling to help participants cope with the fears and challenges they faced as poor and working-class women entering higher education for the first time.[97] The support groups were particularly important for the NCNW's Italian American women, who traditionally remained in the home unless escorted by family members. The women in the support groups stood in for family members and allowed Italian American NCNW members to feel comfortable participating.[98]

In a poor and working-class community where survival depended upon family and kin networks, the threat of social ostracism and the withdrawal of male support worked against collaboration across racial boundaries.[99] Therefore, it was especially important for NCNW members to interrogate the power relations embedded within their ethnic communities, in terms of both racist oppression and male domination. In attempting to confront racial justice by embracing ethnic diversity and emphasizing that everyone is a member of an ethnic group, the NCNW college program shared the approach of the ILGWU's educational programs of the 1930s. As Daniel Katz argues, Fannia Cohn and other Yiddish socialists in the ILGWU implemented mutual culturalism, an approach to ethnic and racial difference that recognizes ethnicity as constituent of class and that considers ethnic differences in the context of power relations within and between groups.[100]

In the NCNW college program, discussions of immigration history and the sociology of poor and working-class families not only helped students break down the categories of "white," "black," and "Spanish" but also to understand a variety of ethnic backgrounds and experiences of oppression.[101] Noschese explained that in the "Labor and Immigration" course, "women saw there was a difference of what it means to come to New York City as a black person, or to come as an Italian or Irish working-class person. The college program helped them to explore these similarities from a different perspective. . . . It provides a forum to get together to see what their problems are without white-washing their differences."[102] Breaking down these racial categories was essential in undoing the racial consolidation of the post-World War II years, which encouraged Americans to perceive racial difference in polarized and antagonistic black-and-white terms.[103] Group projects required "cooperation and collective effort" and encouraged bridge-building among women from different backgrounds.[104]

Students' research into their own family histories sometimes provided inspiring models of activism. Italian American student Elaine Carpenelli discovered that before settling in Williamsburg, her grandmother, Theresa, had taken part in the great 1912 textile mill strike in Lawrence, Massachusetts, known as the "Bread and Roses" strike, which was led by Italian women.[105] For white ethnic women, recovering family members' histories of participation in radical politics as well as their struggles as immigrants—stories that the Italian American community had suppressed during the Palmer and McCarthy eras of anticommunism and government persecution of labor leaders and leftists—led to a rethinking of their own politics and racial identities.[106] African American NCNW member and Cooper Park housing leader Mildred Johnson explained that the college program "helped us to understand that the struggle of white immigrants wasn't so different from ours; and white women, who'd known that their families had been poor, but not *how* poor, felt close to us."[107]

Cooper Park Tenants' Association leader and NCNW graduate Diane Jackson (See figure 4.) remembered the college program as the most important site of interracial dialogue:

> We had to get over a lot of obstacles. . . . There was some racial tension. In working with these other women from outside the community [the instructors], we were able to identify what those racial issues were and talk about it. I remember when the film *Roots* came out and it was part of our assignment to watch it for class. Just to hear some of the responses from other people opened up the door to start talking about race and racism and misunderstandings. We began to find out more about each other, found out that we had a lot in common. . . . Some of the women that I met in the college program, we helped each other, we worked things out.[108]

The program's feminist analysis of social institutions, especially of the family, led members to recognize shared needs, including the right to be safe from domestic violence. Many of the women in the college program were victims of abuse; indeed, for some, participation in the NCNW increased their vulnerability, as husbands and boyfriends came to resent their growing independence. Jewish sociologist Terry Haywoode, who at one time taught in and directed the NCNW college program, recalled white women and women of color coming together to protect each other from abusive husbands and boyfriends: "One woman whose husband didn't want her to go to class would be escorted by four very large women."[109] In another case, when an angry husband came to the NCNW office and began attacking his wife, the other women in the office fought him off and invited her to move in with them until she could find her own housing.[110]

Offering physical protection promoted trust among members and led to collaboration around feminist issues. In 1976, for example, the program sponsored a "speak-out on wife battering," with more than 100 people in attendance as women testified to the need for safe places they could go with their children to escape domestic violence. The speak-out led to the founding of a nonprofit organization, the Center for the Elimination of Violence in the Family, and the establishment of the first publicly funded battered women's shelter in New York State, the Women's Survival Space, a joint effort between the NCNW and YWCA.[111] Jackson was among the NCNW members who helped to found, and then to staff, the shelter. She recalled the special satisfaction she felt in being able to help other women in a similar position and to collaborate across lines of difference:

I didn't feel good about being a battered woman, but I felt good about doing something about my situation. I felt that it was my mission to let other women know that there was help available. My ideal individual goal has been accomplished with the establishment of a battered women's shelter. . . . All of that is what feminism is to me. It's sharing, working with each other for the betterment of all women, on issues that cut across ethnic and racial lines. It doesn't matter whether you're black, white, whatever. I feel very good about that.[112]

With the founding of the Women's Survival Space and Project Open Doors, the federally funded jobs program that staffed nonprofits across the city, the NCNW took on a leadership role within New York's growing feminist movement. At the same time, however, NCNW members also issued class-based critiques of what the media portrayed as "mainstream" and NCNW members saw as middle-class feminism. Continuing to work together across differences of race and class posed ongoing challenges and led the NCNW to develop a leadership-support process to facilitate better communication between allies.

Historians' focus on incidents of white ethnic backlash has resulted in a generally negative assessment of the white ethnic movement of the 1970s and contributed to scholars' skepticism in the potential of progressive change resulting from identity-based politics. In New York City, the divisive conflict between Black Power and Jewish leaders in the 1968 Ocean Hill-Brownsville teachers' strike has come to overshadow other fruitful examples of identity-based organizing. Peterson's successful use of identity-based consciousness-raising for the purpose of multiracial community organizing in Williamsburg reveals a different and equally important aspect of the white ethnic and neighborhood movements, one that Dennis Deslippe terms "ethniclass progressivism." By celebrating the positive aspects of their ethnic and racial identities, exploring their similarities and common needs as well as their differences, and interrogating the ways in which members of some racial/ethnic groups benefited from the oppression of others, Peterson and the women of Cooper Park and Conselyea Street learned to make "antiracist uses of ethnicity" and to use identity-based organizing to form political coalitions.[113] Like for the Mexican American and African American antipoverty activists chronicled by Gordon Mantler in his account of the Poor People's Movement and related organizing efforts, for the women of Williamsburg-Greenpoint, identity politics versus coalitional politics were not antagonistic alternatives but, rather, complementary.[114]

CHAPTER FOUR

It Was Talking about My Life

Developing Working-Class Feminism

In the first half of the 1970s, Peterson and the NCNW participated in and drew from the white ethnic and neighborhood movements; in the second half of the decade, they truly developed their own working-class feminist organization, with affiliates in a dozen cities across the United States, ranging from Bayamon, Puerto Rico to San Francisco.[1] By 1976, between 300 and 400 women regularly participated in local NCNW programs.[2] The NCNW's lightning-quick growth both mirrored the expansion of the feminist movement locally and nationally, and helped drive it. Project Open Doors, the NCNW's federally funded jobs program, placed hundreds of women in feminist nonprofits across New York City, providing a snapshot of the feminist movement and capturing its variety and vibrancy.

Examining the origins and growth of a working-class feminist organization deepens our understanding of feminism as a diverse and powerful social movement. Early histories of the women's movement in the 1960s and 1970s focused on radical women's liberation groups, whose membership was largely white and college-educated. While scholarship on the National Organization for Women (NOW) has shown that its membership in fact varied greatly at the local level in both class and racial/ethnic composition as well as ideological outlook, the organization was nonetheless often associated with the white, middle-class female subjects of NOW founder Betty Friedan's extremely influential *The Feminine Mystique*.[3]

Increasingly, scholars have documented the feminist activism of women of color, focusing particularly on their history of organizing in separate groups, apart from white women, in order to focus on their needs and the needs of their community. These scholars have also shown the role racism and ethnocentrism in the white women's movement had in limiting coalitions between white feminist groups and organizations dedicated specifically to women of color.[4] This chapter joins several recent studies that highlight the achievements of, as well as the tensions and conflicts within, multiracial and cross-class feminist organizing.[5] Taken together, they help round out our understanding of feminism, arguably the largest and most far-reaching social movement in twentieth-century America, and suggest that future coalitions across class and racial difference are not only possible but likely.

NCNW members sought to acknowledge classism and racism within their organization and work it out. Their history suggests that feminism did appeal to working-class women in the 1970s and 1980s, and that women of color and white ethnic women found working together to be pragmatic in terms of both achieving their goals and being personally enriching. Yet, even as Project Open Doors helped staff the offices of the New York Chapter of NOW, and NCNW members participated in major feminist events including the 1977 National Women's Conference in Houston, Texas, they offered a critique of what they perceived as the middle-class bias of mainstream feminist organizations. (See figure 4.) NOW and middle-class feminists, NCNW members charged, overvalued paid work for women and undervalued women's caregiving and the desirability of maintaining stable marriages.

These class-based differences in attitudes toward family, unpaid domestic work, and paid work outside the home must be understood in the context of deindustrialization and economic restructuring, which greatly eroded working-class men's wages and drew more married women with children into the workforce. This shift also contributed to a spike in divorce rates, developments that increasingly left single mothers raising their children in poverty. College-educated feminists often emphasized the benefits of fulfilling work and economic independence that came from working outside the home, but financial necessity and lack of other options meant many working-class women took on low-paying jobs in the service sector that they did not perceive as personally meaningful.[6] The goal of the NCNW college program was to help working-class women obtain the education and skills they needed to access better jobs, both to support their families and for their own empowerment. As the fiscal crisis of the 1970s deepened and many of their husbands lost jobs, NCNW members struggled to reconcile their belief in women's equality and their own growing sense of independence with their desire to maintain family and ethnic traditions in a time of rapidly changing economic circumstances.

The NCNW also experienced growing pains as it drew in new membership from outside of Williamsburg-Greenpoint and wrestled with the difficulties of working together across differences, including those of race, ethnicity, class, sexuality, and religion. African American, East Harlem–based public housing activist Ethel Velez recalled her early experiences with the group as frustrating, stating "I hated it. I did not like it at all. . . . I used to think a lot of the women in the group were real racist. . . . There wasn't a lot of integrating going on."[7] In order to facilitate better communication and relationship building, the NCNW developed its Leadership Support Process (LSP), a more structured form of consciousness-raising that included participation in both "allies' panels"—comprising women of different racial/ethnic and class backgrounds—and "social identity groups"—with women of similar backgrounds. Middle-class professional women made key contributions to the NCNW, including developing the LSP process; nonetheless, their education and class privilege could leave grassroots members feeling silenced or overlooked. Realizing they needed an additional structure for addressing identity-based power differences between members, the NCNW created its Principled Partnership model for how professionals can work with grassroots organizations without taking over control of decision making. Through their own annual Institute on Women and Community Development, the NCNW shared its LSP and Principled Partnership models with other grassroots women's organizations, including rural activists in Appalachia and public housing activists in St. Louis.

In the late 1970s and early 1980s the NCNW encountered external challenges as first the Carter administration cut and then the Reagan administration eliminated CETA funds, the source Project Open Doors depended on. As federal government spending on social welfare programs dramatically decreased, private funders adopted more stringent regulations.[8] These new funding realities shaped the scope, ambition, and direction of NCNW programs in New York, forcing the programs to become less grassroots-driven and less transformative in nature. Yet while American-based feminist organizations struggled in the more conservative political environment of the Reagan era, the global feminist movement took root at the United Nations and blossomed.[9] In response, Peterson steered the NCNW toward international partnerships, achieving consultative status at the United Nations and founding Grassroots Organizations Operating Together in Sisterhood (GROOTS International) at the 1985 Third World Women's Conference in Nairobi, Kenya. The new group aimed to create a global network of women's groups focused on achieving economic justice through women's empowerment in their home communities.

That same year, the NCNW began a five-year restructuring process. A new arm, Neighborhood Women of Williamsburg-Greenpoint, was established as an independent nonprofit administering the organization's remaining locally based programs, including the You Can Community School, a high school for teenage mothers and dropouts. The NCNW continued to exist as a national network of affiliates, but Peterson increasingly focused on international partnerships, the most vibrant area of growth for the organization from the late 1980s on. In 1995, at the World Women's Conference in Beijing the coalition of women's groups from across the globe that GROOTS had brought together in a "Grassroots Tent" received formal recognition from Wally N'Dow, head of the UN Commission on Human Settlements. N'Dow charged the groups with monitoring international development from their perspective as grassroots women. Named the Huairou Commission after the site of their Women's Conference tent in a suburb of Beijing, the coalition is chaired by Peterson and continues to represent grassroots women's organizations at the United Nations.[10]

These international collaborations brought fresh ideas, new perspectives, and opportunities to shape global policymaking. At the same time, however, the NCNW's reduced programs in New York—the college program, for example, closed in 1994—diminished its membership, leaving it less able to reach out to younger generations of women and harming its ability to counteract the threats gentrification posed to its achievements in Williamsburg-Greenpoint.

"That wonderful money": Project Open Doors and the Women's Movement in New York

The NCNW's jobs program, like its college program, played a key role in drawing women to the group. In 1975, the NCNW formed Project Open Doors, a coalition that comprised thirty-three other feminist groups in New York City. The coalition included diverse organizations such as NOW New York, the New York Feminist Credit Union, Feminist Health Works, The National Gay Task Force, the Downtown Welfare Advocacy Center, Women Make Movies, The Council of Asian American Women,

and the Women's Action Alliance, an information clearinghouse and resource center for the women's movement that was founded by Gloria
Steinem. Project Open Doors succeeded in gaining $2.6 million in fed-
eral funds to employ 200 poor and working-class women in public service jobs under the Comprehensive Training and Employment Act
(CETA)—"that wonderful money that allowed people to work in not-for-
profits," as Peterson described it.[11] CETA was signed into law by President
Nixon in 1973; it replaced Johnson's antipoverty job training program,
the 1962 Manpower Development and Training Act, with block federal
grants to state and municipal governments and the stated goal of creating new jobs for the unemployed. As inflation and unemployment skyrocketed in 1974, President Ford increased spending on CETA. President
Carter continued to expand the program in the late 1970s, touting subsidized employment as a form of welfare reform. At its peak in 1978, $6 bil-
lion in CETA funding was used to provide 765,000 jobs nationally, the
majority of which were in cities such as New York, Detroit, and Hartford,
Connecticut, which had played a crucial role in Carter's 1976 election
victory. New York City alone received more than $1 billion in CETA funds
in 1978 to employ 24,946 people.[12]

Project Open Doors funded programs that encompassed the great creativity and breadth of the women's movement in New York and reflected
the passions of the national movement, including securing economic independence and security for women; generating knowledge about wom-
en's lives both in the past and present from their own perspectives;
combating violence against women; enhancing women's reproductive
autonomy; and valuing women's sexuality. The innovative programs
funded by Project Open Doors included Building for Women, in which low-
income women from East Harlem, some of whom were ex-offenders, received training in construction and carpentry skills through sweat-equity
renovation of buildings in which they later received apartments; the Brooklyn Women's Martial Arts Center, which trained CETA employees to conduct free self-defense classes for girls and women; projects that produced
films on battered women and women and aging; counseling services for
victims of rape and domestic abuse; projects that championed the work
of "rediscovered" early American women poets; the development of educational materials on gay men and lesbians; and the operation of a birth
control clinic.[13]

In Williamsburg-Greenpoint, Project Open Doors provided funds to
staff the NCNW office, the Swinging Sixties Senior Center, Small World Day

Care, and the Center for the Elimination of Violence in the Family, with jobs going to neighborhood residents. It also provided a welcome opportunity for NCNW members to acquire training and skills in administration. Since the NCNW oversaw the entire coalition, Peterson explained, its members "literally had to go out and show the women's movement how to set up a board and how to run personnel practices."[14] Many NCNW members experienced personal and professional growth from their participation in the project, as women who had been full-time homemakers or employed as domestic or factory workers trained in accounting and management and ran leadership workshops attended by hundreds of women from all over New York. African American NCNW member and domestic workers' rights activist Geraldine Miller, who previously worked as a housecleaner, recalled her achievements as an administrator for Project Open Doors, exclaiming that "it was exciting, it was interesting. And it was good, because it was the first time that I had ever made over $10,000 a year in my life . . . And we were running it, you know, *the women* were running it. And I think that above all was fantastic. . . . I'm so proud of what we were able to do."[15]

In addition to providing educational opportunities and material benefits to NCNW members, Project Open Doors led Williamsburg/Greenpoint women to greater engagement with the broader women's movement; they interacted with feminist groups from across the city and reflected on their own position within the movement. Some had taken women's studies courses through the NCNW college program, while for others, Project Open Doors was their first exposure to feminism. When Williamsburg homemaker Jean Kowalsky's Russian American husband lost his job in 1977, she got a position through Project Open Doors. At first, Kowalsky said, "I'd no idea it was anything to do with the women's movement, either. The only thing I ever heard about that was bra-burning, and that was a big joke. The women's movement never meant a thing to me. It was the PTA, the church, that's all." After working at the Northside Senior Citizens' Center, Kowalsky became manager of the NCNW office. In a 1979 interview with *Ms. Magazine,* she commented on how her experience with the NCNW had changed her view of feminism, emphasizing her growing sense of self-worth and her belief in equal opportunity for women in the workforce: "I feel more worthwhile. I feel good about myself. And I think the women's movement is wonderful. Because I have daughters, and I want their life to be easier than mine was. I want them to get paid what they're worth, and to get money when they're promoted. I want them to feel good about themselves."[16]

"I like being a mother and happen to like being a wife": Feminism and Class

Like Kowalsky, many NCNW members expressed initial ambivalence or even hostility to what they termed "middle-class feminism," which they perceived as antifamily and either challenging or irrelevant to their lives. And like Kowalsky, other women also testified to supporting feminist goals after participating in the NCNW's programs. However, the group's relationship with the women's movement is more complex than a simple conversion narrative. Although NCNW members criticized second-wave feminists for neglecting working-class women's needs, they also used feminist social-change strategies and incorporated many of the movement's key tenets into their organizing. According to its *Women in Poverty Training Manual*, the NCNW "embraced most of the feminist issues, in fact, but not the movement itself."[17] At times NCNW members offered cogent critiques of elitism within mainstream second-wave thought; at other times they distanced themselves from middle-class feminism in order to deflect the negative connotations the movement's image elicited from their family, friends, and neighbors, as well as from the media and financial supporters.

Mainstream journalists endlessly attacked "man-hating" and "antifamily" middle-class women's liberation groups, who openly critiqued the domestic division of labor along gender lines and promoted more flexible family arrangements.[18] Unsurprisingly, then, the *New York Times* applauded NCNW member Sally Martino Fisher for cooking her family's dinner "without complaining" before heading to Washington, D.C. to testify before a committee on urban and ethnic affairs. Another *Times* reporter noted that "the women of the Northside sound remarkably free of recriminations about men and the past. They identify more than ever with their neighborhood, and their particular self-discovery seems less selfish than that of other revolutionaries."[19]

While the popular press exaggeratedly (and unfairly) charged women's liberation groups with being anti-male because of their call for men to take on a fair share of household duties, there were in fact important class-based differences in attitudes toward women's unpaid caregiving and domestic work. During the NCNW's "Speak Out On Housework," and in subsequent conversations in college courses, members talked about their positive feelings toward caretaking for their families. NCNW member Marie Casella emphasized how gendered domestic labor and cooking in particular was central to her identity as an Italian American woman:

I don't appreciate some middle-class woman telling me to get out of the kitchen who didn't know if there was a kitchen there, and didn't know if the struggles of her home related to the struggles of my home. . . . I happen to like my kitchen. I like being a mother and happen to like being a wife. I don't think you have to give those things up to be a liberated person. . . . I come from a very proud heritage. I know I'm Italian. It was drummed into me what Italian people are: they keep their home; they keep their husband; they keep everything. It was just a proud thing for me.[20]

For Casella, her ability to care for and keep her family together was tied to her ethnic identity. In her study of Italian and Italian American women, Jennifer Guglielmo found that they often saw food as an important means of maintaining tradition and gathering family and friends, and that despite the labor-intensive nature of cooking, women valued their kitchens as spaces that were restorative and autonomous.[21]

Casella's critique of the career-centered nature of mainstream feminism also reflected class consciousness, especially for women who did not have the privilege of choosing whether to enter the workforce or not, and whose paid employment was often not fulfilling. In another interview, Casella argued that by prioritizing equal opportunity for women in the workforce, the women's movement "puts down . . . immigrant women, the women who have always worked. When these women get a chance to stay home a few years, they are being told they are oppressed."[22] For working-class Italian American men and women of Casella's generation, achieving a male breadwinner wage generous enough to allow a wife to stay home with young children was a central aspiration and indeed part of what it meant to make it as an American. The descendants of immigrants who had relied on women's piece and factory work for family survival did not necessarily immediately identify with the subjects of Betty Friedan's *The Feminine Mystique*: college graduates living in prosperous suburbs who felt their skills and knowledge were being wasted and longed for fulfilling professional careers.[23] On the other hand, as deindustrialization and globalization led to stagnation and decline in working-class men's wages and divorce rates skyrocketed, working-class women increasingly needed paid employment outside the home to maintain their standard of living, and stood to greatly benefit from the protections from discrimination and sexual harassment and the affirmative action policies that NOW and other mainstream feminist groups fought to secure.[24]

The women of the NCNW "wanted their marriages to work" and sought economic justice for their husbands and sons as well as for themselves.[25] As Peterson wrote, they recognized that "their men are also discriminated against in the areas of ethnicity, race and class; they need each other to make it in today's world."[26] Yet, they also struggled "to redefine their own roles in relationship to them."[27] Members articulated their goals using feminist language and in ways that evidenced a rethinking of family life. NCNW members sought to help "women identify, perceive and assume power without feeling that it was a threat to family and feeling o.k. about it"; to make "women more aware of abilities and their rights, that they are not necessarily the weaker sex"; to enable "women who didn't get out of the home to meet other women besides family members"; to raise "consciousness on many levels"; and to create "a new sense of identity."[28] Although Peterson argued that the NCNW represented "a brand new kind of feminism—pro-family, pro-church, and pro-neighborhood," that belief wasn't uniform: notes from a consciousness-raising session include "Christianity is also male dominated" as one of the group's "Obstacles."[29]

The tension between preserving or transforming male-dominated institutions such as the patriarchal family and the Roman Catholic Church played out not only within the group's writings and discussions but also within members' personal lives. As NCNW member Candida Tirado explained in a 1976 interview, "I don't think of myself as a feminist, but I think of myself as equal to my husband. But he doesn't think of me as equal."[30] Remembering her late husband's reactions to her participation in civil disobedience and other forms of activism, Elizabeth Speranza recalled, "The only thing he used to say to me was, 'Babe, if you're going on a demonstration and you get arrested, please do not use your married name.'"[31] Another woman recalled her concerns over participating in the NCNW college program: "I was scared. I think I feared I'd wind up losing my husband and family. . . . My husband was as scared as I was. But we've learned you've got to grow. And you can't drop one another by the wayside."[32] NCNW college program counselors worked to help members reconcile their changing roles, as women gained education and better-paying jobs, often at the same time that their blue-collar husbands were being laid off. They did this in part by emphasizing gains to the whole family from women's increasing self-confidence and earnings.[33]

In 1977, tensions in Williamsburg-Greenpoint mounted when a group of local women opposed to the NCNW and Project Open Doors organized themselves into "Neighborhood Women for Home and Family" and issued a formal statement on the NCNW that read "We want not ties with overt homosexuals, communists, and radicals. We believe the basic unit is the family. We are women devoted to our homes and to our husbands, and in good conscience; we must fight any organization against the concept of the family."[34] Not surprisingly, in their response, the NCNW emphasized its own support of families, noting its members' roles "as daughters, mothers, and wives" who "believe the family is the most important aspect of the community."[35]

In the context of Williamsburg-Greenpoint's violently enforced racial segregation and widespread homophobia, NCNW members frequently experienced race- and lesbian-baiting. One African American member said she risked being stigmatized for her association with the NCNW: "The majority of women do not understand . . . if you talk to them about women being independent, they start thinking gay. . . . My husband said 'You'll never go back to the Congress,' after he saw some gay women there." Others accused her of being a race traitor, she noted: "When I went to the Congress, they'd say she's selling out to the white group."[36] Some NCNW members reported a transformation in their own attitudes toward homosexuality as a result of participating in the group. Giordano explained that "Five years ago I would have been scared to death to be seen with a lesbian. Now I say, 'Is she a good human being? Does she work for the community?' Then she's my friend, and I won't apologize for it."[37] Members were willing to speak up in defense of their values of inclusivity, including working across differences of sexuality and race. However, the NCNW's emphasis on preserving family ties, as well as its use of "we're not feminists, but . . . " rhetoric, also served to deflect racist, sexist, and homophobic attacks.

In addition to affirming its pro-family plank, the NCNW avoided taking an organizational stance on controversial issues, including abortion. NCNW member Lisel Burns believed the organization tolerated a wide range of understandings of feminism among its members in order to advance issues they did agree on: "It's very much of a family model, I think, and agreement was not the aim. We have these wonderful thirteen principles but not like on reproductive rights."[38] While the NCNW did not take official positions on matters like abortion and the Equal Rights Amendment (ERA), there was a lot of spirited discussion among NCNW members about these issues. College program instructor Carol Brightman recalled, "There is not a single issue I know of on which the Congress has ever reached unanimous agreement."[39] For the most part, members tolerated women holding different and sometimes changing positions and did not see these as causing major fault lines within the organization. For example, the NCNW elected women with opposing views on the ERA to represent it at the New York State Women's Meeting in July 1977, where participants selected delegates for the November 1977 National Women's Conference in Houston, Texas, at which the ERA was the central issue.[40] This neutrality on abortion rights and the ERA was particularly unusual for feminist groups, as Americans closely identified feminists with support for both.

NCNW members approached feminism from their social location as working-class women, and for some, as single mothers; they noted that in order to achieve equality as women, their basic needs must first be met. Ultimately, the NCNW declared, their one unifying thread was strengthening the position of working-class women, so that their needs and voices would be taken seriously, in their own communities and in state and national politics:

> We are women of varied ethnic backgrounds and just as varied opinions. We are, however, all united on one basic premise: the rights of working class women should be considered, and the voices of working class women should be heard on *all* issues whether the issues raised relate to their own lives and communities, or are city-wide, state-wide, or national in scope. We do not believe that women's choices should be limited because of their economic status.

Regarding other issues, the NCNW statement declared:

> We are free as individual members of NCNW to choose the issues where we want to put our energies. These include all the important social, political, and economic issues of the day: education, day care, sexual preference, employment, women in unions, battered women, control of our own bodies, displaced homemakers, the legal status of homemakers, the Equal Rights Amendment. Members have devoted time to all these matters and many others—not as a monolithic organization but as individual working class women who want their opinions heard on issues relevant to their own lives.[41]

Despite fundamental differences in worldviews, the coalition bound together socialist feminists and devout Roman Catholic women who opposed abortion. The NCNW's emphasis on the long-term development of each member's own leadership capacity and feminist consciousness meant that members accepted each other as they were, while simultaneously working to advance each other's understandings of inequality and social change. Part of what made the group work was being willing to engage with dissimilarities.

"We were fighting all the time": Developing the Leadership Support Process

While NCNW members succeeded in tolerating differences in beliefs on the ERA and abortion rights, bitter disagreements over the management of their own programs posed a serious problem. Over time, they developed a structured consciousness-raising methodology they termed the Leadership Support Process (LSP), which enabled group members to better communicate with each other and reach consensus. As Peterson put it: "We created it because everyone was fighting all the time."[42] Peterson had introduced consciousness-raising at the NCNW's founding conference and continued to promote its use to build trust between members and to establish support networks for sustaining their activism.[43] Rosalyn Baxandall and Linda Gordon describe consciousness-raising, the primary mode of organization for the women's liberation movement, as "a form of structured discussion in which women connected their personal experiences to larger structures of gender" and "came to understand that many of their 'personal' problems . . . were not individual failings but a result of discrimination." During consciousness-raising sessions, participants sat in a circle, gave each other equal talking time, and ideally, refrained from talking over each other or judging one another.[44] NCNW members formed small consciousness-raising groups that met once a week, some for years, and that led to participants organizing larger forms of communitywide events like "speak outs" on topics including welfare, domestic violence, and housework.

Consciousness-raising, with its emphasis on openness and trust building, can be an effective tool for creating a shared sense of identity and group cohesiveness and ultimately for politicizing participants. Italian American Elaine Carpinelli, who joined Project Open Doors in 1975 when she had two small daughters and was looking for work, noted that her participation in consciousness-raising had provided her with a new vocabulary for naming injustices. She explained, "It made you think about certain things in your past, that you knew something was wrong. . . . You didn't like it, but, that's the way it was, in previous jobs with bosses, men, sexual harassment and all of this. . . . And the names began to get attached to all of these different things, and you found yourself really growing."[45] Giordano described the evolution of the group's membership, stating that "there were . . . different phases of feminist consciousness" and "willing-ness to be out there." For Giordano, who had previously attended NOW NY meetings but never felt comfortable at them, the NCNW's consciousness-raising sessions were especially meaningful "because it was relevant; it was what I needed, because it was talking about my life and where I was at."[46] Mexican American Maria Fava had moved to Williamsburg as a young newlywed to an Italian American man; she joined the NCNW in 1974 after her marriage ended and she was raising four children on her own, and said that taking part in consciousness-raising had shifted her self-understanding from being "just a mother" to being "a leader" and a "feminist" and viewing herself as a capable political actor.[47]

Lisel Burns helped the NCNW develop a more advanced form of consciousness-raising in the late 1970s and early 1980s. Burns grew up in a white middle-class suburban household, attended Smith College, and became involved in social change in 1967 when she participated in the civil rights movement in Mississippi as a student. She then moved to New York City and took part in the community-controlled day care movement, where she met Ethel Velez. Burns studied peer counseling and was working at the College for Human Services when Jan Peterson asked her to facilitate a retreat in 1979.[48] She spent the next several years working on developing the NCNW Leadership Support Process (LSP) methodology, which com-bined therapeutic techniques for strengthening individuals' leadership ca-pacities with analysis of social structures and their influence on individ-uals' identities and experiences. The NCNW used the LSP at its home office in Brooklyn, as well as in its conferences and workshops for its affiliate groups.[49]

The LSP first recruited a diverse group of neighborhood women, who worked to develop "personal supportive relationships between them-selves," using "a dialogue format." The dialogue-opening questions in-cluded, "What is great about being female? What are some great memo-ries you have about growing up female? What has been hard about being female? What couldn't you stand about growing up female? What can't you stand about other women? What do you require of another woman in order for her to be your ally?" Other sessions focused on additional aspects of identity, including race, class, religion, and sexuality. As they listened to each other, members came to recognize commonalities as well as differ-ences. Facilitators encouraged participants to reflect upon the ways in which institutions such as the family, the mass media, and the workforce had influenced their lives and worldviews.[50] Additional structured con-versations encouraged participants "to identify their particular concerns, analyze the impact of their concerns on their lives; and work with others to map out strategies that neighborhood women can act upon within their community."[51] Through this process, facilitators encouraged participants to connect their personal histories with societal institutions and structures of power, and to generate their own theories of identity and power. According to Velez, participating in the LSP was a meaningful experience, motivating and sustaining her activism because "for me, social change organizing needs to come out of personal experience, consciousness, and a vision of what should be."[52]

Because the NCNW membership was more diverse than many radical women's liberation groups, the NCNW discussed race and class as well as gender and sexuality and developed an understanding of the intersection of these categories of identity.[53] Working with other members, Burns developed an innovative structure for addressing these differences in identity. Members participated in consciousness-raising in both "allies' panels" and "social identity groups." These panels allowed participants to speak about their "experiences and perceptions as members of a social identity group, both with other members of that group and to those outside the group." Panels could be based on class, race or ethnicity, residence, age, sexual identity, or religion.[54] Within the social identity group panels, members analyzed their own experiences and connected them to social structures. This process allowed NCNW members to overcome class shame and internalized racism and to build upon the positive aspects of their identities—for example, their resilience and their commitment to furthering social justice and improving conditions for their communities.

In the allies' panels, women from different social identity groups discussed the divergences in experience and perspectives among them and outlined what kind of support they needed from each other to be able to work together. The allies' panels helped NCNW members better understand each other and facilitated the development of what the group termed "principled partnerships" between professional and grassroots women. The NCNW defined a principled partnership as "a functional relationship that goes beyond membership in an issue coalition. In a partnership, a combination of organizations or individuals work together to create a comprehensiveness of function they cannot achieve separately, and they do so in a manner that reinforces shared values and goals." The principled partnerships model aimed to create "horizontal" rather than "vertical" relationships between professionals and grassroots women, allowing for "real dialogue" and recognition of expertise on the part of each member in the partnership. The NCNW argued that in order for a partnership to succeed, imbalances in power among members had to be formerly acknowledged and "dealt with" in an ongoing manner in order to promote open communication, including "using processes that help us understand our differences and how to remove difference as an obstacle to working together."[55] NCNW members used the LSP, including the allies' panels, to work out questions of knowledge, responsibility, authority, and appreciation between grassroots and professional women. Miller credited the LSP for enabling members to work out their disagreements, stating "That's where the support part comes in. You know, you can sit down and discuss . . . It was emotional, but they would *do* something about it. They would talk about it, how you felt, what you thought. And I think it's a really good way of clearing up the air."[56]

"Brooklyn to me was a foreign country": The Challenges of Principled Partnerships

Professional women, some from working-class backgrounds like Peterson, and others from upper middle-class backgrounds like Burns, played a key role in the NCNW from the start. Peterson introduced professional women, many of whom were involved in either the civil rights movement and/or women's liberation movements, to the grassroots members. Columbia Law graduate and cofounder of the National Women's Political Caucus Rona Feit met Peterson through Barbara Mikulski, a mutual friend, and joined the NCNW board in 1975. Feit recalled feeling like an outsider during her first visits to Williamsburg, as well as her excitement over the vitality of the NCNW and the recognition that her education and class status made her a useful addition to the membership:

> Brooklyn to me was a foreign country. I lived in Manhattan, my husband was a Wall Street lawyer, this was not my thing. But [Peterson] pulled me in and I found it fascinating from the word go. So she kept me around, I guess I had certain things to offer. A couple of things I think were useful, one is that I'm pretty good at letting people say what they have to say, which was very important to the process. Two, the very fact that I was a Wall Street lawyer by then and came from a somewhat different class, I think helped the women there to feel respected.[57]

In addition to lending her prestige and contacts to the NCNW, Feit wrote proposals and chaired board meetings and tried "to help steer the thing." Feit developed the NCNW's principled partnerships model and said that for her, the organization reflected the combination of professional and grassroots women. She explained that "my position was always, let's be honest. . . . One doesn't happen without the other." Without the specialized knowledge, skills, formal credentials, and networks of the professional members, the NCNW would have been unable to obtain funding for its college, jobs, or housing programs. Grassroots members were aware of this need for help and professional legitimacy. Velez stated that "what I appreciate about the Congress is that they allowed us the opportunity to gain resources and to broaden our perspective on things we want to do."[58] The personal relationships the NCNW cultivated also helped sustain grassroots activism. Giordano described the support she drew from the NCNW's "network of women" as key to sustaining her "constant struggle" to succeed in breaking "the feeling of powerlessness and acceptance" of inequality that was prevalent among residents in Williamsburg.[59]

The process of sharing so intimately with each other created lifelong bonds of friendship between LSP participants. On the other hand, because consciousness-raising requires members to share personal information and emotions, it carries inherent risks, including the misuse of personal knowledge. The NCNW tried to guard against this by requiring participants to pledge confidentiality for all disclosures made during consciousness-raising sessions. Yet when conflicts over decision making within the organization developed, it could be challenging to leave aside the personal knowledge gained during the sessions.[60]

Not all NCNW members were comfortable with Burns's peer counseling techniques, and some members perceived them as a middle-class imposition. Cocounseling, in broad terms, is a movement that tries to increase the affordability and accessibility of therapy by training participants to counsel each other. Among other forms of peer counseling, Burns studied reevaluation counseling, a cocounseling movement founded by Harvey Jackins in which members took turns sharing memories of traumatic events in order to free themselves from emotional distress.[61] In introducing peer counseling techniques to the LSP, Burns emphasized the public airing of conflicts over leadership within a group, in order to speed resolution. Some members disliked the theatrical aspects of this form of conflict resolution and were especially skeptical of reevaluation counseling's tendencies to mute criticism of a group's leader by attributing disagreements to negative emotional reactions.[62]

At times, the NCNW also struggled to reconcile the democratic process of consciousness-raising with the hierarchical structure of a nonprofit organization that had to comply with shifting federal and private funding mandates. Alice Quinn, who headed Project Open Doors, said, "It's very difficult to take a federally funded program like CETA and deal with it in a collective situation. A terrific amount of monitoring went on and it became confusing and difficult."[63] Grassroots members recognized this conflict and challenged professionals in the NCNW to support placing working-class women in positions of power within the organization and its affiliates. In 1978, for example, a group of NCNW members formed the "Ad Hoc Committee to Support Working-Class Women as Leaders." In particular, the committee wrote to the boards of the NCNW and the Women's Survival Space, the battered women's shelter that the NCNW had cofounded, in support of the candidacy of African American NCNW member Mildred Johnson for the position of Assistant Project Director of the shelter.[64]

Johnson was one of twelve children of North Carolina farmers, born in 1930. After settling in the Cooper Park Houses, Johnson became a lifelong community organizer, the long-term president of the Cooper Park Tenants' Association, and an active member of the Crispus Attucks Community Council as well as the NCNW. A devout Southern Baptist, Johnson graduated from the NCNW college program and worked on the NCNW staff as a liaison between "the black, Puerto Rican, Jewish, and white ethnic communities together on projects that are of mutual interest."[65] The Ad Hoc Committee noted Johnson's "dedication" and "commitment" to other working-class women, as well as her considerable experience working with women at the shelter. Most important, the committee argued, was the fact that the board's decision would serve as a "crucial" test of whether "Mildred Johnson and all other working-class women will be given their due leadership roles within our organization." Otherwise, the committee warned, the NCNW will "be labeled 'just another' organization that pushes capable working-class women into the background and renders leadership to professionals."[66] Despite the entreaties of the committee, the board of the Women's Survival Space gave the position to a professional, not to Johnson.[67]

The NCNW was not alone among feminist groups in this struggle to maintain its original social change goals while at the same time conforming to the dictates of the funding agencies and partner organizations that provided the monies it needed to continue its service provision. In her study of women's health groups, Sandra Morgen shows that the process of receiving state funds (either directly from the government or those administered through nonprofits) led directly to increasing bureaucratization within organizations and impeded collective decision making and other practices of participatory democracy. The majority of grant contracts required a hierarchical supervisory structure as well as detailed record-keeping, leading to the specialization of tasks among employees and divisions between paid workers and volunteers. Often, the division of labor resulted in varying degrees of knowledge among members about the organization, which influenced the balance of power among members and shaped an organization's decision-making process.[68] While Peterson hoped to implement MFY's principle of maximum feasible participation in her work with the NCNW, the funding realities she encountered sometimes prevented her from realizing this goal. As Peterson reflected, "It's that ambivalence. If you are successful, things get institutionalized, but not in the ways you expected. They don't run them the way the women's movement ran them."[69]

"I sat there and cried": Social Welfare Funding Realities in an Era of Austerity

By 1978, the American public had grown increasingly weary of high inflation and the slow recovery from the severe recession of the early to mid-1970s. In late 1978–79, changing course from his campaign promises of full employment, President Carter made fighting inflation, rather than joblessness, his top economic priority and initiated a national austerity program that included deep cuts in antipoverty programs.[70] By 1980, the nation was confronted with 18 percent inflation and 20 percent interest rates, and another emerging recession. Carter was facing a tough reelection campaign, and that March, he cut another $13 billion from the federal budget, reducing funding for food stamps, health programs for children, and CETA.[71]

After four exhilarating years of success for Project Open Doors, the New York City Labor Department informed the coalition that it was cutting 24 percent of its budget for fiscal year 1980, which would result in a loss of at least thirty-five jobs.[72] Martino Fisher remembered the feminist groups coming together to decide how to best absorb the painful loss in staff positions: "I sat there and cried. All these women sat together who were heading these different groups and decided where these cuts would take place. . . . I saw how some people could say, 'I'm willing to give up from my group to your group because of its need.'"[73] Despite the cooperation between the Project Open Doors members, the loss of CETA funding led to a dramatic scaling back in feminist social service provision in New York City and portended the greater cuts to come during the Reagan administration.

In an effort to maintain funding for Project Open Doors, the NCNW and NOW NY, represented by attorney Isabelle Pinzler of the Women's Rights

Project of the American Civil Liberties Union (ACLU), filed suit against the city, charging that it was underserving women in its allocation of CETA public service jobs through its categorization of women with children as "ineligible" for employment. The suit contended that the city was violating the CETA requirement that women be served in proportion to their representation within the population; only 43 percent of New York City's CETA jobs went to women, while women made up at least 60 percent of the poor. Therefore, Pinzler argued, the city's funding cut to Project Open Doors was an attack on women's civil rights.[74]

While Pinzler took the case to the U.S. Department of Labor, the NCNW, along with NOW, the Coalition of Labor Union Women, and Women Office Workers, demonstrated at City Hall. Women, many with children in hand, marched and held signs that read "Freezing CETA slots Equals Opening Welfare Rolls!," "Our Mothers Need Jobs," and "It's All [City Labor Commissioner Ronald] Gault's Fault!" Eventually, the NCNW won its claim—in a settlement, the court required the city to submit an affirmative action plan for women's participation in public service jobs and to guarantee, regardless of cutbacks in federal funding, a half-million dollar contract to the NCNW in 1982 and 1983 to run a skills-training program for women.[75]

This victory would soon be undermined by larger changes in social welfare funding. Upon taking office in 1981, President Reagan famously declared "government is the problem" and suggested volunteerism and private sector leadership as the best way to reduce poverty.[76] From 1982 to 1985, Reagan's budgets cut federal funds to nonprofits by 20 percent overall, and by 40 percent to social service organizations.[77] Reductions in government funding were accompanied by new spending stipulations; together, the result was changed priorities within community-based social service agencies, including the replacement of long-term programs such as community organizing with "direct employment search and training programs and emergency assistance."[78] Funding decreases also led to calls for the effectiveness of both government- and nonprofit-administered social programs to be measured using random-control experiments, in which members of a control group were excluded from participating in a program such as job training, in order to have a comparative basis on which to judge the performance of the program.[79]

The NCNW suffered directly from Reagan's budget cuts as well as from the generalized rightward shift of the nonprofit sector that resulted from the restriction in funds for social services in the 1980s. In 1981, President Reagan eliminated the public service job component of CETA, removing the eligibility of most nonprofit community-based organizations from the nation's job training program. In 1983, Reagan replaced CETA entirely with a much more modest and limited program, the Job Training Partnership Act (JTPA), which emphasized private industry's involvement in running training programs. JTPA funds were to be used for training, rather than employment, and did not provide a stipend to participants.[80] After the NCNW's guaranteed job-training contract with New York City ran out at the end of 1983, the City Labor Department rejected their application for administering a JTPA grant. At that point, Peterson said: "We had to first terminate a lot of people . . . You have all these neighborhood people that have been working for you now for five years, and you have to let people go . . . It's a killer. And you find out that you're an administrator and not an organizer."[81] According to NCNW administrator Terry Haywoode, the loss of funding "was very hard" on the organization, because "women lost their jobs and they were very bitter, very, very bitter. . . . That was heartbreaking."[82]

The NCNW faced a reduced staff, a funding shortage, and members' increased need for jobs and social services in the context of New York City's poverty rate of 23.5 percent.[83] Struggling to keep the group together, Peterson secured funding from the Rockefeller Foundation's Minority Female Heads of Households Self Sufficiency Program. In 1982, with the five-year, $900,000 Rockefeller grant, the NCNW established Women's Public Works, an employment program for single mothers in public housing projects in Williamsburg-Greenpoint.[84] Women's Public Works offered training aimed at private sector employment in fields such as "secretarial science/word processing, computer programming and computer repair," as well as child care and building maintenance.[85] This project and other subsequent NCNW employment programs were much more limited in scope than its previous program, Project Open Doors, and devoid of that program's explicitly feminist context. Furthermore, eighteen months into the grant, the Rockefeller Foundation mandated that the NCNW employ random assignment research, requiring the organization to reject a portion of the applicants to the program in order to measure the program's success rate. NCNW members resisted using random assignment research because it would entail turning away needy women who came to the organization for help. When it refused to comply, the Rockefeller Foundation terminated the NCNW contract a year early.[86]

A 1985 list of "Participant Expectations and Regulations" for the NCNW job training program reflected this programmatic shift in the 1980s from community organizing to service provision for the poor. The list warned that "smoking, sleeping, eating, drinking, gum-chewing, and radio playing are not permitted," that "the use of alcoholic beverages or narcotics . . . will result in immediate termination," and that "friends or relatives of trainees are not permitted to accompany students to class at any time."[87] These regulations revealed the extent of the job training program's hierarchy and its deviation from the NCNW's original goals, which emphasized collective decision making, community building, "teaching each other" and "learning from each other."[88] NCNW administrator Sandy Schilen reflected, "We took the money and did as much with the money that reflected our own model as we could. And we didn't coerce and pressure women to do things so we could get money. But . . . you couldn't run those programs and stay on the values of our organization very easily. So for me personally it was a killing time."[89]

Throughout the 1980s and 1990s, the NCNW faced a conflict between securing funding for service provision and remaining faithful to its original mandate of empowering low-income women. As teenage women who became pregnant increasingly declined to get married, politicians and the media focused on teenage pregnancy and single motherhood as social ills.[90] In response, foundations such as Rockefeller earmarked funds specifically to programs to encourage "self-sufficiency" for single mothers. The NCNW responded to these "funding realities" by shifting its programmatic focus to educating teenage mothers as well as teen pregnancy prevention.[91] After that Rockefeller grant ended, the NCNW received a similar $116,000 grant from the New York City Department of Employment Bridge Remediation Program "to run a four-month remediation and job-readiness training program" for seventy young women with "the priority given to young mothers."[92] The NCNW secured additional city funds and in 1986 opened the You Can Community High, an alternative high school serving students who had previously dropped out. You Can provided day care for teen mothers, a GED program, an after-school work program, and counseling services.[93]

In 1989, the NCNW succeeded in securing a federal JTPA grant, allowing it to return to serving women of all ages in its employment training program.[94] The JTPA program's requirements to train the unemployed for what were in practice low-wage and low-status private sector employment jobs greatly restricted the NCNW's ability to use government funding to improve the status of poor and working-class women. According to Peterson, the pressures generated by JTPA's emphasis on performance-based evaluation and measurable job placement success led to changing power dynamics within the NCNW: "The Job Training Partnership comes and you're setting up all these programs for the poor, and then all of a sudden you realize you're a policeperson for the poor. . . . All of the things that we cared about most, in terms of organizing, were being taken away."[95]

Funding cuts and more stringent welfare regulations also affected the NCNW college program, limiting sources of aid as the NCNW's partner institutions raised their costs to administer the degrees. Schilen continued running the NCNW college program until 1994, when rising tuition rates and difficulties working with administrators of the partner institutions led her to end it.[96] The loss of the CETA and college programs represented a considerable setback for the NCNW, not only because it reduced the organization's ability to recruit and retain members through the provision of desperately needed jobs and education but also because it eliminated social spaces in which women had been interacting across differences in race, ethnicity, class, and sexuality in constructive ways. These programs had allowed NCNW members to acquire new knowledge about their abilities to work across differences and to begin solving the social problems that shaped their lives.

A pragmatist as well as an idealist, Peterson adapted to changing political contexts by following the funding. In the mid-1980s, Peterson decided that the NCNW should split into a local and a national organization. Following a five-year transition period, Neighborhood Women of Williamsburg-Greenpoint was established as an independent nonprofit and took over administration of the You Can School as well as the NCNW's remaining local programs. Meanwhile, Peterson focused on national networking with NCNW affiliates in other cities, and increasingly on international collaboration with grassroots women's groups abroad.[97]

"Bread-and-butter concerns": Grassroots Perspectives & the Global Women's Movement

Caroline Pezzullo, a Brooklyn-born Catholic labor activist who was a consultant on Latin America at the United Nations, played a key role in the NCNW's emerging international outreach. Pezzullo traveled widely in South America in the 1960s and 1970s and was running a grassroots leadership training program for Caribbean women when her friend and fellow feminist activist Charlotte Bunch introduced her to Jan Peterson, her "U.S. counterpart." The two women formed a deep and lasting alliance. Pezzullo helped the NCNW obtain status as a nongovernmental organization (NGO) at the United Nations and introduced its leadership support process to groups of grassroots women throughout Latin America.[98]

Estelle Freedman writes that the United Nations "fostered international feminism" through its global women's conferences and its establishment of NGOs that channeled aid to women.[99] For the NCNW, international feminism proved particularly attractive because of its focus on grassroots women's "bread-and-butter concerns." According to Pezzullo, "We found that more poor women had similar problems all over the world than women in general . . . and it was a unifier."[100] The NCNW participated in both the United Nations Decade for Women Conference in Mexico City in 1975 and the Decade for Women forum in Copenhagen, Denmark, in 1980. Beginning in the early 1980s, the NCNW hosted international representatives from the Soviet Union, Togo, Japan, France, Italy, Sweden, Germany, China, Kenya, Costa Rica, and Chile, who came to learn about the NCNW leadership training program and the work of grassroots women activists in the United States.[101]

In 1985 at the Third World Women's Conference in Nairobi, Kenya, the NCNW joined with other leaders to form Grassroots Organizations Operating Together in Sisterhood (GROOTS International) to "end the conference practice of analyzing grassroots women as subjects in the development process without providing them with a chance to participate directly and to present their own ideas and issues." Today, GROOTS has members in Canada, Costa Rica, Germany, Ghana, Jamaica, India, Cameroon, the Czech Republic, Turkey, Kenya, Papua New Guinea, and Zimbabwe. In addition to administrating GROOTS from the Brooklyn office of the NCNW, Peterson also chairs the United Nations Huairou Commission: Women, Homes and Community, an organization founded in 1995 at the United Nations' Fourth Conference on Women in Beijing to "promote the efforts of grassroots women in human settlements and urban development."[102]

Many NCNW members were enthusiastic about this new, international direction. They found it powerful to exchange information and organizing strategies with women from other countries.[103] Their connections with the United Nations also allowed the American women to focus international attention on poverty within the United States. African American public housing leader Rosemary Jackson, a longtime NCNW member and advocate for low-income women, played a key role in the international networking. In 1987, Jackson's Camden Urban Women's Center, in cooperation with the NCNW and Rutgers University, hosted an international conference on women and housing as part of the U.N. International Year for Shelter for the Homeless. The conference brought together grassroots women from 100 different countries, as well as all fifty states.[104]

Following the U.N. conference on housing in Camden, Jackson traveled widely with GROOTS, visiting Jamaica, India, Ghana, Nigeria, Germany, Turkey, Costa Rica, Mexico, Panama, and Fiji. In each country, GROOTS representatives recruited grassroots women leaders to take part in the United Nations' Fourth World Conference on Women. The goal, Jackson explained, was to "ensure that there were poor women speaking for themselves" at international policymaking conferences.[105] This international development has been a fruitful area of growth for the NCNW over the past two decades, partially because it has allowed women's groups to work around and beyond the limitations set by national governments, and provided funds to replace dwindling U.S. government sources of aid.[106]

For some NCNW members, though, the transition to an international focus was painful, and they feared the loss of the vital neighborhood-based women's organization they had fought to establish.[107] The group's local membership declined, and those Williamsburg/Greenpoint residents that were still affiliated with the NCNW no longer regularly participated in the LSP process. Peterson's decision to expand the NCNW's activities to the international arena was driven both by funding opportunities and by her ambitious vision for accomplishing greater social change by working on a global level. Elizabeth Speranza explained, "I always looked at Jan as the person who would start you off and then go on to other things. She's an organizer."[108] Janie Eisenberg, a photographer who worked with the NCNW, noted that the challenge as an organizer is to move on to larger projects "without losing what you have."[109] Currently, Peterson laments that she is refighting "battles from thirty years ago" as New York City funding cuts threaten closure of the Swinging Sixties Senior Center and Small World Day Care.[110]

Legacies

Peterson's vision of organizing was shaped by her experiences in Harlem CORE and in Mobilization for Youth. As described by Charles Payne, the primary themes of the community-based organizing tradition of the civil rights movement were "the developmental perspective, an emphasis on building relationships, respect for collective leadership, for bottom-up change, the expansive sense of how democracy ought to operate in everyday life, the emphasis on building for the long haul, the anti-bureaucratic ethos, [and] the preference for addressing local issues."[111] Certainly all these themes are evident in Peterson's work with the NCNW. Just as Payne chronicled the breakdown of the organizing tradition in the Student Nonviolent Coordinating Committee, the fiscal pressures of running a service agency during the lean times of the 1980s and 1990s at times prevented Peterson from realizing her vision of participatory democracy. This does not diminish the accomplishments of Peterson and the NCNW, however, but rather reveals the importance of the interaction between activists and the state. Under pressure from the conservative attack on the welfare state and the poor, the NCNW did its best to hold on to its accomplishments in empowering low-income women.

The recognition of difference among NCNW members allowed them to work together to improve the status of low-income women. It also helped NCNW members come to a better understanding of the problems they faced as poor and working-class women, by revealing the ways in which categories of identity overlapped and often compounded inequalities. In 1982, outlining the LSP, Jan Peterson demonstrated a holistic conception of identity, writing that "since low and moderate [income] women experience not only sex oppression but other oppressions based on their age, race, class and ethnicity, it is essential to combine this understanding in our work . . . In understanding sexism we will have to understand all other oppressions."[112] This multidimensional understanding of power relations allowed the NCNW to draft a broad and inclusive agenda for social change.

Drawing upon their identities as poor and working-class white women and women of color, NCNW members formed a new, broadened community. It was the NCNW's specific focus on recognizing and analyzing the differences among members, I argue, that allowed the group to build successful cross-race and cross-class partnerships. Rather than allowing differences among them to fracture their coalition, the NCNW members used their holistic understanding of identity and their practice of consciousness-raising to engage in a principled coalitional form of identity-based politics. Once they had established understanding and trust, NCNW members were able to identify areas of mutual need and even to work on issues that did not directly benefit their own group, because they valued the coalition and believed in working to advance the position of all low-income women and communities.

In interviews, many former and current members of the coalition expressed a desire to return to the closer emotional ties between members that they created in the context of daily or weekly contact in the 1970s, when the coalition provided CETA jobs, the college program, and frequent consciousness-raising sessions.[113] Although she has remained active in community organizing, Sally Martino Fisher recalled those years as the best of her life, saying that she felt an unequaled sense of accomplishment and belonging as a result of her participation in the NCNW.[114] Fisher's strong connection to the NCNW, twenty years after she left the organization, highlights the importance of creating nurturing, inclusive activist communities to achieve social change. While most histories of the second wave are only recently beginning to explore the activism of working-class white women and women of color,[115] the NCNW offers an important model for studying the ways in which a holistic concept of identity can help us understand the nature of coalition work across differences, offering insights for broader social justice movements.

CHAPTER FIVE

Turn Anger, Fear, Grief into Action

ACT UP New York

In the 1980s, New York's economy rebounded from the fiscal crisis of the mid-1970s, and real estate developers transformed the cityscape. The recovery was profoundly uneven. Professional workers enjoyed a decade of economic boom in which real household income grew 26 percent across the city. Yet the poverty rate remained at 23 percent citywide—twice the national average—and increased in the Latino and African American neighborhoods of Harlem, East Harlem, the South Bronx, Williamsburg, Bushwick, and Bedford-Stuyvesant. While the dwindling white ethnic working class tried to combat disinvestment and preserve its hold on neighborhoods such as the Northside in Williamsburg-Greenpoint, in Manhattan and brownstone Brooklyn high-end development projects displaced poor, working-class, and lower middle-class residents.[1] The redevelopment of single-occupancy housing, warehouses, and light manufacturing spaces into luxury "lofts" and condominiums was a long-term process that began after World War II and was a result of the city's economic shift from a manufacturing to a finance base. It was particularly visible in the 1980s when, as Sharon Zukin argues, redevelopment was combined with cutbacks in social service provision, creating "a moral type of urban clearance" in which the needs of the investor class trumped those of the mentally ill, gays and lesbians, and low-income people of color in particular.[2]

The spatial transformation of the city went hand in hand with a renewed national emphasis on the primacy of market-based solutions to social problems. President Ronald Reagan and his administration contended that the private sector would solve social problems more efficiently and creatively than government, and that smaller government would permit families and churches to restore a conservative Christian-based morality to the nation.[3] Mayor Ed Koch's administration's pro-investor policies, including tax abatements for commercial developers, resulted in the growth of upscale developments like Trump Tower, which merged luxury apartments, office space, and high-end retail; this in turn contributed to the gentrification of working-class neighborhoods and an explosion in homelessness.

Redevelopment changed consumption as well as residential zones. Real estate developers replaced the inexpensive and raunchy theaters, bars, and small stores of Times Square with "family-friendly" entertainment complexes resembling suburban malls.[4] High-end development transformed the West Village and spread into the East Village, disrupting neighborhoods once known for their visible concentration of gay residents.[5] (See map 3.) This displacement unfolded alongside a national backlash against feminism and the gay and lesbian liberation movement; the backlash was fueled by the rise in prominence of the Religious Right, a coalition of evangelical and fundamentalist Protestants, Mormons, and Roman Catholics opposed to gay rights and abortion. Nationally, the Supreme Court appeared to ratify this moral agenda in 1986 with its 5-4 decision in *Bowers v. Hardwick*, which declared that "the Constitution does not protect homosexual relations between consenting adults, even in the privacy of their own homes." The court declined to rule on the legality of heterosexual sodomy but decided that states could outlaw homosexual sodomy in keeping with "ancient tradition," thus excluding homosexuals from the privacy rights granted to heterosexual couples beginning with the 1965 *Griswold* decision that legalized their use of birth control.[6]

Homophobia along with rising economic inequality shaped public responses to the unfolding AIDS epidemic, leading to city officials' closure of bathhouses and other meeting places for gay men, the stigmatization of those with the disease, and inadequate funding for treatment and research. As gay culture seemed to disappear from the city streets, conservative Christians increasingly claimed public space, protesting in front of abortion clinics.[7] Activist Mary Anne Staniszewski recalled New York in the 1980s as "profoundly conservative. The streets became flooded with homeless. The AIDS epidemic made prejudice more visible. My friends were dying."[8] AIDS activists fought back against the rise in homophobia and misogyny, using participatory democracy and civil disobedience to claim their right to recognition and resources. While they have often been criticized for practicing narrowly focused, single-issue politics, AIDS activists correctly saw cultural and economic issues as linked and sought to combat both antigay sentiment and the ascending neoliberalism of the Reagan era.

In the late 1980s and early 1990s, AIDS activists' stunning visual art and spectacular street theater reshaped the social geography of Lower Manhattan, leading to a dynamic coalition between gay men, lesbians, and feminists supporting not only sexual freedom but also health care for all. The public art and dramatic street theater of the AIDS Coalition To Unleash Power (ACT UP) and its ally, Women's Health Action and Mobilization (WHAM!), brought once-isolated men and women together and gave them an immediate sense of connection. It also changed the way they experienced space in Lower Manhattan, producing a vocal and visible activist queer community that rejected established gender norms and embraced a fluid rather than fixed understanding of sexuality. Like previous gay rights advocates, queer activists reappropriated what had been a derogatory term for homosexuals and used it as a "sly and ironic weapon" against homophobia.[9]

ACT UP chapters quickly sprouted in 147 cities across the country and the globe.[10] Often, these chapters and other AIDS activist groups collaborated with ACT UP New York to mount collective actions at sites outside of New York City with national and international significance to the epidemic; these included dramatic protests at the Food and Drug Administration (FDA) in 1988, the Fifth International Conference on AIDS held in Montreal in June 1989, and at the Centers for Disease Control (CDC) and the National Institutes of Health (NIH) in 1990. These demonstrations were crucial to securing many of ACT UP's most significant policy victories, including speeding up the testing and approval of new treatments, winning the involvement of people with AIDS (PWAs) in drug trial design and testing, and changing the CDC's and Social Services Administration's definitions of AIDS to include opportunistic infections primarily affecting women and low-income people, so that they, too, would qualify for treatment programs and for benefits when they were too ill to work.[11]

Although ACT UP's many chapters and dramatic, highly publicized demonstrations gave it a global presence, a locally based sense of place was essential to the group's identity and targets.[12] ACT UP targeted institutions with particular resonance to New Yorkers, such as Wall Street and the *New York Times*, and leveraged the media to boost their national and international significance. The organization unleashed a flurry of activity in its first several years, holding large and raucous demonstrations periodically as well as smaller, more spontaneous "zap actions" continuously. In addition to medical and public health authorities and the pharmaceutical and financial industries, ACT UP targeted the media for its inaccurate portrayal of the epidemic and especially who was at risk; luxury real estate developers like Donald Trump for exacerbating homelessness; and city hall for its inadequate response to the epidemic.

Because of his vocal and staunch opposition to homosexuality, condom use, and abortion, Cardinal John O'Connor, head of the Roman Catholic Church in New York, emerged as ACT UP New York's leading enemy and the target of its most memorable protests (see figure 13). Hand-selected by Pope John Paul II to be Archbishop of New York in 1983, O'Connor quickly became a leading public figure in the city, installing a press booth in St. Patrick's Cathedral and offering weekly press conferences.[13] O'Connor was combative and controversial, exemplified by his declaration that abortion was equivalent to the Holocaust and his threats to excommunicate Gov. Mario Cuomo for his support of abortion rights. He nonetheless remained highly influential and was seen as the Vatican's leading spokesperson in the United States and the voice of conservative Catholicism nationally.[14]

While courting the press and Mayor Ed Koch, O'Connor worked to restrict abortion, gay rights, and sex education in public schools and to consolidate the archdiocese's role as a key provider of health and social services. This was accomplished through the church's facilities such as the Terence Cardinal Cooke Health Care Center, which was the site of New York's first comprehensive-care ward for AIDS patients and was funded by the New York State Medical Care Facilities Finance Agency.[15] People with AIDS and their allies were painfully aware of the increasing influence the Catholic Church had over the provision of health care, both in New York City and across the United States. As many community hospitals closed and hospital and health-care center mergers and acquisitions increased, by 1985 the Catholic Church operated approximately one third of the nation's health care systems. The Church did so in accordance with its own religious directives for care, while still receiving substantial public financing.[16] In this respect, O'Connor is representative of other conservative Christian leaders in the 1980s and 1990s who sought to gain both the moral high ground in national political discourse and an increasing share of newly privatized social service provision.[17] In its demonstrations against O'Connor, ACT UP sought both to reveal the human costs of ho-

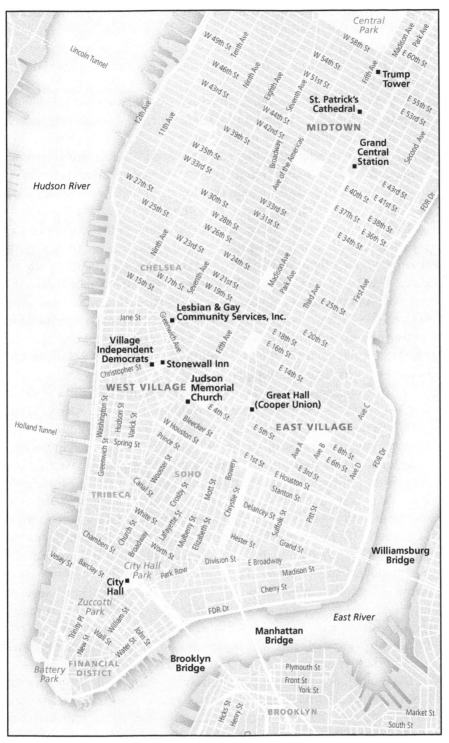

Map 3. Lower Manhattan and Midtown

mophobia and of restriction of abortion and sex education and to call attention to the public funding that the Church received to operate its hospitals, nursing homes, and homeless shelters, all of which banned discussion of contraception (including condoms), sterilization, or abortion with clients.

ACT UP's dramatic confrontation with O'Connor epitomizes the challenges to the dominant gender and sexual order and the backlash against them that came to be known as the "culture wars." The culture wars were directly tied to the Religious Right and pro-family movement's attempts to regulate national morality and to conservatives' successful attacks on the welfare state. Because religious conservatives perceived abortion and gay rights as unwarranted state intrusion into the private realm of family, they supported economic conservatives' efforts to eliminate or shrink social welfare programs, substituting negative liberty and the competitive marketplace for positive liberty and government support of citizens' rights.[18] ACT UP was not a monolith, and not all of its members cared as much about opposing neoliberal reforms as they did about developing better AIDS treatments, but a critical mass of the group's membership understood these two goals to be linked. Collectively, the organization offered one of the most visible and comprehensive defenses of social justice in an era of increasing inequality.

ACT UP's support for abortion stemmed from members' recognition that both AIDS and abortion were "hounded by the moral specter of sex guilt." To leaders of the Religious Right, homosexuality and abortion were key symbols of a corrosive sexual permissiveness based in the severing of sexuality from marital reproduction that was weakening the American family and thus the nation and that should provoke feelings of shame and guilt. In contrast, for feminists and gay and lesbian activists, the separation of sex from reproduction was essential for human well-being. ACT UP members incorporated the gay and lesbian liberation movement's affirmation of the right to sexual pleasure and the feminist health movement's assertion of the right to bodily self-control into their political analysis. Additionally, ACT UP drew on the insights of lesbian feminism that homophobia was rooted in misogyny and therefore gay men and feminists were natural allies, despite the conflicts that often arose within gay and lesbian groups over prioritizing men and women's differing interests.[19]

The group's members were predominantly young, white, gay men with a professional class background, but women, people of color, and veterans of earlier social movements, including the civil rights, anti–Vietnam

War, gay and lesbian liberation, and feminist movements provided key leadership and knowledge. ACT UP member Lei Chou, who was born in Taiwan and joined the group when he was nineteen and a student at Cooper Union, recalled that "it was a great opportunity for learning. There was so much activist history in the room."[20] Chou reflected that "the feminists—particularly the lesbians in the group—provided a lot of the driving force for the whole organization, and leadership. And, their experience from their work in feminism definitely helped ACT UP in its maturing process . . . the best way to organize, and what you can do with people once you get them organized. That kind of technical stuff all came from the feminist movement."[21] The collaboration between gay men and lesbians in ACT UP, Patrick Moore argues, was one of the most significant aspects of the organization, because it allowed for new trust and coalition building "after the divisiveness of the 1970s" and provided a forum "where men were forced to acknowledge the skills and power of women, both personally and in political struggle."[22]

Indeed, the legacy of feminism is apparent in ACT UP's analysis of the health-care system, in its artwork, and in its demonstrations. Like the women's health movement before them, ACT UP members adopted a considered skepticism of biomedical authority, which they critiqued for its heterosexist and patriarchal assumptions that produced erroneous treatment of gays and lesbians as well as women with AIDS. In order to effect change, ACT UP members participated in intense self-education, achieving a level of scientific knowledge that allowed them to challenge medical and public health experts on their own terms.[23] When the state refused to provide clean needles to drug addicts in order to prevent HIV infection, ACT UP members committed civil disobedience and went to court to defend their needle-distribution program (they won); this self-help strategy was similar to the women's health movement's provision of menstrual extractions and abortions prior to *Roe v. Wade*.[24] ACT UP's frequent stenciling of red (symbolizing bloody) hands and chalking or painting of body outlines recalled the methodology of feminist artist Suzanne Lacy, whose 1977 *Three Weeks in May* drew attention to the prevalence of rape in Los Angeles by portraying the outlines of a body along with the notation "a woman was raped here," on sidewalks near locations where rapes were reported.[25] The group's graphic aesthetic, typically using only one color in addition to black and white, along with boldface text, also borrowed from feminist artist Barbara Kruger, whose dramatic poster artwork sought to hold the art world accountable for its depiction of women as sexual objects and for its dismissal of work by female artists.[26]

The group's creative and outrageous zap actions—going in drag to the Republican National Women's Club and disrupting a fundraiser with "Lesbians for BUSH" banners, for example—drew inspiration from those of the women's liberation movement, such as the infamous releasing of mice during a bridal fair at Madison Square Garden. They also drew from the gay and lesbian movement and from the Yippies and other radical performance groups of the 1960s.[27] ACT UP's success in keeping its very large demonstrations nonviolent and ensuring the safety of the participants, some of whom were seriously ill and thus particularly vulnerable, can be attributed in large part to its civil disobedience and marshal trainings. Many of the training sessions were run by Amy Bauer, a lesbian feminist who learned the importance of affinity groups and consensus-based decision making in situations involving civil disobedience from older women in the 1980 Women's Pentagon Action and the 1983 Seneca Women's Peace Encampment, female-led protests against the proliferation of nuclear weapons and the intensification of the Cold War.[28]

Some historians have seen the 1980s as a period of decline in feminist activism, but ACT UP is a good example of the ways in which feminist insights and methodologies, as well as feminist activists themselves, were incorporated into other social justice movements of the era, including the nuclear freeze and the Central American solidarity movements.[29] As has often been the case historically, in the 1980s women's rights activists contributed to progressive social movements that were not exclusively focused on women and, at the same time, sought to advance women's position in society. While members varied in their degree of awareness of the ways in which they built upon the victories of the civil rights and feminist movements and shared their tactics, ACT UP's embrace of participatory democracy and its efforts to make American citizenship more inclusive made it a fitting successor.

"That was when people were not being fed, bathed or touched"

The association of AIDS with homosexuality was early, lasting, and consequential. Though it is likely that IV drug users were dying of AIDS in New York City in the 1970s, from what was then known as "junkie pneumonia" (*Pneumocystis*), AIDS came to medical attention in the United States in 1979–80, when gay men in New York and San Francisco suffered from enlarged lymph nodes and contracted an unusual form of skin cancer, Karposi's sarcoma, which caused purple skin lesions. Although evidence showed that heterosexual drug users (male and female), their children, Haitian immigrants, and hemophiliacs exhibited the same symptoms as gay men, scientists termed the syndrome Gay-Related Immune Deficiency (GRID), leading to the linkage of the disease with homosexuality.[30] (The condition was renamed Acquired Immune Deficiency Syndrome in 1982, two years before the Human Immunodeficiency Virus [HIV] was identified as its cause and the Centers for Disease Control [CDC] assured the public that it was transmitted by blood and other bodily fluids and could not be contracted through casual contact.) Many scientists shared high-ranking Reagan administration members' homophobia; ignorance and antipathy toward gay men resulted in the federal government's slow and inadequate response to the epidemic.[31]

The early years of the AIDS epidemic in New York were marked by uncertainty, false information, and fear about the cause and transmission of the disease. People with AIDS suffered from social isolation, including the loss of homes, jobs, and relationships with partners or family members. The absence of strong federal or local leadership and the prevalent lack of scientific understanding led some New Yorkers to attempt to protect themselves by removing infected people from their communities. In the Rockaways, residents fought to prevent people with AIDS from being placed in a Neponsit nursing home; in Queens, parents launched a school boycott to protest the Board of Education's policy of allowing children with AIDS to attend school.[32]

New York City had roughly half the country's reported AIDS cases, but in the early 1980s, the city did not mount a systematic response to the emerging epidemic, and the care and housing of AIDS patients was left to volunteer groups such as the Gay Men's Health Crisis (GMHC). Cofounded in January 1982 by gay writer Larry Kramer, GMHC provided information services, including a 24-hour hotline, support services such as professional counseling and a buddy program, and assistance negotiating the health insurance and social welfare bureaucracies; it also raised funds and promoted education about safer sex practices.[33] In 1983, Mayor Koch established the Office of Gay and Lesbian Health Concerns under the direction of Dr. Roger Enlow, a move that Kramer and other activists decried as a hugely inadequate and underfunded response to the spiraling number of deaths from AIDS.[34]

Patients experienced stigma and neglect in the city's health care system. Some private hospitals, overwhelmed by the rapidly increasing number of AIDS patients and sensitive to the general public's fears of the spread of the disease, began refusing to admit AIDS patients; hospitals that did admit them, especially public institutions, had too few resources to care for them properly. ACT UP member Keith Cylar stated, "New York City literally had hospital gridlock and that was when they were keeping people out on hospital gurneys in the hallways. That was when people were not being fed, bathed or touched. It was horrendous."[35] The first CDC guidelines for precautions to be taken by healthcare providers were issued in September 1983, and reassurance about the virus's nontransmission by causal contact soon followed. But a few well-publicized cases of accidental occupational exposure and the lack of prophylactic treatment meant that many healthcare providers remained very anxious. Some healthcare providers were so terrified of contracting HIV that they neglected AIDS patients. Robert Vazquez-Pacheco recalled his lover's treatment at New York Hospital: "I went through those early days of the orderly leaving the food tray . . . on the floor outside his room, or the nurse putting on the space suit to come in to talk to him."[36]

Nationally, prominent conservative and religious leaders condemned homosexuality and blamed gay sex for the epidemic.[37] Locally, O'Connor vocally opposed including homosexuality in the city's antidiscrimination law. The Vatican affirmed its support for O'Connor, its stance that homosexuality was a sin, and its seeming acceptance of antigay violence, stating that "when civil legislation is introduced to protect behavior to which no one has any conceivable right . . . irrational and violent reactions increase."[38]

In 1985, to the dismay of safer-sex advocates who argued that gay meeting places were one of the most effective places to provide AIDS education, the Koch administration responded to fears by closing many gay bathhouses and clubs.[39] A marked decline in the vibrant and visible gay public culture that had flourished in New York in the 1970s ensued, while violent attacks on gays and lesbians increased, with many perpetrators referring to AIDS during assaults.[40] In 1986, capturing the rise in homophobic sentiment and AIDS panic, the New Right leader William F. Buckley Jr. issued a call, published by the *New York Times,* to tattoo people with AIDS on the buttocks and upper arms in order to "protect" homosexuals and IV drug users.[41]

In response to the growth in rhetorical and physical attacks on gays and lesbians, a group of graphic artists who had formed an AIDS support group decided to take action as an art collective, which they subsequently named Gran Fury. Emphasizing the fascist implications of Buckley's suggestion, Gran Fury created the Silence = Death project. The poster featured a pink triangle on a black background, a reference to the pink triangle forced on homosexuals by Nazi Germany but inverted "to signify hope." The pink triangle also recalled the legacy of the gay and lesbian liberation movement of the 1960s, which sought to reclaim derogatory images and words associated with homosexuality and to imbue them with new meanings of pride. The poster's slick presentation on a glossy black background drew on advertising techniques and forced the reader to lean in close to read the political text in small font at the bottom: "Why is Reagan silent about AIDS? What is really going on at the Centers for Disease Control, the Federal Drug Administration and the Vatican? Gays and Lesbians are not expendable . . . Use your power . . . Vote . . . Boycott . . . Defend Yourselves . . . Turn anger, fear, grief into action." Gran Fury founder Avram Finkelstein explained that the creators of the Silence = Death project hoped the image would catch people by surprise: "I wanted our work to have a real yuppie graphic, something that would fit where you didn't expect politics."[42] Critic and AIDS activist Adam Rolston noted the success of this technique: "It looked like a corporate logo, like some institution was speaking to me. It's the appropriation of the voice of authority. Like a trick."[43]

In 1986, despite 25,000 AIDS deaths nationwide, President Reagan had not yet publicly acknowledged the disease. While the Silence = Death project singled out the Reagan administration for its muteness, the poster also targeted the media's erasure of the epidemic, from its reluctance to cover the "gay cancer" to newspapers' policies of not naming AIDS as the cause of death in obituaries to avoid "embarrassing" family members. With an initial printing of two thousand posters, Gran Fury set about wheatpasting "Silence = Death" across the city.[44] Directions for hanging posters on temporary construction walls, subway stations, and other public places, later handed out at ACT UP and WHAM! meetings, read: "Wheatpasting: aim for the consistency of potato soup, use big plastic brush, estimate 100 per hour, possible $25 fine."[45]

In March 1987, feeling a strong sense of urgency to stem the epidemic, Larry Kramer gave a speech at the Lesbian and Gay Community Services Center in Greenwich Village, warning the audience that two-thirds of them could be dead within five years. Kramer told his listeners, "If what you're hearing doesn't rouse you to anger, fury, rage, and action, gay men will have no future here on earth." Following Kramer's speech, several hundred people reconvened and took the name AIDS Coalition to Unleash Power (ACT UP).[46] They soon adopted "Silence = Death" as their logo.[47] From the beginning, ACT UP dedicated itself to the use of mass demonstrations and nonviolent civil disobedience to bring public attention to the

AIDS crisis. It pressured both government and drug company officials to increase the availability of treatment for people with AIDS.

ACT UP held its first protest in March 1987 on Wall Street, where gay men, lesbians, and their straight allies criticized drug companies' profiteering, citing the high cost of AIDS drugs. They also deplored the Food and Drug Administration's lengthy process of approval of new treatment regimes. ACT UP charged that by marketing AZT, the first drug approved to combat AIDS, at $10,000 for a year's supply (the most expensive drug to date), the pharmaceutical giant Burroughs Wellcome was immorally putting profits before people. After the protest, the FDA announced it would shorten the drug approval process by two years, and Burroughs Wellcome later reduced the price of AZT to $6,000 a year. ACT UP decided to keep up the pressure on the corporation to reduce further the cost of AZT by affixing "AIDS PROFITEER" stickers to Burroughs Wellcome products in pharmacies and grocery stores, including Sudafed, Actifed, and Neosporin.[48]

ACT UP captured the attention of many New Yorkers with the trademark Silence = Death poster, which was "virtually impossible to miss" on the streets.[49] In one weekend alone, twenty-five ACT UP volunteers wheatpasted more than 1,500 flyers in downtown Manhattan and Brooklyn.[50] In the late 1980s, while development projects were transforming the face of the city, ACT UP plastered its images everywhere, especially on the blue walls designating construction sites that dotted Lower Manhattan, turning the space of the city into a political and cultural forum.[51]

"Just putting that on your jacket was a statement"

New Yorkers who never took part in activism themselves were attracted to and influenced by the Silence = Death project, which created a highly visible and recognizable symbol of opposition to homophobia and governmental policy on AIDS.[52] For ACT UP members, however, part of the power of the Silence = Death logo came when they affixed it, in button form, to their jackets, or wore it on boldly printed T-shirts. (See figures 5 and 12.) Actor Ron Goldberg explained that much of the significance of wearing the logo for him lay in being visibly out as a gay man on the streets of Manhattan, rejecting the shame of homophobia and fear of AIDS: "I remember wearing at that first demonstration my Silence = Death button . . . even just putting that on your jacket was a statement. . . . It was a statement that you were gay, because there was the pink triangle—whether it was true or not. And then, for people who even knew what that was

Figure 12. An ACT UP member wearing a "Silence = Death" button carries the ashes of his partner to the White House, ACT UP Ashes Action, Washington, D.C., October 11, 1992, photograph by Meg Handler. Courtesy of Meg Handler.

about, people just assumed that you must have AIDS. And that was a big deal."[53]

The Silence = Death project built not only a sense of community among gay men and lesbians but also a sense of pride that resulted in personal and group efficacy, fostering the coalition's ability to do something to alleviate the AIDS crisis. The remarkable success of the Silence = Death campaign as well as ACT UP's dramatic demonstrations, including a quarantine or concentration camp float in the 1987 Gay Pride Day parade featuring black-clad AIDS victims surrounded by barbed wire and "guarded" by people wearing military and police uniforms and rubber gloves, resulted in a swift increase in attendance at ACT UP's weekly meetings at the Lesbian and Gay Community Services Center in Greenwich Village.[54] By 1988, the group was attracting between 400 and 600 people to its weekly meetings. Within two years, it grew to more than 1,000 members with an annual budget of more than $500,000, and weekly meetings had to be moved to the Great Hall of Cooper Union.[55]

ACT UP defined itself as "a diverse, nonpartisan group of individuals, united in anger and committed to direct action to end the AIDS crisis." The group's diversity was an asset, allowing it to take on various aspects of the epidemic and to draw on different types of knowledge and skills. *Village Voice* reporter and ACT UP member Donna Minkowitz estimated that during ACT UP's height in the late 1980s and early 1990s, women constituted a quarter of members attending meetings, and people of color a sixth.[56] While many ACT UP members identified as gay, lesbian or, increasingly, as queer, heterosexuals also participated.[57] Some members were HIV-positive; others were not but shared a commitment to combating the epidemic. Most, but not all, members were college-educated; many held professional jobs, contributing to the group's successful fundraising as well as its facility in negotiating with corporate and public officials. Members with backgrounds in art, graphic design, filmmaking, journalism, advertising, theater, academia, medicine, law, and banking put their skills, creativity, and connections to work; while fewer in number, both current and former sex workers and IV drug users contributed important knowledge based in their own experiences. ACT UP successfully pursued an inside/outside strategy, with some members conducting research on AIDS treatment and meeting with government and drug company officials to persuade them to increase the availability of drugs, while others planned dramatic direct actions aimed at bringing public opinion to bear on the same targets.[58]

ACT UP favored a nonhierarchical structure and majority-vote decision making. In large Monday-night meetings, elected rotating facilitators (one man and one woman) imposed *Robert's Rules of Order* and time limits for speakers, with the goal of allowing anyone who wanted to speak the opportunity to do so. Filmmaker and ACT UP member Jean Carlomusto recalled the Monday-night meetings:

> The purpose of these meetings was to inform and to organize. So when you walked into a meeting, you'd walk through a table of different literature about events and about issues that you needed to know about. You would get educated at the meeting or you would find out more. People would propose actions, find out if there was support for the action on the floor, find out maybe if some part of the action needed to be modified so that more people would get on board. And it would go forward. Some very interesting discussions would happen.[59]

The meetings also served as an important social outlet and a source of support for those coping with their own illness or that of their lovers and friends. Despite their length and sometimes contentious tone, ACT UP member and art historian Douglas Crimp remembered "I loved going to meetings, I was hooked on meetings, I never missed a meeting unless I was out of town. I endured them. I sat to the bitter end of every single one. Partly because . . . there was a group of people I would go out to dinner with afterwards."[60]

In addition to the large meetings, smaller caucuses, working groups, and committees were formed to research and plan actions around specific issues, including drug treatment, women and AIDS, IV drug users, housing for people with AIDS, pediatric AIDS, alternative and holistic treatment, health insurance coverage, and sex education. Affinity groups planned civil disobedience in secret and provided members with support during the actions. The entire floor would then vote on anything bearing ACT UP's name.[61] As the group grew larger, it adopted a Coordinating Committee, composed of elected representatives from each of the subcommittees, which met on Sunday nights to determine the agenda for the large Monday meeting and to provide feedback on draft proposals for actions and programs generated by the subcommittees or affinity groups.[62]

Women and people of color in ACT UP successfully pushed the organization to address not only the development of new AIDS treatments but also the larger, structural issues underlying the epidemic, including homophobia, racism, sexism, and class stratification. In May 1988, for example, ACT UP New York coordinated with other ACT UP branches in more than fifty cities around the country to launch nine days of protests focused on "unattended aspects" of the epidemic, including "IV drug use, homophobia, people of color, women, testing programs, prison programs and children with AIDS."[63] In advocating on the behalf of all PWAs, ACT UP drew upon the work of earlier AIDS activists, including Bobbi Campbell and Dan Turner, founders of People With AIDS San Francisco, and Michael Callen and Richard Berkowitz of New York, who developed the first safer-sex guidelines, as well as the others who joined them in drafting the 1983 Denver Principles. In that landmark document, AIDS activists condemned the labels "victim" and "patient" for their implications of defeat and passivity, and urged instead the use of the term "People With AIDS" and the active involvement of *all* PWAs in decision making related to AIDS policy. The Denver Principles urged specifically that PWAs participate in AIDS forums "with equal credibility as other participants" and "share their own experiences and knowledge."[64]

While many ACT UP members were committed to a holistic understanding of the epidemic and to learning from the experiences of all PWAs, identity-based interests at times led to conflict within the group around the prioritization of issues. Minkowitz observed: "This coalition is by no means without its strains. A powerful minority of the group's white men believes that ACT UP should concentrate on getting AIDS drugs approved by the federal bureaucracy—an issue that affects even the wealthiest AIDS patient—while subordinating other struggles, such as obtaining services for indigent PWAs or providing counseling and treatment to IV-drug users."[65] In time, this powerful minority would depart ACT UP to focus exclusively on drug development and testing, but for the first five years of its existence, the affinity group structure of ACT UP allowed members to pursue their sometimes divergent interests while also working together effectively.[66]

"To put the issues of people of color on the agenda": The Majority Action Committee

The Majority Action Committee, so named "because the majority of people dying of AIDS were people of color," addressed the ways in which racial and economic inequalities shaped the epidemic. The committee was formed in late 1987 to represent the "Black, Hispanic, Indian, Asian, and other minority communities."[67] African American law professor Kendall Thomas, who had participated in civil rights activism with his family and church as a child, explained the impetus for its founding. He stated that within ACT UP there was "a degree of ignorance, of such profound ignorance about issues of racial power, privilege—white skin privilege—the racially specific character of people's experiences with the health care system—a whole range of issues—that we felt it necessary, particularly as members of the populations which, together, made up a majority of the people living in the city hardest hit by HIV/AIDS, to have our own presence and our own space, within ACT UP."[68]

Lei Chou explained that "Majority Action was all the people of color in ACT UP that got together . . . to put the issues of people of color on the agenda, because ACT UP was so overwhelmingly white back then."[69] The Majority Action Committee also worked to forge coalitions with community-based organizations that "weren't likely to come to Monday night" ACT UP meetings, such as Baptist churches in Harlem and Asian American groups including Gay Asian Pacific Islander Men of New York (GAPIMNY), and to provide information on safe sex, testing, and treatment options to those communities.[70]

Lack of affordable housing for PWAs quickly emerged as a key issue for the Majority Action Committee. ACT UP estimated that 8,000 homeless people with AIDS, and thousands more infected with HIV, lived in New York City in 1980, while the city provided housing for only 1,316 of them.

Homeless PWAs were particularly susceptible to opportunistic infections, including tuberculosis, which was on the increase after a long decline.[71] The growth in the homeless population was an unintended outcome of the deinstitutionalization movement of the 1960s and 1970s and the subsequent withdrawal of public funding for services to the mentally ill. The development of tranquilizers and antipsychotic drugs in the 1950s, combined with the efforts of advocates who exposed the dismal conditions in many institutions, led to the release of mentally ill patients into the city's single-room-occupancy hotels, supported by public assistance. Seeking to restore its tax base during the financial crisis of the 1970s and early 1980s, the city offered developers substantial tax incentives to convert those hotels into luxury condominiums and apartments, and between 1970 and 1983, the number of single-room-occupancy units decreased 87 percent. The resulting lack of low-income housing and assistance, along with the steep recession of the early 1980s, led to a crisis of homelessness. By 1983, officials estimated there were 40,000 homeless people in New York City, including many families, the mentally ill, and alcoholics.[72] Thousands of homeless poor camped on the streets and in the subway system causing consternation among visiting tourists who were forced to step over their bodies.[73]

Members of the Majority Action Committee, including Chou and Keith Cylar, along with white allies Charles King, Eric Sawyer, and Gedalia Braverman, formed a Housing Committee to press the city to increase the supply of affordable housing for PWAs and coordinated with other advocates for the homeless to stage a series of actions. On Thanksgiving Day 1988 the ACT UP Housing Committee led a demonstration in front of the $200 million Trump Tower. Braverman explained the choice of location:

> The feeling was that instead of these wealthy landlords getting tax abatements and incentives to develop housing for rich people, the city should be providing funds and services to target people who were homeless or on the verge of becoming homeless, because of the conglomeration of problems that occurred as people became ill and lost jobs. So, the idea was to target the Trump Tower which was at that time, the symbol of real estate gigantic-ness in Manhattan.[74]

Trump received the first-ever tax abatement for a commercial developer for his Grand Hyatt Hotel Project, near Grand Central Station. Like other Trump projects such as Trump Plaza at Third Avenue and 61st Street, the huge, mirrored Trump Tower loomed over its smaller neighbors on Fifth Avenue and featured an extravagant pink marble atrium with a $1 million waterfall. The development, with its luxury retail stores on the ground floor, was aimed at what Trump called the "world's best people," with apartments ranging in price from $550,000 to $10 million and doormen dressed like Buckingham Palace guards.[75]

Recognizing Trump as a key symbol of the privatization of New York that contributed to the rapid increase in economic inequality in the 1980s, ACT UP continued to target him. The Housing Committee returned to Trump Tower on February 11, 1989, for the "Soup Kitchen Rally," in which a coalition of city groups protested the city's failure to address homelessness, and again on Halloween 1989, when ACT UP members passed out candy, condoms, and information about AIDS and homelessness.[76] On November 9, 1989, the ACT UP Housing Committee held a "sleep in" at Grand Central Station, itself the site of an upscale redevelopment featuring a privatized Business Improvement District, to protest sweeps of homeless people from the subways.[77] Members also maintained an ongoing presence outside the Department of Housing Preservation and Development. They "set up house" in front of the office building, chaining themselves to "beds, sofas, desks" and demanding a meeting with Commissioner Abraham Biderman. This pressure prompted the Housing Authority to earmark additional units for PWAs and the Koch and Cuomo administrations to dedicate $50 million in capital funds to housing for homeless people with AIDS.[78]

Next on the Housing Committee's agenda was preventing this money from flowing into the Roman Catholic archdiocese's coffers. Cardinal O'Connor had opposed New York City's 1986 Gay Rights Bill and banned masses held by the gay Catholic organization Dignity from taking place in Catholic churches. He denounced the use of condoms to prevent the spread of HIV, even when the National Conference of Catholic Bishops approved condom use as a limited exception to the ban on contraception. At the Vatican's first conference on AIDS, O'Connor announced, "I believe the greatest damage done to persons with AIDS is done by those health care professionals who refuse to confront the moral dimensions of sexual aberrations or drug use." Opposing distribution of clean needles to IV drug users in an effort to curb the spread of HIV, O'Connor said repeatedly, "Good morality is good medicine." Beyond his public statements, O'Connor worked to advance these views in public policy, sitting on the President's Commission on AIDS and placing representatives on the committees determining the sex education curriculum for the New York City schools as well as the schools' Citywide Advisory Council on AIDS.[79]

ACT UP opposed the public subsidies, including tax abatements, tax incentives, and subsidized loans, that went to the Roman Catholic archdiocese's skilled nursing and other health-care facilities designed to treat PWAs. In February 1990, it protested a proposal to allow the archdiocese to operate five new nursing homes, citing the ban on discussion of condoms, clean needle provision, contraceptives, abortion counseling, and gynecological care, and, more fundamentally, the Church's equation of homosexuality and extramarital sex with sin and its opposition to sex education in public schools. Braverman explained: "We thought it was just a great slap in the face to gay people who might be homeless, to have to spend their last days in a nursing facility that was run by the Archdiocese, where they'd be dying and judged simultaneously, and where the state and the city were providing funds to the Catholic Archdiocese for these people's care."[80] Furthermore, ACT UP charged that the archdiocese's request to place a ten-year limit on the city's requirement that the new facilities be specifically for AIDS patients meant that after ten years, the nursing homes would no longer be available to PWAs and would instead house "elderly Catholics."[81] ACT UP members trailed Cardinal O'Connor throughout the city, disrupting his news conferences and public events including an award ceremony honoring his work with the homeless, shouting "You have blood on your hands!" until they were dragged out by police.[82]

Despite some success in provoking public scrutiny of the archdiocese's practices, Housing Committee members realized that "if anyone was going to develop humane, non-institutional housing [for PWAs], it would have to be us." They worked with Nick Rango of the AIDS Institute and architect Richard Jackman to develop a plan for comprehensive housing for PWAs that would allow them to remain in their apartments and receive the care they needed nearby. However, when the Housing Committee brought their proposal to the general meeting, ACT UP members opposed expanding the group's mission, fearing that accepting government contracts and hiring paid staff to provide housing and related services to PWAs would "compromise the voice of the organization."[83] Therefore, the Housing Committee decided to spin off and form a new organization.

In June 1990, along with his partner and fellow homeless advocate, attorney Charles King, and other members of the ACT UP Housing Committee, Keith Cylar founded Housing Works, a service agency dedicated to helping homeless people of color with HIV/AIDS and a history of mental illness or chemical dependency.[84] Since that founding, Housing Works has provided comprehensive services to more than 25,000 low-income PWAs in New York, and it currently operates more than 170 units of housing, including apartments specifically for transgendered people and for formerly incarcerated women, as well as housing facilities with health-care centers attached.[85] Although Housing Works was a separate entity, the split was not acrimonious, and it continued to collaborate with ACT UP. For example, in 1992 and 1993, Housing Works worked with ACT UP and the Coalition for the Homeless to get HIV-positive Haitian political refugees released from a holding facility in the United States' Guantanamo Bay detention center and to provide those who came to New York with housing and medical treatment.[86] Some members continued to participate in ACT UP, and they, along with the Majority Action Committee, frequently collaborated with the ACT UP Women's Caucus.

"They brought an activist history to the group": The ACT UP Women's Caucus

The ACT UP Women's Caucus emerged as one of the most vital subcommittees within the organization, in part due to the political sophistication of its lesbian members who had participated in multiple social justice movements, including the women's health movement, and who drew on their previous activist experience to analyze the social structure of the AIDS epidemic.[87] ACT UP and WHAM! member Emily Nahmanson reflected that the Women's Caucus "was crucially important to the ACT UP community, and to the AIDS activist movement" because "they brought an activist history to the group."[88] Initially, member Liz Tracy explained, the Women's Caucus consisted of informal "dyke dinners" in which lesbians in ACT UP got together to combat feelings of alienation and to do "soul searching" about how AIDS was affecting them and how they should define themselves "within ACT UP and within the crisis."[89] These gatherings generated a sense of solidarity, and the women in the group soon decided they should have their own committee to address issues related to women with AIDS.[90]

The first action of the Women's Caucus was a response to a January 1988 *Cosmopolitan* magazine article suggesting that American women were not at risk for AIDS, and did not need to use condoms, because they did not engage in the "brutal" sex practices of Africans. Members of the Women's Caucus arranged an interview with the psychiatrist who had written the piece "because he had put information out there was really harmful to women."[91] When he refused to retract his article, the Women's Caucus quickly organized a 300-person demonstration in front of *Cosmopolitan*'s office building, stopping traffic and winning TV coverage. They began a campaign to send hundreds of condoms a day to Helen Gurley Brown, *Cosmopolitan*'s editor, who responded by publishing an article on safer-sex practices and urging women to use condoms.[92] ACT UP Women's Caucus members Jean Carlomusto and Maria Maggenti made a film, *Doctors, Liars and Women: AIDS Activists Say No to Cosmo*, that documented the campaign and educated viewers on both safe-sex practices and how to organize a protest. The award-winning film was shown around the country and placed in the permanent collection of the Museum of Modern Art.[93]

Due to the initial framing of AIDS as a gay male disease, many people shared *Cosmo*'s mistaken assumption that women were not at risk for infection. Safe-sex education and the promotion of condom use became the primary focus for the Women's Caucus. In May 1988, they staged a demonstration during a Mets baseball game at Shea Stadium to encourage men to use condoms, holding up banners reading "No Glove/No Love" and "AIDS Kills Women" and passing out condoms and informational flyers.[94] Their efforts increasingly brought them into conflict with Cardinal O'Connor, who had succeeded in 1984 in getting an abstinence-first sex education curriculum adopted for all the public schools and in 1986 in blocking a plan for condom distribution in the schools.[95] In response, the Women's Caucus organized safer-sex education programs outside of nine public high schools in the five boroughs. According to their outcome report:

> We gave out all our information in about 20 minutes flat. Students were hungry for it and took one of each thing. In several instances, officials of the schools came out to talk to us. Some said they were glad we were there because there was hardly any safer sex education going on in their schools and their hands were tied about distributing condoms. Others were dismayed by our presence and were nervous about the outcomes. In some cases, administrators were upset that we had visually explicit information but by the time they expressed concern we had already distributed most of the material.[96]

The caucus focused especially on giving young women knowledge about "how to negotiate safer sex in situations where they may not feel comfortable about sex, and may not feel they have the power to ask for what they want." Handouts included a list of responses to partners' objections to using condoms, such as, "If the partner says 'I can't feel a thing when I wear a condom,' You can say 'Even if you lose some feeling, you'll still have plenty left.'"[97] ACT UP and WHAM! later formed a joint committee, Youth

Education Lifeline (YELL), to work with teenagers to implement ongoing safer sex education in the public schools.

Changing the way the medical and public health establishments treated women and people of color with AIDS was another key objective of the Women's Caucus. In the 1980s, one of the only ways to receive treatment for AIDS was to participate in a drug trial, but the FDA and drug companies restricted trials to white men. Working with the ACLU, the caucus succeeded in gaining the right for women and people of color to be included in clinical drug trials in general, not just for AIDS.[98] The Women's Caucus also fought to change the CDC's definition of AIDS. Medical indicators for AIDS were based on symptoms exhibited by gay men, but women with HIV or AIDS as well as IV drug users and homeless people often presented different opportunistic infections. Thus, they were unable to receive proper diagnoses, and to receive disability and other benefits. The Women's Caucus pressured the CDC to expand its definition of AIDS, and in August 1991 it did so, adding gynecological infections to the diagnostic criteria for AIDS.[99]

Seeking to remedy the widespread lack of information on HIV and women, a subcommittee of the Women's Caucus formed a book group to publish an anthology, *Women, AIDS, and Activism*. The anthology was modeled on the 1971 feminist bestseller, *Our Bodies, Ourselves*, edited by the Boston Women's Health Book Collective, which had roots in the self-help movement.[100] The 1990 anthology is notable for its comprehensive scope as well as its attention to the ways the AIDS epidemic was embedded in specific cultural contexts and therefore affected women in different ways depending on their racial/ethnic, class, religious, sexual, and geographic identities. As Suki Terada Ports and Marion Banzhaf argue in one chapter, "When Asians are all lumped together, there are major problems in AIDS prevention, education and treatment."[101] The book includes chapters on prisoners, IV drug users, bisexuals, prostitutes, heterosexuals, lesbians, pregnant women, mothers, and teenagers. In a chapter on the connections between reproductive rights and AIDS activism, the authors make the case for collaboration, arguing that both movements are fighting for the right to sexual pleasure and that both "address issues at the core of how our society is organized economically and sexually," particularly the distribution of health care and control of decision making over one's body.[102]

As a result of conducting sex education forums and studying the treatment of women in the medical system and the history of the women's health movement, several Women's Caucus members began participating in reproductive rights activism. The Supreme Court's 5-4 decision in *Webster v. Reproductive Health Services*, which restricted women's right to abortion, sparked the founding of WHAM! in New York City in 1989. *Webster* eroded *Roe v. Wade* by upholding a Mississippi law banning abortion counseling, referral, or practice from any institution receiving public funding, such as a state hospital, unless it was to save a woman's life. In anticipation of the decision, a number of women's health activists had been meeting as the Reproductive Rights Coalition (RRC). After the *Webster* decision, thousands joined RRC members at Union Square Park in the largest abortion rights rally in New York City since 1975.[103] Soon, a group of young feminists, mostly white, middle-class women in their twenties who had participated in ACT UP, broke off from the RRC to form WHAM!, a direct-action group dedicated to improving women's health through the use of protest and civil disobedience.[104] (See figure 15.) In one of its first actions, WHAM! organized a boycott of Domino's Pizza, after its owner, Detroit-based Catholic leader Tom Monaghan, funded and led a successful campaign to end all state Medicaid funding for abortions in Michigan.[105]

"Women who were unabashedly pro-abortion, totally unapologetic"

WHAM! modeled its structure and tactics on those of ACT UP, and the two groups successfully partnered around issues of sexual freedom and access to health care.[106] Mobilizing in response to moral interventions by the state and amid a climate of violent right-wing Christian attacks on gay people and abortion clinics, ACT UP and WHAM! members recognized common enemies as well as common goals. As Brian Griffin explained: "The same men and women who don't want women to have abortions also don't want men and women to be gay."[107]

WHAM! member Susan Shaw described the group as "pretty homogenous"—young, "white, college educated. We were very sort of post-college. A few of us had started grad school . . . and a lot of people had stupid day jobs."[108] Charlotte Abbott joined WHAM! at age twenty-two as a newcomer to New York City seeking an activist outlet. In college, Abbott had an abortion at a Planned Parenthood clinic where antiabortion protestors shouted at her. She explained: "That experience completely radicalized me. Being hectored by people under such a private situation was just more than I could bear. WHAM! seemed like a real resource for people who had been through that kind of experience and who could make something out of it and stand up to it. And that was exactly what I was looking for."[109]

Sue Davis, a veteran reproductive rights campaigner who in the 1970s and early 1980s had participated in the Committee for Abortion Rights and Against Sterilization Abuse (CARASA), an interracial organization that advocated for the health-care needs of women of color and poor women as well as for abortion rights, joined the younger women in WHAM! and brought with her a long-term perspective on the struggle for women's rights. The group was overwhelmingly female, with a "definite lesbian sensibility" and an attitude of "general independence."[110] There were, however, several straight men who were long-term members of WHAM!, as well as some gay men, most of whom were also involved in ACT UP. Some members were graphic artists, journalists, and photographers, while others worked in public relations, advertising, law firms, and nonprofits.

Shannon Cain joined WHAM! after seeing a flyer when she was twenty-three and had just moved to New York from Arizona. Her interactions with WHAM! members—"women who were unabashedly pro-abortion, totally unapologetic"—caused her to reflect upon her Catholic mother's attitude toward abortion. Despite self-identifying as a feminist and bringing Cain and her sister with her to feminist demonstrations, "she would tell us that no daughter of mine would have an abortion. It shouldn't be outlawed but you damn well better not have an abortion."[111]

The Catholic hierarchy has led the opposition to legal abortion, which it had described as "the slaughter of innocents," since the 1960s. The Church financed and organized what came to be known as the right-to-life movement and ensured that Catholic hospitals refused to perform abortions. By the 1970s, lay Catholics as well as fundamentalists and evangelical Protestants were drawn into antiabortion activism.[112] The pro-life movement's successful campaign to restrict the availability of abortion not only made race, class, age, religion, family background, and geographic location key factors in determining a woman's access to safe medical abortions but also worked to erode support for women's rights to reproductive self-determination. As Linda Gordon argues, "Making abortion hard to get strengthens its aura of guilt and embarrassment and erodes its legitimacy, despite its continuing legality."[113]

Right-to-life activists adopted increasingly militant tactics as they failed to outlaw abortion entirely.[114] What antiabortion groups called "sidewalk counseling" involved as many as 150 people picketing outside abortion clinics, holding pictures of aborted fetuses and yelling "baby killers" at staff and patients as they attempted to enter the building. In 1988, Operation Rescue head Randall Terry, along with Pro-Life Action League leader Joseph Scheidler, escalated sidewalk counseling into clinic blockades; antiabortion activists would chain themselves in front of clinics' entrances and exits to prevent them from operating. Cardinal O'Connor supported blockades of abortion clinics and urged nuns to direct all their attention to fighting abortion rights.[115]

In fall 1989, WHAM! held a series of demonstrations, known as "October Outrage!", targeting Operation Rescue churches and the National Right to Life Committee Headquarters, located in New York. The protests also sought to unmask "problem pregnancy centers," which enticed women with promises of assistance but then pressured them to continue their pregnancies; despite their deceptive advertising, they did not perform abortions or refer clients to abortion providers. WHAM! planned and held a demonstration every week in October.[116] The demonstrations brought many new members into the group, and, according to Tracy Morgan, "served to make us real to ourselves." It was during the October Outrage that ACT UP asked WHAM! to join them in planning the Stop the Church action, the demonstration that really "brought WHAM! into the spotlight."[117] Membership grew to several hundred, with a core of thirty to forty members consistently attending weekly meetings and "doing a lot of the work."[118]

Stop the Church

On Sunday morning, December 10, 1989, 4,500 protestors massed outside of St. Patrick's Cathedral on Fifth Avenue in New York City. Carrying signs reading, "Stop the Church!" "Public Health Menace," "Curb Your Dogma," "Keep Your Rosaries Off My Ovaries!" and "Know Your Scumbags," they rallied against Cardinal Connor's opposition to gay rights, reproductive rights, sex education, and condom use. (See figure 13.) The cardinal's policies were leading to an increase in AIDS deaths, they charged, while violating the separation between church and state. As thousands rallied outside, several hundred protestors succeeded in entering the cathedral and disrupting the mass. Same-sex couples embraced and participated in a "die-in," dropping to the ground and refusing to move. Others shouted back at the cardinal during his homily, throwing condoms into the air and forcing him to end early. Most notoriously, one demonstrator threw a consecrated Eucharistic wafer to the ground.

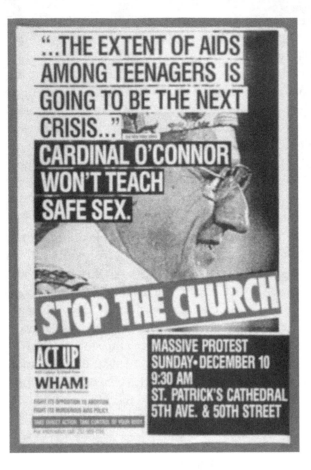

Figure 13. "Stop the Church" poster by ACT UP and WHAM! targeting Cardinal John O'Connor, 1989. NYPL Manuscripts and Archives Division, ACT UP New York Records.

Meanwhile, dozens of protestors lay down in the street across from Rockefeller Center, blocking traffic on Fifth Avenue. Outside, the mood was riotous, with protestors passing along a twenty-foot long, balloon-filled condom bearing the slogan, "Cardinal O'Condom." Clowns threw confetti, blew horns, and distracted the police so that protestors could cross Fifth Avenue. One participant described the clamor: "Christmas carols chimed on one side of the street, while on the other side men and women yelled, 'Racist, sexist, anti-gay, Cardinal O'Connor go away.'" Costumes and drag were an important element of the political theater. Artist Ray Navarro gave interviews dressed as Jesus Christ, alongside men wearing nuns' habits and others in mock clerical vestments.[119] Navarro had AIDS and his health was worsening; his friend and fellow ACT UP member Jean Carlomusto described how Navarro, who was raised Catholic, had sought to reclaim his spirituality as he neared the end of his life. She argued that by dressing as Christ, "Ray was reclaiming this Christ figure as a revolutionary—use of Christ as someone saying, 'Use condoms.' "[120]

Many of the demonstrators had been raised Catholic and shared a sense of anger and alienation from the teachings of the Church. ACT UP member Ron Goldberg served as a civil disobedience marshal at the demonstration, responsible for making sure the demonstrators remained nonviolent and that participants understood which actions could lead to arrest. He described the challenges of keeping everyone calm and safe, which were intensified by the strong, albeit opposing, symbolic resonances that cathedral held for the police as well as the participants. The situation was:

> very volatile and very emotional, on both sides. The police were very emotional about guarding St. Patrick's. There were a lot of people in the organization who were very emotional about St. Patrick's, and what that represented, and in terms of their own Catholicism or not. And there would be people who would take up the barricades and start pushing forward with them. And it wasn't about necessarily stopping them. You might want to—if someone was really blowing their lid, it was about watching them: 'Are you okay?' Trying to defuse the situation.[121]

ACT UP and WHAM! members prepared for the protest by conducting civil disobedience training, as well as working out their chants, press statements, and images, and organizing their own video crews to record the event. For weeks leading up to the protest, activists had wheatpasted posters of Cardinal O'Connor with zombie eyes and the call to "Stop this Man!" all over Lower Manhattan.[122] ACT UP and WHAM! prepped the public and press for the spectacle, and they were delighted by the network news coverage and front-page spreads. The *Daily News* headline read, "SUNDAY PUNCH KOs ST. PAT'S," while the *New York Post* reported "PROTESTS ROCK ST. PAT'S," followed the next day by O'Connor's pledge to prevent another disruption of mass: "OVER MY DEAD BODY." Ultimately, more than 100 people were arrested and charged with criminal trespass, disorderly conduct, and resisting arrest, and the protest remained headline news for several weeks.[123]

The Stop the Church protest, repeated a year later in Stop the Church II, was the most publicized and the most controversial of many direct actions performed by WHAM! and ACT UP. ACT UP members explained that the high mortality rates of people with AIDS, as well as the rapid spread of the disease, had created a "sense of urgency" among activists and a determination to do whatever it took to "get results now." For ACT UP, the disruption of church services, and even the symbolic desecration of the

Eucharist, was not only justified but a necessary step in fighting the "war" on AIDS and homophobia.[124]

Citing the disruption of worship and the infringement of church attendees' rights, the editorial pages of the major dailies, Mayor Koch, mayor-elect David Dinkins, Gov. Mario Cuomo, and Vice President Dan Quayle (who was visiting New York at the time) all condemned the protest. Stop the Church set off an intense public debate within and beyond the gay community.[125] Some gay rights advocates and commentators charged that the demonstration had set the movement back and argued that Catholics should be free to worship as they chose behind the closed doors of the cathedral, just as gay men and lesbians should be free to engage in sexual practices behind the closed door of the bedroom.[126] ACT UP and WHAM! argued that they sought public support for the needs of people with AIDS, for the right of gays and lesbians to express their sexuality openly, and for the recognition of the deleterious social and cultural implications of the Catholic Church's stances on homosexuality, sex education, and abortion rights. For ACT UP and WHAM!, the right to privacy, while important in preventing prosecution for sodomy and for obtaining an abortion, was inadequate in addressing the AIDS crisis, which required massive public education campaigns as well as public funding for research and treatment. Furthermore, Ian Daniels Horst argued, Cardinal O'Connor's and the Catholic Church's leadership's *active intervention* in the affairs of state" necessitated "*active* opposition" by those who felt that the Church's stigmas against homosexuality and nonmarital sex should not shape public policy on reproductive rights, sex education, and health-care provision.[127]

The metaphorical war on AIDS and homophobia being waged by ACT UP and WHAM! was met by real threats of violence, as unknown persons issued bomb threats against ACT UP's offices and left death threats on the group's answering machine.[128] Members whose photographs appeared in the news media's coverage of the Stop the Church protest received threatening calls on their home telephones; some had bricks thrown through their windows.[129] Following the Stop the Church protest, the treatment of gay men by the police became increasingly brutal. Most notably, police clubbed twenty-seven-year-old ACT UP member and former seminarian Christopher Hennelly on the head and yelled homophobic slurs as he was leaving a demonstration in front of the Midtown North Police station to protest earlier incidents of police brutality against ACT UP. They inflicted a severe concussion that put Hennelly in the hospital for six days and led to permanent brain damage, including ongoing seizures.[130] Later, during Hennelly's trial for assault and disorderly conduct, Manhattan Criminal

Court justice Edgar Walker ruled that the only "violent, tumultuous, and threatening behavior . . . was on the part of the police." Walker criticized the police for beating Hennelly without provocation and then lying about the incident.[131]

The trial of six of the protestors who had chained themselves inside the cathedral during Stop the Church kept the action in the local news through the following year. The continued publicity raised awareness of ACT UP and WHAM!'s message and led to dramatic increases in membership.[132] Leaders struggled to incorporate hundreds of new members into a community that had been based on close friendship ties and sought to reconcile diverging visions of its future. Like affordable housing for PWAs and needle exchange, opposition to police brutality drew ACT UP and African American community activists together. Yet, some activists remained critical of the Stop the Church action, fearing that it impeded coalition building with other social change movements.[133] Mindy Nass of WHAM! explained that WHAM!'s partnership with ACT UP and its controversial protest tactics were "great for us" but "also made it difficult for other people to join in with us."[134] This debate points to the fundamental tensions involved in seeking both to create a broad movement for social change and to address the homophobia and misogyny that underlie institutional responses to AIDS and abortion.

"All People with AIDS Are Innocent"

While it was easy for some to dismiss the Stop the Church actions as the fringe identity politics of radical gays and feminists, the demonstration posed a broad challenge to the sweeping changes in American culture and politics ushered in during the Reagan era. In staging demonstrations across from Rockefeller Center during the busiest shopping time of the year, ACT UP and WHAM! highlighted the reduction of citizenship to consumption, as well as the growing political influence of conservative religious leaders such as O'Connor. From the mid-1970s onward, as religious conservatives teamed up with Republican politicians to wage a moral war focused on gender relations and sexuality, WHAM! and ACT UP put forth an alternative vision of an inclusive, egalitarian community and a positive understanding of human sexuality. This in itself was life-sustaining to activists battling the AIDS epidemic and the violence directed against gays, lesbians, and women seeking to regulate their reproduction. In their attacks on drug company profiteering and real estate moguls such as Trump, ACT UP and WHAM! showed how the economic dislocations

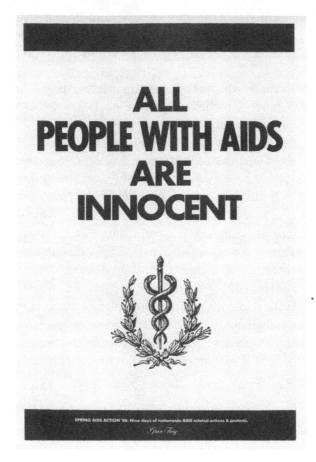

Figure 14. "All People With AIDS Are Innocent," ACT UP poster, 1988. NYPL Manuscripts and Archives Division, Gran Fury Collection, 1987–1995.

and human costs of privatization were masked by the moral veneer offered by religious conservatives.

The sense of community, the collective distribution of information on safer-sex practices, and the visibility of gay men and lesbians within ACT UP helped counter the rabid homophobia of mainstream culture. The group's 1988 "All People with AIDS Are Innocent" poster challenged the press's construction of hemophiliacs as "innocent" AIDS victims and everyone else as implicitly deserving to die from the disease.[135] (See figure 14.) At a time when public officials and the mass media demonized gay sex for creating AIDS, and some insurance companies sought to deny coverage to AIDS patients who had contracted the disease "voluntarily," these posters highlighted the ways in which AIDS itself was socially constructed, showing that AIDS patients were affected as much by homophobia as by the virus and the opportunistic infections it spawned.[136]

As member Robert Garcia explained, the process of collectively demonstrating in public affected ACT UP members personally in addition to strengthening group bonds:

> That's what we do at demonstrations, together, collectively. We all get together and . . . combat AIDS. You're not so fearful in a crowd. When we get in a crowd and that type of dynamic, the energy level reaches a certain pitch, and all of a sudden we look at each other, and we're damn proud of who we are, and we know what we're doing and we know that it's never been seen before—that in the bleakest hour of our history as a community, as a people, we are fighting for our lives. We are not only fighting for our lives but for our right to exist.[137]

Even if, as historian Bradford Martin concludes, ACT UP members "lost the public relations ground war" with their Stop the Church protest, through the very process of confronting the cardinal and all that he stood for, ACT UP and WHAM! members forged an assertive new identity and supportive community that allowed them to counter right-wing Christians' withering attacks on gay people and women.[138]

CHAPTER SIX

It Saved My Life

Creating Queer Politics

In the early 1990s, antiabortion activism escalated as Operation Rescue mounted dramatic sieges that closed women's health clinics and encouraged violence against abortion providers. At the same time, Congressional Republicans led attacks on artists who depicted gay themes or addressed AIDS, arguing that their works were unfit for public display. Responding to the increasing political and cultural influence of the Christian Right, ACT UP and WHAM! generated creative queer politics that sought to reveal and challenge heterosexism's embeddedness in American culture and to claim the right to non-normative, public sexual identities.

"Keeping women from being too intimidated": The Battle for Reproductive Rights

Following the Stop the Church protests, the Catholic hierarchy in New York stepped up its antiabortion activism, and WHAM! directed much of its energies toward countering antiabortion discourse and helping patients get access to clinics. In 1990, the National Conference of Catholic Bishops hired Manhattan-based powerhouse Hill and Knowlton—"the most important public relations agency in history"—to mount a $5 million media campaign to sway public opinion against abortion.[1] Immediately, WHAM! massed several hundred protestors outside the firm's offices.[2] Ultimately, however, the campaign went forward and the Church intensified its local street presence.[3]

Installed as bishop of Brooklyn in April 1990, Thomas Daily declared ending abortion to be his "first priority." Beginning in June 1990, he held monthly prayer vigils in Brooklyn and Queens, known as "Daily's Monthly," gathering 400 to 800 antiabortion activists to march from a Catholic church to a nearby clinic and line up along the sidewalk, creating a gauntlet for patients to walk past. By sending an incognito member to the Church's meetings, WHAM! could find out what clinic Daily was planning to target and then arrange with clinic staff to provide escorts and to meet with the police to encourage them to keep street access open so that clients could be driven to the entrance. Enabling clients to avoid confrontations and remain calm was particularly important, as medical procedures including abortion cannot be performed if a patient's blood pressure is elevated.[4] Daily also sponsored Helpers of God's Precious Infants (HOGPI), a group known for its aggressive sidewalk counseling. HOGPI, composed of mostly white, Catholic men over the age of fifty, would regularly gather at seven A.M. on Saturdays outside of nine clinics in New York City to try to dissuade women from entering.[5] Msgr. Phillip Reilly led similar regular protests and prayer meetings outside of Choices Women's Medical Center in Queens.[6]

U.S. District Court Judge Robert Warn had issued an injunction against Operation Rescue in January 1989, forbidding members from blocking entrances to abortion clinics in New York City and from having more than two antiabortion sidewalk counselors approach women entering the clinics. However, the New York City Police Department interpreted the injunction narrowly and did little to enforce it.[7] WHAM! members therefore spent a lot of time trying to convince police commanders to move antiabortion demonstrators to the opposite side of the street from clinic entrances and to allow cars carrying patients through police barricades.[8] As Susan Davis, who served as WHAM!'s liaison to the police department, explained: "We told them antis were the ones breaking the law and that we were trying to enforce the law, and the cops never got it."[9]

Some WHAM! members regularly escorted patients to Eastern Women's Center in Manhattan for as many as five years. Clinic escorting involved walking with patients from their vehicles or subway stops all the way into the clinic. Escorts wore orange vests (like crossing guards) with identifying signs on the front and back. Their role was to support patients emotionally and shield them physically from the antiabortion picketers, who would try to stop and accost patients on their way in. WHAM! worked closely with the clinic administration, who expressed their gratitude in letters such as the one from Eastern addressed "To All Patients," noting that, "We thank the volunteers from WHAM! and other pro-choice activists, first, for escorting you to our door, and secondly, for publicly defending absolute reproductive freedom and quality health care for all women."[10]

For some WHAM! members, this task was exhausting and emotionally draining.[11] Neil DeMauss explained that he "found escorting very difficult and stopped doing it after a while, because you were having to deal with these people holding signs that said 'Abortion is baby killing,' and who were constantly trying to engage us in conversation. . . . And it was very hard for me to walk people in and not react."[12] Others reported boredom with the predictable confrontations and seemingly endless stalemate. Those who stayed with it found it very satisfying because they personally helped ensure that women got into the clinic that day. Elizabeth Kaltman, who escorted patients every Saturday at a Queens clinic, explained: "It felt good to be successful, and most of what I remember is that we were successful, getting women into clinics. It wasn't solving the bigger problems [of access to reproductive rights], but we were keeping women from being too intimidated to get in."[13]

Clinic defense, in contrast to escorting patients, involved trying to prevent and minimize the effects of Operation Rescue's sieges. Nationally, Operation Rescue grew tremendously from its establishment in spring 1988 through the early 1990s. By 1990, the organization reported that more than 35,000 members had been jailed, with an additional 16,000 risking arrests in attempted "rescues." Karen Ramspacher described clinic defense as like "doing espionage. If there was going to be a big hit and Operation Rescue was coming you were driving around at five in the morning trying to figure out what clinic they were going to close."[14] During a clinic siege, Operation Rescue members would chain themselves to the clinic doors with Kryptonite bicycle locks, while others formed a human chain in front of them. It often took police the better part of a day to remove the phalanx of activists and open the doors, resulting in the shutting out of women seeking access to abortions or other services. From January 28 to February 2, 1991, Operation Rescue targeted all of the abortion clinics in Westchester County, closing one clinic for five days, another for two, and a third for one day.[15]

WHAM! members planned and trained in advance for clinic defense, familiarizing themselves with the municipal injunction that prohibited Operation Rescue from physically blocking clinic entrances and urging police to enforce it. At times, WHAM! acknowledged, the sheer numbers of protestors from both sides overwhelmed patients, while the presence of the press discouraged other women from entering clinics. Following one such confrontation at Eastern Clinic after Cardinal O'Connor led a prayer vigil from St. Patrick's, WHAM! changed strategies, refraining from responding to antiabortion activists' chants.[16] Planned Parenthood of Westchester County credited WHAM! with enabling its clinic to continue to see patients despite Operation Rescue's blockade attempts:

> All of us appreciated your expertise and effectiveness. You were so strong, so knowledgeable—and above all so *there* all day when we needed you. The bottom line for us was that no one was hurt, no one was intimidated, and no one failed to receive a scheduled abortion because of the tactics of a fanatical group. This was in large measure possible because of your efficacy and skill.[17]

Operation Goliath, a local branch of Operation Rescue, stated its goal of closing the Westchester County clinic entirely, or bankrupting the town of Dobbs Ferry with police overtime and processing costs for the dozens of demonstrators arrested every week. This tactic of "stuffing the jails" had been used by civil rights activists in Mississippi, and Operation Rescue members often claimed the mantle of the civil rights movement, arguing that they were fighting for the civil rights of the unborn. Operation Rescue hoped that public opinion would turn against the clinic, especially because of the expense of defending it, but most residents continued to support abortion rights for women. Nonetheless, like the national antiabortion movement, Operation Goliath succeeded in reducing the availability of abortions and other reproductive health services by forcing the clinic to close on weekends. These successes meant WHAM! increasingly found itself playing defense, responding to the Catholic Church and Operation Rescue rather than advancing its own agenda of comprehensive reproductive rights.[18]

Declaring 1991 the "Summer of Rescue," Operation Rescue staged a massive, forty-six-day blockade at three abortion clinics in Wichita, Kansas, gaining the attention of the entire nation.[19] The blockades of clinics, as well as the cumulative violence directed against abortion providers, which according to the National Abortion Federation from 1977 through 1992 included 27 bombings, 101 arsons, 54 attempted bomb and arson attacks, 2 kidnappings, 2 attempted murders, and 88 death threats, led to a marked decline in the number of physicians willing to perform abortions. In 1992 alone, there were 57 butyric acid attacks on clinics and by

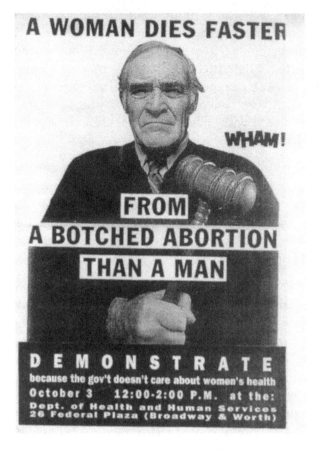

Figure 15. "A Woman Dies Faster From a Botched Abortion than a Man," WHAM! poster, n.d. WHAM! Records, Tamiment Library, NYU. Courtesy of Elizabeth Meixell.

that year, 84 percent of U.S. counties had no physicians providing abortion services.[20] Antiabortion activists were successful in swaying public opinion against abortion and securing laws state laws restricting abortion.[21]

WHAM! members followed the Wichita siege in the news and vowed not to allow something similar to happen in "their" city. In summer 1991, WHAM! created the "Oh, Toto! They're Not in Wichita Anymore!" poster featuring an image of Dorothy walking with the Tin Man and the Lion from the *Wizard of Oz* with text reading "To protect your right to choose abortion, you don't have to go any farther than your own backyard." (See figure 2.) The poster warned that the National Right to Life Committee planned, on September 29, 1991, "to form a human cross smack in the middle of our city by lining up along Fifth Avenue and across 34th Street. This symbolizes their goal: to impose their religious beliefs on all Americans."

The poster invited viewers to "Show them New York isn't Wichita" by joining WHAM! at a rally and march to coincide with the "Life Chain."

To WHAM!'s delight, more than 4,000 people showed up to march down Fifth Avenue in favor of abortion rights, overshadowing the 1,100-person antiabortion demonstration, which WHAM! renamed "The Chain of Fools."[22] Chanting "New York Is Pro-Choice" and holding posters reading "A Woman Dies Faster from a Botched Abortion Than a Man," the marchers passed the antiabortion demonstrators, who held signs reading "Abortion Kills Children" and whose small numbers left them spread out along both sides of Fifth Avenue and 34th Street. (See figure 15.) Participant Abby Scher reported that "the counter-demo took the steam out of the Lifers' symbolism" and was cheered by onlookers, including a group of male construction workers.[23] Davis explained the significance of taking direct action following the Wichita siege:

> You're participating in it and it's liberating you in the process. Any kind of going out into the world and stating who you are and what you believe in strongly is a very empowering thing to do. . . . For us to take to the streets in huge numbers and march in front of St. Patrick's was just an enormously freeing and exciting and exhilarating and actually important thing to do, to be able to stand up to Operation Rescue and all that they represented.[24]

"To Provide an Alternative View": The Church Ladies for Choice

The Church Ladies for Choice organized in 1991 as a response to Operation Rescue and the heated confrontations between antiabortion and pro-choice advocates. The group is composed mostly of gay men from ACT UP, along with several women from WHAM! The group includes WHAM!'s founder, Elizabeth Meixell (see figure 16), who performs as Sister Mary Cunnilingus, and Karen Ramspacher, who performs as Tad, "the altered altar boy." The "Ladies" dress up in drag to sing songs about reproductive rights, AIDS, and homophobia. (See figure 17.) In declaring themselves "the USO [United Servicemen's Organization] of the pro-choice movement," they connected themselves to the military-sanctioned, civilian-run system by which women entertained soldiers in chaperoned dances and cafes, an activity that founder Meixell had participated in with her sister when they were teenagers in the 1960s looking to get out of the house and have

Figure 16. Elizabeth Meixell at a WHAM! demonstration, n.d. WHAM! Records, Tamiment Library, NYU. Courtesy of Elizabeth Meixell.

some fun.[25] The Church Ladies first appeared at the WHAM! picket of St. Patrick's Cathedral after the 1991 *Rust v. Sullivan* Supreme Court decision upholding the abortion gag rule that prevented federally funded family planning clinics from discussing abortion.

Inspired in part by Dana Carvey's popular "Church Lady" character on the comedy show *Saturday Night Live*, in which he appeared in drag and spoofed self-righteous churchgoers, they borrowed Meixell's old bridesmaids' dresses and devised clever, satirical skits and songs. In addition to attending demonstrations and staging fund-raisers, the Church Ladies participated in abortion clinic defenses, mainly to bolster the spirits of pro-choice demonstrators, clinic escorts, and patients. For Steve Quester, an ACT UP member and longtime gay rights activist, support for abortion rights was "a no-brainer. . . . They're the same issue. It's about control over our bodies."[26] Quester helped work on the Church Ladies for Choice song-

Figure 17. Church Ladies for Choice, Buffalo Spring of Life
counterprotest, 1992, unknown photographer. WHAM! Records,
Tamiment Library, NYU. Courtesy of Elizabeth Meixell.

book, which incorporated pro-choice and queer sentiment into the lyrics
of traditional left-wing songs such as "This Land is My Land," renamed
"This Womb is My Womb," with a chorus: "This womb is my womb/It is
not your womb/And there is no womb/For Randall Terry." Another Church
Lady classic is "God is a Lesbian," sung to the tune of "God Save the Queen,"
which is familiar to Americans as "My country 'tis of thee/sweet land of
liberty/of thee I sing."

Brian Griffin, who has been a Church Lady since 1991, observed that by
performing next to the "antis" they could provide an "alternative view" and
"dissipate tension or just direct people's attention away from things. We
learned that these are the ways in which we can be most beneficial, and
one of the best ways was keeping people . . . happy and their spirits up."[27]
As Jan Cohen-Cruz observes, the Church Ladies' use of satire and mim-
icry helped to disrupt the moralistic tone of antiabortion demonstrations.
For example, when antiabortion protestors started singing "Amazing
Grace," the Church Ladies would respond with their own version, substituting "I once was lost, now I'm pro-choice/was blind but now I see."[28]
Quester argued that the Church Ladies' use of "humor" was "much more
effective" than other strategies because "the angry activist thing just feeds
the psycho-Christians," whereas humor "deflates them."[29]

The Church Ladies allowed beards and arm and leg hair to show through their costumes. Yet, police and antiabortion protestors often missed the fact that they were men in drag, misunderstanding the Church Ladies' use of irony and making it that much funnier for spectators who got it. During the Chain of Fools demonstration, the Church Ladies decided to dress as "Transvestites for Life": "as opposed to the Church Ladies being the most upstanding, righteous, pristine and chaste women . . . there could be, the Transvestites for Life wore animal pelts, too much makeup, and they didn't comb out their wigs. They were just, for lack of a better word, the women of ill repute." The Transvestites for Life had their own song repertoire, which included "If you think you own your own womb, show me the deed," and "If you want to get a life, be a wife." Despite the protests of a female police officer who realized that "They're being ironic!" a police sergeant decided that the Transvestites for Life "truly were pro-life" and made them stand behind the barricades with the antiabortion demonstrators for the rest of the day.[30]

The Church Ladies' use of drag allowed them to mock conventions of both gender and religion, a particularly effective combination for pro-abortion and gay rights activism because their opponents in the Christian right based their claims in terms of tradition and faith. Inspired by a group from Pittsburgh and in collaboration with a group from Washington, D.C., they created a "starter kit" for others who wanted to form their own "cheer-leaders for choice." The kit advises would-be Church Ladies to "think of the humor that can be mined by bringing to light certain social conventions that women are constrained to fill without question. . . . Whip your 'opti-comical' self into a drag-driven critique of the patriarchy."[31] For Griffin, putting on drag at clinic defenses "gave [him] the space to react to the surreal quality of it and to really respond back. . . . The minute I put on a dress and a wig it became, like, okay, now it makes sense. It's hard to believe that we could show up and normalize things, but in many ways we did."[32]

ACT UP and WHAM!'s creation of queer and feminist images and texts, exemplified by the Church Ladies' performances, was especially significant in the context of the culture wars of the late 1980s. Conservative Christians attacked representations of gay and lesbian sexuality, which they argued were obscene and unfit for public viewing. Artist David Wojnarowicz described the repressive atmosphere that left him unable to articulate his experience with AIDS: "I'm a prisoner of language that doesn't have a letter or a sign or a gesture that approximates what I'm sensing."[33] While artists such as Wojnarowicz strained to express their sense of urgency and despair over the AIDS epidemic and the loss of so many members of their community, as well as to show positive, vital images of gay sexuality, the Christian right waged moral campaigns that also focused on sexuality, the body, and gender.[34]

The culture wars highlighted the significance of symbolic representations to the distribution of federal funds and, indeed, to citizenship rights. In 1989, Senator Jesse Helms (R-NC) began a campaign against the National Endowment for the Arts (NEA), targeting its support of exhibitions of the work of artists Andres Serrano and Robert Mapplethorpe. Particularly offensive, Helms charged, was Serrano's "Piss Christ," a photograph of a plastic crucifix submerged in the artist's urine. Serrano intended his photograph as a protest against the "commercialization of sacred imagery," but Helms viewed it as sacrilegious. Helms also objected to Mapplethorpe's photographs of men engaged in sex acts with other men, which he argued were obscene. Conservative columnist Patrick Buchanan supported Helms's efforts by employing a language of disease, corruption, and moral decay to describe Mapplethorpe's photographs, labeling the images "trash" and arguing that a "polluted culture, left to fester and stink, can destroy a nation's soul."[35] In contrast, Wojnarowicz wrote that Mapplethorpe's photographs provided him with "comfort in a hostile world. They give me strength."[36]

Helms succeeded in winning Senate approval for restrictions that barred the use of federal arts funds to "promote, disseminate or produce obscene or indecent materials, including but not limited to depictions of sadomasochism, homoeroticism, the exploitation of children, or individuals engaged in sex acts; or material which denigrates the objects or beliefs of the adherents of a particular religion or non-religion."[37] The list coupled homoeroticism with pedophilia, a pervasive allegation made by those who regard homosexuality as sinful and criminal. Under pressure from the courts, Congress added the provision that the banned works, "when taken as a whole, do not have serious literary, artistic political or scientific value." In light of the legislation, the NEA required 1989–90 grant awardees to sign agreements not to produce "obscene" art.[38] The 1990 Congressional reauthorization of the NEA required the agency's chairman to take into "consideration general standards of decency and respect for the diverse beliefs and values of the American public."[39] These laws equating the homoerotic to action such as pedophilia led to a chilling effect on representations of gay sexuality.[40]

The NEA clamped down particularly on artists whose work addressed the AIDS epidemic. In November 1989, NEA chairman John Frohnmayer retracted a $10,000 grant to New York's Artists Space for an AIDS exhibition,

Witnesses: Against Our Vanishing. The show's catalogue included criticism of Cardinal O'Connor, as well as Senator Helms and Rep. William Dannemeyer (R-CA), who sponsored the Helms amendment in the House. Frohnmayer first argued that he needed to protect the NEA from further attacks by Helms, and then stated that the exhibition was "political" and therefore should not be sponsored by the NEA.[41] In June 1990, he rejected funding four of the agency's recommended theater grants, which were to have gone to performance artists Karen Finley, Holly Hughes, John Fleck, and Tim Miller, three of whom were openly gay, and whose work addressed sexuality and AIDS.[42]

Successfully arousing public support for their position, Republicans kept up pressure against the NEA, and in 1996 Congress cut its budget by 39 percent.[43] This attack on public funding for the arts was part of both the Republican drive to dismantle "unnecessary government agencies" and the Religious Right's reactionary sexual agenda.[44] The culture wars constituted a battle over whether gay people could be recognized as citizens with public sexual identities. This matter is especially significant, Carol Vance writes, because "people deprived of images become demoralized and isolated, and they become increasingly vulnerable to attacks on their private expressions of nonconformity, which are inevitable once sources of public solidarity and resistance have been eliminated."[45] The positive depictions of gay sexuality and reproductive rights that were created and disseminated by ACT UP, WHAM!, and the Church Ladies for Choice helped to counter the efforts of Helms and other conservatives to limit what could be represented.

"It helped me become a person":
Forging a Queer Identity

"Queer" connoted an oppositional stance to mainstream culture and institutions that was galvanized in particular by the Religious Right's assertion of a heterosexual, patriarchal norm for American citizenship during the culture wars. Activists in ACT UP, WHAM!, and a constellation of related groups fashioned queer as a social and political identity that was intended to be more inclusive than many perceived the identity-based political movements of the 1960s and 1970s to have been.[46] ACT UP member Maxine Wolfe explained that by the mid-1980s, she had grown frustrated by the "rigid set of politics around which everyone had to agree" in both lesbian-feminist and Marxist groups. She reflected: "Identity politics had gotten to the point where, apparently, the only other person I was supposed to feel comfortable talking to was another working-class, Jewish, lesbian mother of two children from the left. . . . Everybody was in their own separate box and I didn't have a box to fit into."[47] Queer worked to blur, and in the process transcend, these distinctions, in part by emphasizing the constructed nature of identity and unsettling assumptions about the "natural" relationship between sex, gender and desire.[48] Lisa Duggan explains that queer "questions the uniformity of sexual identities" and replaces categories such as "gay" with "flexible, anti-normative, politicized sexualities."[49]

Queer activists sought to broaden the gay and lesbian movement to incorporate bisexual and transgender people and, even more fundamentally, to critique the cultural and political use of sexual and gender categorizations that maintained heterosexual and male privilege. For some, the queer politics of AIDS and reproductive rights activism also provided a retreat from the divisiveness of the feminist "sex wars" of the late 1970s and early 1980s in which one camp, led by Catherine MacKinnon and Andrea Dworkin, argued that pornography led to violence against women and should be banned, while other feminists including Ellen Willis and Gayle Rubin self-identified as "sex positive" and argued against censorship and in favor of sexual pleasure for women, including through pornography.[50] As a social identity, queer was often expressed through non–gender normative self-presentation. Emily Nahmanson described ACT UP as "a whole culture of sex positivity and letting your freak flag fly."[51] Shannon Cain recalled attending her first WHAM! meeting in 1991: "I remember seeing women dressed like men, which was an eye-opener for me. . . . And lesbians. Just totally out lesbians."[52] Similarly, Keith Cylar, who identified as a black man from the South and who had recently lost his lover to AIDS, recalled his first ACT UP meeting: "I saw this table full of paper and all of these people in black leather, this guy in drag with big earrings shouting at everyone and all these dykes. At that point in time, I was very much into wearing black leather. . . . There were all these faggots, people running around, and so I wanted to hear the information. So I listened and I took all of the information off the table."[53]

Queer drew on the gay and lesbian liberation movement's insight that heterosexual monogamy and nuclear families were neither the only nor the preferred way to organize a personal life, and emphasized alternative relationships, often based in bonds of friendship in addition to those based in romantic love and desire. According to ACT UP member Patrick Moore, "flirtations, love affairs, and simple fucking were fairly common between gay men and lesbians who had formed new, powerful relationships that came without the rules of precedent."[54] ACT UP and WHAM! incorporated the erotic potential inherent in queer identity and infused it into their activism; sexual energy helped make queer activism "exciting and compelling" and bound members together.[55] This celebration of sexual expression was particularly important in the context of the AIDS epidemic and the prevalent association of sex with death. In its embrace of safer sex practices, ACT UP provided an alternative understanding of sexuality that was not nihilistic and did not negate the power inherent in sexual expression, which the gay liberation movement had sought to explore. It also reinforced queer activists' desires to be visibly out in public, to partake in the same kinds of public displays of affection as straight couples, and to protect themselves and others from violent homophobic attacks.

For both WHAM! and ACT UP, the formation of an accepting queer community was integral to their activism. For some members, participation in the groups helped to define their identity. Emotional ties between members intensified the passion of their activism but sometimes caused painful schisms within the groups. Heidi Dorow, who when she was in her twenties participated regularly in ACT UP and occasionally in WHAM!, described her experience:

> I really felt like for the first time in my life that I had a community that I was a part of and that I had a role in, and that—I mean, I had friends. I had romantic relationships. I had a mission, a lot which I shared. The urgency that I felt was shared by lots of people. And not only does that create really intense bonds, but it also gives you a kind of energy and inspiration to do more than you ever thought that you could do.
>
> It helped me form my identity as a lesbian and this community that I was part of was not exclusively, but certainly overwhelmingly, gay and queer, and so it helped me form my identity that I didn't have before. I'd had relationships with women before, but I didn't identify as queer. I didn't really know what that meant. And so it helped me become a person. And, there were a lot of intricacies in that. I was always mad and angry about a lot of things, and suddenly I was in a place, in an environment where I was rewarded and praised for that and that felt really good and it felt like home.[56]

Four ACT UP members wrote and distributed the "Queer Nation Manifesto" at New York's Gay Pride Parade in June 1990, proclaiming that "being queer means leading a different sort of life. It's not about the mainstream, profit-margins, patriotism, patriarchy, or being assimilated . . . it's about being on the margins."[57] Precisely what it meant to be "on the margins" became a point of contention, however, in part because many queer activists were white, college-educated professionals, and people of color within ACT UP felt that issues affecting them were often not recognized or prioritized by the majority white membership. Some ACT UP members embraced the manifesto's claim that "being queer" means fighting all forms of oppression, and, like Jan Peterson of the National Congress of Neighborhood Women (NCNW), sought to incorporate a holistic understanding of identity into their activism. For example, the ACT UP New York Women and AIDS Book Group wrote that "fighting AIDS means increasing our own awareness of the connections between all social injustices."[58] However, not all AIDS activists saw their cause this broadly, and these fundamental differences contributed to ACT UP's splintering.

"They were all dying, pretty regularly"

ACT UP and WHAM! collaborated on another large demonstration on January 23, 1991. Declaring a "Day of Desperation," activists disrupted PBS and CBS evening news broadcasts on the night of January 22, demanding that the U.S. government fight AIDS rather than wage war in the Persian Gulf. Three men interrupted the opening of the CBS *Evening News* broadcast, shouting "Fight AIDS, Not Arabs," before anchor Dan Rather announced a commercial break and the CBS security guards apprehended them.[59] The following morning, 800 activists rallied on Wall Street and marched for two hours, leaving empty coffins outside City Hall and the Federal Office Building. Meanwhile, uptown in Harlem, 2,000 protestors marched down Martin Luther King Boulevard to the State Office Building, demanding housing and services for people with AIDS, while twenty-five members of the ACT UP Latino/a caucus broke into the office of Bronx Borough president Fernando Ferrer.

At the height of rush hour, 500 activists took over Grand Central Station, hanging a banner that read "One AIDS Death Every Eight Minutes" over the arrivals board and lying down on the ground to stop foot traffic in and out of the station. Demonstrators released pink-and-red helium balloons that pulled a large sign reading "Money for AIDS, not for war!" toward the station's high ceiling, while others blocked ticket booths and the entrances to tracks. Activists wrapped the information booth in brown paper and red tape and yelled, "We're dying of red tape!," while others poured fake blood on the floor. Police arrested 263 people as demonstrators marched from the station and sat down in the intersection of 42nd Street and Lexington Avenue, blocking traffic.[60]

The Day of Desperation was ACT UP and WHAM!'s last large-scale collaborative demonstration, although they continued to work together on many smaller-scale acts of civil disobedience. While many members felt exhilarated by their success in getting their message out during a national news broadcast, others criticized the antiwar linkage, feeling that it diluted their focus on AIDS. For WHAM! member Meryl Levin, the demonstration marked a turning point in the public's response to direct action:

> I feel like it was an exact moment when there was some switch . . . I remember [previous] actions down at City Hall or outside the Federal Court at lunchtime, and people stopping and taking flyers and we could engage them in conversation.
>
> At a certain point in time, after four years of street action, New Yorkers got sick of it. They stopped taking flyers and they got annoyed by our presence. And that was really a shift, because we weren't only dependent on the work that we did, we also needed receptors to be out there, people who a) we could bring in for new energy and b) on the education level, were willing to hear what we were saying. And something began to shift and the tactics that we had honed and were so good at were almost working against us.[61]

Their perception of public fatigue with demonstrations, particularly those that disrupted daily life, heightened some ACT UP members' sense of desperation, as deaths from AIDS accelerated and few treatment advances had been made. By the early 1990s, AZT was no longer working for many people with AIDS, and the protease inhibitors (drug cocktails) that have since proven effective were still in development. ACT UP member Ron Goldberg described the impact of so many deaths:

> I think for a long while—at least, and what allowed me to stay in the group is—I thought we were clearly making a difference. People who were there were living longer. What became hard for me . . . people who'd been alive for a while, and who I grew up in the group with—and a lot of my personal friends, outside—they were all dying, pretty regularly. And it was . . . this sense of—nothing I do is going to help any of these people. It became incredibly difficult.[62]

As Deborah Gould argues, the emotional habitus of ACT UP was anger, making it difficult for members to share their sadness with one another.[63] Member Maria Maggenti explained: "The understanding was that you would take your grief and you would turn into rage, and you would take that rage and you would do something with it. And, therefore, grief or grieving did not really fit into that idea."[64] Unable to express their feelings of loss, some members left the organization, while others doubled down even harder in their efforts to find successful treatment. Maxine Wolfe reported a resulting decline in the sense of community: "There was a combination of serious politics and joyful living that was so great in ACT UP . . . that people would party really hard. . . . And then, it got to the point where people would say, oh, well, you don't have time for that kind of stuff. And, when you don't have time for that kind of stuff, you basically dehumanize a movement. A movement is about people."[65]

Members of the Treatment and Data Committee, who amassed information on drug effectiveness, wanted ACT UP to moderate its confrontational style in order to improve relations with researchers, government agencies, and pharmaceutical companies. The committee's emphasis was "Drugs into Bodies," and its members were less interested in pursuing underlying social structural causes of the AIDS epidemic than in prioritizing scientific research with a goal of curing the disease. Several Treatment and Data Committee members took positions on government and industry advisory boards.[66] They eventually came to embody the authority and expertise of medical professionals, and they assumed leadership within the organization, bristling when challenged from the floor.[67] As Jennifer Brier has detailed, Treatment and Data Committee members clashed with members of the Women's Caucus over the ethics of a trial testing the use of AZT to prevent transmission of HIV during pregnancy, and the two factions were unable to reconcile.[68]

In January 1992, the Treatment Access Group (TAG) led by Peter Staley, a former Wall Street bond trader, and Mark Harrington split off from ACT UP to focus exclusively on pressuring pharmaceutical corporations and the FDA to increase research on HIV and to release new, more effective antiretroviral drugs. TAG became involved in designing clinical treatment trials with the National Institutes for Health. Jim Eigo, a member of the Treatment and Data Committee who stayed in ACT UP observed that after TAG's departure, "ACT UP divided and large numbers of members left."[69] Some ACT UP members and observers at the time— and subsequent historical accounts of ACT UP such as the 2012 Academy Award–nominated documentary film *How to Survive a Plague* by David France—saw treatment activists as the core of the organization, the true ACT UP, if you will. My interpretation differs in that I believe that ACT UP's most important insights and actions came from the understanding of the epidemic as

Figure 18. Hispanic AIDS Morgue demonstration, cosponsored by the Hispanic AIDS Forum and ACT UP NY, February 26, 1991, photograph by Bill Bytsura. Bill Bytsura ACT UP Photography Collection, Box 13, Folder 7, Fales Library, NYU. Courtesy of Bill Bytsura.

fundamentally social and political rather than medical, shaped by homophobia, racism, and sexism from the start. This radical understanding grew out of the work of the Majority Action Committee and the Women's Caucus; it transformed many but not all members and led the group collectively but not universally to a broad defense of social justice.

Increasingly, ACT UP's iconography focused on death. (See figure 18.) ACT UP members who stayed with the organization following TAG's departure mounted a series of dramatic political funerals, designed to convey the depths of despair within the gay community and to infuse mourning itself with militancy. They were inspired by Wojnarowicz's suggestion that every time someone died of AIDS, there should be a demonstration. Prior to his own death in 1992, the artist reflected: "I imagine what it would be like if, each time a lover, friend or stranger died of this disease, their friends, lovers or neighbors would take the dead body and drive with it in

Figure 19. Demonstrators throwing ashes over the gate onto the
White House lawn, ACT UP Ashes Action, Washington, D.C., October 11, 1992,
photograph by Meg Handler. Courtesy of Meg Handler.

a car a hundred miles an hour to washington d.c. and blast through the gates of the white house and come to a screeching halt before the entrance and dump their lifeless form on the front steps."[70] In October 1992, ACT UP indeed traveled to Washington, D.C. to stage the "Ashes Action," which coincided with the exhibiting of the AIDS memorial quilt on the National Mall. ACT UP member Bob Rafsky argued that the quilt "makes our dying look beautiful" and called for an "angry funeral, not a sad one." People holding urns and boxes with the ashes of loved ones who had died of AIDS led an 8,000-strong procession from the capitol to the White House, where they evaded police in riot gear in order to scatter the ashes on the South Lawn while ACT UP members loudly read the names of people who died of AIDS.[71] (See figures 12 and 19.) In the following years, ACT UP conducted additional political funerals, including carrying the body of Mark Lowe Fisher in an open casket from Judson Memorial Church in Washington Square Park uptown to the New York office of the Republican National Committee on the eve of Election Day 1992, and unsuccessfully attempting to deposit the casket containing Tim Bailey's body on the White House lawn on July 1, 1993.[72]

Bill Clinton's election as president in 1992 changed the dynamics of both ACT UP and WHAM!. As Meryl Levin put it, when Clinton took office, "The bottom fell out. . . . People thought, oh, good, we can just relax. So it was tough to get money and support" for activism.[73] In the context of the American two-party system, it is difficult to sustain oppositional politics when the candidate you are backing takes office. The Clinton administration's crackdown on Operation Rescue and rhetorical, albeit limited, support for gay and reproductive rights "made the target fuzzier" for AIDS and abortion rights activists, diffusing some of the anger and outrage that had fueled their earlier activism.[74] Like their allies in ACT UP, many WHAM! members reported feeling burned out by the years of militant direct action, the focus on combating Operation Rescue, and the loss of friends to AIDS. As member Mindy Nass recalled, "Exhausted, I need[ed] to move on, and I wasn't the only one." At that point, a significant number of WHAM! members departed, many to begin graduate school.[75]

Many AIDS and reproductive rights activists felt that the movement had been co-opted by policy changes that fell far short of their goals. On January 22, 1993, the twentieth anniversary of the *Roe v. Wade* decision and three days after taking office, Clinton lifted multiple Reagan-Bush–era restrictions on abortion. He repealed the gag rule on abortion counseling at federally financed clinics, allowed women to receive abortions at U.S. military hospitals if they paid for them themselves, allowed U.S. funds to go to international family planning programs that offer abortion, and called for review of the ban on RU-486, known as the "abortion pill."[76]

Violence against abortion providers surged following Clinton's lifting of the gag rule. Antiabortion extremists killed two doctors and three abortion clinic workers between March 1993 and December 1994, and attempted the murder of nine others. The violence accelerated the shift in public opinion against Operation Rescue, which denied any link to the murderers but whose slogan proclaimed, "If you think that abortion is murder, act like it."[77] In May 1994, Congress passed the Freedom of Access to Clinic Entrances (FACE) Act, making attacking or blockading abortion clinics a federal crime, punishable by prison terms and heavy fines.[78] The following month, the Supreme Court in *Madsen v. Women's Health Center* upheld a lower-court injunction barring antiabortion activists from demonstrating within thirty-six feet of a clinic.[79] Within a year, all branches of the federal government worked to control the intrusiveness of Operation Rescue and violent antiabortionists.

Following passage of the FACE Act, the Clinton administration stationed U.S. marshals at abortion clinics to protect doctors, workers, and patients.[80] In August 1994, Attorney General Janet Reno instructed the FBI to begin a conspiracy inquiry into six antiabortion extremists who had signed a pledge declaring the killing of abortion providers to be "justifiable homicide."[81] Reno's actions marked a significant departure from the Justice Department's prior inaction to protect clinics under the Reagan administration, and from intervention into legal cases on behalf of Operation Rescue under the George H. W. Bush administration.[82] The mounting fines from civil suit cases, as well as the presence of plainclothes U.S. marshals patrolling the areas around abortion clinics, discouraged antiabortion activists from mounting the aggressive clinic blockades of the early 1990s and led to a decrease in Operation Rescue's membership.[83]

Increased security for women's health clinics was part of Clinton's "third way," a politics of triangulation that moved the Democratic Party closer to the right and embraced neoliberal economic policies while offering comparatively moderate social positions.[84] On abortion, Clinton put forward the libertarian tenet that the government should not make reproductive decisions for middle-class families, yet at the same time he embraced parental rights and refused public funds for abortion except in cases of rape and incest.[85] This contention that only "innocent victims"—girls and women who have been raped—deserve access to publicly funded abortions replicated the moralistic rhetoric around "innocent" AIDS victims. Like the punishment of pregnant women on behalf of the fetus during the "crack baby" scare of the 1980s and 1990s, these policies contributed to the increasing tendency to blame complex social problems on individuals and their bad choices or moral failings.[86] Combined with Clinton's welfare reform—the Personal Responsibility and Work Opportunity Act of 1996, which limited federal support to a maximum of five years—these policies denied poor women full reproductive autonomy. Clinton also adopted a halfhearted position in favor of gay rights, authoring the 1993 "Don't Ask, Don't Tell" policy for gays in the military, which partially reversed a ban on gays in the military by allowing them to serve provided they did not reveal their sexuality.[87] Then, in 1996, as Hawaii moved toward legalizing same-sex marriage, Clinton signed the federal Defense of Marriage Act, which allowed states to refuse to recognize marriages performed in other states.[88]

Influenced by the work of the Committee for Abortion Rights and Against Sterilization Abuse (CARASA) in the 1970s and 1980s, WHAM! developed a broad understanding of reproductive rights, which included the right to control one's reproduction, to have access to quality health care and information regarding health-care options, to rear a family, and to express one's sexuality openly.[89] One of its posters read, "Real freedom of choice means more than just access to abortion" and listed the following steps that must be taken so "that each of us has more control over our bodies, lives, and minds":

Freedom of choice means affordable, quality health care for all.

Freedom of choice means the right to have children, too.

Freedom of choice means being able to care for your family.

Freedom of choice means the right to love whom you want to
without recrimination, regardless of gender, race, or ethnicity.

Freedom of choice means access to proven and affordable medical
options, rather than a research environment held hostage by
the medical establishment and right-wing extremists.

Freedom of choice means protection against and education about
AIDS.

Freedom of choice means freedom from sexual violence in all
its forms.

Freedom of choice means getting and understanding the
information you need to make that choice.[90]

WHAM! members struggled to formulate a broad agenda and to develop new tactics that could effectively respond to attacks on welfare and affirmative displays of sexualities, both of which WHAM! deemed necessary to "full freedom of choice."[91] Just as AIDS activism had brought gay men and lesbians together after political and social divisions in the 1970s, reproductive rights activism helped unite straight feminists and lesbians after frequent lesbian-baiting from critics of feminism and many instances of homophobic responses within the women's movement during the same years.[92]

Member Susan Shaw remembered lesbian feminists within the group in particular urging WHAM! to "take on more issues than just abortion," in particular those issues in which "gender oppression intersect[s] with racial and class oppression."[93] WHAM! members were receptive to this intersectional analysis, but ultimately unable to fully realize Shaw's vision. WHAM! had been founded to respond to the threats to abortion rights posed by Operation Rescue, the Catholic Church, and the Reagan and Bush administrations, and the intensity of defending clients and clinics left members little time to devote to other issues, although some members did participate in sex education for youths, in staffing a domestic violence hotline, and in gynecological self-exams and menstrual extractions.

Given its predominant focus on abortion, WHAM!'s membership was overwhelmingly white.[94] Because of the racialized history of reproductive rights in the United States, including the forced sterilization of African Americans, Puerto Ricans, and Native Americans, activism by women of color has tended to emphasize comprehensive reproductive rights. Attracting a more diverse membership and taking on new issues was a challenge, as Dana Luchiano explained; despite members' good intentions, they did not understand how to move out of their comfort zone and build broader coalitions: "All of our flyers were bilingual, but our meetings were in English. There were no [primarily] Spanish-speaking members of WHAM! . . . What went under the name of outreach wasn't really. Working in coalition with other groups was limited to coming to demonstrations, not cross-migration of memberships."[95]

In 1993, WHAM! formed the Resisting Racism Working Group "out of concern for the different levels of socialized and internalized racism which we became conscious of in ourselves and in those around us."[96] According to member Leslie Wolfe, the group organized a series of intensive workshops led by outside facilitators for WHAM! members to try to understand how racism was limiting the organization's ability to work with women of color.[97] Charlotte Abbott described the workshops as "a pivotal experience" in her development as an activist. She credited the workshops with leading her "to acknowledge how my consciousness was permeated on every level by racism, and to see how my fellow WHAM!ers, whatever their backgrounds, were also struggling with that." They also offered an opportunity for WHAM! to examine its own internal dynamics: how informal leaders developed, how using parliamentary procedure to have discussions and vote on actions could be effective in the short run but leave tensions simmering and unresolved, and how differences of class, sexuality, and age affected the way members treated each other:

Robert's Rules was only going to work so far. When conflicts came up on the floor, Robert's Rules gave us a way to give people space and to move through it, but it didn't clear the air of the personal bitterness that was sometimes left behind by that . . . There was an expectation that we had work to get done, and Robert's Rules was going to get us over the speed bumps. I think it was left to us to work out a lot of that stuff outside of the group, and it didn't always happen and it inhibited us.[98]

As was the case for ACT UP, internal dynamics, members' changing life stages, and new political contexts all contributed to the waning of WHAM! Following his election in 1994, Republican mayor Rudolph Giuliani launched a law-and-order campaign featuring aggressive police tactics, including holding people arrested for civil disobedience overnight in jail, making direct action much riskier to undertake. The Giuliani administration's zero-tolerance policy for wheatpasting and spray-painting eliminated one of WHAM! and ACT UP's most potent means of communication. Poster and street art had attracted new members and delivered messages to the public. Direct-action groups such as WHAM! and ACT UP require both a clear target and a governmental and police power that is dedicated to preserving the right to freedom of expression, including participation in civil disobedience, and lack of both such elements contributed to WHAM! disbanding in 1994–95. ACT UP persists to this day, albeit with a much smaller membership that is dedicated to maintaining the public memory of AIDS activism.

"These folks went out to do other work": Legacies

Robert Vazquez-Pacheco declared that "the legacy of ACT UP, or the great feat of ACT UP, was the ability to bring all of these people together and imbue these people with knowledge, empower them if you want to use that word. And then these folks went out to do other work."[99] Kendall Thomas concluded that "the sex-positive, gay-affirmative, politically empowering force that was in that room and that were in the streets . . . saved my life."[100] In reflecting on the meaning of her experiences with WHAM!, Abbott concluded that in many ways, "We . . . had more of an impact on ourselves than we did on the larger world."[101] Certainly, one of the most important legacies of ACT UP and WHAM! was the personal development of members. Michelle Tepper recalled how formative her experience in the group was to her later activism in the Graduate Employee Organization (GEO) at the University of Michigan, where she succeeded in obtaining health benefits for Graduate Student Instructors (GSIs). Tepper stated: "WHAM! was empowering not only because of the can-do spirit, but precisely the fact that women were going out on the street and doing this fairly outrageous direct action in a very unladylike way. . . . Seeing women out there on the street taking action was a remarkable thing to have and be a part of."[102] Like Tepper, many ACT UP and WHAM! members continued their health-care activism in different venues in the following years, including serving as AIDS research, education, and treatment advocates and coordinators; as social workers; as natural family planning teachers; as lawyers working for reproductive rights organizations; and as administrators in antipoverty programs.

Like MFY and the NCNW before them, ACT UP and WHAM!'s legacy extends far beyond the groups' membership. The changes ACT UP won in the drug treatment process, including involving patients in trial design and including women and people of color in drug testing, reducing the cost of and securing more effective AIDS treatments, and making women, IV drug users, and homeless people with HIV and AIDS eligible for social welfare benefits, have benefited countless people. WHAM!'s legacy also includes its effects on the hundreds of women whom members helped escort into women's health clinics and reassured that others stood by women's integrity in making their own reproductive decisions. ACT UP and WHAM! also contributed to important ongoing debates about the relationship of gender, sexual identity, and motherhood to U.S. citizenship, as well as about the obligations of the state to its citizens.

These debates over sexuality and citizenship are far from settled, and progress on one front has often been accompanied by setbacks on another. In July 2013, for example, Senator Rob Portman (R-OH) embraced efforts to ban abortion twenty weeks after fertilization, seeking to regain the support of his conservative constituents who had objected to his vocal support for same-sex marriage.[103] While homophobic sentiment remains pervasive in American culture, support for same-sex marriage has increased dramatically, along with cultural visibility of and greater tolerance for gays and lesbians. Indeed, the organizers of New York City's St. Patrick's Day Parade, which originates at St. Patrick's Cathedral every year and which had long banned openly gay groups, announced in September 2014 that they were allowing gays and lesbians to march in the parade under their own banner.[104]

ACT UP and WHAM! members take pride in real victories and also recognize these gains to be incomplete and, at times, tenuous. ACT UP's calling attention to the homosexual partners of people dying from AIDS who were unable to make medical decisions or to inherit the partners' estates certainly contributed to support for gay marriage, but in their embrace of a queer imaginary, ACT UP members enacted far more radical relationships that departed from rather than emulated the norms of heterosexual marriage. The 2010 passage of the Patient Protection and Affordable Care Act moved the United States closer to universal health-care coverage, long a goal of ACT UP and WHAM!, while at the same time reenergizing opposition to women's efforts to regulate their reproduction via birth control and abortion.[105] In recent years, the most progressive aspects of ACT UP and WHAM!'s legacy have been taken up by groups like Queers for Economic Justice, dedicated to recognizing the ways that sex and gender shape "issues like immigration, poverty, homelessness, gentrification, and drug use" as well as HIV/AIDS.[106]

Critics on the left have contended that identity politics tend to fracture progressive movements and lead groups to turn inward, away from issues of broad import. But people entering the so-called public sphere of work and politics do not shed their sexual and gender identities any more than those of race and class. As ACT UP, WHAM!, and the Church Ladies for Choice implicitly understood, and as Queers for Economic Justice proclaimed, gay and reproductive rights are not single-issue politics divorced from discussions of political economy, but rather central to broad issues of social justice. As historian Sara Dubow argues, they are also key symbols for the Religious Right concerned "about the cultural fragility of a white Christian America" and opposed to liberalism's redistribution of resources to minority groups.[107] ACT UP and WHAM! left an important visual archive that contests what Lauren Berlant has deemed the Right's sentimentalizing and infantilizing of citizenship with images that value the unborn fetus more than the living woman. This archive in itself constitutes an important legacy to future activists.[108]

Through their coalition with ACT UP, WHAM! members engaged in the creation of alternative family structures or "ways of life" outside of major institutions such as heterosexual marriage. For Michel Foucault, the creation of these new "modes of life" that confound the power relations of normative institutions is the most significant achievement of this social movement. Foucault explained, "The problem is not to discover in oneself the truth of sex but rather to use sexuality henceforth to arrive at a multiplicity of relationships. . . . Therefore we have to work at becoming homosexuals and not be obstinate in recognizing that we are. The development toward which the problem of homosexuality tends is the one of friendship."[109] The creation of a caring community and of deep and sustaining friendships between gay men, lesbians, and heterosexual women and men—relationships that allowed activists to continue their work amid the terrible toll of the AIDS epidemic—along with the memory of that community, was perhaps as significant as the groups' public, political, and sustained struggles to stem the forces of repression and inequality.

Epilogue

ACT UP Will Be Here Again

On a cool but sunny spring morning in April 2012 in Lower Manhattan, more than 1,000 people demonstrated for an end to the AIDS crisis through full funding of treatment, prevention, and research. They gathered at City Hall to hear speeches calling for a "Robin Hood" tax of .05 percent on financial speculation involving stocks, bonds, foreign currency trades, and derivatives, with the revenue to be earmarked for health care. The day marked the twenty-fifth anniversary of the first direct action by the AIDS Coalition to Unleash Power (ACT UP), which took place on Wall Street in the spring of 1987 to draw attention to pharmaceutical corporations' profiteering on AIDS drugs and to demand lower prices and increased access to treatment. Stalwart and graying ACT UP veterans, including playwright Larry Kramer and longtime AIDS activist Eric Sawyer, were joined by newer groups, including members of National Nurses United and a large contingent from Housing Works, an outgrowth of ACT UP dedicated to providing affordable housing and treatment to low-income people with HIV/AIDS.[1]

Most prominent among ACT UP's new coalition were members of Occupy Wall Street, a movement that captivated the nation in the fall of 2011 with its sixty-day encampment at Zuccotti Park near Wall Street and its similar demonstrations in cities across the United States. In the midst of slow and uneven economic recovery from the Great Recession of 2007–9,

Occupy's slogan, "We are the 99 percent," highlighted increasing income stratification and juxtaposed the interests of the majority of Americans against those of the very wealthiest, reinvigorating discussion of the need for greater fairness in economic and social policy. Longtime ACT UP Philadelphia member Julie Davids explained that the two movements share strategies, including calling attention to the financial sector's role in exacerbating social problems: "ACT UP has always looked at the AIDS crisis through an economic justice lens and has always recognized that obstacles were rooted in greed and the profit motive."[2] ACT UP and Occupy Wall Street were similar in their use of direct action, especially a disruptive and theatrical presence in public space, to gain media coverage, influence public opinion, and put pressure on politicians and officials. Like ACT UP, Occupy Wall Street began in New York City but soon spread across the country and around the globe. Both movements emphasize self- and group education and promote a critical consciousness regarding social relations, encouraging members to imagine new ways of being in the world and alternative models for organizing society.[3]

Excitement filled the air as the diverse crowd—men and women, young and old, African American, Latino, Asian, and white—held aloft signs featuring a green-and-black target over the image of the Wall Street bull reading "ACT UP & OCCUPY, TAX WALL ST, END AIDS." (See figure 20.) Chants of "People with AIDS under attack. What do we do? ACT UP, fight back!" grew louder as more people gathered. One group was outfitted in green felt Robin Hood suits; some sported vintage ACT UP T-shirts and black leather jackets; nurses came in scrubs; many wore hoodies; and others were in ordinary office attire.[4] Using Occupy Wall Street's strategy of the "human microphone," the crowd repeated back the speakers' words in unison, both amplifying them and making them their own.

Amanda Lugg, a British and Ugandan ACT UP New York member and Director of Advocacy and Mobilization for the African Services Committee, emphasized that the global AIDS crisis is far from over.[5] "There are eight million people in need of AIDS drugs that don't have them. Is that right? No! A lack of political will means that more than 12,000 people in this country are on waiting lists for AIDS drugs. Is that right?" "No!" the crowd roared. The seventy-seven-year-old Kramer, whose 1987 speech had spurred the formation of ACT UP, remarked on how good it was to "feel the energy coming back" and reminded those gathered to use their anger, as it remains "the healthiest tool" available to fight injustice.[6]

This book has traced the mobilization of New Yorkers who grew angry at injustice and directed their energies to achieving the cause of greater

Figure 20. ACT UP's twenty-fifth anniversary joint demonstration with Occupy, April 25, 2012, photograph by Lars Schumann. Courtesy of Lars Schumann.

equality. New York's dense residential areas along with shared municipal services including public transportation and schools and parks, and its long tradition of ethnic and other forms of identity-based organizing, make the city amenable to both neighborhood-based activism and citywide, issue-oriented coalitions. Over the past five decades, inspired by national movements including the black freedom struggle, feminism, and gay and lesbian liberation, New Yorkers educated themselves, raised conscious-ness, and took to the streets, enacting participatory democracy. The par-ticularly public character of space in New York made it a natural theater for demonstrations that engaged the imagination through use of satire, costumes and props, arresting images, and sheer numbers of participants. Activists drew upon both their own creativity and the rich resources at hand in the nation's media capital to reach passersby and broadcast their messages worldwide. As a result of their actions, social policies changed and democracy expanded. The federal government incorporated an expec-tation of maximum feasible participation into its social programs, and residents crafted Community Action Programs to meet their needs. Decades after the beginning of the AIDS crisis, federal drug regulators and medical researchers have likewise acknowledged that patients must play a greater role in designing and implementing drug treatment trials and, more broadly, in public health and health-care policymaking.

By claiming rights, most importantly the right to participate in decision making about social institutions and policies that shape their everyday lives, these New Yorkers enacted citizenship. They encountered strong opposition to their efforts to craft a state that was robust and responsive to the needs of its citizens, particularly those in marginalized social groups, and some of the gains they made have been rolled back. Indeed, as ACT UP and Occupy Wall Street jointly argue, the primacy of the market and the interests of investors increasingly drive public policy and result in spiraling inequality, to the detriment of our common welfare. Therefore it is especially important to listen to the rich historical stories of Mobilization for Youth, the National Congress of Neighborhood Women, and ACT UP and WHAM!, which can inspire and assist those working in the present and the future to preserve and broaden social citizenship.[7]

Specifically, the histories of these groups teach us that differences of identity need not prevent the formation of coalitions for progressive social change. Rather, when differences of identity are acknowledged, explored, and accounted for, the result is stronger, more vibrant organizations that transform their members personally and enable novel understandings of problems and creative imaginings of solutions. Historian Robert Self explains that in recent decades, rights-based social movements have allowed marginalized groups to coalesce around an identity such as gay in order to claim full citizenship; and yet inevitably participants must confront the ways in which that identity category excludes others, such as black and female.[8] While the relationship between identity and citizenship is indeed "complex" and the claims of particular identity groups can seem to pose a threat to conceptions of universal citizenship, the activists in this study understood that citizenship is not meaningful if it does not recognize them as people with racial, class, gender and sexual identities, or, as Margaret Somers puts it, as citizens "shaped by their relationships to others."[9] By developing a holistic and relational conception of identity that recognizes the ways in which class and race shape gender and sexuality (and vice versa), and by consciously attempting to resist reenacting the privileged categories (for example, white, middle-class, male, heterosexual), the activists in this study provide a positive model for others, even though they themselves could not always achieve that goal. Importantly, they asserted that members of oppressed groups, working together with allies, could identify the problems they faced and create effective solutions, and that government policies should encourage just this sort of meaningful maximum feasible participation. The proximity of and interactions between diverse groups of people in New York was crucial to the development and success of such coalitions, which showed people elsewhere what could be done.

Their stories are particularly important to hear because they counter the pervasive victim-blaming and shifting of responsibilities from the government to the individual that has marked the rise of neoliberalism since the 1970s. Although the 1967 Green Amendment weakened the maximum feasible participation mandate of the Economic Opportunity Act, this book has shown that the ideal of participatory democracy popularized by the civil rights movement and the War on Poverty continued to inspire activism in subsequent decades. For MFY and the NCNW, the availability of federal and foundation funding, as well as the strictures attached to it, shaped what was possible. When funding was available, community activists seized the opportunity to create social programs to meet their needs and, in the process, were drawn into coalitions, often crossing lines of race, ethnicity, gender, class, and sexuality in their efforts to improve living conditions and relationships. Organizers like Jan Peterson were crucial sparks, providing inspiration, instilling confidence, and pushing community activists toward more progressive politics. Through their own commitment and resilience, they also helped activists to sustain their efforts during setbacks and maintain their optimism in the face of opposition.

MFY, which helped inspire the War on Poverty, was founded by social scientists during the height of postwar liberalism, at a moment when, because of the pressure mounted by the civil rights movement, the U.S. government broadened its commitment to ensuring its citizens' rights. By the time Jan Peterson founded the NCNW in 1975, liberalism faced growing opposition from both economic and social conservatives, and Congress changed the Office of Economic Opportunity into the Community Services Administration, signaling an ideological shift from the promise of full employment to the less lofty but practical provision of social welfare. Yet feminists still managed to obtain public and private funding to staff newly created domestic violence shelters and to run employment programs for displaced homemakers and other women entering the paid workforce amid deindustrialization and changes in family structures. In contrast, ACT UP and WHAM! operated in a political context shaped by market fundamentalism and the reactionary sexual politics of the Religious Right. ACT UP and WHAM! were able to raise their own funds, but they did not engage in direct service provision, partially because members wanted to avoid the increasingly prohibitive strictures placed on public and foundation grants. While ACT UP and WHAM! also sought to broaden citizenship rights to include universal health care, sexual privacy, and the protection of sexual minorities, they operated in a political context in which the obligation of the government to ensure access to rights was no longer widely assumed and in which both political parties looked toward the private sector, rather than the public, as the best way to distribute social goods.

The queer identity that ACT UP and WHAM! members forged proved effective in creating feelings of solidarity and the ability to resist the Religious Right's attempts to impose its model of heterosexual marital procreation and the demonization of gays, lesbians, and women controlling their reproduction via birth control and abortion. Because queer resists stable categories of identity in favor of fluidity and change, queer politics require a rethinking of previous social movement models. Participants must not only understand the influence of other dimensions of identity (race, ethnicity, class, gender, and sexuality) on their social identity, but envision and enact new relationships that are not predicated on the assumption that identities are fixed. In order to realize their radical potential, queer politics must both advance remedies to persistent injustices based upon hierarchies of identity and foster new forms of social relations.

ACT UP's Majority Action Committee perhaps best embodies this model and was most successful in forging coalitions with groups that were not queer-identified groups. Like other activists working with highly marginalized populations, the Majority Action Committee's decision to form Housing Works as a separate agency dedicated to service provision to homeless and low-income New Yorkers with AIDS reflects the belief that service provision is just as important a form of activism as nonviolent civil disobedience. Similarly, the Church Ladies for Choice have dedicated themselves in recent years to supporting the Lower Eastside Girls Club in its mission of meeting the needs of underserved girls and young women and building a new facility, the Lower Eastside Girls Club Center for Community on Avenue D between 7th and 8th Streets, just a short walk from MFY's old headquarters. Like MFY and the NCNW before them, Housing Works was dependent upon governmental and foundation funding and regulations that blunted the most radical potential of their organizing, yet also allowed them to improve many people's lives while continuing to work toward lasting progressive social change. Their examples suggest that funding policies that allow community activists greater self-determination will result in deeper, more fundamental problem solving and more lasting change.

Near the conclusion of ACT UP's twenty-fifth anniversary action, the mood turned somber as organizers asked those gathered to call out the names of loved ones who had died of AIDS. Many of those present had long lists, and one ACT UP veteran explained to me: "I never expected to be here, alive, twenty-five years later." It was a bittersweet victory, tinged with loss but also marked by a renewed commitment to the future. "We wanted AIDS treatments to be made available, and they have been. But the fight is not over," ACT UP New York member and Housing Works cofounder Eric Sawyer declared. "In twenty five years, I hope this crisis will be over. But if not, ACT UP will be here again."[10]

Notes

N.B. The WHAM! Records were unprocessed at the time I conducted my research; therefore, no boxes or folder numbers are included in the notes.

PREFACE

1. "NCNW Original Goals and Objectives," n.d., National Congress of Neighborhood Women Records, Box 1, Folder 7, Sophia Smith Collection, Smith College, Northampton, Mass.

2. Though accurate for some women's liberation activists, this description of feminism in the United States during the 1970s is partial and incomplete, as many scholars have emphasized. Nonetheless it is an influential portrayal, found for example in Alice Echols, *Daring to be Bad*, which I had just finished reading before heading to Smith.

3. Patrick Moore, *Beyond Shame*.

4. See, for example, Jefferson Cowie and Nick Salvatore, "The Long Exception," *International Labor and Working Class History* 74, no. 1 (2008); Gary Gerstle, *American Crucible*.

5. John Colapinto, "The Harvey Milk School Has No Right to Exist. Discuss," *New York*, May 21, 2005.

6. Martha Davis, *Brutal Need*; Felicia Kornbluh, *The Battle for Welfare Rights*; Premilla Nadasen, *Welfare Warriors*; Frances Fox Piven and Richard A. Cloward, *Poor People's Movements*; Jacqueline Pope, *Biting the Hand That Feeds Them*; Guida West, *The National Welfare Rights Movement*.

7. Ezra Birnbaum, interview by Tamar Carroll, April 11, 2005, transcript of audio recording, New York City Women Community Activists Oral History Project, Sophia Smith Collection.

8. Ibid.

9. Frances Fox Piven, interview by Tamar Carroll, July 17, 2004, transcript of audio recording, New York City Women Community Activists Oral History Project.

10. Ethel Velez, interview by Tamar Carroll and Martha Ackelsberg, March 30, 2004, transcript of audio recording, New York City Women Community Activists Oral History Project.

11. Karen Stamm, interview by Tamar Carroll, March 25, 2004, audio recording, Oral History of the American Left Collection, Tamiment Library, New York University, New York.

12. Virginia Kennedy, interview by Tamar Carroll, April 29, 2010, audio recording.

13. Velez interview.

14. Elizabeth Meixell, interview by Tamar Carroll, January 24, 2004, transcript of audio recording, WHAM! Oral History Collection, Tamiment Library.

15. Birnbaum interview.

16. On Steinem as a feminist icon, see for example, Sarah Hepola, "A Woman Like No Other," *NY Times*, March 18, 2012.

INTRODUCTION

1. Steve Quester, interview by Sarah Schulman, January 17, 2004, transcript of video recording, p. 15, ACT UP Oral History Project, available at http://www.actuporalhistory. org; Elizabeth Meixell, interview by Tamar Carroll, January 24, 2004, transcript of audio recording, WHAM! Oral History Collection, Tamiment Library, New York University. On *Rust v. Sullivan*, see Linda Greenhouse, "5 Justices Uphold U.S. Rule Curbing Abortion Advice," *NY Times*, May 24, 1991, and "Excerpts from Court Ruling Curbing Family Planning Clinics," *NY Times*, May 14, 1991.

2. See, for example, "Abortion Activists Gag Liberty Statue," *The Register-Guard* (Eugene, Oregon), July 30, 1991, A5, http://news.google.com/newspapers?nid=1310&dat=19 910730&id=nUdWAAAAIBAJ&sjid=1OoDAAAAIBAJ&pg=2902,6623523 (accessed 1 May 2012), and "Abortion Activists Gag Liberty Statue," *The Gainesville (Fla.) Sun*, July 30, 1991, 4A, http://news.google.com/newspapers?nid=1320&dat=19910730&id=_8FPAAAA IBAJ&sjid=xQYEAAAAIBAJ&pg=4701,9269631 (accessed 1 May 2012).

3. Karen Ramspacher, interview by Tamar Carroll, March 5, 2004, transcript of audio recording, WHAM! Oral History Collection.

4. Books on activism in New York City in the twentieth century include: Annelise Orleck, *Common Sense and a Little Fire*; Clarence Taylor, *Knocking at Our Own Door*; Joshua Freeman, *Working-Class New York*; Xiaolan Bao, *Holding up More Than Half the Sky*; Martha Biondi, *To Stand and Fight*; Miguel Melendez, *We Took the Streets*; Sylvie Murray, *The Progressive Housewife*; David Carter, *Stonewall*; Joanne Reitano, *The Restless City*; Peter Eisenstadt, *Rochdale Village*; Darrel Enck-Wanzer, *The Young Lords*; Jennifer Guglielmo, *Living the Revolution*; Michael Abramson and Iris Morales, *Palante*; Clarence Taylor, *Reds at the Blackboard and Civil Rights in New York City*; Brian Purnell, *Fighting Jim Crow in the County of Kings*; Leigh Ann Wheeler, *How Sex Became a Civil Liberty*; Sonia Song-Ha Lee, *Building a Latino Civil Rights Movement*; Roberta Gold, *When Tenants Claimed the City*.

Social movements that had a significant presence in New York City, including labor, civil rights, welfare rights, peace, New Left, counterculture, and ACORN, are discussed in Guida West, *The National Welfare Rights Movement*; Jacqueline Pope, *Biting the Hand That Feeds Them*; Amy Swerdlow, *Women Strike for Peace*; Nan Enstad, *Ladies of Labor, Girls of Adventure*; Jeanne F. Theoharis and Komozi Woodard, *Freedom North* and *Groundwork*; Bradford Martin, *The Theater Is in the Street*; Premilla Nadasen, *Welfare Warriors*; Felicia Kornbluh, *The Battle for Welfare Rights*; Thomas Sugrue, *Sweet Land of Liberty*; John Atlas, *Seeds of Change*; Eileen Boris and Jennifer Klein, *Caring for America*.

5. Guglielmo, *Living the Revolution*; Orleck, *Common Sense and a Little Fire*; David Von Drehle, *Triangle*. See also "Remembering the 1911 Triangle Factory Fire," The Kheel Center, Cornell University, http://www.ilr.cornell.edu/trianglefire/index.html (accessed 31 May 2012), and "The Power and the People," Episode 4 (1898–1918) of *New York: A Documentary Film*, produced and directed by Ric Burns, 1999, DVD.

6. Christopher Klemek, *The Transatlantic Collapse of Urban Renewal*. See also Samuel Zipp, *Manhattan Projects*.

7. Stanley Aronowitz, interview by Tamar Carroll, December 4, 2012, audio recording, transcript available in the New York City Women Activists Oral History Project, Sophia Smith Collection, Smith College, Northampton, Mass. Mary Perot Nichols, "Riding to Utopia on the Monorail," *The Village Voice*, May 29, 1969, 9–10, 55.

8. Anthony Flint, *Wrestling with Moses*, 182.

9. Carter, *Stonewall*, 216. The Stonewall Uprising was profoundly influential in Europe as well as the United States, sparking the formation of gay liberation groups in England and across the continent. Geoff Eley, *Forging Democracy*, 473–4.

10. *Stonewall Uprising*, produced and directed by Kate Davis and David Heilbroner, 2011, DVD.

11. 2011 marked the 100th anniversary of the Triangle Fire, with commemorations held at Washington Place in New York City as well as in Chicago, Washington, D.C., San Francisco, and Los Angeles. Footage of the Washington Place commemoration is available online at http://rememberthetrianglefire.org/centennial/ (accessed 4 June 2012). The Remember the Triangle Fire Coalition is raising funds to build a permanent memorial. Shortly after Jane Jacobs's death in April 2006 at the age of eighty-nine, Mayor Michael Bloomberg proclaimed June 28, 2006, Jane Jacobs Day. The Rockefeller Foundation established the Jane Jacobs Medal in 2007, and in 2007–8 the Municipal Art Society of New York held an exhibition on her legacy, titled "Jane Jacobs and the Future of New York." See Edward Rothstein, "Jane Jacobs, Foe of Plans and Friend of City Life," *NY Times*, September 25, 2007, and Flint, *Wrestling with Moses*, 194. For more about New York City Pride events, see http://www.nycpride.org/about (accessed 4 June 2012).

12. Truman Capote, *Breakfast at Tiffany's*; John Kifter, "Poverty Pickets Get Paper-Bag Dousing on Madison Avenue," *NY Times*, May 28, 1966, p. 1. This protest was portrayed in Matthew Weiner's television series *Mad Men*, about Madison Avenue advertising executives, in episode one of season five, "A Little Kiss, Part I," 2012.

13. "Oh, Toto, They're Not in Wichita Anymore!" poster, WHAM! Records. Robert D. McFadden, "Rally of Foes of Abortion is Outjeered in Manhattan," *NY Times*, September 30, 1991, p. B1. Angela Blake, *How New York Became American*.

14. Robert A. Caro, *The Power Broker*; Zipp, *Manhattan Projects*.

15. On the relative decline of the Northeast and the rise of the Sunbelt, see Bruce Schulman, *The Seventies*; Schulman, *From Cotton Belt to Sunbelt*; "The City: Living It Up," *Time*, April 13, 1962.

16. William Scott and Peter Rutkoff, *New York Modern: The Arts and the City*.

17. Freeman, *Working-Class New York*, 103.

18. Biondi, *To Stand and Fight*, 273. Civil rights activists in Los Angeles pursued similar goals; there, the participation of Jewish activists was important as in New York, but in Los Angeles Mexican and Japanese Americans as well as African Americans were significant participants in interracial civil rights activism from the 1930s through the early 1960s. Shana Bernstein, *Bridges of Reform*.

19. Biondi, *To Stand and Fight*, 132, 35. Suburban-based fair housing activists in Massachusetts also influenced the drafting of federal housing policy. Lily Geismer, "Good Neighbors for Fair Housing."

20. Lisa Levenstein, *A Movement without Marches*.

21. Rhonda Y. Williams, *The Politics of Public Housing*, 6–7.

22. Ethel Velez, interview by Tamar Carroll and Martha Ackelsberg, March 30, 2004, East Harlem, audio recording, transcript available in the New York City Women Activists

Oral History Project. The concept of social citizenship was first developed in T. H. Marshall, *Citizenship and Social Class*.

23. Biondi, *To Stand and Fight*, 223. On segregation in the urban North see especially Thomas Sugrue, *The Origins of the Urban Crisis*.

24. Purnell, *Fighting Jim Crow in the County of Kings*.

25. Mobilization for Youth, "The Lower East Side Story: Emphasizing the Mobilization Area," 1962, p. 27, Frances Fox Piven Papers, Box 57, Folder 9, Sophia Smith Collection. For information on tenements, see Andrew S. Dolkart, *Biography of a Tenement House in New York City*.

26. On labor and radical politics in the Lower East Side, see Orleck, *Common Sense and a Little Fire*; Daniel Katz, *All Together Different*; Elizabeth Ewen, *Immigrant Women in the Land of Dollars*. For information on the settlement houses of the Lower East Side, see Michael Fabricant and Robert Fisher, *Settlement Houses under Siege*; Betty Boyd Caroli, "Settlement Houses"; Doris Groshen Daniels, *Always a Sister*; Helen Hall, *Unfinished Business in Neighborhood and Nation*; Lillian Wald, *The House on Henry Street*.

27. Eric Schneider, *Vampires, Dragons, and Egyptian Kings*, 230. Kitty Hanson, "Youth Mobilized to Give Youth a Chance," *New York Daily News*, July 17 and 18, 1963, reprinted by MFY, Robert F. Kennedy Papers, Attorney General's General Correspondence, Box 39, John F. Kennedy Presidential Library, Boston.

28. Richard A. Cloward and Lloyd E. Ohlin, *Delinquency and Opportunity*.

29. Robert F. Kennedy, "Welcoming Remarks," PCJD to the Citizens Advisory Committee, September 21, 1962, p. 3, Frances Fox Piven Papers, Box 59, Folder 8.

30. Community studies of the civil rights/black freedom movement have also found that women transformed the goals the movement through their enthusiastic participation and prioritization of "areas of daily life commonly perceived as outside the realm of political conflict." (Laurie B. Green, "Challenging the Civil Rights Narrative," 75). In addition to those cited previously, community studies of the civil rights movement outside New York include William H. Chafe, *Civilities and Civil Rights*; John Dittmer, *Local People*; Charles M. Payne, *I've Got the Light of Freedom*; Robert Self, *American Babylon*; Emilye Crosby, *A Little Taste of Freedom* and *Civil Rights History from the Ground Up*; Christina Greene, *Our Separate Ways*; Matthew J. Countryman, *Up South*; Laurie B. Green, *Battling the Plantation Mentality*; Donna Jean Murch, *Living for the City*; Alondra Nelson, *Body and Soul*.

31. George Brager, interview by Noel A. Cazenave, 1992, War on Poverty Project, Columbia University Oral History Archive, New York.

32. Richard A. Cloward and Richard M. Elman, "Advocacy in the Ghetto," 29.

33. As Guian McKee demonstrates, Johnson himself did not understand and later opposed the Community Action Programs and the stipulation of maximum feasible participation of residents in the poverty programs. Nonetheless, as Annelise Orleck argues, the CAPs "galvanized poor people" and led to the creation by residents themselves of innovative and enduring social programs across the country. Orleck, "Introduction," 2; McKee, " 'This Government Is with Us.' "

34. Richard A. Cloward and Frances Fox Piven, "A Strategy to End Poverty," *The Nation*, May 2, 1966.

35. Nadasen, *Welfare Warriors*, 174. Peter Kihss, "City's Welfare Roll Outpacing Forecast," *NY Times*, November 23, 1967, p. 1; Vincent Cannato, *The Ungovernable City*, 539–40.

36. Marisa Chappell, *The War on Welfare*, 67.

37. Cloward and Piven, *The Politics of Turmoil*, 322.

38. David Hackett, interview by John Douglas, October 21, 1970, transcript of audio recording, Robert F. Kennedy Oral History Program, JFK Library, pp. 72, 94–95.

39. Jan Peterson, interview by Tamar Carroll, September 6, 2003, transcript of audio recording, New York City Women Community Activists Oral History Project.

40. Manuel Diaz, interview by Andrew Block, August 17, 2005, p. 4, The Manuel Diaz Papers, Archives of the Puerto Rican Diaspora, Centro de Estudios Puertorriqueños, Hunter College, CUNY.

41. Christina Greene, " 'Someday . . . the Colored and White Will Stand Together,' " 160.

Scholars have documented significant interracial activism in the postwar United States, as well as frequent failures to achieve lasting coalitions. For studies of multiracial activism in New York City see note 4; outside of New York City, see especially Robert Bauman, *Race and the War on Poverty*; Neil Foley, *Quest for Equality*; Brian Behnken, *Fighting Their Own Battles* and *The Struggle in Black and Brown*; Bernstein, *Bridges of Reform*; Carol McKibben, *Racial Beachhead*; Mark Brilliant, *The Color of America Has Changed*; Lilia Fernandez, *Brown in the Windy City*; Lauren Araiza, *To March for Others*; Gordon K. Mantler, *Power to the Poor*; Judy Tzu-Chun Wu, *Radicals on the Road*.

42. Jennifer Frost, *"An Interracial Movement of the Poor"*; Annelise Orleck, *Storming Caesar's Palace*; Susan Youngblood Ashmore, *Carry It On*; Bauman, *Race and the War on Poverty*; Thomas J. Kiffmeyer, *Reformers to Radicals*; William S. Clayson, *Freedom Is Not Enough*; Clayton Howard, "The Closet and the Cul de Sac"; Annelise Orleck and Lisa Hazirjian, *The War on Poverty*; Martin Meeker, "The Queerly Disadvantaged and the Making of San Francisco's War on Poverty"; Robert Bauman, " 'Kind of a Secular Sacrament.' "

43. Sam Roberts, "Introduction," 9.

44. Taylor, *Knocking at Our Own Door*; Purnell, *Fighting Jim Crow in the County of Kings*.

45. Jan Peterson, interview by Tamar Carroll and Lara Rusch, August 16, 2002, transcript of audio recording, New York Women Community Activists Oral History Project.

46. Freeman, *Working-Class New York*, 167.

47. Ida Susser, *Norman Street*, 30.

48. Jonathan Rieder, *Canarsie*.

49. Peterson interview by Carroll and Rusch. In the late 1970s, Women Make Movies enlarged its mission to incorporate the distribution and exhibition of women's films. In 2002, the organization celebrated its thirtieth anniversary and as of this writing, its catalog included more than five hundred films. See http://www.wmm.com/about /general_info.shtml (accessed 30 May 2012).

50. Studies of feminist activism in this period include Sara Evans, *Personal Politics* and *Tidal Wave*; Alice Echols, *Daring to Be Bad*; Nancy Whittier, *Feminist Generations*; Laura Kaplan, *Story of Jane*; Daniel Horowitz, *Betty Friedan and the Making of Women's Liberation*; Rosalyn Baxandall and Linda Gordon, *Dear Sisters*; Ruth Rosen, *The World Split Open*; Marisa Chappell, "Rethinking Women's Politics in the 1970s"; Judith Ezekiel, *Feminism in the Heartland*; Sandra Morgen, *Into Our Own Hands*; Premilla Nadasen, "Expanding the Boundaries of the Women's Movement"; Becky Thompson, "Multiracial Feminism"; Stephanie Gilmore, "The Dynamics of Feminist Activism in Memphis, Tennessee" and *Feminist Coalitions* and *Groundswell*; Jennifer Nelson, *Women of Color*

and the Reproductive Rights Movement; Dorothy Sue Cobble, *The Other Women's Movement*; Benita Roth, *Separate Roads to Feminism*; Kimberly Springer, *Living for the Revolution*; Wini Breines, *The Trouble between Us*; Nancy MacLean, *Freedom Is Not Enough*; Anne Enke, *Finding the Movement*; Anne M. Valk, *Radical Sisters*; Nancy Hewitt, *No Permanent Waves*; Wendy Kline, *Bodies of Knowledge*; Christine Stansell, *The Feminist Promise*; Katherine Turk, "Out of the Revolution, into the Mainstream"; Maylei Blackwell, *Chicana Power*; Carolyn Bronstein, *Battling Pornography*; Lisa Levenstein, "'Don't Agonize, Organize!'"

51. Sally Martino Fisher, interview by Tamar Carroll and Martha Ackelsberg, March 23, 2004, transcript of audio recording, New York Women Community Activists Oral History Project.

52. Peterson interview by Carroll and Rusch. See also Alice O'Connor, *Poverty Knowledge*, 235–39.

53. John H. Mollenkopf and Manuel Castells, "Introduction," 11.

54. Arthur Brown, Dan Collins, and Michael Goodwin, *I Koch*, 290. See also Martin Gottlieb, "Battery Project Reflects Changing City Priorities," *NY Times*, October 18, 1985, p. B1, and Edward Koch, "Welfare Isn't A Way of Life," *NY Times*, March 4, 1988, p. A39.

55. Freeman, *Working-Class New York*, 292.

56. Economic inequality in New York City has increased substantially since the 1980s; see Joshua Freeman, "What Happened to Working-Class New York?," and related articles in the special issue "Mayor Bloomberg's New York," *The Nation,* April 16, 2013.

57. Patrick Moore, *Beyond Shame*, 121–22. Patrick Moore, interview by Sarah Schulman, January 14, 2003, transcript of video recording, Interview 006, ACT UP Oral History Project, http://actuporalhistory.org/interviews/interviews_01.html#moore.

58. Deborah B. Gould, *Moving Politics*, 333.

59. Quester interview, 15.

CHAPTER ONE

1. Marjorie Hunter, "U.S. and City Open 12.6 Million War on Delinquency," *NY Times*, June 1, 1962; Mobilization For Youth, *A Proposal for the Prevention and Control of Delinquency by Expanding Opportunities: A Demonstration Project Conceived and Developed by Mobilization for Youth, Inc.*, December 9, 1961, 2nd ed., August. 1962, MFY Collection, School of Social Work Collection, Lehman Library, Columbia University, New York.

2. Federal government expenditures for social sciences quadrupled between 1960 and 1967. Helfgot, *Professional Reforming*, 118.

3. James Gilbert, *A Cycle of Outrage*; Ruth Feldstein, *Motherhood in Black and White*; Tom Engelhardt, *The End of Victory Culture*; K. A. Cuordileone, *Manhood and American Political Culture in the Cold War*.

4. "Facts about Mobilization for Youth," n.d., Box 55, Folder 11, Frances Fox Piven Papers, Sophia Smith Collection, Smith College, Northampton, Mass. (hereafter cited as FFP Papers).

5. Rosalyn Baxandall, interview by Tamar Carroll, April 19, 2004, transcript of audio recording, New York City Women Community Activists Oral History Collection, Sophia Smith Collection. Baxandall formed a day-care center so that young mothers could participate in the work-training project.

6. *Administrative History of Office of Economic Opportunity*, vol. 1, part 2, pp. 154–57, Lyndon Johnson Presidential Library, Austin, Tex.

7. Cloward and Piven, *The Politics of Turmoil*; George A. Brager and Francis P. Purcell, *Community Action Against Poverty*; Peter Marris and Martin Rein, *Dilemmas of Social Reform*; Harold H. Weissman, *Justice and the Law in the Mobilization for Youth Experience*; Weissman, *Employment and Educational Services*; Weissman, *Community Councils and Community Control*; Daniel Knapp and Kenneth Polk, *Scouting the War on Poverty*; Frances Fox Piven and Richard A. Cloward, *Poor People's Movements*; Helfgot, *Professional Reforming*; Noel A. Cazenave, "Ironies of Urban Reform"; Cazenave, *Impossible Democracy*. For a critique of MFY, see Daniel Patrick Moynihan, *Maximum Feasible Misunderstanding*.

8. I agree with Cazenave that the civil rights movement was the most important factor in furthering democratic participation. My interpretation differs in emphasizing the role of local women in particular and the ways in which they influenced the frontline MFY staff, as opposed to the role of the elite social scientists charged with planning and running MFY. Cazenave, *Impossible Democracy*, xi, 83.

9. Charles M. Payne, "Ella Baker and Models of Social Change"; Barbara Ransby, "Cops, Schools, and Communism"; Ransby, *Ella Baker and the Black Freedom Movement*, 148–57.

10. "Youth: The Scavengers," *Time*, August 12, 1957; "Crime: These Marauding Savages," *Time*, April 28, 1958. For the racial and ethnic organization of gangs and their policing of transitioning neighborhoods, see Robert W. Snyder, "A Useless and Terrible Death," and Schneider, *Vampires, Dragons, and Egyptian Kings*.

11. John Speicher, "The Poverty War—Whose Turf?" *Interplay: The Magazine of International Affairs*, April 1969, pp. 4–8, FFP Papers, Box 1, Folder 2; "Youth, 15, Killed in Park Stabbing," *NY Times*, July 31, 1957, p. 46; Philip Benjamin, "New York Report Notes Strain on Children and Cites Helplessness," *NY Times*, August 15, 1957, p. 1; Robert Alden, "14 Boys Indicted in Two Killings; City Parley Held," *NY Times*, August 21, 1957, p. 1; Jack Roth, "6 Boys Identified at Murder Trial," *NY Times*, February 8, 1958, p. 8; Schneider, *Vampires, Dragons, and Egyptian Kings*, 80–83; Snyder, "A Useless and Terrible Death."

12. For her coworkers' descriptions of Hall as brilliant and dedicated, see Bertram Beck, interview by Greg Raynor, November 14, 1991, transcript of audio recording, and Leona Gold, interview by Greg Raynor, December 16, 1991, audio recording, Henry Street Oral History Collection, Box 152, Henry Street Settlement Collection, Social Welfare Archives, University of Minnesota, as well as Terry Mizrahi, interview by Tamar Carroll, May 4, 2005, transcript of audio recording, New York City Women Community Activists Oral History Project, Sophia Smith Collection. For Hall's "imposing" personality, see Judith Ann Trolander, *Hall, Helen*.

13. Belle M. Steinberg, "Communal Leaders Organize East Side Neighborhoods Association to Improve Living Conditions on the Lower East Side," *East Side News*, May 21, 1955, p. 8; Kitty Hanson, "Youth Mobilized to Give Youth a Chance," *New York Daily News*, July 17, 1963, reprinted by MFY, Robert F. Kennedy Papers, Attorney General's General Correspondence, Box 39, John F. Kennedy Presidential Library, Boston.

14. Wendell Pritchett, *Brownsville, Brooklyn*; Samuel Zipp, *Manhattan Projects*; Richard Plunz, *A History of Housing in New York City*, chap. 8; Martha Biondi, *To Stand and Fight*, chap. 11; Lizabeth Cohen, *A Consumers' Republic*, chap. 5.

15. Digna Sanchez, "Aspira, the Sixties, and Growing Up Puerto Rican," paper presented at the 2008 Puerto Rican Studies Association Conference in San Juan, Puerto Rico, and available online at http://www.drantoniapantojafellowship.org/Other%20Postings/Aspira,%20the%20Sixties.pdf, (accessed 6–7 June 2012.). See also Digna Sanchez, interview by Tamar Carroll, January 5, 2009, transcript of audio recording, New York City Women Community Activists Oral History Project.

16. Daniel Katz, *All Together Different*. See also http://www.coopvillage.coop/cvHistory.html#eastRiver (accessed 7 June 2012).

17. Christopher Mele, *Selling the Lower East Side*, 37, 134.

18. Katz, *All Together Different*; Plunz, *A History of Housing in New York City*, 245. Just to the north of the Lower East Side, Metropolitan Life Insurance Company constructed the enormous Peter Cooper Village and Stuyvesant Town housing developments in the 1940s; they are discussed in Zipp, *Manhattan Projects*, 73–154.

19. Sanchez, "Aspira, the Sixties, and Growing Up Puerto Rican."

20. Nicholas Deagen Bloom, *Public Housing that Worked*, 168–75. Rochdale Village in Jamaica, Queens, a United Housing Foundation cooperative, was an important exception to the pattern of segregation and was racially integrated in the 1960s. Peter Eisenstadt, *Rochdale Village*.

21. Julio Colon, interview by Laurie Norris, 1992, transcript of audio recording, Henry Street Oral History Collection, Box 152, Folder 7.

22. Naomi Barko, "LENA and the 45 Gangs," *The Reporter*, September 29, 1960, Henry Street Settlement Records, Box 74, Folder 7, Social Welfare Archives, University of Minnesota, Minneapolis; Clayton Knowles, "4th Gang Assents to East Side Pact," *NY Times*, August 15, 1956, p. 1; Schneider, *Vampires, Dragons, and Egyptian Kings*, 201–4.

23. Frances Fox Piven, interview by Tamar Carroll, April 21, 2004, transcript of audio recording, New York City Women Community Activists Oral History Project.

24. Helen Hall, interview by Frances Fox Piven, September 12, 1962, FFP Papers, Box 61, Folder 5, p. 3; Winslow Carlton and Helen Hall, "Mobilization for Youth: A Proposal for a Community-Wide Demonstration Project for the Prevention and Control of Juvenile Delinquency," April 1958, FFP Papers, Box 57, Folder 3.

25. Gilbert, *A Cycle of Outrage*, 64.

26. Helfgot, *Professional Reforming*, 25–26.

27. Cloward and Ohlin, *Delinquency and Opportunity*, 105. Cloward and Ohlin brought together the theory of anomie, developed by Emile Durkheim and Robert Merton, and the theory of culture transmission and differential association, developed by Edwin Sutherland. Cloward and Ohlin believed these pressures to succeed materially did not affect young women, because "it is primarily the male who must go into the marketplace to seek employment, make a career for himself, and support a family" (106).

28. Helfgot, *Professional Reforming*, 26, 29.

29. Hall interview, 5.

30. Mitchell Ginsberg, interview by Frances Fox Piven, November 9, 1962, FFP Papers, Box 61, Folder 1, pp. 13–14.

31. Hall interview, 4. Henry Street Settlement House staff member Jeffery Weiner complained that MFY underused the skills and knowledge of Helen Hall, using her rather to "shake glitter." Jeffrey Weiner, interview by Frances Fox Piven, December 21, 1963, FFP Papers, Box 61, Folder 24, p. 8.

32. Richard Cloward, interview by Frances Fox Piven, August 8, 1962, FFP Papers, Box 60, Folder 12, pp. 33–34.

33. Richard Cloward, interview by Noel Cazenave, May 28, 1992, transcript of audio recording, p. 9, War on Poverty Project, Columbia University Oral History Collection; Knapp and Polk, *Scouting the War on Poverty*, 36–37.

34. MFY, *A Proposal for the Prevention and Control of Delinquency*, 2nd ed., 72, 90.

35. In the course of his earlier work in Chicago, Ohlin met Eunice Shriver, who urged Robert Kennedy to tackle juvenile delinquency as a social problem. Kennedy tapped Ohlin to join his brother's administration as a special assistant to Health, Education, and Welfare Secretary Abraham Ribicoff, where he became the "key architect" of the "philosophy behind the program" for combating juvenile delinquency. After Ohlin left for Washington in January 1961, social worker George Brager took his place at MFY and drafted the final MFY proposal with Cloward. Lloyd Ohlin, telephone interview by Noel Cazenave, July 9, 1992, War on Poverty Project; David Hackett, interview by John Douglas, October 21, 1970, transcript of audio recording, Robert F. Kennedy Oral History Program, JFK Library; Piven interview by Carroll.

36. Alvin Shuster, "Kennedy Offers Plan to Combat Juvenile Crimes," *NY Times*, May 12, 1961, p. 1. Robert Manning Washington, " 'Someone the President Can Talk To,' " *NY Times Sunday Magazine*, May 28, 1961, p. 22.

37. Marjorie Hunter, "Congress Passes Delinquency Bill," *NY Times*, September 13, 1961, p. 30; Stanley Kravitz, Program Coordinator, "A Federal View of the Organization of Youth Services: The Program of the President's Committee on Juvenile Delinquency and Youth Crime," March 21, 1964, FFP Papers, Box 59, Folder 8, pp. 2–5; Bertram M. Beck, "Innovations in Combating Juvenile Delinquency," *HEW*, March 1965, FFP Papers, Box 60, Folder 1.

38. Engelhardt, *The End of Victory Culture*, 159–71.

39. Kravitz, "A Federal View of the Organization of Youth Services: The Program of the President's Committee on Juvenile Delinquency and Youth Crime," 5–6.

40. George Brager, "A Report to the Mobilization for Youth Staff: Our First Year of Program," FFP Papers, Box 55, Folder 12, p. 1.

41. "Facts about MFY," FFP Papers, Box 56, Folder 1.

42. Hunter, "U.S. and City Open 12.6 Million War on Delinquency."

43. Neil Sheehan, "Lower East Side: Profile of a Slum," *NY Times*, August 25, 1964, p. 18.

44. Helfgot, *Professional Reforming*, 5, 14; Henry Heifetz, "Introduction," 20.

45. Notes from interview with Harold Weissman, by Paige and Daniel Knapp, December 4, 1967, Daniel Knapp Papers, Box 51, JFK Library (hereafter cited as DK Papers).

46. Richard Cloward, "Orientation Speech," September 6, 1962, FFP Papers, Box 60, Folder 12.

47. Ezra Birnbaum, interview by Tamar Carroll, April 11, 2005, transcript of audio recording, New York City Women Community Activists Oral History Project.

48. Heifetz, "Introduction," 21; Frank Reissman, "Mobilizing the Poor: The Role of the Professional," *Commonweal*, May 21, 1965, p. 285, FFP Papers, Box 55, Folder 10.

49. Marilyn Bibb Gore, interview by Tamar Carroll, April 6, 2005. See also Marilyn Bibb Gore and Sidney Pinsky, interview by Noel Cazenave, May 19, 1992, War on Poverty Project.

50. Barbara Hunter Randall Joseph, interview by Tamar Carroll, March 21, 2005, transcript of audio recording, New York City Women Community Activists Oral History Project.

51. Mary Anne Dowery, interview by Tamar Carroll, April 21, 2005, transcript of audio recording, New York City Women Community Activists Oral History Project.

52. Knapp and Polk, *Scouting the War on Poverty*, 164.

53. Dowery interview.

54. Harold H. Weissman, "Overview of Educational Opportunities," 119.

55. MFY, "Report on Principals' Dispute with Mobilization for Youth," February 19, 1964, DK Papers, Box 28, Folder titled "MOM School Dispute," pp. 5–6.

56. Heifetz, "Parent Education Program," 127.

57. Biondi, *To Stand and Fight*, 241–49; Taylor, *Knocking at Our Own Door*, 51–53.

58. Dowery interview.

59. Charles Grosser, quoted in Knapp and Polk, *Scouting the War on Poverty*, 160–61.

60. Cloward and Elman, "Advocacy in the Ghetto," 29.

61. Stephen Wizner, interview by Tamar Carroll, October 25, 2010, transcript of audio recording, New York City Women Community Activists Oral History Project.

62. Cloward and Elman, "Advocacy in the Ghetto," 27–32.

63. "Resume" and "Petra Santiago Biography," 1992, Petra Santiago Papers, Box 1, Folder 2, p. 7, Archives of the Puerto Rican Diaspora, Centro de Estudios Puertorriqueños, Hunter College, CUNY.

64. "Petra Santiago Biography," p. 7.

65. Dowery interview; Heifetz, "Parent Education Program," 127–28.

66. MFY, "Mobilization of Mothers," n.d., DK Papers, Box 28, Folder titled "MOM School Dispute," p. 1. MOM had a precedent in Parents in Action, founded by Ella Baker in Harlem in 1954 to empower African American and Puerto Rican mothers who shared concerns over the poor quality of education their children were receiving. Ransby, "Cops, Schools, and Communism."

67. MFY, "Mobilization of Mothers," 3–4.

68. MFY, "Report on Principals' Dispute with Mobilization for Youth," 9.

69. Ibid, 8–11.

70. George Brager, "Addenda to Mobilization of Mothers," December 16, 1963, DK Papers, Box 28, Folder "MOM School Dispute."

71. "Voter Registration Drive Slated on Lower East Side," *NY Times*, September 11, 1963, p. 22.

72. George Brager to Chiefs and Assistant Chiefs, "Re: Voter Registration Campaign," June 3, 1963, in *MFY: The Crisis*, vol. 5, DK Papers, Box 29.

73. Richard Cloward, "MFY Participation in the March on Washington and in Initiating a Voter Registration Campaign," notes from all-staff meeting, August 6, 1963, in *MFY: The Crisis*, vol. 1, MFY Collection, School of Social Work, Columbia University.

74. Harry Specht, "Organizing the Unaffiliated: Annual Report," July 8, 1963, p. 4, FFP Papers, Box 56, Folder 5.

75. Martin Tolchin, "Project's Road Has Been Rocky," *NY Times*, August 17, 1964, p. 12. Piven interview by Carroll; Frances Fox Piven and Richard Cloward, "Echoes from the Old Left," FFP Papers, Box 72, Folder 14; Mary Dowery, "Progress Report on Parent Education Program," December 3, 1963, FFP Papers, Box 56, Folder 3.

76. Manny Diaz, interview by Lillian Jiménez, March 14, 2001, transcript of audio recording, Latino Educational Media Center Oral History Project, New York, NY, information available at http://www.lemctr.org/main/index_oral.html (accessed 22 August 2014), p. 34; Sonia Lee and Ande Diaz, " 'I Was the One Percenter,' " 64–65. Indeed, Sonia Lee argues that it was the "catalyst" for the political mobilization of Puerto Ricans in New York, and for their collaboration with African Americans in both the school desegregation movement and the War on Povety. *Building a Latino Civil Rights Movement*, 119. My own reading of the MOM dispute suggests that local mobilizations began before the March on Washington but intensified and gained support as a result of the visibility of Puerto Rican participation in the March.

77. Photographs from the March, in *MFY: The Crisis*, vol. 1, MFY Collection.

78. Frances Fox Piven, *Who's Afraid of Frances Fox Piven?*, 253.

79. Sidney Pinsky, joint interview with Marilyn Gore by Noel A. Cazenave, May 19, 1992, pp. 22–23, War on Poverty Project. By 1965, the YAAG was engaged in consciousness-raising around African American history and culture and race relations, and most of the group's membership was black. The young adults themselves decided to mount a demonstration against police brutality, and to picket New York's Ninth Precinct for alleged brutality against Puerto Rican girls. Bloom, *Public Housing That Worked*, 153–55.

80. Marilyn Bibb, "Memorandum Re: MFY-Engaged Actions in Which a Civil Rights Component Was Present," p. 2, in *MFY: The Crisis*, vol. 5, DK Papers, Box 29. For more on CORE, see Brian Purnell, *Fighting Jim Crow in the County of Kings*.

81. "Report Prepared by the Principals of Districts 1–4," February 24, 1964, in *MFY: The Crisis*, vol. 5, pp. 5–10; Helfgot, *Professional Reforming*, 76–77.

82. The Harlem Parents Committee, founded in 1963 and led by Isaiah Robinson and Thelma Johnson, also played an important role in channeling grassroots activism for integrated schools (Taylor, *Knocking at Our Own Door*, 120). Harlem mothers initiated school boycotts in 1958, providing an important example for the leaders of the citywide boycotts of 1964. Adina Back, "Exposing the 'Whole Segregation Myth.' "

83. MFY took pains to assert that the local community groups, such as NAG, made their own decisions over whether to participate in the boycott and that MFY staffers that were involved were not participating in their official capacities. However, they acknowledged that MFY paraprofessionals and staffers worked with the community groups to organize picket lines and assist in distributing information about the boycott. "Memorandum Re: Mobilization for Youth and the School Boycotts," October 7, 1964, in *MFY: The Crisis*, vol. 5; Memo to All Staff from Allen Simpson, "Re: Boycott," February 17, 1964, FFP Papers, Box 56, Folder 3; Lee and Diaz, " 'I Was the One Percenter,' " 66–68.

84. Torres emphasizes the "joint efforts" of Puerto Ricans and African Americans in New York, but also notes that "within the overall context of unity, junctures of competition and sometimes of confrontation could threaten interethnic solidarity." Andres Torres, *Between Melting Pot and Mosaic*, 84–86.

85. Pritchett, *Brownsville, Brooklyn*, 139. See also Jesse Hoffnung-Garcia, *A Tale of Two Cities*, 109–13.

86. Lee and Diaz, " 'I Was the One Percenter,' " 53. See also Lee, *Building a Latino Civil Rights Movement*, 117–21.

87. Leonard Buder, "Galamison Maps Integration Plan," *NY Times*, February 26, 1964, p. 1; Fred Powledge, "Civil Rights and Labor Groups Join for March on Albany Today,"

NY Times, March 10, 1964, p. 19; Marilyn Bibb, "Memorandum Re: MFY Engaged Actions in Which a Civil Rights Component Was Present," in *MFY: The Crisis,* vol. 5.

88. The decrease in citywide participation from the first boycott was due in part to withdrawal of Puerto Rican support in response to the African American leadership's failure to attend a March 2 demonstration sponsored by the National Association for Puerto Rican Civil Rights. Taylor, *Knocking at Our Own Door,* 161–62.

89. Ibid., 116–46. Marilyn Bibb, "Memorandum Re: Mobilization for Youth-Engaged Actions in Which a Civil Rights Component Was Present," "Notes on the Meeting of the Civil Rights Committee," January 24, 1964, and "A Draft Policy Statement on School Integration for Mobilization for Youth," all in *MFY: The Crisis,* vol. 5; Fred Powledge, "Boycotters Push Grassroot Drive," *NY Times,* February 9, 1964, p. 52. On opposition to school desegregation, see Clarence Taylor, "Conservative and Liberal Opposition to the New York City School-Integration Campaign."

90. The full MFY Board approved the Statement on School Integration on February 5, 1964. "Memorandum Re: MFY and the School Boycotts," October 7, 1964, in *MFY: The Crisis,* vol. 5.

91. Gene Currivan, "Principals Assail Juvenile Agency," *NY Times,* January 31, 1964, p. 29.

92. MFY, "Report on Principals' Dispute with Mobilization for Youth," 4; "Hearing is Planned on Youth Program," *NY Times,* February 3, 1964, p. 17; Susan Goodman, "Bitterness Revealed Over E. Side Schools," in "Appendices to a Report on the Principals' Dispute with Mobilization for Youth," February 19, 1964, FFP Papers, Box 55, Folder 9.

93. Susan Goodman, "Puerto Ricans Turn Out: Bitterness Revealed Over East Side Schools," *The Village Voice,* February 20 1964, in *MFY: The Crisis,* vol. 1.

94. "Report on Principals' Dispute," 4.

95. Samuel Kaplan, "Youth Aide Backs East Side Groups," *NY Times,* February 1, 1964.

96. From the start, MFY positioned itself as outside of local systems of power, including the school system. It was only under pressure from the President's Committee that MFY invited Superintendent Florence Becker to join the MFY Board of Directors. Becker resented being left out of the planning process and remarked in an interview that MFY "made a big mistake" by not involving her sooner. Florence Becker, interview by Frances Fox Piven, October 31, 1962, FFP Papers, Box 60, Folder 2.

97. "Report Prepared by the Principals of Districts 1–4," February 24, 1964, in *MFY: The Crisis,* vol. 5, pp. 1–2, 15, 19.

98. David Seeley to David Hackett, February 17, 1964, DK Papers, Box 28, Folder titled "MOM School Dispute," pp. 2–3.

99. "Report Prepared by the Principals of Districts 1–4," February 24, 1964, in *MFY: The Crisis,* vol. 5, p. 23.

100. Ibid., 19.

101. MFY, "Report on Principals' Dispute with Mobilization for Youth," February 19, 1964, DK Papers, Box 28, Folder titled "MOM School Dispute," p. 13.

102. Winslow Carlton, interview by Noel Cazenave, May 11, 1992, War on Poverty Project.

103. George A. Brager, "Effecting Organizational Change Through a Demonstration Project."

104. Harold H. Weissman, "Educational Innovation," 218.

105. Heifetz, "Parent Education Program," 131.

106. Frank Riessman, "Mobilizing the Poor: The Role of the Professional," *Commonweal*, May 21, 1965, pp. 285–86; FFP Papers, Box 55, Folder 10.

107. Ibid., 287.

108. Gore, joint interview with Pinsky, 16.

109. Ibid., 30–31.

110. Dowery went on to direct two of the first community mental health sites as demonstration projects for the War on Poverty. Dowery interview.

111. Adina Back, " 'Parent Power,' " 196.

112. Taylor, "Conservative and Liberal Opposition to the New York City School-Integration Campaign."

113. Virginia Korrol, "Building the New York Puerto Rican Community," 13–15; Lorrin Thomas, *Puerto Rican Citizen*, 200–244.

114. Anthony De Jesus and Madeline Perez, "From Community Control to Consent Decree."

115. James Jennings and Francisco Chapman, "Puerto Ricans and the Community Control Movement," 284.

116. Ella Baker, interview by Sue Thrasher, April 19, 1977, transcript of audio recording, pp. 59–60, Interview G-008, Southern Oral History Program Collection, Wilson Library, University of North Carolina at Chapel Hill.

117. For the important history of civil rights organizing in New York City prior to the 1960s, see Biondi, *To Stand and Fight*. As Theoharis points out in her introduction to *Freedom North*, the civil rights movement in the North also inspired southern activism; nationally, civil rights groups engaged in an ongoing dialogue on goals and tactics.

CHAPTER TWO

1. Francis P. Purcell and Harry Specht, "Selecting Methods and Points of Intervention in Dealing with Social Problems," 231.

2. Biondi, *To Stand and Fight*, 112–36; Mandi Isaacs Jackson, "Harlem's Rent Strike and Rat War"; George Tood, "Gray: Have Fair Visitors Visit Slums in Harlem," *Amsterdam News*, February 22, 1964, p. 46. Matthew Countryman's study of black activism in Philadelphia reveals that direct-action campaigns grew in popularity there as residents' frustration with the slow pace of change pursued by political parties and city bureaucracies mounted. Countryman, *Up South*.

3. Frances Fox Piven, interview by Noel Cazenave, May 28, 1992, transcript of audio recording, War on Poverty Project, Columbia University Oral History Archives, New York.

4. Marilyn Bibb Gore, interview by Tamar Carroll, April 6, 2005, transcript of audio recording, New York City Women Community Activists Oral History Project, Sophia Smith Collection, Smith College, Northampton, Mass.

5. Craig Wilder, *A Covenant with Color*.

6. "Rent and Rookeries: I," *NY Times*, December 26, 1963, p. 26; Plunz, *A History of Housing in New York City*, 47.

7. Biondi, *To Stand and Fight*, 135.

8. Charles Grutzner, "100,000 Waiting for City Homes," *NY Times*, October 6, 1957, p. 113; Jackson, "Harlem's Rent Strike and Rat War," 57–58.

9. Purcell and Specht, "Selecting Methods and Points of Intervention in Dealing with Social Problems," 231. As Purcell and Specht point out, lead poisoning was a major

public health problem for New York's poor children. The Puerto Rican activists in the Young Lords Party made the health hazards posed by lead paint a key organizing issue in the late 1960s and early 1970s in New York City. Johanna Fernandez, "Between Social Service Reform and Revolutionary Politics"; Johanna Fernandez, "Radicals in the Late 1960s."

10. Homer Bigart, "Harlem Tenants Cope with Cold," *NY Times*, January 1, 1964, p. 1.

11. McCandlish Phillips, "Harlem Tenants Open Rent Strike," *NY Times*, September 28, 1963, p. 1; Homer Bigart, "Rent Striker Bids for Red Cross Aid," *NY Times*, December 25, 1963; Freeman, *Working-Class New York*, 183–85.

12. Quoted in Purcell and Specht, "Selecting Methods and Points of Intervention in Dealing with Social Problems," 237.

13. Ezra Birnbaum, "The Community Organization Housing Program: Report to the Ad Hoc Committee on Community Organization," January 7, 1964, pp. 4–6, U.S. Senate Internal Security Files, Box 157, Folder titled "MFY 1965–1968," National Archives, Washington, D.C.

14. Gore interview.

15. Roberta Gold, "City of Tenants," 141–42. According to Gold's interview with O'Dell, both O'Dell and Gray joined the Communist Party in the 1950s. Robert Sullivan, in contrast, writes that Gray was "probably not" a Communist, although he was certainly dedicated to promoting radical social change. Robert Sullivan, *Rats*, 66.

16. Martin Gansberg, "Tenants in 34 Tenements Join Growing Rent Strike in Harlem," *NY Times*, December 2, 1963, p. 30; "Powell Urges City Hall March to Support Harlem Rent Strike," *NY Times*, December 16, 1963, p. 27; "Harlem Slum Fighter," *NY Times*, December 31, 1963; Jackson, "Harlem's Rent Strike and Rat War," 66–67.

17. MFY's Housing Program also organized tenants in the Seward Park neighborhood to oppose city plans to site a middle-income cooperative there with no provision for low-income housing. Birnbaum, "The Community Organization Housing Program," 8. See also "Harlem Boycott on Rents Spreads," *NY Times*, November 5, 1963, p. 23, and "MFY Tenant News," vol. 1 (April 10, 1963), Frances Fox Piven Papers, Box 56, Folder 5, Sophia Smith Collection, Smith College, Northampton, Mass (hereafter cited as FFP Papers).

18. At least part of MFY's motivation in forming an independent tenants' movement was to protect the organization from the wrath of landlords and city agencies. In this they failed spectacularly. Birnbaum, "The Community Organization Housing Program," 5–7.

19. The majority of the buildings where tenants went on strike were located in lower central Harlem, in the area between 111th and 120th Streets and Park and Eighth Avenues. Residents in East Harlem also participated in the rent strikes. Samuel Kaplan, "Slum Rent Strike Gains Momentum," *NY Times*, January 1, 1964, p. 28.

20. "Harlem Boycott on Rents Spreads," *NY Times*, November 5, 1963, p. 23; "Rent Strike Plan Pushed in Harlem," *NY Times*, December 23, 1963, p. 42.

21. Bigart, "Rent Striker Bids for Red Cross Aid."

22. MFY, "Community News," vol. 1, no. 1 (January 1964), FFP Collection, Box 56, Folder 4; "Lower East Side Plans Rent Rally," *NY Times*, January 12, 1964, p. 80.

23. "Rent Strike Due to Double in Size," *NY Times*, February 1, 1964, p. 23.

24. "Conference Follow-Up Meetings Map Action: Spanish Organizing Committee," *Metropolitan Council on Housing Tenant News* 2, no. 4 (December 1963), p. 1, FFP Papers, Box 56, Folder 5.

25. Annelise Orleck, *Common Sense and a Little Fire*, 30.

26. Jose Fuentes, interview by Noel A. Cazenave, May 27, 1992, transcript of audio recording, p. 5, War on Poverty Project, Columbia University Oral History Archives, New York.

27. Andres Torres, *Between Melting Pot and Mosaic*, 61–89. Sonia Song-Ha Lee argues that the civil rights movement—in particular the March on Washington—and the War on Poverty helped to "catalyze Puerto Ricans' political association with African Americans." *Building a Latino Civil Rights Movement*, 11 and 119.

28. Patrick Doyle and William Rice, "Ricans Riot After Slaying," *Daily News*, August 31, 1964, in *MFY: The Crisis*, vol. 1, MFY Collection, School of Social Work, Columbia University, New York.

29. Ken Gross, "Lower E. Side Question: Why All the Anger?" *New York Post*, April 3, 1964, in *MFY: The Crisis*, vol. 1.

30. "Agency Assails City on Housing Action," *NY Times*, February 2, 1964, p. 88.

31. Birnbaum, "The Community Organization Housing Program," 1.

32. "Rent and Rookeries: II," *NY Times*, December 27, 1963, p. 24.

33. Quoted in Martha Davis, *Brutal Need*, 30.

34. Ibid., chapter 3. Davis notes that in their first full year of operation, the four MFY lawyers "handled 250 housing cases, 60 workers' compensation matters, 50 consumer credit cases, and 200 criminal cases" (31).

35. Michael Appleby and Harold H. Weissman, "Legal Enforcement of Laws Affecting Private Housing," 82.

36. "Jesse Gray Guilty of Hindering Police," *NY Times*, February 29, 1964, p. 10.

37. Freeman, *Working-Class New York*, 182.

38. "Rent Strike March on Police Planned," *NY Times*, March 22, 1964, p. 48.

39. Appleby and Weissman, "Legal Enforcement of Laws Affecting Private Housing," 83. Theodore Jones, "Rent Strike Gets a Woman's Touch," *NY Times*, March 20, 1964, p. 66.

40. Fuentes interview, 6.

41. Jones, "Rent Strike Gets a Woman's Touch."

42. Bigart, "Harlem Tenants Cope with Cold."

43. Martin Tolchin, "Youth Agency-Aim Stirring Debate," *NY Times*, August 22, 1964, p. 22.

44. "Rent Strike Due to Double in Size," *NY Times*, February 1, 1964, p. 23.

45. "Mother Hysterical at Boy's Bier," *NY Times*, July 19, 1964, p. 54.

46. Biondi, *To Stand and Fight*, 70.

47. Witnesses later testified that Powell had not been carrying a knife and that the policeman shot him without warning. Jack Roth, "Hogan Issues Call for Witnesses to Shooting of Boy by Gilligan," *NY Times*, August 11, 1964, p. 1. On September 1, 1964, however, the grand jury exonerated Gilligan, ruling in essence that he had acted in self-defense. Lawrence R. Samuel, *New York City 1964*, 153.

48. Freeman, *Working-Class New York*, 192.

49. Junius Griffin, " 'Guerilla War' Urged in Harlem," *NY Times*, July 20, 1964, p. 16.

50. Peter Kihss, "Gray Denies Role in Inciting Riots," *NY Times*, July 30, 1964, p. 12.

51. Gray sought the Democratic nomination for mayor in 1965 but was forced to withdraw after a court found false names on his nominating petitions. Morris Kaplan, "Gray Pulls Out of Mayoral Race; Council Finds Invalid Names," *NY Times*, August 28, 1965, p. 22.

52. Joel Schwartz, "Tenant Power in the Liberal City," 183; Sydney H. Schanberg, "Gray Reports Improvement in Slums," *NY Times*, August 11, 1964, p. 25.

53. Clayton Knowles, "New Housing Law Urged by Wagner," *NY Times*, March 22, 1965, p. 35; Samuel Kaplan, "Zaretzki Sees Passage of Bill to Legalize City Rent Strikes," *NY Times*, May 12, 1965, p. 39.

54. Cloward and Piven also argued that the strikes would have been more disruptive and thus more successful had tenants pocketed the rent money, rather than placing it in escrow accounts with the courts. Cloward and Piven, *The Politics of Turmoil*, 153–54. For additional assessments of the rent strike, see Joel Schwartz, "The New York City Rent Strikes of 1963–1964" and Jackson, "Harlem's Rent Strike and Rat War."

55. "Rent Strike Law Gets Court Test," *NY Times*, August 4, 1965, p. 37.

56. Harold H. Weissman, "The Housing Program 1962 to 1967," 61, 66.

57. Gold, "City of Tenants," 175.

58. Fuentes interview, 22.

59. "U.S. Fund to Help Slum Youth Here," *NY Times*, July 9, 1964, p. 1.

60. Peter Kihss, "Screvane Links Reds to Rioting: Says Other 'Radical Groups' Also Incited Violence," *NY Times*, July 22, 1964, p. 1.

61. Maurice Isserman, "Communism"; Isserman, "American Labor Party."

62. Ellen Schrecker, *No Ivory Tower*, 75–82.

63. Clarence Taylor, *Reds at the Blackboard*, 6.

64. Freeman, *Working-Class New York*, 72–95; Ellen Schrecker, *Many Are the Crimes*; Reitano, *The Restless City*, 156–59; Gerald Horne, *Black Liberation/Red Scare*. The Roman Catholic Church championed anticommunism in New York City; see Joshua M. Zeitz, *White Ethnic New York*.

65. Josephine Oravetz of The Research Center of the Columbia University School of Social Work assembled a five-volume documentary record of the anticommunist attacks on the organization, titled *The Crisis*. The records include newspaper clippings, official reports, and internal agency documents. "Mobilization for Youth Minutes of the Meeting of the Committee on Social Issues and Public Policy," August 4, 1964, Pan American Building, in *MFY: The Crisis*, vol. 1.

66. William Federici, Edward O'Neill, and Henry Lee, "Anti-JD Agency Probed for Red Ties," *The Daily News*, August 16, 1964, pp. 1–2; "The Hunt's on for Reds in E. Side Youth Project," *New York Journal American*, August 17, 1964, p. 1, in *MFY: The Crisis*, vol. 1.

67. Homer Bigart, "Youth Project Chief Is Called to Capital," *NY Times*, August 18, 1964, p. 1.

68. Martin Tolchin, "Project's Road Has Been Rocky," *NY Times*, August 17, 1964, p. 12.

69. Jack Newfield, "The Story of Mobilization for Youth: An Old Theory Is Put to the Test," *New York Post Sunday Magazine*, August 20, 1964, in *MFY: The Crisis*, vol. 1.

70. James Edward Smethurst, *The Black Arts Movement*, 138–39.

71. Homer Bigart, "Youth Aide Ran as a Leftist," *NY Times*, August 27, 1964, p. 30. The three MFY employees belonged to the Socialist Workers Party and the Progressive Labor Party, which had both split from the Communist Party USA. Piven and Cloward contended that the communist allegations stemmed from sectarian factions within the Old Left; because of the split between the Trotskyites and the Communist Party in the 1930s, members of the Trotskyite faction had reported MFY to the New York Police Department's "Red Squad." Piven and Cloward summarized: "It seems clear that MFY had got-

ten caught in the lingering vendettas carried on by elements of the Old Left. The few ex-Communists on MFY's staff had been singled out by former Trotskyites and Socialists who were now trusted members of the Liberal-Democratic coalition, and depended upon to keep track of their ancient enemies." Frances Fox Piven, interview by Tamar Carroll, July 14, 2004, transcript of audio recording, New York City Women Community Activists Oral History Project; Frances Fox Piven and Richard Cloward, "Echoes from the Old Left," FFP Papers, Box 72, Folder 14. Regardless of where these charges originated, they carried weight with city administrators and agencies angry at MFY's attacks on their policies.

72. Homer Bigart, "9 in Youth Project Linked to Leftists," *NY Times*, August 19, 1964, p. 1. The *Daily News* held other MFY staff members' travel abroad, to Cuba or the Soviet Union in particular, as evidence of communism. "A Statement of the Undersigned Staff Members of Mobilization for Youth," n.d., FFP Papers, Box 55, Folder 11.

73. Barbara Hunter Randall Joseph, interview by Tamar Carroll, March 21, 2005, transcript of audio recording, New York City Women Community Activists Oral History Project.

74. Schrecker, *Many Are the Crimes*, 266–305.

75. Frances Fox Piven, interview by Tamar Carroll, April 21, 2004, transcript of audio recording, New York City Women Community Activists Oral History Project.

76. Bigart, "9 in Youth Project Linked to Leftists."

77. Tolchin, "Youth Agency Aim in Stirring Debate."

78. "A Statement of the Undersigned Staff Members of Mobilization for Youth," n.d., FFP Papers.

79. Tolchin, "Project's Road Has Been Rocky."

80. Newfield, "The Story of Mobilization for Youth."

81. "MFY Notes," no. 3 (October 8, 1964) FFP Papers, Box 55, Folder 11.

82. George Younger, Haydee Ortiz, and Esther Gollobin, "A Statement Defends Mobilization for Youth," *East Side News*, August 28, in *MFY: The Crisis*, vol. 1.

83. "A Rally Is Held for Youth Agency," *NY Times*, August 30, 1964, p. 56.

84. "13,500 Sign Petitions Backing MFY," *Daily News*, September 5, 1964, in *MFY: The Crisis*, vol. 1. The Council of Puerto Rican Organizations, the Lower East Side Neighborhood Association, CORE, and the NAACP also sent telegrams backing MFY. Fred Gilman, "What's So 'Natural' About Hounding of MFY," *The Worker*, November 17, 1964, p. 8, in Senate Internal Security Subfiles, Box 157, Folder titled "MFY: 2," National Archives, Washington, D.C.

85. Junius Griffin, "Youth Unit Wins Experts' Praise," *NY Times*, November 17, 1964, p. 1.

86. "The Right to Fight City Hall," *NY Times*, November 11, 1964, in Richard Cloward Collection, Box 2, Folder M, Sophia Smith Collection.

87. Paul Ylivisaker, Director, Ford Foundation to George Brager, MFY, September 14, 1964, FFP Papers, Box 58, Folder 7.

88. Jack Mallon and Edward O'Neill, "MFY Exec Blew $1,000 Monthly on Food and Booze," *Daily News*, September 1, 1964, p. 5, in Senate Internal Security Files, Box 157, Folder titled "MFY: 2," National Archives, Washington, D.C.

89. For an example of Lindsay's support of MFY, see the transcript of his interview with WABC-TV on October 17, 1965, in FFP Papers, Box 72, Folder 14. Ultimately, Screvane's redbaiting backfired, and he lost the Democratic primary to Abraham Beame. Terry

Smith, "Buckley, Communism, and Mayoral Campaign," *New York Herald Tribune*, September 29, 1965, FFP Papers, Box 72, Folder 14. Daniel Patrick Moynihan ran for City Council president on Screvane's team, and *The Village Voice* reported that Moynihan had boasted of playing a role in ordering FBI loyalty checks into the agency's staff. Jack Newfield, "Moynihan Says He Helped Extract Mobilization Reds," *The Village Voice*, August 1, 1965, in FFP Papers, Box 72, Folder 14.

90. "MFY Staff Fighting Witch Hunt," *National Guardian*, September 16, 1964, p. 1, in Senate Internal Security Files, Box 157, Folder titled "MFY '65-'68," National Archives, Washington, D.C.

91. Homer Bigart, "Marchi Is Challenged to Prove Aide of M.F.Y. Is 'Extremist'," *NY Times*, January 1, 1965, p. 24.

92. Homer Bigart, "4 in Youth Agency Retort to Marchi," *NY Times*, January, 1965, p. C26.

93. Fred Powledge, "Mobilization for Youth Receives $1,542,820 and a Clean Slate," *NY Times*, August 24, 1965, p. 18.

94. Homer Bigart, "Director Resigns at Youth Agency," *NY Times*, December 29, 1964, p. 16. Richard Cloward also resigned as codirector, although he continued to direct the research efforts of MFY from his base at the Research Center at the Columbia University School of Social Work. Bertram M. Beck, "Mobilization for Youth," 146.

95. Bertram Beck, interview by Noel Cazenave, May 18, 1992, transcript of audio recording, War on Poverty Project. Cazenave argues that Beck was an elitist professional social worker who opposed maximum feasible participation and implemented a strong commitment to professionalism during his tenure at MFY. Cazenave, *Impossible Democracy*, 163-66.

96. Harry Specht, "Report to the Ad Hoc Committee to Review the Community Organizing Program," March 4, 1964, p. 4, FFP Papers, Box 56, Folder 5. Specht and Brager, who earned a PhD at NYU in 1968 and eventually became dean of the social work school at Columbia, coauthored *Community Organizing*, the best-known handbook on the subject.

97. Ezra Birnbaum, interview by Tamar Carroll, April 11, 2005, transcript of audio recording, New York City Women Community Activists Oral History Project, Sophia Smith Collection.

98. Ibid.

99. Marilyn Bibb Gore and Sidney Pinsky, interview by Noel A. Cazenave, May 19, 1992, transcript of audio recording, War on Poverty Project.

100. Joseph interview. For more on Women Strike for Peace, see Swerdlow, *Women Strike for Peace*; Andrea Estepa, "Taking the White Gloves Off."

101. Joseph interview.

102. Baxandall interview.

103. For the larger history of the welfare rights movement, see Chappell, *The War on Welfare*; Kornbluh, *The Battle for Welfare Rights*; Nadasen, *Welfare Warriors*; Pope, *Biting the Hand That Feeds Them*; West, *The National Welfare Rights Movement*.

104. John Kifner, "Welfare Clients Indict City Aid," *NY Times*, March 11, 1966, p. 21. Davis, *Brutal Need*, 40-41.

105. Davis, *Brutal Need*, 42.

106. Kifner, "Welfare Clients Indict City Aid."

107. Birnbaum interview.

108. Davis, *Brutal Need*, 47–50. Karen Tani documents the development of a right to a fair hearing among the administrators of the Social Security Board as early as 1936. Karen M. Tani, "Welfare and Rights Before the Movement."

109. Davis, *Brutal Need*, 43–44.

110. Ibid., 51.

111. "City Inquiry Sought on Welfare Costs," *NY Times*, January 3, 1964, p. 24.

112. Davis, *Brutal Need*, 53.

113. Linda Greenhouse, "New Look at an 'Obscure' Ruling, 20 Years Later," *NY Times*, May 11, 1990. Fritz Umbach argues that the expansion of "individual rights in relation to state institutions" through the fair-hearing rights that MFY secured had a detrimental effect: it limited the ability of community groups to achieve self-determination. Specifically, he found that public housing residents experienced the 1971 *Escalera vs. New York City Housing Authority* consent decree that gave public housing tenants greater protection from eviction as weakening their community's safety by making it very difficult to evict tenants expediently, even when they had committed crimes. When coupled with disinvestment, Umbach concludes that "in public housing, the disparity between increasingly robust legal rights and increasingly dismal day-to-day circumstances had the effect of making life for the majority of law-abiding tenants worse, not better." *The Last Neighborhood Cops*, 9–11, 149–59, 169.

114. Davis, *Brutal Need*.

115. Chappell, *The War on Welfare*, 65–105.

116. George Brager, interview by Noel Cazenave, May 19, 1992, transcript of audio recording, War on Poverty Project.

117. The 1966 Scheurer Amendments to the EOA authorized $3.3 million for the New Careers Program. The New Careers Program, as well as the previous Community Action Program provision within the EOA, allowed for the hiring of paraprofessionals in human service agencies, including community organizers, day-care workers, counselors, and teachers' aides. Nancy A. Naples, *Grassroots Warriors*, 2.

118. Harold J. Rothwax, "The Law as an Instrument of Social Change." Nancy LeBlanc, interview by Tamar Carroll, July 27, 2005, audio recording.

119. Herbert Mitgang, "The Storefront Lawyer Helps the Poor," *The NY Times Sunday Magazine*, November 10, 1968. For more on the development of legal services across the country, see Earl Johnson Jr., *Justice and Reform*.

120. Cazenave, *Impossible Democracy*, 166–69. Rosenbloom, "The Neighborhood Movement," 7.

121. Stanley Aronowitz, interview by Tamar Carroll, December 4, 2012, transcript of audio recording, New York City Women Community Activists Oral History Project. Mary Perot Nichols, "Riding to Utopia on the Monorail," *The Village Voice*, May 29, 1969, pp. 9–10, 55.

122. The original *Waiting for Lefty* featured cab drivers planning a labor strike and was the first critical success to come out of New York's Group Theater, which was founded to support new plays documenting social reality during the Great Depression.

123. For the history of the black arts movement broadly, see especially Smethurst, *The Black Arts Movement*. On the MFY Cultural Arts Program specifically, see Woodie King Jr., *The Impact of Race*, 33–40. Woodie King Jr., interview by Tamar Carroll, December 13, 2012, transcript of audio recording, p. 11, New York City Women Community Activists Oral History Project; Henry Heifetz, "Training Youth in the Arts"; James R. Sikes,

"Play's the Thing in Poverty Areas: Youth Perform in Realistic Dramas in City Programs," *NY Times*, August 7, 1966.

124. In summer 1964, Baraka came under criticism for producing "anti-white" plays with OEO funding at his Harlem-based Black Arts Repertory Theater. An OEO report concluded that "collectively" the plays *The Super, The Liberal, Black Ice, Jello,* and *The Experimental Death Unit* "denounced Martin Luther King's philosophy of nonviolence, advocated rebellion by black people, challenged the liberal rhetoric as hypocritical, exposed white capitalist exploitation of the ghetto, and invoked a quasi-Marxist form of political and social revolution." While the plays were well-received in Harlem, according to the OEO, critics were particularly offended by the use of "black-face-in-reverse" and the term "whitey," and OEO funding was eventually cut. Administrative History, Office of Economic Opportunity, vol. 1, pp. 116–120, Lyndon Baines Johnson Library, Austin, Tex. MFY's Cultural Arts Program, in contrast, received critical praise.

125. King interview, 13–18.

126. King, *The Impact of Race*, 38.

127. King interview, 22–23.

128. Elenore Lester, "Cut Off from American Life?" *NY Times*, August 27, 1967.

129. King, *The Impact of Race*, 39.

130. King interview, 8.

131. Evelyn Thomas, interview by Tamar Carroll, April 13, 2013, transcript of audio recording in author's possession, 24.

132. Smethurst, *The Black Arts Movement*, 105–6.

133. Ibid., 10.

134. King interview, 18.

135. Hattie Gossett, "in the window/monk," printed in Norma Rogers, "Introduction to the Lower East Side Retrospective," *African American Review* 27, no. 4 (1993): 571–72.

136. Marilyn Bibb Gore and Sidney Pinsky, interview by Noel A. Cazenave, May 19, 1992, transcript of audio recording, War on Poverty Project.

137. Brager interview.

138. Lee and Diaz, " 'I Was the One Percenter,' " 71–72.

139. Terry Mizrahi, interview by Tamar Carroll, May 3, 2005, transcript of audio recording, New York City Women Community Activists Oral History Project.

140. Birnbaum interview. For information on Lower East Side residents' participation in the community health movement of the late 1960s and early 1970s, see Mizrahi interview.

141. Janet Peterson, interview by Tamar Carroll, September 6, 2003, transcript of audio recording, New York City Women Community Activists Oral History Project; Karen M. Tani, "The House That 'Equality' Built"; Cazenave, *Impossible Democracy*, 174. In 1975, the OEO was renamed the Community Services Administration (CSA) and in 1981, the CSA was closed, replaced by block grants to the states.

CHAPTER THREE

1. Orleck and Hazirjian, *The War on Poverty*, especially chapters 5–7.

2. On Ocean Hill-Brownsville, see Jerald E. Podair, *The Strike That Changed New York*; Marilyn Gittell and Maurice R. Berube, *Confrontation at Ocean-Hill Brownsville*. For the

backlash against school busing for racial integration, see Rieder, *Canarsie*; Ronald D. Formisano, *Boston against Busing*; Matthew Lassiter, *The Silent Majority*. On white ethnic attitudes toward racial integration more broadly, see Zeitz, *White Ethnic New York*; Kenneth D. Durr, *Behind the Blacklash*.

3. Schulman, *The Seventies*, 53–77.

4. Michael Novak, *The Rise of the Unmeltable Ethnics*; Matthew Frye Jacobson, *Roots Too*.

5. Richard Rogin, "Joe Kelly Has Reached His Boiling Point: Why the Construction Workers Holler, 'U.S.A., All the Way!'," *NY Times Sunday Magazine*, June 28, 1970. See also Pete Hamill, "The Revolt of the White Lower Middle Class," *New York Magazine*, April 14, 1969.

6. Novak, *The Rise of the Unmeltable Ethnics*, 28–29.

7. Richard Sennett and Jonathan Cobb, *The Hidden Injuries of Class*.

8. David R. Roediger, *Working Towards Whiteness*; Theodore Sorenson, *Kennedy*, 9–17; Theodore H. White, *The Making of the President 1960*, 258–61.

9. Jan Peterson, interview by Tamar Carroll and Lara Rusch, August 16, 2002, transcript of audio recording, New York City Women Community Activists Oral History Project, Sophia Smith Collection, Northampton, Mass.

10. The full text of the Port Huron Statement is available at http://www.lsa.umich.edu/phs/resources/porthuronstatementfulltext (accessed 21 August 2013).

11. Robert Rosenbloom, "The Neighborhood Movement," 9. Baroni, the Catholic Church's coordinator for the 1963 March on Washington for Jobs and Freedom, advocated the formation of political coalitions between urban whites and minority groups, as well as community organizing, local control of social services, and Catholic Church funding for antipoverty work. See Geno Baroni, *Pieces of a Dream*; Philip Shabecoff, "Msgr. Geno Baroni, a Leader in Community Organizing," *NY Times*, August 29 1984; Lawrence O'Rourke, *Geno*; Dennis Deslippe, "'We Must Bring Together a New Coalition'"; Robert Bauman, "'Kind of a Secular Sacrament.'" Wade Rathke began his activism as an organizer for the National Welfare Rights Organization. For more on Rathke and ACORN, see Gary Delgado, *Organizing the Movement*; Robert Fisher, *The People Shall Rule*; John Atlas, *Seeds of Change*.

12. On the origins and consequences of redlining, see David M. P. Freund, *Colored Property*, 111–39. On urban renewal in New York, see Zipp, *Manhattan Projects*.

13. Suleiman Osman, *The Invention of Brownstone Brooklyn*; Rosenbloom, "The Neighborhood Movement," 7. The exemplar of neighborhood-based program building was the Black Panther Party. Murch, *Living for the City*; Nelson, *Body and Soul*.

14. Kaplan, *Story of Jane*; Morgen, *Into Our Own Hands*; Enke, *Finding the Movement*; Kline, *Bodies of Knowledge*.

15. For an overview of The Feminists, see Echols, *Daring to Be Bad*, 167–85. On Flo Kennedy, see Sherie Randolph, *Women's Liberation or . . . Black Liberation, You're Fighting the Same Enemies*.

16. Held at the Marriage License Bureau, this was The Feminists' most famous direct action. For coverage of the demonstration and the group's hard-line policy on attendance and its quota on married members, see Sara Davidson, "An 'Oppressed Majority' Demands Its Rights," *Life Magazine*, December 12, 1969, 67–78.

17. Kate Millet, *Sexual Politics*; Susan Brownmiller, *Against Our Will*. On New York Radical Feminists, see Echols, *Daring to Be Bad*, 186–97.

18. Donna Sammons, "Jan Peterson: Bringing the Movement Home," *Herald-Dispatch* (Huntington, West Virginia), November 4, 1975, NCNW Records, Box 28, Folder 12, Sophia Smith Collection, Smith College, Northampton, Mass. Jan Peterson, interview by Tamar Carroll and Lara Rusch, August 16, 2002, transcript of audio recording, New York City Women Community Activists Oral History Project, Sophia Smith Collection. Jan Peterson, interview by Tamar Carroll, December 7, 2012.

19. Nancy Seifer, *Nobody Speaks for Me!*; Peterson, interview by Rusch and Carroll, August 16, 2002.

20. Jan Peterson, "A Bridge to the Neighborhoods for the Women's Movement," n.d., NCNW Records, Box 1, Folder 23.

21. Ellen M. Synder-Grenier, *Brooklyn!*, 31, 34, 45; Susser, *Norman Street*, 30.

22. Themis Chronopoulos, "Politics of Race and Class," 4.

23. Nadine Brozan, "A Community Where Family Togetherness Is a Thing of the Past," *NY Times*, February 14, 1972, p. 34.

24. Janie Eisenberg, interview by Tamar Carroll, Manhattan, May 31, 2006.

25. David Gonzales, "Still Taking to the Streets to Honor Their Saints," *NY Times*, June 7, 2010, A16.

26. John T. McGreevy, *Parish Boundaries*, 20. A similar but larger Italian festival in East Harlem is chronicled in vivid detail in Robert A. Orsi, *The Madonna of 115th Street*.

27. Emanuel Perlmutter, "Our Changing City: Northern Brooklyn," *NY Times*, July 22, 1955, p. 25; Brozan, "A Community Where Family Togetherness Is a Thing of the Past."

28. McGreevy, *Parish Boundaries*, 13–28.

29. Wilder, *A Covenant with Color*, 181–97.

30. Susser, *Norman Street*, 93–96, 99–100; Phillip Thompson, "Public Housing in New York City," 121. Rochdale Village, a large United Housing Foundation cooperative in Jamaica, Queens, was an important exception to the pattern of racial segregation; in the 1960s it was racially integrated with a population that was approximately 20 percent African American, although by the mid-1970s most of its white residents had moved out. Eisenstadt, *Rochdale Village*, 4.

31. "Cornerstone is Laid in Greenpoint for Project to Have 11 Buildings," *NY Times*, October 22, 1952, p. 29.

32. Steven Roberts, "Housing Hearing Sets Off Debate," *NY Times*, April 26, 1966, p. 35; Brozan, "A Community Where Family Togetherness Is a Thing of the Past." Throughout the late 1970s and 1980s, the neighborhood's white ethnics did succeed in blocking restoration of the McCarren Park Pool, which they contended brought African American and Puerto Ricans into their neighborhood. Chronopoulos, "Politics of Race and Class," 7–9. For more on white ethnics' attempts to preserve racial segregation in Greenpoint, see Judith DeSena, *Protecting One's Turf*. On segregated recreation facilities more broadly, see Jeff Wiltse, *Contested Waters*; Victoria W. Wolcott, *Race, Riots and Roller Coasters*.

33. Mildred Tudy (later Tudy-Johnston), interviewed in *Metropolitan Avenue*, produced and directed by Christine Noschese, 1985, videocassette, NCNW Records, Box 145, Tape 1. Themis Chronopoulos argues that "white ethnics felt that they had to protect the areas around subway stations because otherwise their access to Manhattan would be severely limited and the commercial centers adjacent to them would fail." He found that the Graham Avenue LL (later L) train stop, in the center of Italian Williamsburg, was the most hotly defended, and some nonwhite residents of Cooper Park would walk

to more distant stops to avoid confrontations there. Chronopoulos, "Politics of Race and Class," 4.

34. Tudy quoted in Anne Witte Garland, *Women Activists Challenging the Abuse of Power*, 69. On segregation in Greenpoint's churches, see DeSena, *Protecting One's Turf*, 74–75.

35. Susser, *Norman Street*, 92–93.

36. Sally Martino Fisher, interviewed in *Metropolitan Avenue*. The quotation is from Sally Martino Fisher, interview by Tamar Carroll and Martha Ackelsberg, March 23, 2004, transcript of audio recording, New York City Women Community Activists Oral History Project, Sophia Smith Collection, p. 19.

37. Rieder, *Canarsie*, 1; Sugrue, *The Origins of the Urban Crisis*, chapter 9.

38. Thomas A. Guglielmo, *White on Arrival*, 159. Guglielmo demonstrates that as Italians immigrated to the United States, immigration officials categorized their color as "white" but their "race" as either Northern or Southern Italian. It was not until the early 1940s that race and color conflated and Italian Americans began to mobilize politically as white, often to maintain racial segregation of housing.

39. Jennifer Guglielmo and Salvatore Salerno, *Are Italians White?*, 4.

40. Guglielmo, *White on Arrival*, 170; Guglielmo and Salerno, *Are Italians White?*, 13.

41. Diane Henry, "A Survey on Italian-Americans Finds Government Is Ignoring Their Needs," *NY Times*, February 6, 1975, p. 29.

42. Elizabeth Speranza, Tillie Tarantino, Angie Giglios, and Jan Peterson, group interview by Mary Belenky, February 26, 1992, transcript titled "NCNW," p. 1, NCNW Records, Box 8, Folder 4.

43. Guglielmo, *Living the Revolution*, 3.

44. Women's workplaces were often more racially integrated than men's, as men of certain ethnicities dominated and controlled the "skilled" branches. Tillie Tarantino, group interview by Tamar Carroll, December 12, 2012; Guglielmo, *Living the Revolution*, 4. On Italian immigrant women's participation in labor unions, see also Orleck, *Common Sense and a Little Fire*. On the ILGWU in particular, see Katz, *All Together Different*. As Katz shows, in the 1930s the ILGWU celebrated the ethnic identities of its members and encouraged women's leadership and participation in education programs that fostered understanding across racial and ethnic differences, but by 1940 the leadership of the ILGWU had grown much more conservative and abandoned its educational efforts. Thus, over time the union diminished as a space for interracial socialization. On racial discrimination against Puerto Rican and African American workers within the ILGWU in the post–World War II years, see Lee, *Building a Latino Civil Rights Movement*, 61–94.

45. Guglielmo, *Living the Revolution*, 267.

46. Peterson, interview by Carroll, August 16, 2002.

47. Ibid.

48. Speranza, group interview by Belenky, 1.

49. Peterson, interview by Carroll, August 16, 2002. Tillie Tarantino and Peterson, group interview by Carroll, December 12, 2012.

50. Garland, *Women Activists Challenging the Abuse of Power*, 65–68.

51. Colin Campbell, "A Lifetime of Leadership: An Interview with Mildred Tudy," NCNW Records, Box 97, Folder 23.

52. Garland, *Women Activists Challenging the Abuse of Power*, 69.

53. Ibid.

54. *Metropolitan Avenue*.

55. Freeman, *Working-Class New York*, chapter 15; Steven R. Weisman, "City in Crisis II."

56. The Northside runs from Grand Street north to 15th Street in Greenpoint, from the East River to the Brooklyn-Queens Expressway. It was a primarily Polish neighborhood with many senior citizens. Susser, *Norman Street*, 218–19.

57. Brozan, "A Community Where Family Togetherness Is a Thing of the Past," 34.

58. *Metropolitan Avenue*; Susser, *Norman Street*, 170–71.

59. Freeman, *Working-Class New York*, 277.

60. Fredelle Maynard, "Woman Power," *Woman's Day*, November 16, 1982, NCNW Records, Box 28, Folder 12; "Demographics," NCNW Records, Box 67, Folder 22.

61. Interview with Rosalie Wysoboski, NCNW Records, Box 143, Tape 1 Side A. Pollution remained a pressing concerns for Williamsburg residents and led to environmental justice activism in the 1980s and 1990s, documented in Julie Sze, *Noxious New York*.

62. Susser, *Norman Street*, 162.

63. Janie Eisenberg, interview by Tamar Carroll, Manhattan, May 31, 2006.

64. For accounts of the fires in the South Bronx, see Jill Jonnes, *South Bronx Rising*; Jonathan Mahler, *Ladies and Gentlemen, the Bronx Is Burning*.

65. Lena Williams, "Brooklyn Drive Pressed to Open Local Firehouse," *NY Times*, November 28, 1976; Frank J. Prial, "Protest Is Planned on an Alleged Shift of Rescue Company," *NY Times*, January 2, 1977, p. 11; Paul Schneider, *People's Firehouse #1*, DVD, 1979; Eisenberg interview.

66. Schneider, *People's Firehouse #1*.

67. Susser, *Norman Street*, 180–81.

68. "'People's Firehouse' to Resume Services," *NY Times*, March 4, 1977, p. 19.

69. People's Firehouse Housing and Community Development Co. 10th anniversary brochure, November 23, 1985, NCNW Records, Box 135, Folder 19; Susser, *Norman Street*, chapter 10. On May 25, 2003, Mayor Michael Bloomberg, marshaling overwhelming police force, finally succeeded in closing the firehouse. Sadly, the following November, a five-alarm fire spread quickly down Monitor Street in the Northside, blazing for more than eight hours and destroying a half-block of homes and displacing 29 families. Shaila K. Dewan, "Police Snatch a Fire Engine from Its Die-Hard Guardians in Brooklyn," *NY Times*, August 13, 2003, p. B1; Michael Brick, "Greenpoint Fire Guts Half-Block and Displaces 29 Families," *NY Times*, November 20, 2003, p. B1. Currently, Paul Veneski, Adam's son, is leading a campaign to turn the building into a community center with offices for the People's Firehouse Inc. and an environmental group, Neighbors Allied for Good Growth, with the ground floor to be used as a performance space for arts groups. Lore Croghan, "Williamsburg Activists Running Kickstarter Campaign for 'People's Firehouse' Makeover," *New York Daily News*, September 5, 2012.

70. Peter Freiberg, "Neighborhoods: Woman Power," *New York Post*, June 25, 1976.

71. Orsi, *The Madonna of 115th Street*, 129–49. As Orsi notes, these gender norms "compelled women to exercise their authority and influence in subterranean ways" (147). Jennifer Guglielmo shows that because Italian American women's activism often occurred in the home and through female networks, it was overlooked by historians as well as contemporaries. Guglielmo, *Living the Revolution*. See also Virginia Yans-McLaughlin,

Family and Community; Micaela di Leonardo, *Varieties of Ethnic Experience*; Miriam Cohen, *Workshop to Office*.

72. Speranza, Tarantino, Giglios, and Peterson, group interview by Belenky, 7.

73. Tillie Tarantino, quoted in Mary Field Belenky, Lynne A. Bond, and Jacqueline S. Weinstock, *A Tradition That Has No Name*, 212.

74. Speranza, Tarantino, Giglios, and Peterson, group interview by Belenky, 13.

75. *Working Class Women Changing Their World*, produced by Jan Peterson and Christine Noschese, 1975, videocassette, NCNW Records, Box 145, Tape 4.

76. Speranza, Tarantino, Giglios, and Peterson, group interview Belenky, 5.

77. In his study of Elmhurst-Corona, Queens, Roger Sanjeck found that women were more likely to work across racial ties for the purpose of community activism than men were, because women related to each other as women more quickly than men related to each other as men. Additionally, because of their gender socialization and the structure of the workplace, women valued "improvisation and abilities to involve others," while men valued hierarchy. Roger Sanjek, *The Future of Us All*, 374–75.

78. Danielle Furfaro, "Williamsburg's Beloved Swinging Sixties Center Closing," *The Brooklyn Paper*, October 15, 2012. As of this writing, Peterson, Tarantino's daughter and granddaughter, and other residents were fighting the city's plans to close the center in a new round of budget cuts and had won a temporary stay to keep the center going. As of June 2014, the nonprofit St. Nick's Alliance was challenging the new lease agreement, which included a dramatic rent increase and tenant liability to fix $500,000 in outstanding repairs, in court. Julie Strickland, "Politicians, Landlord in Battle over Williamsburg Senior Center," *The Real Deal: New York Real Estate News*, June 25, 2014, http://therealdeal.com/blog/2014/06/25/pols-push-for-city-purchase-of-williamsburg -senior-center/ (accessed 28 August 2014).

79. Speranza, Tarantino, Giglios, and Peterson, group interview by Belenky, 13–27.

80. Peterson, interview by Carroll and Rusch, August 16, 2002.

81. *National Congress of Neighborhood Women Quarterly*, vol. 1, no. 1 (Spring 1976), NCNW Records, Box 29, Folder 4.

82. The consciousness-raising session was recorded by Italian American NCNW member Christine Noschese, a pioneer in feminist filmmaking.

83. *Working Class Women Changing Their World*.

84. Peterson, interview by Carroll and Rusch, August 16, 2002.

85. Lindsay Van Gelder, "National Congress of Neighborhood Women: When the Edith Bunkers Unite!" *Ms.*, February 1979, NCNW Records, Box 28, Folder 10. The funds came from the pilot for the Comprehensive Employment Act (CETA). Peterson, interview by Carroll and Rusch, August 16, 2002.

86. Wooten, "Report of Activities for 1980–1981."

87. Speranza, Tarantino, Giglios, and Peterson, group interview by Belenky, 4–5.

88. Deborah Esposito and Antoinette Rohan, "The Counseling Program at NCNW," NCNW Records, Box 59, Folder 12.

89. Noschese was challenged by her best friend, black filmmaker Carol Olegrario, to diversify the NCNW. Christine Noschese, telephone interview by Tamar Carroll, March 15, 2006.

90. "Neighborhood Studies and Leadership Development: The NCNW College Program," 1982, NCNW Records, Box 69, Folder 22.

91. Jan Peterson and Christine Noschese, "Our College Program," NCNW Records, Box 69, Folder 19, p. 6.

92. Jan Peterson and Christine Noschese, "An Overview of the College Program from the First Year Report," in "Our College Program," NCNW Records, Box 69, Folder 19, p. 1. See also Terry Haywoode and Laura Scanlon, "World of Our Mothers."

93. *National Congress of Neighborhood Women Quarterly*, vol. 1, no. 1 (Spring 1976): 2, NCNW Records, Box 29, Folder 4; Judy Janda to Sandy Lowe, April 4, 1979, NCNW Records, Box 31, Folder 4.

94. "Progress Report Education Committee," June 17, 1977, NCNW Records, Box 3, Folder 5.

95. Jan Peterson to Marilyn Levy, March 12 1980, NCNW Records, Box 18, Folder 19. In fall 1982, the NCNW offered a B.A. in Community Development and Special Studies through Empire State College in conjunction with the College at Old Westbury. In January 1982, it began offering courses in elementary and special education for accreditation through Brooklyn College. "Neighborhood Studies and Leadership Development: The NCNW College Program," 1982, NCNW Records, Box 69, Folder 22.

96. Alice Quinn to Ralph Perrotta, May 22, 1975, NCNW Records, Box 31, Folder 1.

97. Esposito and Rohan, "The Counseling Program at NCNW."

98. Belenky, Bond, and Weinstock, *A Tradition That Has No Name*, 208–9.

99. Johanna Brenner, *Women and the Politics of Class* (New York: Monthly Review Press, 2000), 4.

100. Katz, *All Together Different*, 1–16.

101. The NCNW's Latina membership was primarily Puerto Rican but also included some Cuban and Mexican Americans. "Neighborhood Studies and Leadership Development: The NCNW College Program," 2.

102. "A Dialogue on the Organization, Goals and Needs of the National Congress of Neighborhood Women," June 1978, p. 1–2, NCNW Records, Box 3, Folder 8.

103. John T. McGreevy, *Parish Boundaries*.

104. Peterson and Noschese, "An Overview of the College Program from the First Year Report."

105. Francis X. Clines, "About New York: A Quiet Revolution in Northside," *NY Times*, January 21, 1978.

106. Guglielmo, *Living the Revolution*, 200–201.

107. Barbara Grizzuti Harrison, "Hers," *NY Times*, May 22, 1980.

108. Diane Jackson, interview by Martha Ackelsberg, New York, April 28, 2004, tape recording.

109. Terry Haywoode, interview by Tamar Carroll and Martha Ackelsberg, April 30, 2004, transcript of audio recording, New York City Women Community Activists Oral History Project, Sophia Smith Collection.

110. Jackson interview.

111. Lindsay Van Gelder, "Battered Wives Hit Back at the System," *New York Post*, December 2, 1976, NCNW Records, Box 28, Folder 10. The Women's Survival Space, now part of the Center Against Domestic Violence, is the longest-operating domestic violence emergency shelter in New York. http://www.cadvny.org/2009/08/17/our-history/.

112. Diane Jackson, "Diane Jackson," NCNW Records, Box 75, Folder 24.

113. Deslippe, "'We Must Bring Together a New Coalition,'" 166. Jim Sleeper similarly argues that "only in granting the integrity of one another's experience of

uprooting can New Yorkers discover what they share." Sleeper, *The Closest of Strangers*, 122.

114. Mantler, *Power to the Poor*, 5.

CHAPTER FOUR

1. "Affiliates," *Neighborhood Woman*, vol. 1, no. 3 (November/December 1977), NCNW Records, Box 29, Folder 5. An examination of the affiliate organizations is beyond the scope of this study; however, more information on the affiliate organizations is available in Tamar Carroll, "How Did Feminists Meet the Challenges of Working across Differences?"

2. Enid Nemy, "For Working-Class Women, Own Organization and Goals," *NY Times*, January 24, 1976, p. L20.

3. Evans, *Personal Politics*; Echols, *Daring to Be Bad*; Whittier, *Feminist Generations*; Horowitz, *Betty Friedan and the Making of Women's Liberation*; Rosen, *The World Split Open*; Chappell, "Rethinking Women's Politics in the 1970s"; Ezekiel, *Feminism in the Heartland*; Evans, *Tidal Wave*; Gilmore, *Groundswell*.

4. Nadasen, "Expanding the Boundaries of the Women's Movement"; Roth, *Separate Roads to Feminism*; Springer, *Living for the Revolution*; Breines, *The Trouble between Us*; Blackwell, *Chicana Power!*

5. Nancy A. Naples, *Community Activism and Feminist Politics*; Thompson, "Multiracial Feminism"; Nelson, *Women of Color and the Reproductive Rights Movement*; Cobble, *The Other Women's Movement*; MacLean, *Freedom Is Not Enough*, chapter 4; Enke, *Finding the Movement*; Valk, *Radical Sisters*; Gilmore, *Feminist Coalitions*; Hewitt, *No Permanent Waves*.

6. Historians Katherine Turk and Lisa Levenstein argue that NOW chapters in the late 1960s and early 1970s were diverse and included activists that prioritized the needs of working-class women and displaced homemakers reentering the workforce and that sought recognition of the economic value of women's unpaid domestic and caregiving work; over the course of the 1970s, however, the organization streamlined to a sole focus on achieving ratification of the Equal Rights Amendment. Turk, "Out of the Revolution, into the Mainstream"; Levenstein, " 'Don't Agonize, Organize!' " On changes in women's labor force participation, family structure, and female and child poverty, see also Susan Thistle, *From Marriage to Market*; Natasha Zaretsky, *No Direction Home*; Chappell, *The War on Welfare*; Robert O. Self, *All in the Family*.

7. Ethel Velez, interview by Tamar Carroll and Martha Ackelsberg, March 30, 2004, transcript of audio recording, New York City Women Community Activists Oral History Project, Sophia Smith Collection, Smith College, Northampton, Mass.

8. Peter Passell, "Like a New Drug, Social Programs Are Put to the Test," *NY Times*, March 9, 1993, p. C1.

9. Stansell, *The Feminist Promise*, 355–94.

10. http://www.huairou.org/

11. Jan Peterson, interview by Tamar Carroll and Lara Rusch, August 16, 2002, transcript of audio recording, New York City Women Community Activists Oral History Project, Sophia Smith Collection.

12. "Portrait of the Artist as a Civil Servant," *The Economist*, Sept. 20, 1975; John Berry and Art Pine, "19 Years of Job Programs—Question Still Is 'What Works'," *Washington*

Post, April 24, 1979; Ronald Smothers, "CETA Cutbacks Leaving Thousands Unemployed," *NY Times*, April 11 1981; "Why CETA Is in Trouble," *Business Week*, October 2, 1978, p. 124.

13. "New York Groups Win $2.6 Million Federal Job Grant," *Women's Agenda* 5, NCNW Records, Box 75, Folder 22, Sophia Smith Collection; Elise Piquet, "Those Women: The Story of Project Open Doors," n.d., NCNW Records, Box 75, Folder 24.

14. Peterson, interview by Carroll and Rusch, August 16, 2002.

15. Geraldine Miller, interview by Tamar Carroll and Lara Rusch, August 16, 2002, transcript of audio recording, New York City Women Community Activists Oral History Project.

16. Lindsay Van Gelder, "National Congress of Neighborhood Women: When the Edith Bunkers Unite!, *Ms.*, February 1979, NCNW Box 28, Folder 10; Constance Rosenblum, "The Old-Fashioned Feminists of Brooklyn," *Sunday News Magazine*, New York, August 7, 1977, p. 7, NCNW Records, Box 28, Folder 10; Carol Brightman, "The Women of Williamsburg," NCNW Records, Box 28, Folder 12.

17. "Overview: A Women's Perspective on Community Problems," NCNW Records, Box 3, Folder 23.

18. Susan Faludi, *Backlash*.

19. Jan Peterson, "The NCNW," n.d., NCNW Records, Box 4, Folder 22; Barbara Grizzuti Harrison, "Hers," *NY Times*, May 22, 1980, p. C2, NCNW Records, Box 28, Folder 12; Francis X. Clines, "About New York: A Quiet Revolution in Northside," *NY Times*, January 21, 1978, NCNW Records, Box 28, Folder 12.

20. Untitled term paper, n.d., NCNW Records, Box 69, Folder 28, p. 9. Video footage from the "Speak Out on Housework" and other NCNW programs and events has recently been digitized and is now available to watch streaming from the Sophia Smith Collection website at: http://media.smith.edu/departments/ssc/ncnw/ncnw_playlist.html.

21. Guglielmo, *Living the Revolution*, 133.

22. Nemy, "For Working-Class Women, Own Organization and Goals."

23. Friedan, *The Feminine Mystique*.

24. Nancy MacLean, *Freedom Is Not Enough*; MacLean, "The Hidden History of Affirmative Action."

25. Harrison, "Hers."

26. Jan Peterson to Counseling Staff, February 29, 1988, p. 7, NCNW Records, Box 99, Folder 9.

27. Jan Peterson, "The National Congress of Neighborhood Women College Model," p. 14, NCNW Records, Box 69, Folder 24.

28. "Goals/Objectives Staff," November 20, 1979, NCNW Records, Box 1, Folder 11.

29. Jan Peterson, "The NCNW," n.d., NCNW Records, Box 4, Folder 22; "Obstacles," n.d., NCNW Records, Box 1, Folder 11; "NCNW: Original Goals and Objectives," n.d., NCNW Records, Box 1, Folder 7.

30. Nemy, "For Working-Class Women, Own Organization and Goals."

31. Elizabeth Speranza, Tillie Tarantino, Angie Giglios, and Jan Peterson, group interview by Mary Belenky, February 26, 1992, transcript titled "NCNW," p. 7, NCNW Records, Box 8, Folder 4.

32. Untitled term paper, NCNW Records, Box 69, Folder 28, p. 12.

33. Deborah Esposito and Antoinette Rohan, "The Counseling Program and NCNW," NCNW Records, Box 59, Folder 12.

34. Neighborhood Women for Home & Family, "New Women's Group Attacks," 1977, NCNW Records, Box 28, Folder 12.

35. The NCNW, "On Women: The Old Welcomes the New," 1977, NCNW Records, Box 28, Folder 12.

36. "Ethnic Heritage Cooper Park," audiocassette, NCNW Records, Box 143, Tape 10.

37. Harrison, "Hers."

38. Lisel Burns, interview by Tamar Carroll, February 12, 2004, transcript of audio recording, New York City Women Community Activists Oral History Project, Sophia Smith Collection. The thirteen principles the NCNW committed itself to supporting after a 1982 national meeting are: "values-based processes, empowerment, economic self-determination, women's leadership, neighborhood, families, support groups and networks, government responsibility, coalitions, diversity, including environmental concerns, and our health and well-being." The National Congress of Neighborhood Women, *The Neighborhood Women's Training Sourcebook,* 1993, pp. 10–22, in author's possession.

39. Carol Brightman, "The Women of Williamsburg," *Working Papers,* January/February 1978, p. 54, NCNW Records, Box 28, Folder 12.

40. Sally Martino Fisher, interview by Tamar Carroll and Martha Ackelsberg, March 23, 2004, transcript of audio recording, New York City Women Community Activists Oral History Project, Sophia Smith Collection. Nan Robertson, "Women's Meeting Friday in Albany Will Have a National Focus," *NY Times,* July 5, 1977.

41. "We are Women," n.d., NCNW Records, Box 4, Folder 22.

42. Jan Peterson, interview by Tamar Carroll, December 7, 2013.

43. *Working Class Women Changing Their World,* produced by Jan Peterson and Christine Noschese, 1975, videocassette, NCNW Records, Box 145, Tape 4.

44. Baxandall and Gordon, *Dear Sisters,* 13.

45. Maria Fava, Ann Giordano, Elaine Carpinelli, Sandy Schilen, and Jan Peterson, group interview by Mary Belenky, March 26, 1992, transcript titled "NCNW," pp. 3–4, NCNW Records Box 8, Folder 4.

46. Ibid., 1–2, 18–19.

47. Ibid., 1–2, 10–11, 32.

48. Burns interview.

49. NCNW, *The Neighborhood Women's Training Sourcebook,* 180.

50. Support group topics included, "Self-confidence as women," "Ethnic and racial identities as women," "Learning and the oppression of schools," "Goal setting and planning as women," "Class and its effect on our lives as women," and "Housing and our lives as women." Lisel Burns, "General Curriculum Ideas for Support Groups," February 8, 1983, NCNW Records, Box 15, Folder 24.

51. "Summary," n.d., NCNW Records, Box 98, Folder 5, pp. 2–3; Jan Peterson to Counseling Staff, February 29, 1988, NCNW Records, Box 99, Folder 9, pp. 11–14; Lisel Burns, "NCNW Training Materials: General Ideas for Support Groups," January 24, 1983, NCNW Records, Box 115, Folder 18.

52. Ethel Battle Velez, "Why Do You Do Community Work?" n.d., NCNW Records, Box 101, Folder 34.

53. Echols, *Daring to Be Bad*; Anne Valk, "Living a Feminist Lifestyle"; Ezekiel, *Feminism in the Heartland*; Whittier, *Feminist Generations.* I am not claiming that the

NCNW was the first or the only group to employ an analysis of intersectionality; rather, I am arguing that using a conception of multiple, overlapping identities allowed the NCNW to treat seriously the differences between members while also identifying areas of mutual need. For an early and eloquent statement of intersectionality, see Combahee River Collective, "Combahee River Collective Statement." Similarly, Kimberly Springer writes that "black feminists . . . enacted interstitial politics focused on articulating their race, gender and class identities as interconnected." Springer, *Living for the Revolution*, 4.

54. NCNW, *The Neighborhood Women's Training Sourcebook*, 56.

55. Ibid., 72–75.

56. Miller, interview by Carroll and Rusch.

57. Rona Feit, interview by Tamar Carroll, January 9, 2004, transcript of audio recording, New York City Women Community Activists Oral History Project, Sophia Smith Collection.

58. Velez interview.

59. Fava, Giordano, Carpinelli, Schilen, and Peterson, group interview by Belenky, 30.

60. Christine Noschese, interview by Tamar Carroll and Martha Ackelsberg, March 30, 2004, transcript of audio recording, New York City Women Community Activists Oral History Project.

61. Former clients of Jackins have since accused him of misusing his authority in counselor-patient relationships.

62. Fisher interview.

63. Elise Piquet, "Those Women: The Story of Project Open Doors," n.d., NCNW Records, Box 75, Folder 24, p. 10.

64. "Memo to the Board of the Battered Women's Shelter and the NCNW Board from the Ad Hoc Committee to Support Working-Class Women as Leaders," 1978, NCNW Records, Box 31, Folder 3.

65. "Mildred Johnson: Community Organizer," *Neighborhood Woman*, vol. 1, no. 3, (November/December 1977): 3, NCNW Records, Box 29, Folder 5.

66. "Memo to The Board of the Battered Women's Shelter."

67. Jan Peterson to author, email communication, April 26, 2006.

68. Morgen, *Into Our Own Hands*, chapter 7. Kimberly Springer also found that "direction of fund-raising and organization often fell to black feminist organizations' leaders, raising conflicts among black feminist activists over power, privilege, and the future of black feminism." Springer, *Living for the Revolution*, 18.

69. Peterson, interview by Carroll and Rusch, August 16, 2002.

70. Bruce Schulman, "Slouching Toward the Supply Side," 56. William E. Leuchtenburg, "Jimmy Carter and the Post–New Deal Presidency," 19.

71. Leuchtenburg, "Jimmy Carter and the Post–New Deal Presidency," 12–13; Schulman, "Slouching Toward the Supply Side," 60–61.

72. Alice Quinn to Subcontractors/Worksites, August 9, 1979, NCNW Records, Box 54, Folder 9.

73. Fisher interview.

74. Isabelle Katz Pinzler to Ronald Gault, n.d., NCNW Records, Box 55, Folder 9; *NCNW, NOW NY et al vs. City of New York Dept. of Employment and U.S. Dept. of Labor*, NCNW Records, Box 55, Folder 2.

75. Initial Determination, *NCNW et al vs. City of New York*, May 30 1980, NCNW Records, Box 55, Folder 5; Stipulation of Settlement, Case No. 81-CETA-147, NCNW Records, Box 55, Folder 7.

76. Gil Troy, *Morning in America*, 57; Gareth Davies, "The Welfare State," 217.

77. Robert Pear, "Nonprofit Groups Are Losing U.S. Aid," *NY Times*, September 2, 1982, p. A18.

78. Richard P. Nathan and Fred C. Doolittle, "Federal Grants," 65.

79. Peter Passell, "Like a New Drug, Social Programs Are Put to the Test," *NY Times*, March 9, 1993, p. C1.

80. Kenneth B. Noble, "After 20 Years, Is It Time to Retire the Jobs Corps?" *NY Times*, April 21, 1985, Section 4, p. 5; Nathan and Doolittle, "Federal Grants," 68.

81. Peterson, interview by Carroll and Rusch.

82. Terry Haywoode, interview by Tamar Carroll and Martha Ackelsberg, April 30, 2004, transcript of audio recording, New York City Women Community Activist Oral History Project, Sophia Smith Collection.

83. Suzanne Daley, "Soup Kitchens Rise Sharply, Report Finds," *NY Times*, June 25, 1987, p. B1.

84. "Fall 1982 Press Release," n.d., NCNW Records, Box 1, Folder 24.

85. "NCNW Narrative Description of Project," n.d, NCNW Records, Box 55, Folder 7; "Annual Report, 1982–83," n.d., NCNW Records, Box 1, Folder 26; Alice Quinn to Tony Torres, December 3, 1982, NCNW Records, Box 101, Folder 1.

86. Jan Peterson to Board of Directors, November 20, 1986, NCNW Records, Box 45, Folder 10; "Educational and Employment Program for Adult Women," ca. 1990, in author's possession.

87. "Participant Expectations and Regulations," September 5, 1985, NCNW Records, Box 85, Folder 17.

88. NCNW, "Original Goals and Objectives," NCNW Records, Box 1, Folder 7.

89. Sandy Schilen, interview by Tamar Carroll and Martha Ackelsberg, April 20, 2004, transcript of audio recording, New York City Women Community Activists Oral History Project, Sophia Smith Collection.

90. See for example, Leslie Bennetts, "Teen-Age Pregnancies: Profiles in Ignorance," *NY Times*, December 20, 1981, p. 57; William J. Haskins, "A Black Responsibility," *NY Times*, October 4, 1982, p. A19; Paul Bass, "New Group Seeks Strategies for Curbing Teen Pregnancies," January 12, 1986, p. A1; "Cost of Teen-Age Pregnancies," *NY Times*, February 20, 1986, p. C11.

91. NCNW, *The Neighborhood Women's Training Sourcebook*, 8.

92. "Our Training Programs," NCNW Records, Box 97, Folder 13.

93. "Governor Cuomo Believes 'You Can,'" *NCNW Newsletter*, November 1986, NCNW Records, Box 29, Folder 10, pp. 6–7; NCNW, "Educational and Employment Program for Adult Women," ca. 1990, in author's possession.

94. Untitled, "The 1989–1991 JTPA contract year . . . ," NCNW Records, Box 7, Folder 12.

95. Peterson, interview by Carroll and Rusch.

96. Schilen interview.

97. NCNW, *The Neighborhood Women's Training Sourcebook*, 8.

98. Caroline Pezzullo, interview by Tamar Carroll, August 19, 2002, transcript of audio recording, New York City Women Activists Oral History Project, Sophia Smith Collection.

99. Estelle B. Freedman, *No Turning Back*, 107–12.

100. Pezzullo interview.

101. NCNW, *The Neighborhood Women's Training Sourcebook*, 181–82.

102. Sandy Schilen, "Presentation at the Global Coalitions for Voices for the Poor," World Bank Consultation, July 31–August 1, 2000, NCNW office, Brooklyn. Although Neighborhood Women of Williamsburg-Greenpoint, the NCNW, and GROOTS are separate nonprofits, they all share the same Williamsburg office and staff and membership overlap.

103. Velez interview.

104. Rosemary Jackson, telephone interview by Tamar Carroll, May 7, 2006.

105. Ibid.

106. Janet Peterson, interview by Carroll and Rusch, August 16, 2002.

107. Schilen interview.

108. Elizabeth Speranza, Tillie Tarantino, Angie Giglios, and Jan Peterson, group interview by Mary Belenky, February 26, 1992, transcript titled "NCNW," p. 12, NCNW Box 8, Folder 4.

109. Janie Eisenberg, interview by Tamar Carroll, Manhattan, May 31, 2006.

110. Peterson, interview by Carroll, December 7, 2012; Danielle Furfaro, "New Bid to Save Williamsburg's Swinging Sixties Senior Center," *The Brooklyn Paper*, March 28, 2013.

111. Payne, *I've Got the Light of Freedom*, 364.

112. Jan Peterson, "Draft of Leadership Training Program," September 3 1982, NCNW Records, Box 3, Folder 19.

113. The job and college programs were closed due to a lack of funding, stemming from federal and state cuts in social service spending and a shift in private foundations' grant-allocating priorities.

114. Fisher interview.

115. Nancy MacLean, "The Hidden History of Affirmative Action: Working Women's Struggles in the 1970s and the Gender of Class," *Feminist Studies* 25 (1999).

CHAPTER FIVE

1. John H. Mollenkopf, *New York City in the 1980s*, 5, 41–49; Mollenkopf and Castells, "Introduction," 7–9.

2. Sharon Zukin, *Loft Living*, 175, 86.

3. Schulman, *The Seventies*, 246–52.

4. Samuel R. Delaney, *Times Square Red, Times Square Blue*; Plunz, *A History of Housing in New York City*; Peter Marcuse, "Abandonment, Gentrification, and Displacement."

5. Moore, *Beyond Shame*; Schulman, *Gentrification of the Mind*.

6. Stuart Taylor, "Division Is Bitter," *NY Times*, July 1, 1986, p. A1.

7. See, for example, Donald Kaplan, "Bishop Daily Leads 600 in S'Park Abortion Protest," *The Park Slope Paper*, July 27, 1990, p. 1; Mary Papenfuss, "Bishop's Abortion Clinic Crusade: Brooklyn Cleric Vows to Hit the Streets with Prayer Vigils," *New York Post*, May 7, 1990, p. 1, 5.

8. Mary Anne Staniszewski, group interview by Tamar Carroll, Albany, N.Y., December 16, 2005, digital video recording, WHAM! Oral History Collection, OH-66-012, Tamiment Library, New York University.

9. "Queer Nation Manifesto," June 1990, http://www.actupny.org/documents/QueersReadThis.pdf (accessed 15 May 2013).

10. *United in Anger*, directed by Jim Hubbard. 2012. DVD.

11. On the history and influence of ACT UP in changing treatment design and testing, see especially Jennifer Brier, *Infectious Ideas*; Gould, *Moving Politics*; Steven Epstein, *Impure Science*. On the CDC definition of AIDS and its exclusion of conditions affecting women, IV drug users, and homeless people, see ACT UP/NY Women & AIDS Book Group, eds., *Women, AIDS and Activism*.

12. Douglas Crimp and Adam Rolston, *AIDS Demographics*, 13.

13. Leslie Bennetts, "Man in New York," *Vanity Fair*, August 1990.

14. Peter Steinfels, "Death of a Cardinal," *NY Times*, May 4, 2000.

15. Felicia Lee, "At a Catholic Health Center, a Haven for AIDS Patients," *NY Times*, April 21, 1989; Bruce Lambert, "A Nursing Home Ward is Approved for AIDS," *NY Times*, August 12, 1988.

16. Increased competition from for-profit hospital networks led to the closure of more than 600 community hospitals in the 1980s. Some Catholic congregations had already been operating more than one health care institution and were well positioned to expand their systems. According to Barbra Wall, "by 1985 there were 91 Catholic health systems out of a total of 268" (Wall, *American Catholic Hospitals*, 16–17). According to Susan Berke Fogel and Lourdes A. Rivera, "from 1990–2001 there were 171 mergers or acquisitions of secular hospitals by Catholic health systems" nationally (Fogel and Rivera, "Saving Roe is Not Enough," 730). The increase in Catholic-sponsored or affiliated hospitals intensified in the following decade so that by 2011, "about one in nine beds was in a Catholic-sponsored or affiliated hospital." It is argued that the growth in Catholic-affiliated hospitals "may reduce or eliminate women's health services in the affected communities, especially abortion, contraception, sterilization, infertility services, and emergency contraceptives for rape survivors. Low-income, minority, and rural residents are most affected because they have fewer options." (Monica Slodoba, "The High Cost of Merging with a Religiously-Controlled Hospital," 140–41). In many rural areas, Catholic hospitals are the only provider. (Lois Uttley et al., *Miscarriage of Medicine*). My thanks to Sara Dubow for pointing me toward these sources.

17. While scholars have rightly focused attention on the Charitable Choice Provision of the Personal Responsibility and Work Opportunity Act of 1996 (P.L. 104–938 section 104) because it allows religious groups including churches, mosques, and synagogues to receive government funds directly (as opposed to receiving them through a nonprofit), the privatization of social welfare provision started in the early 1980s as the Reagan administration began this shift toward government funding of faith-based initiatives. Carol J. De Vita and Sarah Wilson, "Faith-Based Initiatives: Sacred Deeds and Secular Dollars," in *Emerging Issues in Philanthropy* (The Urban Institute, 2001), available online at http://www.urban.org/UploadedPDF/310351_philanthropy_5.pdf (accessed 30 March 2010); William Saletan, *Bearing Right*; Robert Wineburg et al., "Leveling the Playing Field: Epitomizing Devolution through Faith-Based Organizations," *Journal of Sociology and Social Welfare* 35, no. 1 (March 2008): 17–42.

18. Self, *All in the Family*, Prologue.

19. Marion Banzhaf, Tracy Morgan, and Karen Ramspacher, "Reproductive Rights and AIDS," 203–4; Self, *All in the Family*, 183, 258.

20. Lei Chou, interview by Sarah Schulman, May 5, 2003, transcript of video recording, p. 21, ACT UP Oral History Project.

21. Ibid., 28.

22. Moore, *Beyond Shame*, 131. Anne Cvetkovich also points to the importance of friendships between gay men and lesbians in ACT UP, and argues that these friendships, political alliances, and sometimes romantic partnerships constituted a working out of what it meant to be queer, and were the basis for the organization's power. Cvetkovich, *An Archive of Feelings*, chapter 5. Cvetkovich examines the experiences of lesbians in ACT UP New York in chapters five and six of her work. Sarah Schulman, in her novel *People in Trouble* based on her experiences on ACT UP, makes the working out of her main characters' (two women and a man) sexual identities the central drama.

23. Epstein, *Impure Science*. On the women's health movement, see Morgen, *Into Our Own Hands*; Nelson, *Women of Color and the Reproductive Rights Movement*; Kline, *Bodies of Knowledge*.

24. Ronald Sullivan, "Needle-Exchangers Had Right to Break Law, Judge Rules," *NY Times*, June 26, 1991; Kaplan, *Story of Jane*.

25. Norma Broude and Mary D. Garrard, *The Power of Feminist Art*, 171–72.

26. Mary Anne Staniszewski, *Believing Is Seeing*, 40. Mary Anne Staniszewski, group interview by Tamar Carroll.

27. Maria Maggenti, interview by Sarah Schulman, January 20, 2003, transcript of video recording, pp. 39–42, ACT UP Oral History Project; Gloria Steinem, "After Black Power, Women's Liberation," *New York Magazine*, April 4, 1969; Martin, *The Theater Is in the Street*; Bradford Martin, *The Other Eighties*, 173.

28. Amy Bauer, interview by Sarah Schulman, March 7, 2004, transcript of video recording, pp. 15–25, 47–50, ACT UP Oral History Project.

29. Self, for example, argues that feminism began to decline as a social movement and lose influence politically by the second half of the 1970s (Self, *All in the Family*, 321). For an overview of progressive social movements in the 1980s, see Martin, *The Other Eighties*.

30. Douglas Crimp, *Melancholia and Moralism*, 59. Recent studies suggest that people were infected with HIV in Congo in the 1950s, and that by the mid-1960s, HIV was present in Haiti, and from there emerged in the United States around 1969 in Haitian immigrants. Phil Tiemeyer, *Plane Queer*, 139–40.

31. Paula A. Treichler, *How to Have Theory in an Epidemic*, 25; Brier, *Infectious Ideas*, 80–81; Self, *All in the Family*, 388.

32. Michael Daly, "AIDS Anxiety," *New York Magazine*, June 20, 1983; Dudley Clendinen, "AIDS Spreads Pain and Fear Among Ill and Health Alike," *NY Times* June 17, 1983; Susan M. Chambre, *Fighting for Our Lives*, 20–24; Jennifer Brier, "'Save Our Kids, Keep AIDS Out.'"

33. In his influential history of the early AIDS epidemic in the United States, journalist Randy Shilts attributes the lack of city attention to AIDS to the fact that Koch, a longtime bachelor, had been gay-baited during his 1977 mayoral campaign against, among other candidates, Mario Cuomo, with signs that said "Vote for Cuomo Not The Homo." Shilts suggests that Koch wanted to prevent any further association with homosexuality and therefore avoided meeting with gay leaders to discuss the emerging epidemic. However, Democratic governors Cuomo and Michael Dukakis (Mass.) also

blocked funding for AIDS in the early 1980s, and the Republican Reagan administration was notoriously slow to respond on the federal level as well. (Randy Shilts, *And the Band Played On*, 181, 245, 340, 559.) Debate over Koch's sexuality and whether it influenced his response to the emerging AIDS epidemic continues today.

Both Shilts and Kramer attempted through their writing to draw attention to what they perceived to be an inadequate governmental and societal response to the AIDS crisis rooted in homophobia, yet both argued that gay men needed to abandon promiscuity and adopt monogamy, thus reinforcing the belief that AIDS was a result of gay immorality. For a critique of moralism and homophobia in writings by Shilts and Kramer, see Crimp, *Melancholia and Moralism*, 42–82; Tiemeyer, *Plane Queer*, 136–93. For an overview of GMHC, see Chambre, *Fighting for Our Lives*.

34. "The City: New AIDS Office Set Up for City," *NY Times*, March 10, 1983; Larry Kramer, "1,112 and Counting," *New York Native* 59, March 14–27, 1983, available online at http://www.bilerico.com/2011/06/larry_kramers_historic_essay_aids_at_30.php (accessed 28 August 2014).

35. Benjamin Shepard, "Building a Healing Community from ACT UP to Housing Works," 355.

36. Robert Vazquez-Pacheco, interview by Sarah Schulman, December 14, 2002, transcript of video recording, ACT UP Oral History Project, p. 11.

37. Clendinen, "AIDS Spreads Pain and Fear."

38. Roberto Suro, "Vatican Reproaches Homosexuals with a Pointed Allusion to AIDS," *NY Times*, October 31, 1986.

39. Joyce Purnick, "City Closes Bar Frequented By Homosexuals, Citing Sexual Activity Linked to AIDS," *NY Times*, November 8, 1985.

40. William Greer, "Violence Against Homosexuals Rising, Groups Seeking Wider Protection Say," *NY Times*, November 23, 1986.

41. William F. Buckley Jr., "Crucial Steps in Combating the AIDS Epidemic; Identify All the Carriers," *NY Times*, March 18, 1986.

42. Douglas Crimp, "Gran Fury Talks to Douglas Crimp," *Artforum International*, April 1 2003; Richard Goldstein, "How AIDS Activists Tapped the Power of Art," *Village Voice*, March 25, 1997, pp. 43–44. Gran Fury took the name of the Plymouth model used by the NYC Police Department in 1987, after its "Let the Record Show" display at the New Museum.

43. Richard Meyer, "This Is to Enrage You," 62.

44. May 31, 1987, was the date of President Reagan's first speech on AIDS, which focused mainly on testing and avoided using the words gay or homosexual (Shilts, 559). See also Jennifer Brier, *Infectious Ideas*, 80. In Chapter 3 of her book, Brier argues that after 1985, the Reagan administration did begin to address the AIDS epidemic, but that its approach was divided, reflecting different camps within modern American conservatism. Surgeon General Everett Koop and the State Department promoted sex education and condom distribution as methods to reduce the spread of AIDS, while presidential advisor and Christian Right member Gary Bauer emphasized instead "personal responsibility" and "heterosexual marriage."

45. Reproductive Rights Coalition Meeting Minutes, June 20, 1991, WHAM! Records, Tamiment Library Archives, New York University. Prior to Republican mayor Rudolph Giuliani's campaign to clean up New York in the mid-1990s, wheatpasting was

tolerated by the police, with only a nominal fine imposed if one was caught in the act, and noncommercial images were much more common in the city.

46. In addition to the Gay Men's Health Crisis, some audience members had participated in the Gay and Lesbian Alliance Against Defamation (GLAAD), formed in 1985 to combat homophobia, and in the Lavender Hill Mob, a small gay and lesbian group that did zap actions and met with government officials about AIDS policy. Laraine Sommella, "This Is About People Dying," 410–11.

47. Jason DeParle, "Rude, Rash, Effective, ACT-UP Shifts AIDS Policy," *NY Times*, January 3, 1990, pp. B1–B4.

48. Ibid., B1, B4; Mark Schoofs, "The AIDS Shock Troops Who Changed the World," *Village Voice*, March 25, 1997, pp. 42–44; No author, "ACT UP Marks Tenth Anniversary Founding at Center," *Center Voice: Newsletter of the Lesbian and Gay Community Services Center*, April/May 1997, 1–4, WHAM! Records. "ACT UP Background: A Capsule History of ACT UP/NY," n.d., WHAM! Records.

49. Cynthia Crossen, "Shock Troops: AIDS Activist Group Harasses and Provokes to Make Its Point," *Wall Street Journal*, December 7, 1989, p. 1.

50. ACT UP NY Minutes, February 22, 1988, Box 3, Folder 1, Reel 2, ACT UP New York Records, Manuscripts and Archives Division, The New York Public Library.

51. Jesse Green, "When Political Art Mattered: ART=CHANGE," *NY Times Magazine*, December 7, 2003, p. 69.

52. For example, Lauren Monroe, who was in high school in New York in the late 1980s, recalled herself and her friends hanging the Silence = Death posters in their bedroom and following the news coverage of ACT UP demonstrations. Lauren Monroe, interview by Tamar Carroll, July 29, 2010, audio recording.

53. Some heterosexuals wore a pink triangle to affirm their solidarity with gays and lesbians, particularly during the AIDS epidemic, just as some non-Jews who resisted Nazi occupation had worn yellow stars in solidarity with Jews but were assumed to be, and were treated as, Jewish themselves. Ron Goldberg, interview by Sarah Schulman, October 25, 2003, transcript of video recording, p. 7, ACT UP Oral History Project.

54. Eric Sawyer, interview by Carlos Motta, March 1, 2011, transcript of audio recording, We Who Feel Differently Project, http://wewhofeeldifferently.info/interview.php?interview=100 (accessed 29 May 2013).

55. Crossen, "Shock Troops: AIDS Activist Group Harasses and Provokes to Make Its Point," 6–8.

56. Donna Minkowitz, "ACT UP at a Crossroads," *Village Voice*, June 5, 1990, pp. 19–22.

57. Rebecca Cole, interview by Sarah Schulman, ACT UP Oral History Project, June 30, 2008, transcript of video recording, p. 56.

58. Peter Cohen links the "inside" approach to the "class style" of upper middle-class white men in ACT UP who were used to being treated with respect and given access to power and preferred negotiating to staging demonstrations. Peter F. Cohen, *Love and Anger*, 49.

59. Jean Carlomusto, interview by Sarah Schulman, December 19, 2002, transcript of video recording, p. 31, ACT UP Oral History Project.

60. Douglas Crimp, interview by Sarah Schulman, May 16, 2007, transcript of audio recording, p. 30, ACT UP Oral History Project.

61. Minkowitz, "ACT UP at a Crossroads," 19–22.

62. Maggenti interview; Sawyer interview by Motta, 8.

63. "ACT UP/NY Capsule History," p. 1, WHAM! Records.

64. The text of the Denver Principles is available online at http://www.actupny.org/documents/Denver.html (accessed 15 August 2013).

65. Minkowitz, "ACT UP at a Crossroads," 19–22.

66. Brier, *Infectious Ideas*, 179–84.

67. Gould, *Moving Politics*, 334. "Invitation to ACT/UP Majority Action Committee Meeting," July 13, 1988, Box 2, Folder 37, Robert Garcia Papers, 1988–1993, Cornell University Library, Division of Rare and Manuscript Collections. Subsequently, a Latino/Latina caucus and an Asian Pacific Islander caucus formed.

68. Kendall Thomas, interview by Sarah Schulman, May 3, 2003, transcript of video recording, p. 13, ACT UP Oral History Project.

69. Lei Chou, interview by Sarah Schulman, May 5, 2003, transcript of video recording, p. 21, ACT UP Oral History Project.

70. Thomas interview, 14, 20; Chou interview, 22.

71. Robert Sullivan, "Tuberculosis in City Reported on Rise," *NY Times*, March 3, 1980, p. B3; Crimp and Rolston, *AIDS Demographics*, 122–29.

72. Edward Gargan, "Ducking for Cover Over the Homeless," *NY Times*, November 27, 1983, p. E7.

73. Russell Baker, "A Cold Hard Net," *NY Times*, December 18, 1982, p. 27.

74. Gedalia Braverman, interview by Sarah Schulman, April 20, 2003, transcript of video recording, pp. 13–16, ACT UP Oral History Project.

75. William Geist, "The Expanding Empire of Donald Trump," *NY Times Sunday Magazine*, April 8, 1984, p. 31. Trump had sought a $20 million tax abatement and was granted $6 million. Crimp and Rolston, *AIDS Demographics*, 122.

76. "An ACT UP Chronology," 1994, WHAM! Records.

77. "ACT UP/NY Capsule History," WHAM! Records.

78. Braverman interview, 16; Eric Sawyer, interview by Sarah Schulman, March 10, 2004, transcript of video recording, pp. 26–27, ACT UP Oral History Project; Bruce Lambert, "In Spite of Crisis, New York Lacks Basic Services for AIDS Patients," *NY Times*, January 3, 1989.

79. The Reagan administration chose Cardinal O'Connor for its AIDS panel, despite his claim that homosexuality was sinful and his opposition to promoting condom use as a way to prevent the spread of AIDS. "Reagan's AIDS Panel: Who the Members Are," *NY Times*, July 24, 1987, p. A12; "Vatican AIDS Meeting Hears O'Connor Assail Condom Use," *NY Times*, November 14, 1989, p. A10; Bruce Lambert, "Nursing Homes to Increase Beds for AIDS Cases: New York State to Help Archdiocese in Plan," *NY Times*, January 10, 1990, p. B3; Bruce Lambert, "A Church-State Conflict Arises Over AIDS Care," *NY Times*, February 23, 1990, p. B2.

80. "Clinic Will Become AIDS Nursing Home," *NY Times*, March 19, 1989, ACT UP/NY Capsule History, p. 3; Braverman interview, p. 17.

81. Sawyer, interview by Schulman, 27–29.

82. Cole interview, 63–64.

83. Sawyer interview by Schulman, 21, 35.

84. Shepard, "Building a Healing Community from ACT UP to Housing Works," 358. See also http://www.housingworks.org/aboutus/history.html.

85. *Housing Works 2012 Annual Report*, http://www.housingworks.org/annual_report.html#page/4 (accessed 10 July 2013).

86. "An ACT UP Chronology," 8, WHAM! Records.

87. Cvetkovich, *An Archive of Feelings*, chapters 5 and 6.

88. Emily Nahmanson, interview by Sarah Schulman, April 27, 2003, transcript of video recording, p. 23, ACT UP Oral History Project.

89. Kimberly Smith, "Tough Act to Follow: AIDS, ACT UP, and Women: An Interview with Liz Tracey," n.d., 3 pp., WHAM! Records.

90. Maggenti interview, p. 24.

91. Carlomusto interview, 18.

92. Maria Maggenti et al., *The ACT UP Women's Caucus Women and AIDS Handbook*, March 1989, p. 91, WHAM! Records. The handbook was later published as ACT UP/NY Women & AIDS Book Group, eds., *Women, AIDS and Activism*.

93. The film can be viewed at http://www.jeancarlomusto.com/doctorsliars&women.html.

94. Also at the 1988 Lesbian and Gay Pride March, the Women's Caucus passed out information about safe sex for lesbians and 200 women subsequently came to their Safer Sex Forum. "Action at Shea Stadium: Women and AIDS Day," May 4, 1988, ACT UP NY Records, Reel 53, pp. 94–96.

95. "City Council Swallows the Wafer," *Village Voice*, January 9, 1990, p. 41.

96. Ibid., 93.

97. Ibid., 93-A.

98. Maggenti et al., *The ACT UP Women's Caucus Women and AIDS Handbook*, 48–52; Gina Kolata, "AIDS Research on New Drugs Bypasses Addicts and Women," *NY Times*, January 5, 1988. Cole interview.

99. "An ACT UP Chronology," 1994, p. 6, WHAM! Records.

100. For more information on *Our Bodies, Ourselves*, see Kline, *Bodies of Knowledge*.

101. Suki Terada Ports and Marion Banzhaf, "Many Cultures, Many Approaches," 107.

102. Banzhaf, Morgan, and Ramspacher, "Reproductive Rights and AIDS," 200–202.

103. Karen Davy, Laura Bird, and Jessie Mangaliman, "Abortion Rights Rally in Union Square," *Newsday*, July 6, 1989, 4, 25.

104. Sue Davis to Reproductive Rights Coalition, "Re: Proposal to reconcile the need for action and structure," n.d., p. 1, WHAM! Records; Karen Ramspacher, interview by Tamar Carroll, September 8, 2003, transcript of audio recording, p. 6, WHAM! Oral History Collection, Tamiment Library.

105. Mary Lou Greenberg, "New Yorkers Working for Pro-Choice Victory," *New Directions for Women*, November/December 1989, p. 18, WHAM! Records.

106. Brian Griffin, interview by Tamar Carroll, March 16, 2004, transcript of audio recording, p. 2, WHAM! Oral History Collection, Tamiment Library.

107. Griffin interview, 12.

108. Susan Shaw, interview by Tamar Carroll, July 26, 2004, transcript of audio recording, p. 2, WHAM! Oral History Collection, Tamiment Library.

109. Charlotte Abbott, Panel 2, "A Retrospective Assessment of WHAM!," WHAM! Forum and Reunion, Tamiment Library, New York University, October 15, 2005, video recording.

110. Shaw interview, 6.

111. Shannon Cain, telephone interview by Tamar Carroll, October 2004.

112. Self, *All in the Family*, 143–44, 55, 59, 285.

113. Linda Gordon, "Back-Alley Antiabortion," *The Nation*, 1998.

114. Self, *All in the Family*, 368, 96.

115. Douglas Crimp and Adam Rolston, "Stop the Church," 132; DeParle, "111 Held in St. Patrick's AIDS Protest"; Mary Papenfuss, "New Bishop Plans Abortion Pray-Ins," *New York Post*, May 7, 1990, p. 5.

116. Elizabeth Meixell to Tamar Carroll, email communication, March 9, 2004.

117. Tracy Morgan, "From WHAM! to ACT UP," 146.

118. Karen Ramspacher, interview with Tamar Carroll, March 5, 2004, audio recording, WHAM! Oral History Collection, Tamiment Library.

119. Kate Walter, "A View from St. Marks Place," *New York Press*, December 22, 1989, p. 8; Griffin interview. The clowns were part of a direct-action group "Operation Ridiculous," a satire of the antiabortion group Operation Rescue. They chanted, "Save the clown babies." *Like a Prayer: Stop the Church*, produced by Damned Interfering Video Activists (DIVA TV), 1990, DVD, in author's possession.

120. Carlomusto interview, 34.

121. Ron Goldberg, interviewed by Sarah Schulman, Manhattan, October 25, 2003, transcript of video recording, pp. 26–27, ACT UP Oral History Project

122. Amy Pagnozzi, "Catholics' Dilemma: Thinking They Can Pick the Loopholes," *New York Post*, December 11, 1989, pp. 3, 14.

123. Crimp and Rolston, "Stop the Church." Coverage of the Stop the Church demonstration was extensive in all the New York papers. See, for example, Manuel Perez-Rivas and Ji-Yeon Yuh, "Protest Siege at St. Pat's: 111 Arrests in abortion, AIDS Sit-in," *Daily News*, December 11 1989, p. 1, 3, 25; Linda Stevens, "Protests: Mass Turns into Nightmare for Cardinal," *New York Post*, December 11 1989, p. 1–3; Charles Bell, "Mass Will Go On: O'Connor Pledges," *Daily News*, December 12 1989, p. 5; and Jason DeParle, "111 Held in St. Patrick's AIDS Protest," *NY Times*, December 11, 1989, p. B3. The protest also received national coverage. See, for example, Joyce Price, "Protestors Interrupt Mass at St. Patrick's," *Washington Times*, December 11, 1989, p. 1, 7. Posters from the WHAM! Records. See also, "Media Report: 'Stop the Church,'" WHAM! Records.

124. Robert Hilferty, director, *Issues and Outrage: Stop the Church*, 1990, DVD, in author's possession. For the controversy over airing Hilferty's film on public television, see B. J. Bullert, *Public Television*, 123–45.

125. Andrew Miller and Rex Wockner, "AIDS/Abortion Rights Demo Halts High Mass at St. Pat's: Condemnations, Controversy Sweep through Community," *Outweek*, December 24, 1989, pp. 12–20.

126. Mike McAlary, "Shame on O'Connor—and Shame on ACT-UP, Too," *New York Post*, December 10, 1990, p. 3, 24, WHAM! Records. See also Maralyn Matlick, "Backlash-Wary Gays Rip Protest at St. Pat's," *New York Post*, December 13, 1989, WHAM! Records, and Miller and Wockner, "AIDS/Abortion Rights Demo Halts High Mass at St. Pat's."

127. Ian Daniels Horst, "No Regrets," *Outweek*, January 7, 1990, p. 8, WHAM! Records.

128. Miller and Wockner, "AIDS/Abortion Rights Demo Halts High Mass at St. Pat's," 14.

129. Esther Kaplan, "ACT UP Under Siege," *The Village Voice*, July 16, 1991, pp. 35–36.

130. Jon Nalley and Stacey Mink, "Police Violence Proliferates," *Guardian*, February 27, 1991, p. 15, WHAM! Records. Also in February 1991, shortly before Hennelly's beating, police beat and arrested three ACT UP members for spray-painting "O'Connor Spreads Death" on the sidewalk near John O'Connor's residence. Police held Scott Sensenig for thirty-three hours and gave him a severe beating that left him with black eyes, a broken nose, and nasal damage. Guy Trebay, "Slugfest: ACT UP, O'Connor, and the Cops," *The Village Voice*, February 26, 1991, p. 20.

131. James Barron, "Judge Denounces 'Lawless' Beating by Police at Rally," *NY Times*, October 1, 1991, pp. B1, B4.

132. WHAM!'s membership doubled over the course of 1991. "Proposal for Project Support of Clinic Defense and Escorting Activities," January 6, 1992, p. 3, WHAM! Records.

133. James E. Keenan, "Act Down," *Outweek*, January 7, 1990, p. 11.

134. Mindy Nass, Panel 1, "Activist Legacies," WHAM! Forum and Reunion, Tamiment Library, New York University, October 15, 2005, video recording, WHAM! Oral History Collection.

135. Crimp and Rolston, *AIDS Demographics*, 62–63, 54.

136. In January 1990, ACT UP conducted a "phone zap," in which members deluged the switchboard of Galaxy Carpet Mills, whose employees had to prove "involuntary" HIV infection in order to get coverage or HIV-related treatments under the company's health insurance policy. "An ACT UP Chronology," 1994, p. 3, WHAM! Records.

137. Robert Garcia, untitled essay, n.d., 1 page, WHAM! Records.

138. Martin, *The Other Eighties*, 178.

CHAPTER SIX

1. Karen S. Miller, *The Voice of Business*.

2. Mary Papenfuss, "Pro-Choicers Picket Church's PR Firm," *New York Post*, May 10, 1990, WHAM! Records, Tamiment Library Archives, New York University.

3. "Public Relations Firm to Present Anti-Abortion Effort to Bishops," *NY Times*, August 14, 1990.

4. Mary Papenfuss, "New Bishop Plans Abortion Pray-Ins," *New York Post,* May 7, 1990, p. 5; Donald Kaplan, "Bishop Daily Leads 600 in S'Park Abortion Protest," *The Park Slope Paper* 13, no. 27 (July 27–August 2, 1990), WHAM! Records; Dan Colarusso, "Pro-Life Group Rallies for 'God's Precious Infants,'" *The Tablet*, March 31, 1990, p. 32, WHAM! Records; Letter to Mr. Adams, Flushing Gynecology Center, from Yasha Buncik, WHAM!, March 18, 1991, WHAM! Records. Note: because of their use of civil disobedience tactics, WHAM! members frequently used pseudonyms in telephone conversations and written communications.

5. Alfred Lubrano, "Clinic Combat," *New York Newsday*, March 12, 1995, pp. A4, A48.

6. Colarusso, "Pro-Life Group Rallies for 'God's Precious Infants.'"

7. Alfred Lubrano, "Judge Says City Not Following His Order," *New York Newsday*, March 12, 1995, pp. A4, A48. See also *New York State National Organization for Women et al vs. Randall Terry et al*, United States District Court Southern District of New York, 88 Civ. 3017, January 10, 1989; WHAM! to Ruth W. Messinger, Borough President of Manhattan, October 18, 1990, WHAM! Records.

8. Susan Davis, interview by Tamar Carroll, Manhattan, March 3, 2004, audio recording, WHAM! Oral History Collection, Tamiment Library.

9. Susan Davis, WHAM! Forum and Reunion, October 15, 2005, Tamiment Library, New York University, video recording, WHAM! Oral History Collection, Tamiment Library.

10. Letter "To All Patients," from Eastern Women's Center Administration, dated February 1990, WHAM! Records.

11. Laura Daniels, "A Clinic Escort on the Front Lines," Flyer, "Pro-Choice Clinic Escort," dated April 8, 1990, WHAM! Records.

12. Neil DeMauss, interview by Tamar Carroll, Brooklyn, March 22, 2004, audio recording, WHAM! Oral History Collection, Tamiment Library.

13. Elizabeth Kaltman, telephone interview by Tamar Carroll, August 31, 2004. Karen Ramspacher reported feeling bored by the repetition of clinic escorting; Karen Ramspacher, interview by Tamar Carroll, March 5, 2004, transcript of audio recording, WHAM! Oral History Collection, Tamiment Library.

14. Ramspacher interview.

15. Letter to "Supporter of Choice," from Mitzi Mayfair, WHAM! treasurer, February 1991, WHAM! Records.

16. Chris Gannon, no title, June 17, 1992, WHAM! Records.

17. Letter to WHAM! from Kathleen McIntosh, Executive Director, Planned Parenthood, February 6, 1991, WHAM! Records.

18. Alison Gendar, "Women's Clinic to Stop Saturday Practice," *The Journal-News*, November 29, 1990, WHAM! Records.

19. Faye Ginsburg, "Rescuing the Nation," 227–28; Sara Diamond, *Not by Politics Alone*, 131–55.

20. National Abortion Federation "Violence and Disruption Statistics," http://www .prochoice.org/pubs_research/publications/downloads/about_abortion/violence_statis tics.pdf (accessed 15 August 2013); Marcy C. Wilder, "The Rule of Law, the Rise of Violence, and the Role of Morality," 84. Physician Warren Hern provides a moving account of the threats and attempts on his life as a result of his work as an abortion provider in Boulder, Colorado, from the late 1970s to the present. Warren Hern, "Life on the Front Lines," 311–14.

21. Wilder, "The Rule of Law, the Rise of Violence, and the Role of Morality," 85.

22. Robert D. McFadden, "Rally of Foes of Abortion Is Outjeered in Manhattan," *NY Times*, September 30, 1991, p. B1.

23. Abby Scher, "Right to Lifers Line Fifth: Choicers March the Gauntlet," *GF Student Newsletter*, September 30, 1991, p. 5, WHAM! Records.

24. Susan Davis, Panel 2, "A Retrospective Assessment," WHAM! Forum and Reunion, October 15, 2005, Tamiment Library, New York University, video recording, WHAM! Oral History Collection, Tamiment Library.

25. Elizabeth Meixell, interview by Sarah Schulman, September 30, 2010, ACT UP Oral History Project, video recording, DVD in author's possession.

26. Steve Quester, interview by Sarah Schulman, January 17, 2004, transcript of video recording, p. 17, ACT UP Oral History Project.

27. Brian Griffin, interview by Tamar Carroll, March 16, 2004, transcript of audio recording, pp. 10–11, 17, WHAM! Oral History Collection, Tamiment Library.

28. Jan Cohen-Cruz, "At Cross Purposes," 239.

29. Quester interview, 34.

30. Griffin interview, 15.

31. "The Church Ladies for Choice Starter Kit," p. 3, WHAM! Records.

32. Griffin interview, 38.

33. David Wojnarowicz, "Postcards from America," 75.

34. Carole S. Vance, "The War on Culture."

35. Patrick Buchanan, "How Can We Clean Up Our Art Act?" *Washington Post,* June 19, 1989.

36. Wojnarowicz, "Postcards from America," 80; William H. Honan, "Congressional Anger Threatens Arts Endowment's Budget," *NY Times,* June 20, 1989, p. C15.

37. Michael Oreskes, "Senate Votes to Bar U.S. Support of 'Obscene or Indecent' Artwork," *NY Times,* July 27, 1989, pp. A1, C18.

38. In 1991, the U.S. District Court in California ruled this requirement unconstitutional in *Bella Lewitzky Dance Foundation v. Frohnmayer,* and the NEA abandoned it. Kathleen Sullivan, "Are Content Restrictions Constitutional?," 236.

39. Ibid., 237.

40. Vance, "The War on Culture."

41. William H. Honan, "Arts Endowment Withdraws Grant for AIDS Show," *NY Times,* November 9, 1989, p. A1; David Deitcher, "What Does Silence Equal Now?," 101. Frohnmayer ultimately reinstated the grant, and was subsequently forced to resign by the Bush administration.

42. Barbara Gamarekian, "Arts Agency Denies 4 Grants Suggested by Advisory Panel," *NY Times,* June 30, 1989, p. 1.

43. NEA chairwoman Jane Alexander said that she was pleased that her agency still existed, given that it was listed as one of the top ten Republican targets for elimination. Robert Pear, "With New Budget, Domestic Spending Is Cut $24 Million," *NY Times,* April 27, 1996, p. 10.

44. Lewis Hyde, "The Children of John Adams," 253.

45. Vance, "The War on Culture," 229.

46. ACT UP members formed other queer activist groups including Queer Nation, the Church Ladies for Choice, and the Lesbian Avengers.

47. Maxine Wolfe, "AIDS and Politics," 233–34.

48. Annamarie Jagose, *Queer Theory,* 3.

49. Lisa Duggan, *The Twilight of Equality?,* 58.

50. On the "sex wars" see Laura Lederer, *Take Back the Night*; Ann Snitow, Christine Stansell, and Sharon Thompson, *Powers of Desire*; Carol S. Vance, *Pleasure and Danger*; Amber L. Hollibaugh, *My Dangerous Desires*; Lisa Duggan and Nan D. Hunter, *Sex Wars*; and Carolyn Bronstein, *Battling Pornography,* as well as the Autumn 1984 special issue of the journal *Signs* (10:1).

51. Emily Nahmanson, interview by Sarah Schulman, April 27, 2003, transcript of video recording, p. 27, ACT UP Oral History Project.

52. Shannon Cain, telephone interview by Tamar Carroll.

53. Shepard, "Building a Healing Community from ACT UP to Housing Works." ("Cylar" is misspelled in the original publication); Wolfgang Saxon, "Keith Cylar, 45; Found Homes for AIDS Patients," *NY Times,* April 8, 2004.

54. Moore, *Beyond Shame,* 123.

55. Liz Highleyman, "Radical Queers or Queer Radicals?"

56. Heidi Dorow, interview by Tamar Carroll, April 13, 2004, transcript of audio recording, 6–7, WHAM! Oral History Collection, Tamiment Library.

57. "Queer Nation Manifesto," June 1990, http://www.actupny.org/documents/Queers ReadThis.pdf (accessed 15 May 2013).

58. Rachel Lurie, "Translating Issues into Actions," 211.

59. Verne Gay and Ben Kubasik, "AIDS Activists Disrupt News Shows," *Newsday*, January 23, 1991, p. 8.

60. Don Broderick, Paul Schwartzman, and Bill Hoffman, "It's Crush Hour," *New York Post*, January 24, 1991, WHAM! Records; "Rush Hour Protest Calls Attention to AIDS," *NY Times*, January 24, 1991, WHAM! Records; "An ACT UP Chronology," p. 5, WHAM! Records; Catharine Woodard, "ACT UP Hits Grand Central," *Newsday*, January 24, 1991, p. 37.

61. Meryl Levin, Panel 1, "Activist Legacies," WHAM! Forum and Reunion, Tamiment Library, New York University, October 15, 2005, video recording, WHAM! Oral History Collection.

62. Ron Goldberg, interviewed by Sarah Schulman, October 25, 2003, Manhattan, transcript of video recording, pp. 33, 36, ACT UP Oral History Project.

63. Gould, *Moving Politics*.

64. Maria Maggenti, interview by Sarah Schulman, January 20, 2003, transcript of video recording, p. 46, ACT UP Oral History Project.

65. Maxine Wolfe, interview by Jim Hubbard, February 19, 2004, transcript of video recording, pp. 112–113, ACT UP Oral History Project.

66. Ramspacher interview. See also TAG's webpage http://www.aidsinfonyc.org/tag/about.html.

67. Moises Agosto, interview by Sarah Schulman, December 14, 2002, transcript of video recording, pp. 41–42, ACT UP Oral History Project.

68. Brier, *Infectious Ideas*, 179–84.

69. Jim Eigo, "The City as Body Politic/The Body as City Unto Itself," 182.

70. Wojnarowicz, "Postcards from America," 81.

71. James Wentzy, "Fight Back, Fight AIDS: 15 Years of Act UP," transcription of video documentary, http://www.actupny.org/divatv/synopsis75.html (accessed 29 July 2013).

72. James Wentzy, "Political Funerals," transcript of compilation video of political funerals, originally telecast January 31, 1995, http://www.actupny.org/diva/polfunsyn.html.

73. Meryl Levin, Panel 1, "Activist Legacies," WHAM! Forum and Reunion, Tamiment Library, New York University, October 15, 2005, video recording, WHAM! Oral History Collection.

74. Mindy Nass, Panel 1, "Activist Legacies," WHAM! Forum and Reunion, Tamiment Library, New York University, October 15, 2005, video recording, WHAM! Oral History Collection.

75. WHAM! Forum and Reunion, Tamiment Library, New York University, October 15, 2005, video recording, WHAM! Oral History Collection.

76. Robin Toners, "A Flurry of Edicts," *NY Times*, January 23, 1993, p. A1.

77. Ginsburg, "Rescuing the Nation," 228–29, 36–37; Adam Clymers, "Reno Urges Senate to Curb Anti-Abortion Violence," *NY Times*, May 13, 1993, p. A21.

78. Michael Wines, "Senate Approves Bill to Protect Abortion Clinics," *NY Times*, May 13, 1994, p. A1.

79. Sara Diamond, *Roads to Dominion*, 303–4. In its 2014 decision in *McCullen v. Coakley*, the Supreme Court struck down a Massachusetts state law that had established a

35 foot buffer zone in front of all reproductive health clinics in Massachusetts as an overly broad restriction on free speech, while allowing that individual clinics could still make the case that a buffer zone was necessary to reduce violence. New York Civil Liberties Union, "The Impact of the U.S. Supreme Court's *McCullen v. Coakley* decision on Reproductive Health Clinic Access Laws in New York State," June 30, 2014, http://www.nyclu.org/files/issues/NYCLU_McCullen_Decision_20140707.pdf (accessed 2 September 2014).

80. David Johnston, "Marshals Sent to a Dozen Abortion Clinics in Drive to Halt Violence," *NY Times*, August 2, 1994, p. A14; Ginsburg, "Rescuing the Nation," 237.

81. David Johnston, "FBI Undertakes Conspiracy Inquiry in Clinic Violence," *NY Times*, August 4, 1994, p. A1.

82. Wilder, "The Rule of Law, the Rise of Violence, and the Role of Morality," 82.

83. Ginsburg, "Rescuing the Nation," 237–42.

84. Kim Phillips-Fein, *Invisible Hands*, 264–65.

85. Saletan, *Bearing Right*, chapter 10.

86. Sara Dubow, *Ourselves Unborn*, 152.

87. Richard Berke, "President Backs a Gay Compromise," *NY Times*, May 28, 1993, p. A1.

88. Christine Guilfoy, "Gay Voters Rethink Support of Clinton," *Worcester Telegram and Gazette*, September 29, 1996, p. A17.

89. Susan Davis, interview by Tamar Carroll, Manhattan, March 3, 2004, transcript of audio recording, WHAM! Oral History Collection, Tamiment Library.

90. Poster, "Real freedom of choice means more than just access to abortion," WHAM! Records.

91. Ibid.

92. In her study of NOW chapters in Memphis, Columbus, and San Francisco, Stephanie Gilmore found pervasive divides over issues of hetero- and same-sex sexuality in all three local chapters. (Gilmore, *Groundswell*). Wendy Kline argues that health feminists in Chicago in the late 1970s and early 1980s experienced abortion rights activism as divisive, with grassroots comprehensive reproductive rights activists unable to draw groups like NARAL and NOW into coalition. In New York, WHAM! believed it was complementing the work of NOW and the Reproductive Rights Coalition, viewing itself as the direct-action wing of the broader reproductive rights movement. Kline, *Bodies of Knowledge*, 94–96.

93. Susan Shaw, interview by Tamar Carroll, Northampton, Mass., July 26, 2004, transcript of audio recording, p. 1, WHAM! Oral History Collection, Tamiment Library.

94. Nelson, *Women of Color and the Reproductive Rights Movement*.

95. Dana Luciano, telephone interview by Tamar Carroll, September 20, 2004.

96. "We are the Resisting Racism Working Group," 3 pages, WHAM! Records.

97. Leslie Wolfe, Panel 1, "Activist Legacies," WHAM! Forum and Reunion, Tamiment Library, New York University, October 15, 2005, video recording, WHAM! Oral History Collection.

98. Charlotte Abbott, Panel 2, "A Retrospective Assessment of WHAM!," WHAM! Forum and Reunion, Tamiment Library, New York University, October 15, 2005, video recording, WHAM! Oral History Collection.

99. Robert Vazquez-Pacheco, interview by Sarah Schulman, December 14, 2002, transcript of video recording, p. 63, ACT UP Oral History Project.

100. Kendall Thomas, interview by Sarah Schulman, May 3, 2003, transcript of video recording, p. 22, ACT UP Oral History Project.

101. Abbott, "A Retrospective Assessment of WHAM!"

102. Michelle Tepper, Panel 1, "Activist Legacies," WHAM! Forum and Reunion, Tamiment Library, New York University, October 15, 2005, video recording, WHAM! Oral History Collection.

103. Jeremy Peters, "G.O.P. Senators See an Upside in a Problematic Issue: Abortion," *NY Times*, July 28, 2013.

104. Marc Santora, "Gay Groups to Join St. Patrick's Parade in New York as a Ban Falls," *NY Times*, September 5, 2014, p. 1.

105. For extensive coverage of the debates over insurance coverage of contraception and abortion, see http://topics.nytimes.com/top/news/health/diseasesconditionsand healthtopics/health_insurance_and_managed_care/health_care_reform/contracep tion/index.html and http://topics.nytimes.com/top/reference/timestopics/subjects/a/ abortion/index.html?8qa&module=Search&mabReward=relbias%3As%2C{%221%22 %3A%22RI%3A6%22} (accesssed 3 September 2014).

106. Queers for Economic Justice, "A New Queer Agenda," http://www.q4ej.org/new _queer_agenda, full text available at http://sfonline.barnard.edu/a-new-queer-agenda / (accessed 4 September 2014). Queers for Economic Justice was based in New York City and active from 2002 to early 2014, when it closed due to lack of funding; however, some of its projects continue and the group's writings remain influential. http://www.auto straddle.com/queers-for-economic-justice-closes-its-doors-thanks-to-lack-of-econo mic-justice-224520/ (accessed 4 September 2014).

107. Dubow, *Ourselves Unborn*, 157; Self, *All in the Family*; Duggan, *The Twilight of Equality?*

108. Lauren Berlant, *The Queen of America Goes to Washington City*, chapter 3.

109. Michel Foucault, "Friendship as a Way of Life," 308.

EPILOGUE

1. ACT UP's twenty-fifth anniversary demonstration took place on April 25, 2012. Footage and still images from the protest are available at http://actupny.com/actions/index .php/act-up-news/70-latest-news/119—act-up-protests-wall-street-over-1000-taken -to-the-streets-demanding-a-wall-street-tax-for-health-care-sp-418696566 (accessed 3 September 2014). National Nurses United was formed in 2009 by the California Nurses Association's National Nurses Organizing Committee, United American Nurses, and the Massachusetts Nurses Association and is affiliated with the AFL-CIO: http://www .nationalnursesunited.org/pages/19 (accessed 20 August 2013). In a June 21, 2011 interview with the *Nation*, NNU Executive Director Rose Ann Demoro explained why her organization and its members launched a campaign to demand a strong social safety net, including access to health care and a living wage: http://www.thenation.com/audio /161575/nation-conversations-rose-ann-demoro-demanding-decent-standard-living -all-americans# (accessed 20 August 2013).

2. Verna Dobnik, "Chained AIDS Protesters Arrested in Wall St. Area," *Associated Press*, April 25, 2012, http://www.foxnews.com/us/2012/04/25/chained-aids-protesters -arrested-in-wall-st-area/ (accessed 29 May 2012).

3. For more information on Occupy Wall Street, see http://occupywallst.org/ (accessed 30 May 2012); Todd Gitlin, *Occupy Nation*. ACT UP's twenty-fifth anniversary demonstration was organized by ACT UP New York, but included participants from ACT UP Philadelphia and the newly re-formed ACT UP chapters in Boston and Rhode Island. See "Newly Revived ACT UP Chapters," http://actupny.com/actions/index.php/act-up-news/70-latest-news/118-newly-revived-act-up-chapters (accessed 3 September 2014).

4. A month before ACT UP's anniversary demonstration, in nearby Union Square, marchers donned hooded sweatshirts in honor of the unarmed black Florida teenager, Trayvon Martin, who was killed by a neighborhood watchman. Edgar Sandoval and Helen Kennedy, "'Million Hoodie' March Takes Union Square," *New York Daily News*, March 21, 2012, http://articles.nydailynews.com/2012-03-21/news/31222229_1_chief-bill-lee-arrest-jumaane-williams (accessed 30 May 2012).

5. Founded in 1981 by Ethiopian refugee Asfaha Haders, the African Services Committee is a Harlem-based group that provides services to refugees and immigrants from conflict zones in Africa. Combating HIV/AIDS is among its highest priorities. http://www.africanservices.org/about-us/mission-history (accessed 20 August 2013).

6. "Amanda Lugg," http://www.africanservices.org/about-us/our-staff/26-about-us/staff-list/104-amanda-lugg (accessed 3 September 2014); Andy Humm, "ACT UP Pushes Dedicated Tax to Fight AIDS," *Gay City News*, May 5, 2012, http://gaycitynews.com/act-up-pushes-dedicated-tax-to-fight-aids/ (accessed 29 May 2012).

7. I am indebted to Margaret Somers's definition of citizenship as "the right to have rights." Somers, *Genealogies of Citizenship*, 5.

8. Self, *All in the Family*, 167–68.

9. Somers, *Genealogies of Citizenship*, 18–19.

10. Digital audio recording of joint ACT UP/Occupy Wall Street demonstration, April 25, 2012, in author's possession.

Bibliography

MANUSCRIPT COLLECTIONS

ACT UP New York Records. Manuscripts and Archives Division. The New York Public Library, Astor, Lenox, and Tilden Foundations.

Bytsura, Bill. ACT UP Photography Collection. Fales Library. New York University.

Cloward, Richard. Collection. Sophia Smith Collection. Smith College, Northampton, MA.

Diaz, Manuel. Papers. Archives of the Puerto Rican Diaspora. Centro de Estudios Puertorriqueños, Hunter College, CUNY.

Garcia, Robert. Papers, 1988–1993. Division of Rare and Manuscript Collections, Cornell University Library, Ithaca, NY.

Henry Street Settlement Records. Social Welfare Archives, University of Minnesota, Minneapolis.

Klein, Alan. Papers. Fales Library. New York University.

Knapp, Daniel. Personal papers. John F. Kennedy Presidential Library, Boston.

Mobilization for Youth. Records. Rare Books and Manuscript Library, Columbia University, New York.

Mobilization for Youth Collection. School of Social Work Collection. Lehman Library, Columbia University, New York.

National Congress of Neighborhood Women Records. Sophia Smith Collection. Smith College, Northampton, MA.

Office of Economic Opportunity Records. Lyndon Johnson Presidential Library, Austin, TX.

Piven, Frances Fox. Papers. Sophia Smith Collection. Smith College, Northampton, MA.

Santiago, Petra. Papers. Archives of the Puerto Rican Diaspora. Centro de Estudios Puertorriqueños, Hunter College, CUNY.

Signorile, Michelangelo. Papers. Fales Library. New York University.

U.S. Senate Internal Security Committee Subfiles. National Archives, Washington, D.C.

Women's Action Alliance Collection. Sophia Smith Collection. Smith College Archives, Northampton, MA.

Women's Health Action and Mobilization Records. Tamiment Library Archives, New York University.

ORAL HISTORY COLLECTIONS

ACT UP Oral History Project. Available at http://www.actuporalhistory.org.

Cazenave, Noel. War on Poverty Project. Columbia Center for Oral History Archives, Columbia University Libraries. New York.

Henry Street Oral History Collection, Henry Street Settlement Collection, Social Welfare Archives, University of Minnesota, Minneapolis.

Kennedy, Robert F. Oral History Program. John F. Kennedy Presidential Library, Boston.

Knapp, Daniel. Working Files Interviews. Daniel Knapp Papers. John F. Kennedy Presidential Library, Boston.

Piven, Frances Fox. Mobilization for Youth Project Interviews. Frances Fox Piven Papers. Sophia Smith Collection. Smith College, Northampton, MA.

Southern Oral History Program Collection. Wilson Library, University of North Carolina at Chapel Hill.

We Who Feel Differently Project, by Carlos Motta, available at http://wewhofeel differently.info/interviews.php.

PARTIAL LIST OF ORAL HISTORIES BY AUTHOR

AbuBakr, Rashida Ismaili, interview by author, Harlem, NY, April 20, 2005, audio recording, available in the New York City Women Community Activists Oral History Project, Sophia Smith Collection, Smith College.

Alexander II, Charles K., Mark Jacquinot, and Mary Anne Staniszewski, interview by author, Albany, NY, December 16, 2005, digital video recording, available in the WHAM! Oral History Collection, Tamiment Library, NYU.

Aronowitz, Stanley, interview by author, Manhattan, NY, December 4, 2012, audio recording.

Baxandall, Rosalyn, interview by author, Manhattan, NY, April 19, 2004, audio recording, available in the New York City Women Community Activists Oral History Project, Sophia Smith Collection, Smith College.

Birnbaum, Ezra, interview by author, Manhattan, NY, April 11, 2005, audio recording, available in the New York City Women Community Activists Oral History Project, Sophia Smith Collection, Smith College.

Burns, Lisel, interview by author, Northampton, MA, February 21, 2004, audio recording, available in the New York City Women Community Activists Oral History Project, Sophia Smith Collection, Smith College.

Cain, Shannon, telephone interview by author, August 8, 2004.

Curtis, Diane, interview by author, Northampton, MA, July 19, 2004, audio recording, available in the WHAM! Oral History Collection, Tamiment Library, NYU.

Davis, Susan, interview by author, Manhattan, NY, March 3, 2004, audio recording, available in the WHAM! Oral History Collection, Tamiment Library, NYU.

DeMauss, Neil, and Mindy Nass, interview by author, Brooklyn, NY, March 22, 2004, audio recording, available in the WHAM! Oral History Collection, Tamiment Library, NYU.

Dorow, Heidi, interview by author, Manhattan, NY, April 13, 2004, audio recording, available in the WHAM! Oral History Collection, Tamiment Library, NYU.

Dowery, Mary Anne, interview by author, Manhattan, NY, April 21, 2005, audio recording, available in the New York City Women Community Activists Oral History Project, Sophia Smith Collection, Smith College.

Duke, Linda, interview by author, Northampton, MA, February 21, 2004, audio
    recording, available in the New York City Women Community Activists Oral
    History Project, Sophia Smith Collection, Smith College.

Feit, Rona, interview by author, Washington, DC, January 9, 2004, audio recording,
    available in the New York City Women Community Activists Oral History Project,
    Sophia Smith Collection, Smith College.

Fisher, Sally Martino, interview by author and Martha Ackelsberg, Queens, NY,
    March 23, 2004, audio recording, available in the New York City Women
    Community Activists Oral History Project, Sophia Smith Collection,
    Smith College.

Goldenberg, Dahlia, interview by author, Brooklyn, NY, January 22, 2004, audio
    recording, available in the New York City Women Community Activists Oral
    History Project, Sophia Smith Collection, Smith College.

Gore, Marilyn, interview by author, Manhattan, NY, April 6, 2005, audio recording,
    available in the New York City Women Community Activists Oral History Project,
    Sophia Smith Collection, Smith College.

Griffin, Brian, interview by author, Queens, NY, March 16, 2004, audio recording,
    available in the WHAM! Oral History Collection, Tamiment Library, NYU.

Haywoode, Terry, interview by author and Martha Ackelsberg, Boston, MA,
    April 30, 2004, audio recording, available in the New York City Women Community
    Activists Oral History Project, Sophia Smith Collection, Smith College.

Jackson, Rosemary, interview by author and Martha Ackelsberg, Northampton, MA,
    February 20, 2004, audio recording.

Joseph, Barbara Hunter Randall, interview by author, audio recording, Manhattan,
    NY, March 21, 2005, available in the New York City Women Community Activists
    Oral History Project, Sophia Smith Collection, Smith College.

Kaltman, Elizabeth, telephone interview by author, August 31, 2004.

Kennedy, Virginia, interview by author, Ithaca, NY, April 29, 2010, audio recording.

King, Woodie, Jr., interview by author, Manhattan, NY, December 13, 2012, audio
    recording.

LeBlanc, Nancy, interview by author, Wilmington, NY, July 27, 2005.

Luciano, Dana, telephone interview by author, September 20, 2004.

Matuschka, interview by author, Harlem, NY, May 2, 2005, audio recording, available
    in the WHAM! Oral History Collection, Tamiment Library, NYU.

Meixell, Elizabeth, interview by author, Manhattan, NY, January 24, 2004,
    audio recording, available in the WHAM! Oral History Collection, Tamiment
    Library, NYU.

Meixell, Elizabeth, interview by author, Manhattan, NY, February 21, 2004,
    audio recording, available in the WHAM! Oral History Collection, Tamiment
    Library, NYU.

Miller, Geraldine, interview by author and Lara Rusch, Brooklyn, NY, August 16, 2002,
    audio recording, available in the New York City Women Community Activists Oral
    History Project, Sophia Smith Collection, Smith College.

Mizrahi, Terry, interview by author, Manhattan, NY, May 3, 2005, audio recording,
    available in the New York City Women Community Activists Oral History Project,
    Sophia Smith Collection, Smith College.

Monroe, Lauren, interview by author, Ithaca, NY, July 29, 2010, audio recording.

Morgan, Tracy, interview by author, Manhattan, NY, April 5, 2004, audio recording, available in the WHAM! Oral History Collection, Tamiment Library, NYU.

Noschese, Christine, interview by author and Martha Ackelsberg, Manhattan, NY, March 30, 2004, audio recording.

Orengo, Juanita, interview by author, Brooklyn, NY, May 27, 2012, audio recording.

Peterson, Jan, interview by author and Lara Rusch, Brooklyn, NY, August 16, 2002, audio recording, available in the New York City Women Community Activists Oral History Project, Sophia Smith Collection, Smith College.

Peterson, Jan, telephone interview by author, September 17, 2002.

Pezzullo, Caroline, interview by author, Manhattan, NY, August 19, 2002, audio recording, available in the New York City Women Community Activists Oral History Project, Sophia Smith Collection, Smith College.

Piven, Frances Fox, interview by author, Manhattan, NY, April 21, 2004, audio recording, available in the New York City Women Community Activists Oral History Project, Sophia Smith Collection, Smith College.

Piven, Frances Fox, interview by author, Barrington, NY, July 14, 2004, audio recording, available in the New York City Women Community Activists Oral History Project, Sophia Smith Collection, Smith College.

Ramspacher, Karen, interview by author, Manhattan, NY, September 8, 2003.

Ramspacher, Karen, interview by author, Manhattan, NY, March 5, 2004, audio recording, available in the WHAM! Oral History Collection, Tamiment Library, NYU.

Sanchez, Digna, interview by author, Manhattan, NY, January 5, 2009, audio recording, available in the New York City Women Community Activists Oral History Project, Sophia Smith Collection, Smith College.

Schilen, Sandy, interview by author and Martha Ackelsberg, Brooklyn, NY, April 20, 2004, audio recording, available in the New York City Women Community Activists Oral History Project, Sophia Smith Collection, Smith College.

Shaw, Susan, interview by author, Northampton, MA, July 26, 2004, audio recording, available in the WHAM! Oral History Collection, Tamiment Library, NYU.

Stamm, Karen, interview by author, Manhattan, NY, March 25, 2004, audio recording, available in the Oral History of the American Left Collection, Tamiment Library, NYU.

Thomas, Evelyn, interview by author, Oakland, CA, April 13, 2013, audio recording.

Velez, Ethel, interview by author, Northampton, MA, February 21, 2004, audio recording, available in the New York City Women Community Activists Oral History Project, Sophia Smith Collection, Smith College.

Velez, Ethel, interview by author and Martha Ackelsberg, East Harlem, NY, March 30, 2004, audio recording available in the New York City Women Community Activists Oral History Project, Sophia Smith Collection, Smith College.

Wizner, Stephen, interview by author, New Haven, CT, July 29, 2010, audio recording, available in the New York City Women Community Activists Oral History Project, Sophia Smith Collection, Smith College.

ADDITIONAL RECORDINGS

Jackson, Diane, interview by Martha Ackelsberg, New York, April 28, 2004, audio recording.

Neighborhood Women Legacy Project Leadership Walking Tour Inauguration, May 27, 2013, multiple audio interviews and video recording, in author's possession and the NCNW Collection, Sophia Smith Collection, Smith College.

WHAM! Forum and Reunion, Tamiment Library, New York University, October 15, 2005, video recording, WHAM! Oral History Collection, Tamiment Library, NYU.

SELECTED SECONDARY WORKS

Abramson, Michael, and Iris Morales, eds. *Palante: Voices and Photographs of the Young Lords, 1969–1971*. Chicago: Haymarket Books, 2011.

ACT UP/NY Women & AIDS Book Group, eds. *Women, AIDS & Activism*. Boston: South End Press, 1990.

Appleby, Michael, and Harold H. Weissman. "Legal Enforcement of Laws Affecting Private Housing." In *Justice and the Law in the Mobilization for Youth Experience*, edited by Harold H. Weissman, 79–87. New York: Association Press, 1969.

Araiza, Lauren. *To March for Others: The Black Freedom Struggle and the United Farm Workers*. Philadelphia: University of Pennsylvania Press, 2013.

Ashmore, Susan Youngblood. *Carry It On: The War on Poverty and the Civil Rights Movement in Alabama, 1964–1972*. Athens: University of Georgia Press, 2008.

Atlas, John. *Seeds of Change: The Story of Acorn, America's Most Controversial Antipoverty Community Organizing Group*. Nashville: Vanderbilt University Press, 2010.

Back, Adina. "Exposing the 'Whole Segregation Myth': The Harlem Nine and New York City's School Desegregation Battles." In *Freedom North: Black Freedom Struggles Outside the South, 1940–1980*, edited by Jeanne F. Theoharis and Komozi Woodard, 65–92. New York: Palgrave Macmillan, 2003.

———. "'Parent Power': Eveline Lopez Antonetty, the United Bronx Parents, and the War on Poverty." In *The War on Poverty: A New Grassroots History*, edited by Annelise Orleck and Lisa Gayle Hazirjian, 184–208. Athens: University of Georgia Press, 2011.

Banzhaf, Marion, Tracy Morgan, and Karen Ramspacher. "Reproductive Rights and AIDS: The Connections." In *Women, AIDS & Activism*, edited by The ACT UP/ New York Women and AIDS Book Group, 199–209. Boston: South End Press, 1990.

Bao, Xiaolan. *Holding up More Than Half the Sky: Chinese Women Garment Workers in New York City, 1948–92*. Urbana: University of Illinois Press, 2001.

Baroni, Geno, ed. *Pieces of a Dream: The Ethnic Worker's Crisis with America*. New York: Center for Migration Studies, 1972.

Bauman, Robert. "'Kind of a Secular Sacrament': Father Geno Baroni, Monsignor John J. Egan, and the Catholic War on Poverty." *The Catholic Historical Review* 99, no. 2 (April 2013): 298–317.

———. *Race and the War on Poverty: From Watts to East L.A.* Norman: University of Oklahoma Press, 2008.

Baxandall, Rosalyn, and Linda Gordon, eds. *Dear Sisters: Dispatches from the Women's Liberation Movement.* New York: Basic Books, 2000.

Beck, Bertram M. "Mobilization for Youth: Reflections About Its Administration." In *Justice and the Law in the Mobilization for Youth Experience,* edited by Harold H. Weissman, 145–66. New York: Association Press, 1969.

Behnken, Brian. *Fighting Their Own Battles: Mexican Americans, African Americans, and the Struggle for Civil Rights in Texas.* Chapel Hill: University of North Carolina Press, 2011.

———, ed. *The Struggle in Black and Brown: African American and Mexican American Relations during the Civil Rights Era.* Lincoln: University of Nebraska Press, 2011.

Belenky, Mary Field, Lynne A. Bond, and Jacqueline S. Weinstock. *A Tradition That Has No Name: Nurturing the Development of People, Families, and Communities.* New York: Basic Books, 1997.

Berlant, Lauren. *The Queen of America Goes to Washington City: Essays on Sex and Citizenship.* Durham, NC: Duke University Press, 1997.

Bernstein, Shana. *Bridges of Reform: Interracial Civil Rights Activism in Twentieth-Century Los Angeles.* New York: Oxford University Press, 2011.

Biondi, Martha. *To Stand and Fight: The Struggle for Civil Rights in Postwar New York City.* Cambridge, MA: Harvard University Press, 2003.

Blackwell, Maylei. *Chicana Power!: Contested Histories of Feminism in the Chicano Movement.* Austin: University of Texas Press, 2011.

Blake, Angela. *How New York Became American, 1890–1924.* Baltimore: Johns Hopkins University Press, 2006.

Bloom, Nicholas Deagen. *Public Housing That Worked: New York in the Twentieth Century.* Philadelphia: University of Pennsylvania Press, 2008.

Boris, Eileen, and Jennifer Klein. *Caring for America: Home Health Workers in the Shadow of the Welfare State.* New York: Oxford University Press, 2012.

Brager, George A. "Effecting Organizational Change through a Demonstration Project: The Case of the Schools." In *Community Action against Poverty: Readings from the Mobilization Experience,* edited by George A. Brager and Francis P. Purcell, 104–18. New Haven, CT: College and University Press, 1967.

Brager, George A., and Francis P. Purcell, eds. *Community Action against Poverty.* New Haven, CT: College and University Press, 1967.

Brager, George, and Harry Specht. *Community Organizing.* New York: Columbia University Press, 1973.

Breines, Wini. *The Trouble between Us: An Uneasy History of White and Black Women in the Feminist Movement.* New York: Oxford University Press, 2006.

Brier, Jennifer. *Infectious Ideas: U.S. Political Responses to the AIDS Crisis.* Chapel Hill: University of North Carolina Press, 2009.

———. " 'Save Our Kids, Keep AIDS Out': Anti-AIDS Activism and the Legacy of Community Control in Queens, New York." *Journal of Social History* 39, no. 4 (Summer 2006): 965–87.

Brilliant, Mark. *The Color of America Has Changed: How Racial Diversity Shaped Civil Rights Reform in California, 1941–1978.* New York: Oxford University Press, 2012.

Bronstein, Carolyn. *Battling Pornography: The American Feminist Anti-Pornography Movement, 1976–1986.* New York: Cambridge University Press, 2011.

Broude, Norma, and Mary D. Garrard, eds. *The Power of Feminist Art: The American Movement of the 1970s, History and Impact.* New York: Harry Abrams, 1994.

Brown, Arthur, Dan Collins, and Michael Goodwin. *I Koch.* New York: Dodd, Mead, 1985.

Brownmiller, Susan. *Against Our Will: Men, Women and Rape.* New York: Simon and Schuster, 1975.

Bullert, B. J. *Public Television: Politics and the Battle over Documentary Film.* New Brunswick, NJ: Rutgers University Press, 1997.

Cannato, Vincent. *The Ungovernable City: John Lindsay and His Struggle to Save New York.* New York: Basic Books, 2001.

Capote, Truman. *Breakfast at Tiffany's.* New York: Random House, 1958.

Caro, Robert A. *The Power Broker: Robert Moses and the Fall of New York.* New York: Vintage Books, 1974.

Caroli, Betty Boyd. "Settlement Houses." In *The Encyclopedia of New York City*, edited by Kenneth T. Jackson, 1059–61. New Haven, CT: Yale University Press, 1995.

Carroll, Tamar. "How Did Feminists Meet the Challenges of Working across Differences?" *Women and Social Movements in the U.S., 1600–2000* 10, no. 4 (Dec. 2006).

Carter, David. *Stonewall: The Riots That Sparked the Gay Revolution.* New York: St. Martin's Press, 2004.

Cazenave, Noel A. *Impossible Democracy: The Unlikely Success of the War on Poverty Community Action Programs.* Albany: State University of New York Press, 2007.

———. "Ironies of Urban Reform: Professional Turf Battles in the Planning of the Mobilization for Youth Program Precursor to the War on Poverty." *Journal of Urban History* 26, no. 1 (Nov. 1999): 22–43.

Chafe, William H. *Civilities and Civil Rights: Greensboro, North Carolina, and the Black Struggle for Freedom.* New York: Oxford University Press, 1981.

Chambre, Susan M. *Fighting for Our Lives: New York's AIDS Community and the Politics of Disease.* New Brunswick, NJ: Rutgers University Press, 2006.

Chappell, Marisa. "Rethinking Women's Politics in the 1970s: The League of Women Voters and the National Organization for Women Confront Poverty." *Journal of Women's History* 13, no. 4 (Winter 2002): 155–79.

———. *The War on Welfare: Family, Poverty, and Politics in Modern America.* Philadelphia: University of Pennsylvania Press, 2010.

Chronopoulos, Themis. "The Politics of Race and Class and the Changing Spatial Fortunes of McCarren Pool in Brooklyn, New York." *Space and Culture* 20, no. 10 (2013): 1–19.

Clayson, William S. *Freedom Is Not Enough: The War on Poverty and the Civil Rights Movement in Texas.* Austin: University of Texas Press, 2010.

Cloward, Richard A., and Richard M. Elman. "Advocacy in the Ghetto: Social Workers Fight the 'Welfare Establishment' to Secure Legal Rights of the Poor." *Society* 4, no. 2 (1966): 27–35.

Cloward, Richard A., and Lloyd E. Ohlin. *Delinquency and Opportunity: A Theory of Delinquent Gangs.* New York: The Free Press, 1960.

Cloward, Richard A., and Frances Fox Piven. *The Politics of Turmoil: Essays on Poverty, Race, and the Urban Crisis.* New York: Pantheon Books, 1965.

Cloward, Richard A., and Frances Fox Piven. "A Strategy to End Poverty." *The Nation*, May 2, 1966, 510–17.

Cobble, Dorothy Sue. *The Other Women's Movement: Workplace Justice and Social Rights in Modern America*. Princeton, NJ: Princeton University Press, 2004.

Cohen-Cruz, Jan. "At Cross Purposes: The Church Ladies for Choice." In *From ACT UP to the WTO: Urban Protest and Community Building in the Era of Globalization*, edited by Benjamin Shepard and Ronald Hayduk, 234–41. New York: Verso, 2002.

Cohen, Lizabeth. *A Consumers' Republic: The Politics of Mass Consumption in Postwar America*. New York: Alfred A. Knopf, 2003.

Cohen, Miriam. *Workshop to Office: Two Generations of Italian Women in New York City, 1900–1950*. Ithaca, NY: Cornell University Press, 1992.

Cohen, Peter F. *Love and Anger: Essays on AIDS, Activism, and Politics*. New York: The Haworth Press, 1998.

Combahee River Collective. "The Combahee River Collective Statement." In *Home Girls: A Black Feminist Anthology*, edited by Barbara Smith, 272–82. New York: Kitchen Table: Women of Color Press, 1983.

Countryman, Matthew J. *Up South: Civil Rights and Black Power in Philadelphia*. Philadelphia: University of Pennsylvania Press, 2006.

Crimp, Douglas. "Gran Fury Talks to Douglas Crimp." *Artforum International*, April 1, 2003, 70–74.

———. *Melancholia and Moralism: Essays on AIDS and Queer Politics*. Cambridge, MA: MIT Press, 2002.

Crimp, Douglas, and Adam Rolston, eds. *AIDS Demo Graphics*. Seattle: Bay Press, 1990.

Crosby, Emilye, ed. *Civil Rights History from the Ground Up: Local Struggles, a National Movement*. Athens: University of Georgia Press, 2011.

———. *A Little Taste of Freedom: The Black Freedom Struggle in Claiborne County, Mississippi*. Chapel Hill: University of North Carolina Press, 2005.

Cuordileone, K. A. *Manhood and American Political Culture in the Cold War*. New York City: Routledge, 2005.

Cvetkovich, Ann. *An Archive of Feelings: Trauma, Sexuality, and Lesbian Public Cultures*. Durham, NC: Duke University Press, 2003.

Daniels, Doris Groshen. *Always a Sister: The Feminism of Lillian D. Wald*. New York: The Feminist Press at CUNY, 1989.

Davies, Gareth. "The Welfare State." In *The Reagan Presidency: Pragmatic Conservatism and Its Legacies*, edited by W. Elliot Brownlee and Hugh Davis Graham, 209–32. Lawrence: University of Kansas Press, 2003.

Davis, Martha. *Brutal Need: Lawyers and the Welfare Rights Movement*. New Haven, CT: Yale University Press, 1993.

Deitcher, David. "What Does Silence Equal Now?" In *Art Matters: How the Culture Wars Changed America*, edited by Brian Wallis, Philip Yenawine, and Marianne Weems, 93–135. New York: New York University Press, 1999.

De Jesus, Anthony, and Madeline Perez. "From Community Control to Consent Decree: Puerto Ricans Organizing for Education and Language Rights in 1960s and '70s New York City." *Centro Journal* XI, no. 2 (Fall 2009): 7–31.

Delaney, Samuel R. *Times Square Red, Times Square Blue*. New York: New York University Press, 1999.

Delgado, Gary. *Organizing the Movement: The Roots and Growth of Acorn.*
Philadelphia: Temple University Press, 1986.

DeSena, Judith. *Protecting One's Turf.* Rev. ed. Lanham, MD: University Press of
America, 2005.

Deslippe, Dennis. " 'We Must Bring Together a New Coalition': The Challenge of
Working-Class White Ethnics to Color-Blind Conservativism in the 1970s."
International Labor and Working Class History, no. 74 (Fall 2008): 148–70.

Diamond, Sara. *Not by Politics Alone: The Enduring Influence of the Christian Right.*
New York: The Guilford Press, 1998.

———. *Roads to Dominion: Right-Wing Movements and Political Power in the United
States.* New York: The Guilford Press, 1995.

di Leonardo, Micaela. *The Varieties of Ethnic Experience: Kinship, Class and Gender
among California Italian-Americans.* Ithaca, NY: Cornell University Press, 1984.

Dittmer, John. *Local People: The Struggle for Civil Rights in Mississippi.* Urbana:
University of Illinois Press, 1994.

Dolkart, Andrew S. *Biography of a Tenement House in New York City: An Architectural
History of 97 Orchard Street.* Santa Fe, NM: Center for American Places, 2007.

Dubow, Sara. *Ourselves Unborn: A History of the Fetus in Modern America.* New York:
Oxford University Press, 2011.

Duggan, Lisa. *The Twilight of Equality? Neoliberalism, Cultural Politics, and the Attack
on Democracy.* Boston: Beacon Press, 2003.

Duggan, Lisa, and Nan D. Hunter. *Sex Wars: Sexual Dissent and Political Culture.*
10th Anniversary ed. New York: Routledge, 2006.

Durr, Kenneth D. *Behind the Blacklash: White Working-Class Politics in Baltimore,
1940–1980.* Chapel Hill: University of North Carolina Press, 2003.

Echols, Alice. *Daring to Be Bad: Radical Feminism in America, 1967–1975.* Minneapolis:
University of Minnesota Press, 1989.

Eigo, Jim. "The City as Body Politic/the Body as City unto Itself." In *From ACT UP to
the WTO: Urban Protest and Community Building in the Era of Globalization,*
edited by Benjamin Shepard and Ronald Hayduk, 178–95. New York: Verso, 2002.

Eisenstadt, Peter. *Rochdale Village: Robert Moses, 6,000 Families, and New York City's
Great Experiment in Integrated Housing.* Ithaca, NY: Cornell University Press, 2010.

Eley, Geoff. *Forging Democracy: The History of the Left in Europe, 1850–2000.* New
York: Oxford University Press, 2002.

Enck-Wanzer, Darrel, ed. *The Young Lords: A Reader.* New York: New York University
Press, 2010.

Engelhardt, Tom. *The End of Victory Culture: Cold War America and the Disillusioning
of a Generation.* Amherst: University of Massachusetts Press, 1995.

Enke, Anne. *Finding the Movement: Sexuality, Contested Space, and Feminist Activism.*
Durham, NC: Duke University Press, 2007.

Enstad, Nan. *Ladies of Labor, Girls of Adventure: Working Women, Popular Culture,
and Labor Politics at the Turn of the Twentieth Century.* New York: Columbia
University Press, 1999.

Epstein, Steven. *Impure Science: AIDS, Activism, and the Politics of Knowledge.*
Berkeley: University of California Press, 1996.

Estepa, Andrea. "Taking the White Gloves Off: Women Strike for Peace and 'the
Movement,' 1967–73." In *Feminist Coalitions: Historical Perspectives on Second-Wave*

Feminism in the United States, edited by Stephanie Gilmore, 84–112. Urbana: University of Illinois Press, 2008.

Evans, Sara. *Personal Politics: The Roots of Women's Liberation in the Civil Rights Movement and the New Left*. New York: Alfred A. Knopf, 1979.

———. *Tidal Wave: How Women Changed America at Century's End*. New York: The Free Press, 2003.

Ewen, Elizabeth. *Immigrant Women in the Land of Dollars: Life and Culture on the Lower East Side, 1890–1925*. New York: Monthly Review Press, 1985.

Ezekiel, Judith. *Feminism in the Heartland*. Columbus: Ohio State University Press, 2002.

Fabricant, Michael, and Robert Fisher. *Settlement Houses Under Siege: The Struggle to Sustain Community Organizations in New York City*. New York: Columbia University Press, 2002.

Faludi, Susan. *Backlash: The Undeclared War against American Women*. New York: Anchor Books, 1991.

Feldstein, Ruth. *Motherhood in Black and White: Race and Sex in American Liberalism, 1930–1965*. Ithaca: Cornell University Press, 2000.

Fernandez, Johanna. "Between Social Service Reform and Revolutionary Politics: The Young Lords, Late Sixties Radicalism, and Community Organizing in New York City." In *Freedom North: Black Freedom Struggles Outside the South, 1940–1980*, edited by Jeanne F. Theoharis and Komozi Woodard, 255–86. New York: Palgrave Macmillan, 2003.

———. "Radicals in the Late 1960s: A History of the Young Lords Party in New York City, 1969–1974." PhD diss., Columbia University, 2004.

Fernandez, Lilia. *Brown in the Windy City: Mexicans and Puerto Ricans in Postwar Chicago*. Chicago: University of Chicago Press, 2012.

Fisher, Robert, ed. *The People Shall Rule: ACORN, Community Organizing, and the Struggle for Economic Justice*. Nashville: Vanderbilt University Press, 2009.

Flint, Anthony. *Wrestling with Moses: How Jane Jacobs Took on New York's Master Builder and Transformed the American City*. New York City: Random House, 2009.

Fogel, Susan Berke, and Lourdes A. Rivera. "Saving Roe Is Not Enough: When Religion Controls Health Care." *Fordham Urban Law Journal* 33, no. 3 (2003): 725–49.

Foley, Neil. *Quest for Equality: The Failed Promise of Black-Brown Solidarity*. Cambridge, MA: Harvard University Press, 2010.

Formisano, Ronald P. *Boston against Busing: Race, Class, and Ethnicity in the 1960s and 1970s*. Chapel Hill: University of North Carolina Press, 1991.

Foucault, Michel. "Friendship as a Way of Life." In *Foucault Live: Collected Interviews, 1961–1984*, edited by Sylvere Lotringer, 308–13. New York: Semiotext(e), 1989.

Freedman, Estelle B. *No Turning Back: The History of Feminism and the Future of Women*. New York: Ballantine Books, 2002.

Freeman, Joshua. *Working Class New York: Life and Labor since World War Two*. New York: The New Press, 2000.

Friedan, Betty. *The Feminine Mystique*. New York: Dell Publishing, 1963.

Frost, Jennifer. *"An Interracial Movement of the Poor": Community Organizing and the New Left in the 1960s*. New York: New York University Press, 2001.

Garland, Anne Witte. *Women Activists Challenging the Abuse of Power*. New York: The Feminist Press at CUNY, 1988.

Geismer, Lily. "Good Neighbors for Fair Housing: Suburban Liberalism and Racial Inequality in Metropolitan Boston." *Journal of Urban History* 39, no. 3 (2012): 454–77.

Gilbert, James. *A Cycle of Outrage: America's Reaction to the Juvenile Delinquent in the 1950s.* New York: Oxford University Press, 1986.

Gilmore, Stephanie. "The Dynamics of Feminist Activism in Memphis, Tennessee, 1971–1982: Rethinking the Liberal/Radical Divide." *NWSA Journal* 15 (Spring 2003): 94–117.

———, ed. *Feminist Coalitions: Historical Perspectives on Second-Wave Feminism in the United States.* Urbana: University of Illinois, 2008.

———. *Groundswell: Grassroots Feminist Activism in Postwar America.* New York: Routledge, 2013.

Ginsburg, Faye. "Rescuing the Nation: Operation Rescue and the Rise of Anti-Abortion Militance." In *Abortion Wars: A Half Century of Struggle, 1950–2000,* edited by Rickie Solinger, 227–50. Berkeley: University of California Press, 1998.

Gitlin, Todd. *Occupy Nation: The Roots, the Spirit, and the Promise of Occupy Wall Street.* New York: Harper Collins, 2012.

Gittell, Marilyn, and Maurice R. Berube. *Confrontation at Ocean Hill-Brownsville: The New York School Strikes of 1968.* New York: Praeger, 1969.

Gold, Roberta. "City of Tenants: New York's Housing Struggles and the Challenge to Postwar America, 1945–1974." PhD diss., University of Washington, 2004.

———. *When Tenants Claimed the City: The Struggle for Citizenship in New York City Housing.* Urbana: University of Illinois Press, 2014.

Gould, Deborah B. *Moving Politics: Emotion and ACT UP's Fight against AIDS.* Chicago: University of Chicago Press, 2009.

Green, Laurie B. *Battling the Plantation Mentality: Memphis and the Black Freedom Struggle.* Chapel Hill: University of North Carolina Press, 2007.

———. "Challenging the Civil Rights Narrative: Women, Gender and the 'Politics of Protection.'" In *Civil Rights History from the Ground Up: Local Struggles, a National Movement,* edited by Emilye Crosby, 52–80. Athens: University of Georgia Press, 2011.

Greene, Christina. *Our Separate Ways: Women and the Black Freedom Movement in Durham, North Carolina.* Chapel Hill: University of North Carolina Press, 2005.

———. "'Someday . . . The Colored and White Will Stand Together': The War on Poverty, Black Power Politics, and Southern Women's Interracial Alliances." In *The War on Poverty: A New Grassroots History, 1964–1980,* edited by Annelise Orleck and Lisa Gayle Hazirjian, 159–83. Athens: University of Georgia, 2011.

Guglielmo, Jennifer. *Living the Revolution: Italian Women's Resistance and Radicalism in New York City, 1880–1945.* Chapel Hill: University of North Carolina Press, 2010.

Guglielmo, Jennifer, and Salvatore Salerno, eds. *Are Italians White?: How Race Is Made in America.* New York City: Routledge, 2003.

Guglielmo, Thomas A. *White on Arrival: Italians, Race, Color, and Power in Chicago, 1890–1945.* New York: Oxford University Press, 2003.

Hall, Helen. *Unfinished Business in Neighborhood and Nation.* New York: Macmillan, 1971.

Haywoode, Terry, and Laura Scanlon. "World of Our Mothers: College for Neighborhood Women." *Women's Studies Quarterly* 34, nos. 3 and 4 (1984): 101–09.

Heifetz, Henry. "Introduction." In *Employment and Educational Services in the Mobilization for Youth Experience,* edited by Harold H. Weissman, 13–21. New York: Association Press, 1969.

———. "Parent Education Program." In *Employment and Educational Services in the Mobilization for Youth Experience*, edited by Harold H. Weissman, 125–35. New York: Association Press, 1969.

———. "Training Youth in the Arts." In *Individual and Group Services in the Mobilization for Youth Experience*, edited by Harold H. Weissman, 172–79. New York: Association Press, 1969.

Helfgot, Joseph H. *Professional Reforming: Mobilization for Youth and the Failure of Social Science*. Lexington, MA: D. C. Heath and Co., 1981.

Hern, Warren. "Life on the Front Lines." In *Abortion Wars: A Half Century of Struggle, 1950–2000*, edited by Rickie Solinger, 307–19. Berkeley: University of California Press, 1998.

Hewitt, Nancy, ed. *No Permanent Waves: Recasting Histories of U.S. Feminism*. New Brunswick, NJ: Rutgers University Press, 2010.

Highleyman, Liz. "Radical Queers or Queer Radicals? Queer Activism and the Global Justice Movement." In *From ACT UP to the WTO: Urban Protest and Community Building in the Era of Globalization*, edited by Benjamin Shepard and Ronald Hayduk, 106–20. New York: Verso, 2002.

Hirsch, Arnold R. *Making the Second Ghetto: Race and Housing in Chicago, 1940–1960*. Chicago: University of Chicago Press, 1998.

Hoffnung-Garcia, Jesse. *A Tale of Two Cities: Santo Domingo, New York, and a Changing World since 1950*. Princeton, NJ: Princeton University Press, 2008.

Hollibaugh, Amber L. *My Dangerous Desires: A Queer Girl Dreaming Her Way Home*. Durham, NC: Duke University Press, 2000.

Horne, Gerald. *Black Liberation/Red Scare: Ben Davis and the Communist Party*. Newark: University of Delaware Press, 1994.

Horowitz, Daniel. *Betty Friedan and the Making of Women's Liberation*. Amherst: University of Massachusetts Press, 1998.

Howard, Clayton. "The Closet and the Cul de Sac: Sex, Politics, and Suburbanization in Postwar California." PhD diss., University of Michigan, 2010.

Hyde, Lewis. "The Children of John Adams: A Historical View of the Fight over Arts Funding." In *Art Matters: How the Culture Wars Changed America*, edited by Brian Wallis, Marianne Weems, and Philip Yenawine, 252–75. New York: New York University Press, 1999.

Isserman, Maurice. "American Labor Party." In *The Encyclopedia of New York City*, edited by Kenneth T. Jackson, 29–30. New Haven, CT: Yale University Press, 1995.

———. "Communism." In *The Encyclopedia of New York City*, edited by Kenneth T. Jackson, 268–70. New Haven, CT: Yale University Press, 1995.

Jackson, Mandi Isaacs. "Harlem's Rent Strike and Rat War: Representation, Housing Access and Tenant Resistance in New York, 1958–1964." *American Studies* 47, no. 1 (2006): 53–79.

Jacobson, Matthew Frye. *Roots Too: White Ethnic Revival in Post-Civil Rights America*. Cambridge, MA: Harvard University Press, 2006.

Jagose, Annamarie. *Queer Theory: An Introduction*. New York: New York University Press, 1996.

Jennings, James, and Francisco Chapman. "Puerto Ricans and the Community Control Movement: An Interview with Luis Fuentes." In *The Puerto Rican*

Movement: Voices from the Diaspora, edited by Andres Torres and Jose E. Velazquez, 280–95. Philadelphia: Temple University Press, 1998.

Johnson, Earl, Jr. *Justice and Reform: The Formative Years of the American Legal Services Program*. New Brunswick, NJ: Russell Sage/Transaction Books, 1974.

Jonnes, Jill. *South Bronx Rising: The Rise, Fall, and Resurrection of an American City*. New York City: Fordham University Press, 2002.

Kaplan, Laura. *The Story of Jane: The Legendary Underground Feminist Abortion Service*. New York: Pantheon Books, 1995.

Katz, Daniel. *All Together Different: Yiddish Socialists, Garment Workers, and the Labor Roots of Multiculturalism*. New York: New York University Press, 2011.

Kiffmeyer, Thomas J. *Reformers to Radicals: The Appalachian Volunteers and the War on Poverty*. Lexington: University Press of Kentucky, 2008.

King, Woodie, Jr. *The Impact of Race: Theatre and Culture*. New York: Applause Theatre and Cinema Books, 2003.

Klemek, Christopher. *The Transatlantic Collapse of Urban Renewal: Postwar Urbanism from New York to Berlin*. Chicago: University of Chicago, 2011.

Kline, Wendy. *Bodies of Knowledge: Sexuality, Reproduction and Women's Health in the Second Wave*. Chicago: University of Chicago Press, 2010.

Knapp, Daniel, and Kenneth Polk. *Scouting the War on Poverty: Social Reform Politics in the Kennedy Administration*. Lexington, MA: Heath Lexington Books, 1971.

Kornbluh, Felicia. *The Battle for Welfare Rights: Poverty and Politics in Modern America*. Philadelphia: University of Pennsylvania Press, 2007.

Korrol, Virginia. "Building the New York Puerto Rican Community, 1945–1965: A Historical Interpretation." In *Boricuas in Gotham: Puerto Ricans in the Making of Modern New York City*, edited by Gabriel Haslip-Viera, Angelo Falcon, and Felix Matos Rodriguez, 1–20. Princeton, NJ: Markus Wiener Publishers, 2005.

Lassiter, Matthew. *The Silent Majority: Suburban Politics in the Sunbelt South*. Princeton, NJ: Princeton University Press, 2006.

Lederer, Laura, ed. *Take Back the Night: Women on Pornography*. New York: Harper Perennial, 1980.

Lee, Sonia, and Ande Diaz. "'I Was the One Percenter': Manny Diaz and the Beginnings of a Black-Puerto Rican Coalition." *Journal of American Ethnic History* 26, no. 3 (Spring 2007): 52–80.

Lee, Sonia Song-Ha. *Building a Latino Civil Rights Movement: Puerto Ricans, African Americans, and the Pursuit of Racial Justice in New York City*. Chapel Hill: University of North Carolina Press, 2014.

Leuchtenburg, William E. "Jimmy Carter and the Post-New Deal Presidency." In *The Carter Presidency: Policy Choices in the Post-New Deal Era*, edited by Gary M. Fink and Hugh Davis Graham, 7–28. Lawrence: University of Kansas Press, 1998.

Levenstein, Lisa. "'Don't Agonize, Organize!': The Displaced Homemakers Campaign and the Contested Goals of Postwar Feminism." *The Journal of American History* 100, no. 4 (March 2014): 1114–36.

———. *A Movement without Marches: African American Women and the Politics of Poverty in Postwar Philadelphia*. Chapel Hill: University of North Carolina Press, 2009.

Lurie, Rachel. "Translating Issues into Actions: Introduction." In *Women, AIDS, and Activism*, edited by The ACT UP/New York Women and AIDS Book Group, 211-14. Boston: South End Press, 1990.

MacLean, Nancy. *Freedom Is Not Enough: The Opening of the American Workplace.* Cambridge, MA: Harvard University Press, 2006.

———. "The Hidden History of Affirmative Action: Working Women's Struggles in the 1970s and the Gender of Class." *Feminist Studies* 25 (Spring 1999).

Mahler, Jonathan. *Ladies and Gentlemen, the Bronx Is Burning: 1977, Baseball, and the Battle for the Soul of a City.* New York: Farrar, Straus, and Giroux, 2005.

Mantler, Gordon K. *Power to the Poor: Black-Brown Coalition and the Fight for Economic Justice, 1960-1974.* Chapel Hill: University of North Carolina Press, 2013.

Marcuse, Peter. "Abandonment, Gentrification, and Displacement: The Linkages in New York City." In *Gentrification of the City*, edited by Neil Smith and Peter Williams, 153-77. New York: Routledge, 1986.

Marris, Peter, and Martin Rein. *Dilemmas of Social Reform: Poverty and Community Action in the United States.* Chicago: University of Chicago Press, 1967.

Marshall, T. H. *Citizenship and Social Class, and Other Essays.* Cambridge: Cambridge University Press, 1950.

Martin, Bradford. *The Other Eighties: A Secret History of America in the Age of Reagan.* New York: Macmillan, 2011.

———. *The Theater Is in the Street: Politics and Public Performance in Sixties America.* Amherst: University of Massachusetts Press, 2004.

McGreevy, John T. *Parish Boundaries: The Catholic Encounter with Race in the Twentieth-Century Urban North.* Chicago: University of Chicago Press, 1996.

McKee, Guian. " 'This Government Is with Us': Lyndon Johnson and the Grassroots War on Poverty." In *The War on Poverty: A New Grassroots History, 1964-1980*, edited by Annelise Orleck and Lisa Gayle Hazirjian, 31-62. Athens: University of Georgia Press, 2011.

McKibben, Carol. *Racial Beachhead: Diversity and Democracy in a Military Town.* Stanford, CA: Stanford University Press, 2011.

Meeker, Martin. "The Queerly Disadvantaged and the Making of San Francisco's War on Poverty, 1964-1967." *Pacific Historical Review* 81, no. 1 (Feb. 2012): 21-59.

Mele, Christopher. *Selling the Lower East Side: Culture, Real Estate, and Resistance in New York City.* Minneapolis: University of Minnesota Press, 2000.

Melendez, Miguel. *We Took the Streets: Fight for Latino Rights with the Young Lords.* New York: St. Martin's Press, 2003.

Meyer, Richard. "This Is to Enrage You: Gran Fury and the Graphics of AIDS Activism." In *But Is It Art?: The Spirit of Art as Activism*, edited by Nina Felshin, 51-83. Seattle: Bay Press, 1995.

Miller, Karen S. *The Voice of Business: Hill and Knowlton and Postwar Public Relations.* Chapel Hill: University of North Carolina Press, 1999.

Millet, Kate. *Sexual Politics.* Garden City, NY: Doubleday, 1970.

Mollenkopf, John H. *New York City in the 1980s: A Social, Economic, and Political Atlas.* New York: Simon and Schuster, 1993.

Mollenkopf, John H., and Manuel Castells. "Introduction." In *Dual City: Restructuring New York*, edited by John H. Mollenkopf and Manuel Castells, 1-22. New York: Russell Sage Foundation, 1991.

Moore, Patrick. *Beyond Shame: Reclaiming the Abandoned History of Radical Gay Sexuality.* Boston: Beacon Press, 2004.

Morgan, Tracy. "From WHAM! to ACT UP." In *From ACT UP to the WTO: Urban Protest and Community Building in the Era of Globalization,* edited by Benjamin Shepard and Ronald Hayduk, 141–49. New York: Verso, 2002.

Morgen, Sandra. *Into Our Own Hands: The Women's Health Movement in the United States, 1969–1990.* New Brunswick, NJ: Rutgers University Press, 2002.

Moynihan, Daniel Patrick. *Maximum Feasible Misunderstanding: Community Action in the War on Poverty.* New York: The Free Press, 1969.

Murch, Donna Jean. *Living for the City: Migration, Education, and the Rise of the Black Panther Party in Oakland, California.* Chapel Hill: University of North Carolina Press, 2010.

Murray, Sylvie. *The Progressive Housewife: Community Activism in Suburban Queens, 1945–1965.* Philadelphia: University of Pennsylvania Press, 2003.

Nadasen, Premilla. "Expanding the Boundaries of the Women's Movement: Black Feminism and the Struggle for Welfare Rights." *Feminist Studies* 28 (Summer 2002): 271–301.

———. *Welfare Warriors: The Welfare Rights Movement in the United States.* New York: Routledge, 2005.

Naples, Nancy A., ed. *Community Activism and Feminist Politics: Organizing across Race, Class, and Gender.* New York: Routledge, 1998.

———. *Grassroots Warriors: Activist Mothering, Community Work, and the War on Poverty.* New York: Routledge, 1998.

Nathan, Richard P., and Fred C. Doolittle. "Federal Grants: Giving and Taking Away." *Political Science Quarterly* 100, no. 1 (Spring 1985): 53–74.

Nelson, Alondra. *Body and Soul: The Black Panther Party and the Fight against Medical Discrimination.* Minneapolis: University of Minnesota Press, 2011.

Nelson, Jennifer. *Women of Color and the Reproductive Rights Movement.* New York: New York University Press, 2003.

Novak, Michael. *The Rise of the Unmeltable Ethnics.* New York: Macmillan, 1971.

O'Connor, Alice. *Poverty Knowledge: Social Science, Social Policy, and the Poor in Twentieth-Century U.S. History.* Princeton, NJ: Princeton University Press, 2001.

Orleck, Annelise. *Common Sense and a Little Fire: Women and Working-Class Politics in the United States, 1900–1965.* Chapel Hill: University of North Carolina Press, 1995.

———. "Introduction: The War on Poverty from the Grass Roots Up." In *The War on Poverty: A New Grassroots History, 1964–1980,* edited by Annelise Orleck and Lisa Gayle Hazirjian, 1–28. Athens: University of Georgia Press, 2011.

———. *Storming Caesar's Palace: How Black Mothers Fought Their Own War on Poverty.* Boston: Beacon Press, 2005.

Orleck, Annelise, and Lisa Gayle Hazirjian, eds. *The War on Poverty: A New Grassroots History.* Athens: University of Georgia Press, 2011.

O'Rourke, Lawrence. *Geno: The Life and Mission of Geno Baroni.* New York: Paulist Press, 1991.

Orsi, Robert A. *The Madonna of 115th Street: Faith and Community in Italian Harlem, 1880–1950.* New Haven, CT: Yale University Press, 1985.

Osman, Suleiman. *The Invention of Brownstone Brooklyn: Gentrification and the Search for Authenticity in Postwar New York.* New York: Oxford University Press, 2011.

Payne, Charles M. "Ella Baker and Models of Social Change." *Signs* 14, no. 4 (Summer 1989): 885–99.

———. *I've Got the Light of Freedom: The Organizing Tradition and the Mississippi Freedom Struggle.* Berkeley: University of California Press, 1995.

Phillips-Fein, Kim. *Invisible Hands: The Businessman's Crusade against the New Deal.* New York: Norton, 2009.

Piven, Frances Fox. *Who's Afraid of Frances Fox Piven?: The Essential Writings of the Professor Glenn Beck Loves to Hate.* New York: The Free Press, 2011.

Piven, Frances Fox, and Richard A. Cloward. *Poor People's Movements: Why They Succeed, How They Fail.* New York: Vintage Books, 1977.

Plunz, Richard. *A History of Housing in New York City: Dwelling Type and Social Change in the American Metropolis.* New York: Columbia University Press, 1990.

Podair, Jerald E. *The Strike That Changed New York: Blacks, Whites, and the Ocean Hill-Brownsville Crisis.* New Haven, CT: Yale University Press, 2002.

Pope, Jacqueline. *Biting the Hand That Feeds Them: Organizing Women on Welfare at the Grassroots Level.* New York: Praeger, 1989.

Ports, Suki Terada, and Marion Banzhaf. "Many Cultures, Many Approaches." In *Women, AIDS, and Activism*, edited by ACT UP/New York Women & AIDS Book Group, 107–11. Boston: South End Press, 1990.

Pritchett, Wendell. *Brownsville, Brooklyn: Blacks, Jews, and the Changing Face of the Ghetto.* Chicago: University of Chicago Press, 2002.

Purcell, Francis P., and Harry Specht. "Selecting Methods and Points of Intervention in Dealing with Social Problems: The House on Sixth Street." In *Community Action against Poverty: Readings from the Mobilization Experience*, edited by George A. Brager and Francis P. Purcell, 229–42. New Haven, CT: College and University Press, 1967.

Purnell, Brian. *Fighting Jim Crow in the County of Kings: The Congress of Racial Equality in Brooklyn.* Lexington: University Press of Kentucky, 2013.

Randolph, Sherie. " 'Women's Liberation or . . . Black Liberation, You're Fighting the Same Enemies': Florynce Kennedy, Black Power, and Feminism." In *Want to Start a Revolution? Women in the Black Revolt*, edited by Dayo F. Gore, Jeanne Theoharis, and Komozi Woodard, 223–47. New York: New York University Press, 2009.

Ransby, Barbara. "Cops, Schools, and Communism: Local Politics and Global Ideologies—New York City in the 1950s." In *Civil Rights in New York City: From World War II to the Giuliani Era*, edited by Clarence Taylor, 32–51. New York: Fordham University Press, 2011.

———. *Ella Baker and the Black Freedom Movement: A Radical Democratic Vision.* Chapel Hill: University of North Carolina Press, 2003.

Reitano, Joanne. *The Restless City: A Short History of New York from Colonial Times to the Present.* New York: Routledge, 2006.

Rieder, Jonathan. *Canarsie: The Jews and Italians of Brooklyn against Liberalism.* Cambridge, MA: Harvard University Press, 1985.

Roberts, Sam. "Introduction." In *America's Mayor: John V. Lindsay and the Reinvention of New York*, edited by Sam Roberts, 4–9. New York: Columbia University Press, 2010.

Roediger, David R. *Working toward Whiteness: How America's Immigrants Became White*. New York: Perseus, 2005.

Rosen, Ruth. *The World Split Open: How the Modern Women's Movement Changed America*. New York: Viking, 2000.

Rosenbloom, Robert A. "The Neighborhood Movement: Where Has It Come From? Where Is It Going?" *Nonprofit and Voluntary Sector Quarterly* 10, no. 2 (April 1981): 4-26.

Roth, Benita. *Separate Roads to Feminism: Black, Chicana, and White Feminist Movements in America's Second Wave*. Cambridge: Cambridge University Press, 2004.

Rothwax, Harold J. "The Law as an Instrument of Social Change." In *Justice and the Law in the Mobilization for Youth Experience*, edited by Harold H. Weissman, 137-44. New York: Association Press, 1969.

Saletan, William. *Bearing Right: How Conservatives Won the Abortion War*. Berkeley: University of California Press, 2003.

Samuel, Lawrence. *New York 1964: A Cultural History*. Jefferson, NC: McFarland and Co., 2014.

Sanjek, Roger. *The Future of Us All: Race and Neighborhood Politics in New York City*. Ithaca, NY: Cornell University Press, 1998.

Schneider, Eric. *Vampires, Dragons, and Egyptian Kings: Youth Gangs in Postwar New York*. Princeton, NJ: Princeton University Press, 1999.

Schrecker, Ellen. *Many Are the Crimes: McCarthyism in America*. Boston: Little, Brown and Co., 1998.

———. *No Ivory Tower: McCarthyism and the Universities*. New York: Oxford University Press, 1996.

Schulman, Bruce. *From Cotton Belt to Sunbelt: Federal Policy, Economic Development, and the Transformation of the South, 1938-1980*. New York: Oxford University Press, 1991.

———. *The Seventies: The Great Shift in American Culture, Society, and Politics*. New York: The Free Press, 2001.

———. "Slouching toward the Supply Side: Jimmy Carter and the New American Political Economy." In *The Carter Presidency: Policy Choices in the Post-New Deal Era*, edited by Gary M. Fink and Hugh Davis Graham, 51-71. Lawrence: University of Kansas Press, 1998.

Schulman, Sarah. *The Gentrification of the Mind: Witness to a Lost Imagination*. Berkeley: University of California Press, 2012.

———. *People in Trouble*. New York: E. P. Dutton, 1990.

Schwartz, Joel. "The New York City Rent Strikes of 1963-1964." *Social Service Review* (December 1983): 545-64.

———. "Tenant Power in the Liberal City, 1943-1971." In *The Tenant Movement in New York City, 1904-1984*, edited by Ronald Lawson, 134-208. New Brunswick, NJ: Rutgers University Press, 1986.

Scott, William, and Peter Rutkoff. *New York Modern: The Arts and the City*. Baltimore: Johns Hopkins University Press, 2001.

Seifer, Nancy. *Nobody Speaks for Me! Self-Portraits of American Working Class Women*. New York: Simon and Schuster, 1976.

Self, Robert. *American Babylon: Race and the Struggle for Postwar Oakland*. Princeton, NJ: Princeton University Press, 2003.

Self, Robert O. *All in the Family: The Realignment of American Democracy since the 1960s.* New York: Hill and Wang, 2012.

Sennett, Richard, and Jonathan Cobb. *The Hidden Injuries of Class.* New York: Alfred A. Knopf, 1972.

Shepard, Benjamin. "Building a Healing Community from ACT UP to Housing Works: Benjamin Shepard Interviews Keith Cyler." In *From ACT UP to the WTO: Urban Protest and Community Building in the Era of Globalization*, edited by Benjamin Shepard and Ronald Hayduk, 351–59. New York: Verso, 2002.

Shilts, Randy. *And the Band Played On: Politics, People, and the AIDS Epidemic.* New York: St. Martin's Press, 1987.

Sleeper, Jim. *The Closest of Strangers: Liberalism and the Politics of Race in New York.* New York: Norton, 1990.

Slodoba, Monica. "The High Cost of Merging with a Religiously-Controlled Hospital." *Berkeley Women's Law Journal* 16, no. 1 (2001): 140–217.

Smethurst, James Edward. *The Black Arts Movement: Literary Nationalism in the 1960s and 1970s.* Chapel Hill: University of North Carolina Press, 2005.

Snitow, Ann, Christine Stansell, and Sharon Thompson, eds. *Powers of Desire: The Politics of Sexuality.* New York: Monthly Review Press, 1983.

Snyder, Robert W. "A Useless and Terrible Death: The Michael Farmer Case, 'Hidden Violence,' and New York City in the Fifties." *Journal of Urban History* 36, no. 2 (2010): 226–50.

Somers, Margaret R. *Genealogies of Citizenship: Markets, Statelessness, and the Right to Have Rights.* New York: Cambridge University Press, 2008.

Sommella, Laraine. "This Is About People Dying: The Tactics of Early ACT UP and Lesbian Avengers in New York City: An Interview with Maxine Wolfe." In *Queers in Space: Community, Public Places, Sites of Resistance*, edited by Gordon Brent Ingram, Anne-Marie Bouthillette, and Yolanda Retter, 407–37. Seattle: Bay Press, 1997.

Sorenson, Theodore. *Kennedy.* New York: Harper & Row, 1965.

Springer, Kimberly. *Living for the Revolution: Black Feminist Organizations, 1968–1980.* Durham, NC: Duke University Press, 2005.

Staniszewski, Mary Anne. *Believing Is Seeing: Creating the Culture of Art.* New York: Penguin Books, 1995.

Stansell, Christine. *The Feminist Promise: 1792 to the Present.* New York: Modern Library, 2010.

Sugrue, Thomas. *The Origins of the Urban Crisis: Race and Inequality in Postwar Detroit.* Princeton, NJ: Princeton University Press, 1996.

———. *Sweet Land of Liberty: The Forgotten Struggle for Civil Rights in the North.* New York: Random House, 2008.

Sullivan, Kathleen. "Are Content Restrictions Constitutional?" In *Art Matters: How the Culture Wars Changed America*, edited by Brian Wallis, Marianne Weems, and Philip Yenawine, 235–39. New York: New York University Press, 1999.

Sullivan, Robert. *Rats: Observations on the History and Habitat of the City's Most Unwanted Inhabitants.* New York: Bloomsbury Publishing, 2005.

Susser, Ida. *Norman Street: Poverty and Politics in an Urban Neighborhood.* New York: Oxford University Press, 1982.

Swerdlow, Amy. *Women Strike for Peace: Traditional Motherhood and Radical Politics in the 1960s.* Chicago: University of Chicago Press, 1993.

Synder-Grenier, Ellen M. *Brooklyn!: An Illustrated History.* Philadelphia: Temple University Press, 1996.

Sze, Julie. *Noxious New York: The Racial Politics of Urban Health and Environmental Justice.* Cambridge, MA: MIT Press, 2007.

Tani, Karen M. "The House That 'Equality' Built: The Asian American Movement and the Legacy of Community Action." In *The War on Poverty: A New Grassroots History, 1964–1984,* edited by Annelise Orleck and Lisa Gayle Hazirjian, 411–36. Athens: University of Georgia Press, 2011.

———. "Welfare and Rights before the Movement: Rights as a Language of the State." *Yale Law Journal* 122, no. 2 (2012): 314–83.

Taylor, Clarence, ed. *Civil Rights in New York City: From World War II to the Giuliani Era.* New York: Fordham University Press, 2011.

Taylor, Clarence. "Conservative and Liberal Opposition to the New York City School-Integration Campaign." In *Civil Rights in New York City: From World War II to the Giuliani Era,* edited by Clarence Taylor, 95–117. New York: Fordham University Press, 2011.

———. *Knocking at Our Own Door: Milton A. Galamison and the Struggle to Integrate New York City Schools.* New York: Columbia University Press, 1997.

———. *Reds at the Blackboard: Communism, Civil Rights, and the New York City Teachers Union.* New York: Columbia University Press, 2011.

Theoharis, Jeanne F., and Komozi Woodard, eds. *Freedom North: Black Freedom Struggles Outside the South, 1940–1980.* New York: Palgrave Macmillan, 2003.

———, eds. *Groundwork: Local Black Freedom Movements in America.* New York: New York University Press, 2005.

Thistle, Susan. *From Marriage to Market: The Transformation of Women's Lives and Work.* Berkeley: University of California Press, 2006.

Thomas, Lorrin. *Puerto Rican Citizen: History and Political Identity in Twentieth-Century New York City.* Chicago: University of Chicago Press, 2010.

Thompson, Becky. "Multiracial Feminism: Recasting the Chronology of Second Wave Feminism." *Feminist Studies* 28, no. 2 (Summer 2002): 337–60.

Thompson, Phillip. "Public Housing in New York City." In *Housing and Community Development in New York City,* edited by Michael Schill, 119–42. Albany: State University of New York Press, 1999.

Tiemeyer, Phil. *Plane Queer: Labor, Sexuality, and AIDS in the History of Male Flight Attendants.* Berkeley: University of California Press, 2013.

Torres, Andres. *Between Melting Pot and Mosaic: African Americans and Puerto Ricans in the New York Political Economy.* Philadelphia: Temple University Press, 1995.

Treichler, Paula A. *How to Have Theory in an Epidemic: Cultural Chronicles of AIDS.* Durham, NC: Duke University Press, 1999.

Trolander, Judith Ann. "Hall, Helen. Jan. 4, 1892–Aug. 31, 1982." In *Notable American Women: Completing the Twentieth Century,* edited by Susan Ware. Cambridge, MA: Harvard University Press, 2004.

Troy, Gil. *Morning in America: How Ronald Reagan Invented the 1980s.* Princeton, NJ: Princeton University Press, 2005.

Turk, Katherine. "Out of the Revolution, into the Mainstream: Employment Activism in the Now Sears Campaign and the Growing Pains of Liberal Feminism." *The Journal of American History* 97, no. 2 (2010): 399–423.

United in Anger: A History of ACT UP. Directed by Jim Hubbard. 2012. New York: United in Anger Inc., 2012. DVD.

Uttley, Lois, Sheila Reynertson, Lorraine Kenny, and Louise Melling. *Miscarriage of Medicine: The Growth of Catholic Hospitals and the Threat to Reproductive Health Care*. New York: ACLU and Merger Watch, 2013.

Valk, Anne M. "Living a Feminist Lifestyle: The Intersection of Theory and Action in a Lesbian Feminist Collective." *Feminist Studies* 28, no. 2 (Summer 2002): 303-34.

———. *Radical Sisters: Second-Wave Feminism and Black Liberation in Washington, D.C.* Urbana: University of Illinois Press, 2008.

Vance, Carole S., ed. *Pleasure and Danger: Exploring Female Sexuality*. New York: Routledge, 1984.

———. "The War on Culture." In *Art Matters: How the Culture Wars Changed America*, edited by Brian Wallis, Marianne Weems, and Philip Yenawine, 220-31. New York: New York University Press, 1999.

Von Drehle, David. *Triangle: The Fire That Changed America*. New York: Grove Press, 2003.

Wald, Lillian. *The House on Henry Street*. New York: H. Holt and Company, 1927.

Wall, Barbra. *American Catholic Hospitals: A Century of Changing Markets and Missions*. New Brunswick, NJ: Rutgers University Press, 2011.

Weisman, Steven R. "City in Crisis II." In *America's Mayor: John V. Lindsay and the Reinvention of New York*, edited by Sam Roberts, 192-213. New York: Columbia University Press, 2010.

Weissman, Harold H. *Community Councils and Community Control: The Workings of Democratic Mythology*. Pittsburgh: University of Pittsburgh Press, 1970.

———. "Educational Innovation: The Case of an External Innovating Organization." In *Employment and Educational Services in the Mobilization for Youth Experience*, edited by Harold H. Weissman, 206-20. New York: Association Press, 1969.

———, ed. *Employment and Educational Services*. New York: Association Press, 1969.

———. "The Housing Program 1962 to 1967." In *Community Development in the Mobilization for Youth Experience*, edited by Harold H. Weissman, 44-70. New York: Association Press, 1969.

———, ed. *Justice and the Law in the Mobilization for Youth Experience*. New York: Association Press, 1969.

———. "Overview of Educational Opportunities." In *Employment and Educational Services in the Mobilization for Youth Experience*, edited by Harold H. Weissman, 119-24. New York: Association Press, 1969.

West, Guida. *The National Welfare Rights Movement: The Social Protest of Poor Women*. New York: Praeger, 1981.

Wheeler, Leigh Ann. *How Sex Became a Civil Liberty*. New York: Oxford University Press, 2013.

White, Theodore H. *The Making of the President 1960*. New York: Atheneum, 1988.

Whittier, Nancy. *Feminist Generations: The Persistence of Radical Women's Activism*. Philadelphia: Temple University Press, 1994.

Wilder, Craig. *A Covenant with Color: Race and Social Power in Brooklyn*. New York: Columbia University Press, 2000.

Wilder, Marcy C. "The Rule of Law, the Rise of Violence, and the Role of Morality: Reframing America's Abortion Debate." In *Abortion Wars: A Half Century of*

Struggle, 1950–2000, edited by Rickie Solinger, 73–94. Berkeley: University of California Press, 1998.

Williams, Rhonda Y. *The Politics of Public Housing: Black Women's Struggles against Urban Inequality*. New York: Oxford University Press, 2004.

Wiltse, Jeff. *Contested Waters: A Social History of Swimming Pools in America*. Chapel Hill: University of North Carolina Press, 2007.

Wojnarowicz, David. "Postcards from America: X-Rays from Hell." In *Art Matters: How the Culture Wars Changed America*, edited by Brian Wallis, Marianne Weems, and Philip Yenawine, 74–81. New York: New York University Press, 1999.

Wolcott, Victoria W. *Race, Riots, and Roller Coasters: The Struggle over Segregated Recreation in America*. Philadelphia: University of Pennsylvania Press, 2012.

Wolfe, Maxine. "AIDS and Politics: Transformation of Our Movement." In *Women, AIDS, and Activism*, edited by ACT UP/New York Women & AIDS Book Group, 233–37. Boston: South End Press, 1990.

Wu, Judy Tzu-Chun. *Radicals on the Road: Internationalism, Orientalism, and Feminism During the Vietnam Era*. Ithaca, NY: Cornell University Press, 2013.

Yans-McLaughlin, Virginia. *Family and Community: Italian Immigrants in Buffalo, 1880–1930*. Ithaca, NY: Cornell University Press, 1971.

Zaretsky, Natasha. *No Direction Home: The American Family and the Fear of National Decline, 1968–1980*. Chapel Hill: University of North Carolina Press, 2007.

Zeitz, Joshua M. *White Ethnic New York: Jews, Catholics, and the Shaping of Postwar Politics*. Chapel Hill: University of North Carolina Press, 2007.

Zipp, Samuel. *Manhattan Projects: The Rise and Fall of Urban Renewal in Cold War New York*. New York: Oxford University Press, 2010.

Zukin, Sharon. *Loft Living: Culture and Capital in Urban Change*. Baltimore: Johns Hopkins University Press, 1982.

Acknowledgments

Researching and writing this book was a lengthy process, and many people helped me along the way. I am pleased to be able to acknowledge some of them here. My thanks to everyone who allowed me to interview them for this book, and gave generously of their time and insight. Without their stories, this book would not be possible. Special thanks to Jan Peterson and Elizabeth Meixell, both of whom permitted me to interview them multiple times, gave me access to archives, and put me in touch with other interviewees. Most importantly, through their examples, they inspire me. Political scientist Martha Ackelsberg welcomed my attendance at an NCNW reunion she had organized at Smith College, conducted several interviews with me, and generously gave me access to her own interviews with NCNW members. When we were both graduate students, political scientist Lara Rusch helped me conduct my very first oral history interviews; throughout the years, I have learned so much from her about social change and listening to people. Thanks also to Sarah Schulman and Jim Hubbard of the ACT UP Oral History Project, Frances Fox Piven, and Noel Cazenave for sharing their oral history interviews, which were key sources for this book. Mark Jacquinot gave me his own personal archive of WHAM! materials; Woody King Jr. let me make copies of the amazing films he made with MFY Cultural Arts students in the 1960s. Janie Eisenberg, Meg Handler, Donna Binder, and Bill Bytsura gave me permission to use their wonderful photographs in this book. Thanks to Liz Hauser, Abby Woodroffe, and the staff at the Audio Transcription Center for painstakingly transcribing my interviews. At the University of Michigan, Erica Buher provided research assistance.

Feedback from other scholars has greatly improved this book. In particular, Annelise Orleck's extensive comments helped me rethink and rewrite an earlier version of the manuscript, making it a much richer book and a better read. Grey Osterud helped me find my voice and clarify my arguments as well as my prose. Gina Morantz Sanchez and Matthew Lassiter taught me how to write history and patiently read numerous versions of this manuscript. I am equally grateful for their sharp editorial eyes, their vast knowledge of American history, and their steadfast support and friendship. An anonymous reader for the University of North Carolina Press provided valuable feedback. Maria Cotera and Sonya Rose helped me think expansively and urged me to be both rigorous in my research and creative in my analysis. Members of the Metropolitan History Workshop at the University of Michigan read an early draft of the entire manuscript and assisted me in identifying areas for further development.

Many others colleagues have commented on parts of this book. Stephanie Gilmore and Tom Dublin edited earlier versions of this research for publication and asked great questions. Thanks in particular to Felice Batlan, Rebecca Brannon, Lily Geismer, Andrew Highsmith, Clay Howard, Sonia Song-Ha Lee, Will Mackintosh, Robert Maclean, Molly Michelmore, Jennifer Palmer, Lara Rusch, Rebecca Scales, Corinna Schlombs, and LaKisha Simmons, all of whom read parts of this book. I also benefited from the response of organizers and participants in a number of seminars, including the American History Workshop and the Institute for Women and Gender's Community of Scholars summer research colloquium at the University of Michigan; the Schlesinger Library's 2008 Summer Seminar on Gender History "Sequels to the 1960s" at Harvard University; the New York Metro American Studies Association 2010 Summer Institute "Re-Visiting the Lower East Side" at Hunter College; the Americas Colloquium and the 2009–10 and 2010–11 Mellon Humanities Seminars at Cornell University; a College of Liberal Arts women's faculty reading group at Rochester Institute of Technology; and the Rochester U.S. History Group. Commentators, fellow panelists, and audience members at the Berkshire Conference on the History of Women; the annual meetings of the American Historical Association, the Organization of American Historians, and the Social Science History Association; and the biennial Urban History Association and Puerto Rican Studies Association Conferences; all helped me think through this material. I would particularly like to thank Jennifer Briar, Robert Fisher, Deborah Gould, Susan Reverby, Heather Thompson, and Rhonda Williams for their commentary on my papers.

Since I began studying history as an undergraduate, I have benefited from the mentorship and support of many individuals, only some of whom I can acknowledge individually here. At the University of Massachusetts, Madeleine Blais, Karen List, Kathy Peiss, and Norm Sims inspired me to become a scholar. The faculty and graduate students of the University of Michigan's History Department provided an amazingly vibrant intellectual community, and I am grateful to the many scholars there who shaped my intellectual development and who continue to influence my practice as a scholar and a teacher. I would particularly like to thank Geoff Eley, Myron Gutmann, Mary Kelly, Terry McDonald, and Susan Juster. I was fortunate to spend two years as a Mellon Postdoctoral Fellow at the Cornell University History Department, where many faculty and graduate students welcomed me into their community, offered exciting discussions of history, gave me feedback on my book, and swapped teaching strategies. Thanks especially to Mary Beth Norton, Derek Chang, Maria Christina Garcia, Mary Katzenstein, Aaron Sachs, and Margaret Washington. Members of the Department of History at the College of the Holy Cross inspired me with their passion for excellent teaching and made my year there enjoyable with their fabulous humor. Marisa Chappell, Nancy Hewitt, Georgina Hickey, Alison Parker, Benita Roth, and Victoria Wolcott have all offered crucial encouragement and wonderful models of engaged scholarship and pedagogy in women's history. I am so lucky to have landed in the History Department at the Rochester Institute of Technology, where Rebecca Edwards, Joseph Henning, Christine Keiner, Michael Laver, Rich Newman, Eric Nystrom, Rebecca Scales, and Corinna Schlombs, along with their families, have extended warm friendship and collegiality and made me and Lars feel at home.

Financial support from a number of institutions allowed me to work on this book. Thanks to the University of Michigan and the Eisenberg Institute for Historical Studies, the Mellon Foundation and Cornell University, and the Rochester Institute of Technology for fellowships. In particular, the Paul and Francena Miller Research Fellowship from RIT's College of Liberal Arts provided crucial time for the final revisions. I am particularly grateful to my department chair, Rebecca Edwards, and my dean, James Winebrake, for granting me teaching release and subvention funds. I also deeply appreciate the efforts of Peggy Noll and Israel Brown to smooth the bureaucratic waters on my behalf. Travel grants allowed me to conduct archival research on-site, and I am thankful to have received the Margaret Storrs Grierson Scholar-in-Residence Fellowship from Smith College, the Clark Chambers Travel Grant from the Social Welfare Archives at the University of Minnesota, and the Moody Grant from the Lyndon Baines Johnson Foundation. Along with my grandmother, many kind friends gave me a place to stay while I was conducting research for this book. For their generous hospitality, I am deeply grateful to Lorraine Andon, Marge and the late Paul Barnett, Madeline Blais, Lisa Di Donato and Bill Walsh, Marta Peimer and Ashton Stewart, Robyn Phillip-Norton, and Norm Sims.

To complete this book, I depended on the goodwill and skills of many archivists and librarians and who went above and beyond to help me track down sources. Thank you to the staff at the Centro de Estudios Puertorriqueños, Hunter College, CUNY; Fales Library, Tamiment Library, and the Robert F. Wagner Archives at New York University; Lehman Library and the Rare Book and Manuscript Library, Columbia University; the National Archives; the New York Public Library Manuscripts and Archives Division; the John F. Kennedy and Lyndon Baines Johnson Presidential Libraries; and the Sophia Smith Collection at Smith College. Special thanks to the late Michael Nash of New York University's Tamiment Library, who hosted and helped me organize a WHAM! reunion, and to Margaret Jessup of the Sophia Smith Collection, who has cheerfully and efficiently fielded dozens of queries over many years.

Sian Hunter acquired this book for the University of North Carolina Press; after her departure Charles Grench extended his faith in the project and ably guided me through the publishing process. My thanks to Chuck and the staff at UNC, especially Dino Battista, Paul Betz, Kim Bryant, Lucas Church, Katherine Fisher, and Susan Raines Garrett. Thanks to Brett Keener for copyediting, to Melody Negron for production assistance, and Lohnes+Wright for making the maps. Thank you to Laurie Prendergast for assistance in preparing the index. Thanks also to the editors of the Gender and American Culture Series.

Over the many years I was at work on this book, friends and family kept my spirits up and reminded me occasionally to stop and smell the roses, too. My dear friends since childhood Megan Blake, Brie Donnally, Kara Larcome, and Kristy Streeter help me stay grounded. In addition to those already named for their help with my manuscript, Saskia Coenen, Robert Kruckeberg, Amanda Moniz, Roberta Pergher, Rebekah Pite, Nick Syrett, Lenny Ureña, Tamara Walker, and my fellow co-opers and housemates made graduate school at Michigan a lot of fun. Patty Keller and Rhiannon Welch made our time in Ithaca unforgettable. Thanks to Sarah Thompson, Hinda Mandell, and Kelly Norris Martin for making me laugh every time I see them and for sharing their perspectives with me. My brother, David, and his lovely wife, Jill, brighten my life. My parents, Ted and Susan Carroll, have believed in me and offered their support throughout this endeavor, and I cannot thank them enough. Lars Schumann has lived with this book nearly as long as I have, and I thank him especially for his patient help with all things technical, for being my cameraman and sounding board, for keeping me sane, and most of all, for sharing his life with me. As I write this, we are expecting our first child, and I am so excited to begin this next leg of our adventure together. This book is dedicated to Lars with love and gratitude.

Index

Abbott, Charlotte, 153–54, 183, 184

Abortion rights, xii–xiii, 5, 89, 114, 116, 132, 159, 186, 192, 237–38 (n. 79); access to based on identity, 154; and ACT UP, 136, 153, 168; and Cardinal O'Connor, 155, 165; and Catholic opposition to, 20, 115, 134, 149, 154, 158, 162–63, 227 (n. 16); clinic defense, 164–65, 168, 237–38 (n. 79); clinic escorting, 163–64, 235 (n. 13); and Clinton administration, 80–181; and coalition building, 153, 154; and comprehensive reproductive rights, 182, 183; and direct actions, x, 153, 155, 162–63, 167, 184; and feminism, 1, 53, 170; gay male support for abortion rights, x, 1, 20, 154, 167, 168; media impact on public opinion, 162; and reproductive rights activism, 1–2, 20, 82, 153, 155, 164–65, 167, 170; restrictions on, 19, 136, 153, 166, 168, 180, 185; and women's health movement, 137, 238 (n. 92). *See also* Antiabortion activism; Reproductive rights

Abzug, Bella, 98

Affinity group, 138, 145, 146

Affirmative action, 112, 123

Affordable housing, 7, 43, 49, 52, 59, 73

African Americans, 7, 32, 34–35, 41, 45, 47, 48, 74; and block-busting, 85; and high school education, 90; and HIV/AIDS, 146, 159, 188; and juvenile delinquency, 8–9, 29; and living conditions, 26, 49, 51–52, 55; and poverty, 11, 23, 131; relations with police, 56–58, 159, 205 (n. 79); and reproductive rights, 183; and residential segregation, 8, 26–27, 49,

87; support for Communist Party, 60–61; and voter registration, 40; and Williamsburg-Greenpoint, 86, 88, 89, 95. *See also* African American Women; Civil rights movement; Puerto Ricans

African American women, 52, 58, 97, 127; and community activism, xii, 7–8, 9, 15, 23–25, 48, 89, 121; and education activism, 25, 38, 43, 46; and feminism, 82, 110, 114, 224 (n. 68); and interracial coalitions, 81, 88, 90, 102–3, 107; and welfare rights, 68

African Services Committee, 188, 240 (n. 5)

AIDS. *See* HIV/AIDS

AIDS Coalition to Unleash Power (ACT UP), x, 1–2, 17–20; and "Ashes Action," 179; and Church Ladies for Choice, 167–70; and Clinton's election, 180; and Day of Desperation, 175–76; and feminism, 137–38; founding of, 140–41; Housing Committee, 147, 148, 149; and Latino/a Caucus, 175; and Legacies, 185–86; Majority Action Committee, 146–47, 150, 178, 192; meetings, 144–45; membership, 143, 144, 230 (n. 58); and political funerals, 178–79; and public memory of AIDS activism, 184; and queer identity, 172–75; and service provision, 191–92; and social justice, 136, 188; and Stop the Church, 155–61; and targets, 133–34, 234 (nn. 130, 136); Treatment and Data Committee split, 177, 227 (n. 11); and 25th anniversary action, 187–88, 190, 193, 239 (n. 1), 240 (n. 3); and WHAM!, 153, 154, 155; Women's Caucus, 150–53, 175, 177, 178

—poor people, 9, 24, 34, 36, 57, 87, 95, 102; and citizenship, 8, 32; and housing, 17, 51, 53, 59, 82, 131, 147; and maximum feasible participation, 10, 11–12, 19, 25, 71, 72; Poor People's Movement, 104; and rights, 47, 56, 65, 66, 67, 70, 72; and service provision to, 14, 93, 124, 125, 126, 146; and social protest, 5, 10, 13, 46, 48, 66, 70; War on Poverty, xi, 10–13, 23–24, 47, 78, 79, 89, 99, 191; and women, ix, 15–16, 83, 99, 101, 109, 123, 127, 128, 129, 154, 221 (n. 6). *See also* Mothers, low-income

—professional, 24, 25, 33, 50, 78, 82, 121, 131; and ACT UP, 136, 144, 175, 230 (n. 58); and NCNW Principled Partnership model, 107, 118–20; and paraprofessionals, 10, 25, 33–36, 46, 57, 66, 67, 72, 78, 213 (n. 117); and WHAM!, 154

—working, 14, 15, 32, 67, 72, 80, 82, 86–87, 88, 97, 100, 131; and feminism, 15, 83, 98, 111–12, 113, 114, 115–17, 130, 221 (n. 6); and men, 86–87, 106, 112; and progressive politics, 104; and women, ix, 83, 98, 99–100, 101, 106, 112, 115, 121, 173, 221 (n. 6)

Clinton, Bill, 180, 181

Cloward, Richard: and disruptive social protest, 66, 210 (n. 54); and MFY, 24, 32, 36, 40, 64, 212 (n. 94); and Old Left, 210–11 (n. 71); and opportunity theory, 9, 23, 30–31, 202 (n. 27); and Piven, 10; and rent strikes, 59; and welfare rights, 10, 69, 70

Coalition of Labor Union Women, 123

Coalitions, ix–x, xiv, 1–2, 10, 20, 189; and abortion, 153, 154; and AIDS, 133, 136, 145–46, 159; and CAPS, 79; and consciousness raising, 81, 107, 129; cross-class coalitions, xiv, 15, 25, 46, 57, 99; and group education, 100–103; interracial coalitions, 13, 15, 42–43, 46, 57, 73, 75, 77, 81, 88, 90, 99, 102–3, 104, 107, 199 (n. 41); and Principled Partnership model, 107, 118–20; for

progressive social change, 190, 191, 192; racist limitations on, 106, 107, 114, 183; in Williamsburg-Greenpoint, 90, 99, 101. *See also* Solidarity

Cold War, 5, 8, 22, 23, 45, 50, 68, 138

Colon, Julio, 27–29

Columbia University School of Social Work, 30, 33

Commission on Human Rights, 90

Committee for Abortion Rights and Against Sterilization Abuse (CARASA), 154, 181–82

Committee of Welfare Families, 66

Communism: African American support for, 60–61; allegations against MFY, 50, 60–66, 78, 210 (n. 65), 210–11 (n. 71), 211 (n. 84); and anticommunism, 50, 60–66, 102, 210 (n. 64); and civil rights, 7, 60; Communist left, 63; Communist Party (CP), 60–64, 66–67; and Jewish support for, 61; and Lower East Side, 63; Puerto Rican support for, 60; red-baiting, 44, 57, 114; Roman Catholics' anticommunism, 210 (n. 64)

Community Action Program (CAP), 13, 23–24, 50, 69, 72, 78, 79, 189, 198 (n. 33)

Community activism, xi–xv, 7, 41, 67, 73, 189, 191, 192, 219 (n. 77); in Williamsburg-Greenpoint, 90–92, 97, 100

Community control, 13, 47, 79, 117

Community Council on Housing, 52

Community organizers, 21, 97, 124 128–29, 191, 213 (n. 117); and MFY, xi, 13, 34, 36, 41, 43, 46, 47, 50, 73; and public housing, xii, 121; and welfare rights, 66–67, 68; and white ethnic movements, 81, 88–89, 104

Community Services Administration (CSA), 191, 214 (n. 141)

Comprehensive Employment and Training Act (CETA), 15–16, 107, 109, 121, 122, 123, 124, 126, 129, 219 (n. 85)

Condoms, 18, 20, 134, 136, 148, 149, 150, 151, 155, 156, 157, 229 (n. 44), 231 (n. 79)

Economic Opportunity Act, 10, 23–24, 50, 62, 72; Green and Quie Amendments, 72, 191; Scheurer Amendments, 213 (n. 117)

Education Action Center, 89

Eigo, Jim, 177

Eisenberg, Janie, 128

Elder, Lonnie, III, 74

England, Marshall, 13, 79

Enlow, Roger, 139

Equal Rights Amendment (ERA), 114, 115, 116, 221 (n. 6)

Espada, Frank, 47

European immigrants, ix, xii, 3, 8, 14, 60, 80, 83, 87, 88, 90, 102, 112; Irish, 8, 26, 29, 83, 101, 102; Russians, 110; Ukrainians, 36, 83. *See also* Italians; Jews; White ethnics

Evening News (CBS), 175

Fair hearing, 70–71, 213 (nn. 108, 113)

Fair housing, 7, 49, 53, 197 (n. 19)

Farmer, Michael, 26, 29

Fava, Maria, 117

Federal Bureau of Investigation (FBI), 60–64, 181

Feit, Rona, 119–20

Feminine Mystique, The (Friedan), 105, 112

Feminism, ix–xv, 1–2, 13–15, 97, 103, 105–6, 122, 189, 199 (n. 50), 228 (n. 29); and abortion, 1, 53, 170; and ACT UP, 137; attack on by Religious Right, 19, 20, 132; and domestic violence, 103–4; and international women's movement, 17, 107–8, 126, 127, 128; and lesbians, 136, 172, 182; and Project Open Doors, 108–10, 120–21, 122–23, 124, 191; and "sex wars," 173, 236 (n. 50); and women of color, 106, 130, 223–24 (n. 53), 224 (n. 68); and women's health, 82, 99, 136, 150, 152–53, 183, 228 (n. 23); and women's liberation movement, 78, 82, 105, 111, 116, 118, 119, 138, 195 (n. 2); and working-class, 15, 83, 98, 111–12, 113, 114, 115–17, 130, 221 (n. 6)

Feminist Health Works, 108

Feminists, The, 82, 215 (nn. 15–16)

Ferlinghetti, Lawrence, 74

Ferrer, Fernando, 175

Finkelstein, Avram, 141

Finley, Karen, 172

Fisher, Mark Lowe, 179

Fisher, Sally Martino, 15, 86, 111, 122, 129–30

Fleck, John, 172

Food and Drug Administration (FDA), 133, 141, 142, 152, 177

Ford, Gerald, 93, 109

Ford Foundation, 8, 22–23, 30, 43, 65, 73

France, David, 177

Franklin Settlement (Detroit), 74

Frazier, Cliff, 74

Freedom of Access to Clinic Entrances (FACE) Act, 180

Friedan, Betty, 105, 112

Frohnmayer, John, 171–72, 236 (n. 41)

Fuentes, Jose, 54–55, 57, 59

Fuentes, Luis, 47–48

Fundamentalists, 132, 154

Galamison, Milton, 42–43, 49

Game, The (1967), 74–75

Gangs (youth), 25–26, 29–30, 33, 67, 73, 201 (n. 10)

Garcia, Robert, 161

Gay and Lesbian Alliance Against Defamation (GLADD), 230

Gay Asian Pacific Islander Men of New York (GAPIMNY), 146

Gay bathhouses, 17, 140

Gay men, 4, 132, 158, 159, 170, 171, 173, 192; gay bathhouses, 17, 140; and HIV/AIDS, xiii, 18, 19, 136, 138, 139, 140, 141, 142, 151, 152, 160; and support for abortion rights, x, 1, 20, 154, 167, 168

Gay men and lesbians, 109, 131, 228 (n. 22); and AIDS activism, 133, 137, 143, 159, 173–74, 182, 186; Defense of Marriage Act, 181; differences between, x, 136; gay and lesbian liberation movement, 4, 132, 136, 137, 138, 141, 173, 174, 189; gay and lesbian

Heterosexuality: and AIDS, 139, 152; and
  AIDS activism, 144, 186, 230 (n. 53);
  Defense of Marriage Act, 181; and
  normative, 18, 154, 172, 173, 185, 186,
  190, 192, 229 (n. 44); and privacy
  rights, 132. *See also* Sexuality
Hicks, Calvin, 66
HIV/AIDS, xiii, 17–20; and activism, 133,
  142, 144, 145, 155–61, 167, 175, 178–79,
  184, 186, 187, 230 (n. 46), 234 (n. 136);
  and art, 170–72, 236 (n. 41); deaths
  from, 141, 155, 176–77, 180; definition
  of, 19, 133, 152, 227 (n. 11); and early
  years, 138–40; and Haitians, 139, 150,
  228 (n. 30); prevention and treatment
  of, 20, 136, 146, 152, 176–77, 185, 189–90,
  227 (n. 11); and queer politics, 173, 174;
  and racism, 145, 156; social context
  of, 177–78, 188; and stigma, 132, 139.
  See also AIDS Coalition to Unleash
  Power
Hodes, Roberta, 74–75
Homelessness, 17, 132, 134, 146, 147, 148,
  149, 152, 185, 186
Homophobia, 114, 185; activism against,
  4, 18, 133, 142, 174, 182, 230 (n. 46); and
  Catholic Church, xiii, 134–36, 158; and
  HIV/AIDS, 132, 139, 145, 159, 160, 167,
  178, 228–29 (n. 33)
Homosexuality, 4, 186; and attitudes
  towards, 114, 141; and Catholic
  Church, 134, 140, 149, 158; Defense of
  Marriage Act, 181; gay and lesbian
  liberation movement, 4, 132, 136, 137,
  138, 141, 173, 174, 189; and HIV/AIDS,
  138, 139, 140, 228 (n. 33), 231 (n. 79);
  and Religious Right, 136;
  representations of, 171; same-sex
  marriage, 185. *See also* Sexuality
House Un-American Activities
  Committee (HUAC), 61
Housework (Domestic labor), 11, 106, 116,
  221 (n. 6), 222 (n. 20)
Housing: ACT UP Housing Committee,
  146–47, 148, 149–50; affordable, 7,
  43, 49, 52, 59, 73; and civil rights

movement, 7, 49; fair, 7, 49, 53, 197
  (n. 19); gentrification, 17, 81–82, 108,
  132, 186; homelessness, 17, 132, 134,
  146, 147, 148, 149, 152, 185, 186; housing
  cooperatives, 27, 202 (n. 20); Lower
  East Side activism, 53–57, 59, 73;
  luxury real estate development, 17,
  131, 132, 147; Metropolitan Council on
  Housing, 54; and MFY, 9–10, 47, 48, 50,
  52–60, 73, 208 (n. 17); middle-class, 6,
  59, 81–82, 85, 131; New York City
  Department of Housing Preservation
  and Development, 148; New York City
  Housing Authority, 51, 85–86, 90; and
  poor people, 17, 51, 53, 59, 82, 131, 147;
  and public housing activism, xii, xiv,
  7–8, 15, 17; and racial segregation and
  housing cooperatives, 27–29, 216
  (n. 30); racial transitions, 29, 83, 85–86;
  redlining, 81, 85, 99, 215 (n. 12); rent
  control, 53, 54, 59, 73; rent strikes, 10,
  25, 48, 49, 50, 53, 58–60, 62, 73, 208
  (n. 19), 210 (n. 54); and school
  segregation, 35; and Scottish Tenants'
  Movement, 53; single-occupancy
  housing, 131, 147; slum clearance, 27;
  slum landlords, 24, 50, 52, 55–56, 57;
  suburbanization, 6, 8, 13, 26, 32, 33,
  51, 81, 98; Tenants' Councils, 53, 57,
  66; tenements, 8, 27, 32, 49, 51–52;
  and United Nations, 127, 128;
  Williamsburg-Greenpoint activism,
  91–92, 95. *See also* Disinvestment;
  Public housing;
  Williamsburg-Greenpoint
Housing Clinic, 53, 54
Housing Works, 149–50, 187, 192, 193, 231
  (n. 77)
How to Survive a Plague (2012), 177
Hughes, Holly, 172

Identity, x, 5; and abortion access, 154;
  and class, 98, 100, 101, 121; collective
  identities, 19, 59, 161; and differences,
  107, 126, 129, 130, 145–46, 183, 190;
  feminist identities, 113, 117; and

United Federation of Teachers, 47; United Retail and Wholesale Employees, 60; University of Michigan Graduate Employee Organization, 184; and white working-class masculinity, 87

Lacy, Suzanne, 137

LaGuardia Community College, 100

Latino/as, 23, 36, 51, 86, 131, 175, 188, 220 (n. 101). *See also* Mexicans; Puerto Ricans

Lavender Hill Mob, 230 (n. 46)

Leadership training, 46, 47, 66, 73, 101, 110, 127

Lee, Maryat, 74

Legal Aid Society, 70

Legal services, xi, xiv, 10, 36, 48, 50, 56, 57, 70; expansion of under OEO, 72; and tenants' rights, 59; and welfare rights, 69, 70

Lesbian and Gay Community Services Center, 141, 143

Lesbians, 131, 132; and AIDS activism, 133, 142, 143, 144, 150, 152, 158, 160, 173; attacks on, 140, 159; and feminism, 109, 114, 136, 137, 138; and identity politics, x, 172–73; and liberation movements, 4, 13, 141; and queer identity, 174; and reproductive rights activism, 154, 169, 170, 182, 228 (n. 22). *See also* Gay men and lesbians

Levin, Meryl, 1–2, 176, 180

Liberalism, 8–9, 15, 19, 22, 26, 186, 191

Lindsay, John, 13, 65; and New York City budget crisis, 10, 91

Lorenzi, Maria, 37, 39, 43–44

Lower East Side, 65, 79, 83; and Black Arts Movement, 73; and Communist left, 63; and community health movement, 78, 214 (n. 140); and housing activism, 53–57, 59, 73; and Labor and radical politics, 198 (n. 26); living conditions and characteristics, 8–9, 26–29, 51–52, 59, 73; Lower East Side Civil Rights Committee, 40–43;

Lower East Side Girls Club, 192; Lower East Side Neighborhood Association (LENA), 26, 29, 31, 78; opposition to expansion of Lower Manhattan Expressway, 73; residents of, 32, 36, 50; and school boycotts, 41–43; support for MFY, 64–65; and welfare rights, 69; and women, 57, 67

Lower East Side Civil Rights Committee, 40–43

Lower East Side Girls Club, 192

Lower East Side Neighborhood Association (LENA), 26, 29, 31, 78

Luchiano, Dana, 183

Lugg, Amanda, 188

Lurie, Ellen, 41, 47

Lyons Law, 56

MacKinnon, Catherine, 173

Madsen v. Women's Health Center, 180

Magee, Judith, 69

Maggenti, Maria, 151, 176–77

Mapplethorpe, Robert, 171

Marcantonio, Vito, 61

Marchi, John, 66

March on Washington for Jobs and Freedom (1963), 40–41, 50, 64, 205 (n. 76), 215 (n. 11)

Martinez, Ernesto, 44, 73

Martinez, Peter, 74

Maximum feasible participation (MFP), xi, 10–12, 24–25, 45, 71, 72, 78, 89, 122, 189, 190, 212 (n. 95)

McCarren Park Pool, 86

McCarthy, James, 33, 44, 62, 64, 65

McCarthyism. *See* Anticommunism; Red-baiting

McLean, Jackie, 74

McRae, LeRoy, 63, 65–66

Media, 29, 117, 125; and coverage of AIDS, 134, 141, 158, 160; coverage of civil rights movement, 8; New York City as center of, 5, 189; and portrayal of feminism, 104, 111; and public opinion on abortion, 162; and reach of direct

N'Dow, Wally, 108
Needle exchange, 137, 148, 149, 159
Negro Action Group (NAG), 41, 54
Neighborhood movement, 81–83, 97, 104, 105, 215 (n. 13)
Neighborhood service center, 23, 36, 38, 46, 68
Neoliberalism, 133, 136, 181, 191
New Federal Theater, 77
New Left, the, 13, 81
Newman, Pauline, 54
New York Artists Space, 71
New York City Board of Education, 34, 35, 38, 41–43, 46, 47, 61, 139
New York City Department of Housing Preservation and Development, 148
New York City fiscal crisis, 10, 14, 91, 106–7, 131, 147
New York City Housing Authority (NYCHA), 51, 85–86, 90
New York City Labor Department, 122, 123, 124
New York Community Trust, 10
New York Feminist Credit Union, 108
New York Radical Feminists, 82, 215 (n. 17)
New York State Assembly, 59
New York State Medical Care Facilities Finance Agency, 134
New York Times, 22, 43, 56, 57, 65, 85, 111, 134, 140
Nixon, Richard, 10–11, 71, 109
Noschese, Christine, 98, 100–101, 102, 219 (nn. 82, 89)

Obscenity, 170, 171, 236 (n. 38)
Occupy Wall Street, 187, 188, 190, 240 (n. 3)
Ocean Hill-Brownsville, 79, 104, 214–15 (n. 2)
O'Connor, Cardinal John Joseph, 135, 159, 172, 231 (n. 79); and ACT UP, 19–20, 134, 136, 149, 151, 155, 158, 161, 234 (n. 130); and antiabortion, 155, 165; opposition to gay rights, 140, 148
O'Dell, Jack, 53
Odet, Clifford, 73

Office of Economic Opportunity (OEO), 5, 72, 191
O'Hagan, John T., 93, 94, 95
Ohlin, Lloyd, 9, 23, 24, 30–31, 202 (n. 27), 203 (n. 35)
Operation Rescue, 20, 155, 162, 163, 164, 165, 167, 180, 181, 182, 233 (n. 119)
Oral history, xi–xiv, 21, 23
Ortiz, Haydee, 64
Our Bodies, Ourselves (Boston Women's Health Book Collective), 152, 232 (n. 100)

Pantoja, Antonia, 47
Paraprofessionals, 10, 25, 33–36, 46, 57, 66, 67, 78; and New Careers, 72, 213 (n. 117)
Parents' Workshop for Equality in New York City Schools, 42
Participatory democracy, 20, 24–25, 33, 72, 81, 121, 129, 133, 138, 189, 191
Paterson, Basil, 95
Patient Protection and Affordable Care Act (2010), 185, 239 (n. 105)
Patriarchal, 113, 137, 172, 174
Peace activism: antinuclear movement, 63, 68, 138; antiwar movement, xii, 34, 80, 136–37, 175
Peer counseling, 117, 120
People's Firehouse, 93–96, 97, 218 (n. 69)
People with AIDS (PWA), 134, 139, 142, 145, 146, 159, 185, 187, 188; and homelessness, 146–47, 149, 152
Personal Responsibility and Work Opportunity Act of 1996, 181, 227 (n. 17)
Peterson, Jan, 13–14, 17; and community organizing in Williamsburg-Greenpoint, 79, 81, 88–89, 91, 92, 96, 97, 191; and GROOTS, xiv, 17, 107–8, 127; and Huariou Commission, 108, 127; and MFY, xiv, 11–12, 78; and NCNW, ix, 14–15, 83, 97, 99, 100, 104, 105, 113, 117, 119, 122, 124, 125–26, 128, 129, 175; and Women's Liberation movement, 82
Pezzullo, Caroline, 126, 127

Puerto Rican studies, 47; juvenile delinquency of, 8–9; living conditions of, 7, 26, 49, 51–52, 54, 55; Nuyorican writers, 77; and Pentecostal Church, 6 7; Puerto Rican women, 15, 38, 46, 52, 67, 68, 86, 91; Puertorriqueños Unidos, 54; relations with police, 56–58; and reproductive rights, 183; residential segregation, 26–29, 49; and South Williamsburg, 83; Support for Communist Party, 60; and welfare rights, 67–71; and Williamsburg-Greenpoint, 86, 91, 95

Quayle, Dan, 158
Queens County, 26, 139, 163, 164, 202 (n. 20), 216 (n. 30), 219 (n. 77)
Queers, 18, 133, 144, 162, 169, 170–74, 192, 228 (n. 22)
Queers for Economic Justice, 186
Quester, Steve, 21, 168, 169
Quill, Michael, 61
Quinn, Alice, 101, 120–21

Racial segregation, 7–8, 26, 35, 49, 53; and fair housing, 7, 49, 53, 197 (n. 19); and housing cooperatives, 27–29, 216 (n. 30); and public spaces, 29, 86, 216 (n. 32); in Williamsburg-Greenpoint, 85–86, 96, 114, 216 (n. 32), 216–17 (n. 33), 217 (n. 34). See also Civil rights movement; School segregation
Racism, 8, 24, 75, 97, 103, 106, 145, 178; and HIV/AIDS, 145, 156; internalized, 118, 183; and racial transition, 29, 83, 85–86; and white flight, 27, 51, 86; and white racial backlash, 14–15, 57, 79, 80, 104, 214–215 (n. 2); and white violence, 86, 87, 96, 216–17 (n. 33), 240 (n. 4). See also Racial segregation; School segregation
Rafsky, Bob, 179
Ramspacher, Karen, 2, 164, 167, 235 (n. 13)
Randolph, A. Phillip, 40
Rango, Nick, 149

Rape, 82, 109, 137, 181, 227 (n. 16)
Rapp-Coudert Committee, 61
Rather, Dan, 175
Rathke, Wade, 81, 215 (n. 11)
Rats, 51, 52, 53, 57, 59
Reagan, Ronald, 19, 132, 133, 159, 181; and AIDS, 139, 141, 148, 229 (n. 44), 229–30 (n. 33), 231 (n. 79); and social spending cuts, 16, 107, 122, 123
Real estate development, luxury, 17, 131, 132, 147. See also Trump, Donald; Trump Tower
Red-baiting, 44, 57, 114; and MFY, 10, 50, 60–66, 210–11 (n. 71), 211 (n. 72), 211–12 (n. 89)
Redlining, 81, 85, 99, 215 (n. 12)
Reevaluation counseling, 120
Reilly, Phillip, 163
Reissman, Frank, 46
Religious Right, 19–20, 132, 136, 161, 170, 171, 172, 186, 191, 192
Reno, Janet, 181
Rent control, 53, 54, 59, 73
Rent strikes, 10, 25, 48, 49, 50, 53, 58–60, 62, 73, 208 (n. 19), 210 (n. 54)
Reproductive rights, ix, 109, 114, 115, 132, 154, 162, 180, 185, 238 (n. 92); and AIDS activism, x, 1–2, 152, 153, 155, 158; and health care, 20, 154, 164, 182, 239 (n. 105); and queer politics, 167, 172, 173, 186; and race, 181–83; and sterilization, 136, 183, 227 (n. 16); and welfare reform, 181–82; women's access to, 164, 165. See also Abortion rights; Antiabortion activism; Birth control
Reproductive Rights Coalition (RRC), 1, 53
Republican National Women's Club, 138
Republicans, 7, 10, 13, 19, 21, 65, 70, 159, 162, 172, 179, 184
Right-to-life movement. See Antiabortion activism
Robert's Rules of Order, 144, 183
Robeson, Paul, 61
"Robin Hood" tax, 187, 188

Social work, xi, 29, 33–35, 46, 65, 74, 185; and client advocacy, 9, 11, 34–36, 52, 55; and welfare rights, 10, 67, 69

Solidarity, 32, 42, 57, 138, 150, 161, 172, 192, 205 (n. 84), 230 (n. 53). *See also* Coalitions

South Bronx, 51, 54, 93, 131, 218 (n. 64)

Sparer, Ed, 56

"Speak-out," 82, 103, 111, 116, 222 (n. 20)

Specht, Harry, 40, 66, 212 (n. 96)

Speranza, Elizabeth, 87, 89, 97, 113, 128

Staley, Peter, 177

Staniszewski, Mary Anne, 132–33

Starr, Roger, 93

Statue of Liberty protest, 1–2, 21

Steinem, Gloria, ix, xv, 109, 196 (n. 16)

Stonewall Uprising, 4, 197 (n. 9)

Stop the Church protest, 20, 155–61, 233 (nn. 123–24)

St. Patrick's Cathedral, 20, 82, 134, 155, 157, 165, 167, 168, 185

Street theater, 17, 74, 133, 156, 189. *See also* Church Ladies for Choice

Students for a Democratic Society (SDS), 69, 81

Stuyvesant Town, 6, 51

Suburbanization, 6, 8, 13, 26, 32, 33, 51, 81, 98

Susser, Ida, 86

Swinging Sixties Senior Center and Small World Day Care, 14, 97, 109, 128, 219 (n. 78)

Tarantino, Millie, 97

Tarantino, Molly, 97

Tarantino, Tillie, 89, 96, 97, 99

Tax revenue, 91, 93

Tenants' Councils, 53, 57, 66

Tepper, Michelle, 184

Terence Cardinal Cooke Health Care Center, 134

Terry, Randall, 155, 169

Texter, Eva, 74

Thomas, Evelyn, 75–77

Thomas, Kendall, 1, 46, 184

Time (magazine), 6, 25

Times Square, 5, 132

Tirado, Candida, 113

Tracy, Liz, 150

Transgender people, 150, 173

Treatment Access Group (TAG), 177

Triangle Shirtwaist Factory Fire, 3–4, 197 (n. 11)

Truman, Harry, 63

Trump, Donald, 17, 134, 148, 159, 231 (n. 75)

Trump Tower, 132, 147, 148

Tudy, Mildred, 86, 89–91

Turner, Dan, 145

Ukrainians, 36, 83

Union Square Park, 153

United Bronx Parents, 47

United Nations, 5, 6, 17, 107–8, 126, 127, 128

United Nations Conferences on Women, 108, 127, 128

United Servicemen's Organization (USO), 167

United States Supreme Court, 1, 35, 71, 132, 153, 168, 180, 237 (n. 79)

—decisions: *Bowers v. Hardwick*, 1, 32; *Goldberg v. Kelly*, 71; *Griswold v. Connecticut*, 132; *King v. Smith*, 71; *Madsen v. Women's Health Center*, 180; *Roe v. Wade*, 137, 153, 180; *Rust v. Sullivan*, 1, 168; *Shapiro v. Thompson*, 71; *Webster v. Reproductive Health Services*, 153

Urban crisis, 15

Urban renewal, 3–4, 6, 8, 26–27, 75, 79, 81, 83, 215 (n. 12)

Vaneski, Adam, 94

Vatican, the, 134, 140, 141, 148

Vazquez-Pacheco, Robert, 140, 184

Velez, Ethel, xii, xiv, 7, 107, 117, 118, 120

Village Voice, 144

Volunteer In Service to America (VISTA), 39

Wagner, Robert F., 7, 22, 43, 56, 58–59, 65

Waiting for Lefty (Odets), 73, 213 (n. 122)

Wakowski, Diane, 74

Wald, Lillian, 26

Walker, Edgar, 159

Wall Street, 119, 133, 142, 175, 177, 187, 188

Warn, Robert, 163

War on Poverty, the, xi, 10–13, 23–24, 47, 78, 79, 89, 99, 191; and maximum feasible participation (MFP), xi, 10–12, 24–25, 45, 71, 72, 78, 89, 122, 189, 190, 212 (n. 95)

Webster v. Reproductive Health Services, 153

Weissman, Harold, 56

Welfare rights, xi, 9–10, 25, 48, 50, 66–71, 78, 98, 212 (n. 103). *See also* Social welfare

Westchester County, 164, 165

West Village, 18, 73, 132

Wheatpasting, 141, 142, 157, 184, 229–30 (n. 45)

White ethnics: movements of, 13–14, 80–83, 97, 100, 104, 105; and white flight, 27, 51, 86; racial backlash of, 14–15, 57, 79, 80, 104, 214–15 (n. 2); and white violence, 86, 87, 96, 216–17 (n. 33), 240 (n. 4)

White flight, 27, 51, 86

White House, 179

Wichita, Kans., 165, 166, 167

Wiley, George, 70

Williamsburg-Greenpoint, 14, 78, 79, 80, 131; activism in, 91–92, 95; and African Americans, 86, 88, 89, 95; and coalitions, 90, 99, 101; community activism in, 90–92, 97, 100; direct actions in, 93–94; and environmental activism, 218 (n. 61); and Jews, 14, 83, 86, 103, 121; and NCNW, 99–101, 108, 109, 119, 120, 128; and Neighborhood Women for Home and Family, 113–14; overview of, 83–88; and People's Firehouse, 93–96; and planned shrinkage, 93; public housing in, 85–86, 88, 90, 124; and Puerto Ricans, 83, 86, 91, 95; racial tensions in, 86, 90, 91, 97, 114, 216 (n. 32), 216–17 (n. 33), 217

(n. 34); rezoning of Northside neighborhood, 91–92, 96, 218 (n. 56); and Roman Catholics, 85, 86. *See also* Peterson, Jan

Willis, Ellen, 173

Will-o-Way School of Theater, 74

Wilson, Malcolm, 91

Witnesses: Against Our Vanishing (exhibition), 172

Wizard of Oz (1939), 166

Wizner, Steven, xiv, 36

Wojnarowicz, David, 170, 171, 178–79

Wolfe, Leslie, 183

Wolfe, Maxine, 172, 177

Women: feminism and women's health, 82, 99, 136, 150, 152–53, 183, 228 (n. 23); Italian, 82, 86, 87, 88, 89, 91, 98, 102, 217 (n. 41), 218–19 (n. 71); and Lower East Side, 57, 67; and middle-class activists, 46, 68, 98, 104, 105, 106, 107, 111, 112, 153; paid work participation, 23, 86–87, 99, 106, 110, 112, 115, 123, 191, 221 (n. 6); poor, ix, 15–16, 83, 99, 101, 109, 123, 127, 128, 129, 154, 221 (n. 6); Puerto Rican, 15, 38, 46, 52, 67, 68, 86, 91; working-class, ix, 83, 98, 99–100, 101, 106, 112, 115, 121, 173, 221 (n. 6). *See also* Feminism; Mothers, low-income; National Congress of Neighborhood Women; National Organization for Women; Peterson, Jan; Women's Health Action and Mobilization

Women, AIDS, and Activism (ACT UP New York Women and AIDS Book Group), 152, 175

Women Make Movies, 108, 199 (n. 49)

Women Office Workers, 123

Women's Action Alliance, 109

Women's Health Action and Mobilization (WHAM!), x, xiii, 150, 190; and Church Ladies for Choice, 167–70; and clinic access, 162–66, 182, 185; and Clinton's election, 180; and "Day of Desperation," 175–76; disbanding of, 184; Domino's Pizza boycott, 153; founding of, 153; legacies of, 185–86;

CPSIA information can be obtained
at www.ICGtesting.com
Printed in the USA
LVHW112008040123
736293LV00007B/556